NINETEENTH-CENTURY STORIES
BY WOMEN

NINETEENTH-CENTURY STORIES BY WOMEN

EDITED BY GLENNIS STEPHENSON

broadview literary texts

Canadian Cataloguing in Publication Data

Nineteenth-century stories by women
Includes bibliographic references.

ISBN 1-55111-000-8
I. Literature —Women authors. 2. Literature, Modern —
19th century. I. Stephenson, Glennis, 1955-   .

PN6069.W65B64 1993   808.8'99287   C93-093031-2

Broadview Press
Post Office Box 1243, Peterborough, Ontario, Canada. K9J
7H5

In the United States of America:
269 Portage Road, Lewiston, New York, USA. 14092

In the United Kingdom:
c/ o: Drake Marketing Services, Market Place, Deddington,
Banbury, Oxford, UK. OX15 0SF

Cover: "The Kiss of Peace" by Julia Margaret Cameron, 1869.
Reproduced by permission of the Royal Photographic Society.

Broadview Press gratefully acknowledges the support of the
Canada Council, the Ontario Arts Council, and the Ontario
Publishing Centre.

Printed in Canada

1 2 3 4 5 6 7 8 9 10 11

FOR FRANK AND OLIVE STEPHENSON

Picture Credits

Louisa May Alcott (p. 22) Concord Free Public Library.
Mary Elizabeth Braddon (p. 70) Harry Ransom Humanities Research Center, The University of Texas at Austin.
Kate Chopin (p. 104) Missouri Historical Society.
Isabella Valancy Crawford (p. 114) National Archives of Canada (item number C6720).
Ella D'Arcy (p. 130). From: The *Bookman* vol. 2. New York: 1895
Rebecca Harding Davis (p. 164). From: Langford, Gerald. The *Richard Harding-Davis Years: A Biography of Mother and Son.* New York: Rinehart Winston, 1961.
Alice Dunbar-Nelson (p. 182) University of Delaware Library, Special Collections.
George Egereton (p. 195) photograph courtesy of Virago Press.
Annie Howells Fréchette (p. 218) Herrick Memorial Library, Alfred University.
Mary Wilkins Freeman (p. 231) University of Virginia, Alderman Library, Special Collections/Manuscripts.
Elizabeth Gaskell (p. 248) Portrait by George Richmond, reproduced by permission of The National Portrait Gallery, London.
Charlotte Perkins Gilman (p. 310) Bryn Mawr College Archives, Mariam Coffin Canaday Library, Bryn Mawr College.
Sarah Orne Jewett (p. 330) Special Collections, Dimond Library, University of New Hampshire.
Vernon Lee (p. 348) Portrait by John Singer Sargent, reproduced by permission of The Tate Gallery, London
L.M. Montgomery (p. 384) Public Archives and Records Office of Prince Edward Island (Acc# 3110/1).
Margaret Oliphant (p. 402) Trustees of the National Library of Scotland.
Mary Shelley (p. 429) Portrait by R. Rothwell, reproduced by permission of The National Portrait Gallery, London.
Harriet Prescott Spofford (p. 442) Special Collections, Smathers Libraries, University of Florida, Gainsville.
Flora Annie Steel (p. 462) From: Steel, Flora Annie, *The Garden of Fidelity.* London: Macmillan, 1921.
Constance Fenimore Woolson (p. 472) Department of College Archives and Special Collections, Olin Library, Rollins College, Winter Park, Florida (Acc# 1326-C).

Contents

Acknowledgements

I am grateful to the Social Sciences and Humanities Research Council of Canada and the University of Alberta for their support in the production of this anthology. And I would like to thank both Erika Rothwell, a superb research assistant who proved admirably adaptable in accommodating my quirks about method, and Heidi Jacobs, who searched diligently for various obscurities. I would also like to acknowledge the kindess of all those who helped me with suggestions about stories to be included, with translations, and with tracing photographs and identifying references. For such help I am indebted to, among others, Shymal Bagshee, Duncan Fishwick, Gordon Moyles, Lady Violet Powell, Bob Solomon, Rebecca Sutcliffe, Jennifer Stark, Avice Stephenson, Paul Stephenson, Martha Vicinus, and Christine Wiesenthal. And finally, I would like to thank all the people who helped me trace photographs, and in particular Gregory Johnson, Special Collections, Alderman Library, University of Virginia; Bill Ross, Special Collections, University of New Hampshire; Rebecca Johnson, Senior Assistant Librarian, University of Delaware, and Leo M. Dolenski, Manuscripts Librarian, Mariam Coffin Canaday Library, Bryn Mawr College.

Introduction

WHILE MUCH HAS BEEN DONE OVER THE PAST THIRTY YEARS TO reclaim women's literary tradition, the focus of interest has been, particularly in the case of British authors, primarily on the novel. As a result, we have ended up with a somewhat misleading view of women's literature and women's relationship to the literary market. The female novelist of the nineteenth century may have frequently encountered opposition and interference from the male literary establishment, but the female short story writer, working in a genre that was seen as less serious and less profitable, found her work to be actively encouraged. As increased literacy and leisure among middle and upper-class women created a greater demand for literary periodicals, magazines, and annuals, this in turn led to an increased need for women writers to cater to the tastes of this growing market. From the very beginning of the nineteenth century, women played a significant role in the production of short stories, and, for the first time, they became professional writers.

Women even exerted a surprising amount of editorial control over the periodical literature of the time: Louisa May Alcott was the editor of *Merry's Museum*, and Sarah Josepha Hale of *Godey's Lady's Book*; Mary Elizabeth Braddon was founder and editor of the *Belgravia*, and Charlotte Perkins Gilman of the *Forerunner*. At the beginning of the century, Letitia Landon served as editor for at least four annuals, and probably contributed to at least three-quarters of the others; and, at the end of the century, Ella D'Arcy's position as unofficial assistant editor was no doubt responsible for the large number of women's stories that were published in *The Yellow Book*. For those women with no inclination to edit, there was at least a ready market for their work in such publications, and their contributions were actively sought: Margaret Oliphant became closely associated with both *Blackwood's* and the *Cornhill*, Elizabeth Gaskell with *Household Words*, and Mary Shelley with the *Keepsake*. Carole Gerson has even found that women produced 70 percent of the fiction for the Canadian periodical *The Literary Garland* (McMullen 58).

During the first part of the nineteenth century, there was, admittedly, a price that had to be paid by the women who entered the literary market: they were expected to produce stories based in the feminine and domestic sphere. The degree to which critics and readers could dictate the type of fiction they produced is strikingly demonstrated by the case of Lydia Maria Child, author of the highly successful *Hobomok, A Tale of Early Times* (1824) and founder and editor of the popular American magazine, *The Juvenile Miscellany*. As soon as Child stepped into the masculine sphere of politics with the publication of *An Appeal in Favor of That Class of Americans Called Africans* (1833), and then implicitly challenged the prevalent notions concerning "woman's sphere" in the *History of the Condition of Women, in Various Ages and Nations* (1835), the domestic advice books that provided her main source of income were boycotted, and her magazine failed for lack of subscribers.[1]

As critics have recently begun to recognize, however, these restrictions had their positive side: rather than simply imitating the works of their male contemporaries, many women adopted a self-consciously "feminine" perspective, and created a distinctive female voice. Others turned limitation into opportunity by covertly challenging the very roles that they appeared to be supporting. And while some critics have suggested that the restrictions the women encountered led to a pose of authorial innocence, to a denial of any sense of professionalism or serious en-

---

1   Child's short story "The Quadroons," which first appeared in the abolitionist literary annual, *The Liberty Bell* in 1842, introduces what is generally considered the prototype of the character who has come to be known as the "tragic mulatto"; Rosalie's story draws upon and brings together two of Child's primary concerns: inter-racial relations and the fallen woman (reprinted in Koppelmann *The Other Woman*).

gagement with writing, and even to an "anxiety of author-ship,"[2] my own reading in preparing this anthology has led me to the same conclusion as that reached by Judith Fetterley in her *Provisions: A Reader from Nineteenth-Century American Women*: "What I discovered," she writes, "was not 'innocence' but awareness. Indeed many of the women whose work I read exhibited a considerable degree of self-consciousness about writing and a serious, sometimes di-rect, sometimes indirect, engagement with the issues raised by the conjunction of woman and writer" (Fetterley, 2). The representative annual story chosen for inclusion here, Mary Shelley's "The Parvenue," certainly supports this conclusion.

While the women's ability to fill the needs created by the growing literary market was at least partly responsible for their success in the nineteenth century, it was also responsible for a later tendency to devalue their achieve-ments once the whole notion of "woman's sphere" began to be rejected. For much of this century, their short stories have been dismissed as sentimental, trivial, or artless: the reason that we know so little about the women and their short stories does not seem to be because they were un-dervalued by their contemporaries. In 1855, the *Cyclopedia of American Literature*, edited by Evert and George Duyckinck, listed eighty-two women authors, including Catherine Sedgewick, Alice Cary, Elizabeth Stuart Phelps, Fanny Fern, Gail Hamilton, and Harriet Spofford. Yet in 1891, as women began to assume more power in the social and political sphere, Horace Scudder, editor of the Houghton Mifflin anthology, *Masterpieces of American Lit-erature*, did not include even one.

Most of the recovery work so far with respect to nine-teenth-century women's short stories has taken place in

---

2   See, for example, Ann Douglas's "The 'Scribbling Woman' and Fanny Fern: Why Women Wrote." The "anxiety of authorship" is discussed both by Gilbert and Gubar in *The Madwoman in the Attic* and by Mary Kelley in *Private Woman, Public Stage*.

the field of American literature. Such series as Rutgers' "American Women Writers" have done much to make these texts available for study. And as more American women short story writers of the nineteenth century have been reprinted and anthologized, so they have become the focus of more scholarly studies. British women short story writers, with the exception of Gaskell and Oliphant, remain generally ignored, and there is an urgent need for their stories to be collected and published in scholarly editions so that the general work of reevaluation can proceed in a more informed manner. The problems facing critics wishing to re-inscribe women into Canadian literary history are even more acute. It is often difficult to locate the periodicals in which Canadian women wrote—sometimes they are simply untraceable; and, for various reasons, women's manuscripts, letters, and journals have often not been preserved.[3]. As a result, there is a self-replicating tendency in Canadian anthologies: the same stories by women are chosen for inclusion over and over again. This can, of course, be regarded as a positive move towards "mainstreaming."[4] Although Isabella Valancy Crawford is best known as a poet, her "Extradited," with its striking portrait of a petulant and narcissistic woman and its devastating examination of jealousy, has deservedly become a standard entry in anthologies of Canadian short stories. Annie Howells Fréchette, however, who produced some equally deserving stories, has, as far as I am aware, never been reprinted. "A Widow in the Wilderness," which proves Fréchette to be quite as adept as D.C. Scott at the vignette of Indian life, is particularly interesting for its links with the early Canadian sketch. Many of the early nineteenth-century Canadian women writers, including Susanna Moodie and Catherine Parr Traill, focused on producing sketches which drew on their experiences as

---

3   For more information on these problems, see the essays by Marion Beyea, Carrie MacMillan, and Carole Gerson in McMullen.

4   See Gerson on this point in McMullen.

pioneer women in a new world, and when they turned to the short story, the influence of these sketches remained, often resulting in an innovative hybrid that is not easily identified as either fact or fiction.[5] Lucy Maud Montgomery, one of the most familiar names in Canadian women's fiction, has fared far better than either Crawford or Fréchette, and the recent publication of three volumes of her short stories shows her to be a writer of far more varied talents than might be assumed by those who associate her only with the children's classic, *Anne of Green Gables*.

There are a number of other nineteenth-century Canadian women, apart from those represented here, whose stories are beginning to be reprinted and are well worth exploring. Rosanna Leprohon, best known for *Antoinette de Mirecourt* (1864), was a regular writer for the *Literary Garland* and also contributed to such magazines as *The Canadian Illustrated News*. Susie Frances Harrison, a practitioner of romantic local color fiction, produced an interesting collection of eleven stories entitled *Crowded Out! and Other Sketches* in 1886 under the pseudonym "Seranus." Her best story, "The Idyl of the Island," concerns the chance encounter of an English visitor with a young Canadian woman, and effectively uses the Canadian wilderness to create a psychological landscape.[6] And just after the turn of the century, and therefore unfortunately out of the scope of this anthology, the journalist Sara Jeannette Duncan published *The Pool in the Desert* (1903), a collection of four short stories which includes the frequently reprinted "A Mother in India."

In America, the large amount of reclamation work has allowed critics to explore in some detail the development of women's literary tradition. Numerous studies produced over the last ten or fifteen years identify two main streams

---

5   See, for example, Moodie's "A Well in the Wilderness," recently reprinted in *Voyages*.
6   "The Idyl of the Island" has been recently reprinted in Sullivan.

of writing. The first includes those women writing primarily in the first half of the century that Mary Kelley has designated the "literary domestics": socially respectable women whose perspective was "private and familial" and who produced "a prose of heroines with only a sprinkling of heroes; a prose mostly of women" who "were intimately involved with and derived their identity from the domestic sphere" (Kelly, ix). The most significant achievement of this group, as Kelley's definition suggests, lies in the endorsement of women as significant subjects. Although most of the women Kelley identifies as "literary domestics" are primarily novelists,[7] some of the short stories in this anthology, such as Rebecca Harding Davis's "Anne" and Harriet Prescott Spofford's "Circumstance," may be said to have grown out of this tradition. Both can, however, also be seen to problematize, as well as draw upon, the tradition. The focus of Davis's *Life in the Iron Mills* certainly qualifies her allegiance to this school of writing: she did not always choose to write about the lives of women.

In the second half of the nineteenth century, American women short story writers, particularly those designated local color or regionalist writers, began to reject what they saw as the worn-out conventions and mannerisms of their predecessors. This tradition is represented here by Mary Wilkins Freeman, Sarah Orne Jewett, and Constance Fenimore Woolson. Both Freeman and Jewett belong to the school of New England local color literature, which also included Rose Terry Cooke and Elizabeth Stuart Phelps, and which had a significant influence on such later writers as Edith Wharton, Willa Cather, Flannery O'Connor, and Eudora Welty. In determining the movement towards literary realism, these women made a significant contribution to American women's literature. As Josephine Donovan has noted, they:

> presented the first women's literary tradition

---

7   She includes, for example, Harriet Beecher Stowe, Susan Warner, and E.D.E.N. Southworth

which moved beyond a negative critique of reified male-identified customs and attitudes. The New England women created a counter world of their own, a rural realm that existed on the margins of patriarchal society, a world that nourished strong free women. (Donovan, 3)

In Britain, the dominant trends in nineteenth-century women's short fiction have not yet been as clearly identified as those in America. At the beginning of the century some of the most interesting work was done in the area of the sketch or tale. Such series of interconnected sketches as Mary Mitford's *Our Village*, begun in the *Lady's Magazine* in 1819, Anna Maria Hall's *Sketches of Irish Character* (1829), and many of the short satiric pieces published by Letitia Landon in the *New Monthly Magazine* reveal links with the essay. Elizabeth Gaskell, who used this type of sketch in *Cranford* (1851-53), and Margaret Oliphant were the most skilful and popular short story writers of mid-century Britain. While the styles of the two women differ significantly, they share a number of common interests. Both, for example, frequently explored the impact of male sexuality upon women, a subject that forms the basis for both "Lizzie Leigh" and "A Story of a Wedding Tour." And both produced some exceptional ghost stories. Some of the best supernatural stories of the nineteenth century were written by women; indeed, as Rosemary Jackson notes, "supernatural fiction written in English in the last two hundred years has been *predominantly* women's literature" (Salmonson ix).[8] Vernon Lee, Rosa Mulholland,

---

8   Salmonson suggests that "as much as seventy percent of the supernatural fiction" in Victorian periodicals "was the work of women" (Salmonson, x). The two best supernatural anthologies are those edited by Dalby and Salmonson. The reader who wishes to explore this area further might start with Mary Wilkins Freeman, "Luella Miller," and Elizabeth Stuart Phelps, "Since I Died" (both reprinted in Salmonson); Margaret Oliphant, "The Open Door" and Lanoe Falconer

Amelia B. Edwards, Rhoda Broughton, Charlotte Riddell, Louisa Hunt, and Mary Wilkins Freeman are just a few of the numerous women in Britain and America who achieved popular and critical success in this field. Women's ghost stories are often quite different from those written by men, and speak specifically to a female readership, particularly those, like Gaskell's "The Old Nurse's Story," which deal with haunted houses. Hauntings, as Lynette Carpenter and Wendy Kolmar have suggested, are inevitably tied to domestic gender politics, and women who wrote about haunted houses drew on Gothic fiction to comment indirectly upon "woman's sphere":

> From the Gothic, women ghost story writers inherited a context for describing what Kate Ferguson Ellis calls the "failed home" (ix), and a precedent for addressing issues that could not be confronted openly. . . . From the female Gothic, they inherited a series of themes and images—of women victimized by violence in their own homes, of women dispossessed of homes and property, of the necessity of understanding female history, and of the bonds between women, living and dead, which help to ensure women's survival. (Carpenter and Kolmar, 10)

Gaskell's "The Old Nurse's Story," generally considered one of the best ghost stories of the century, provides a striking example not only of the disruptive threat of sexuality and the power of the repressive father, but also of the manner in which the female spectre can become

---

"Cecilia de Noël" (both reprinted in Dalby); Bitha Mary Croker, "To Let" (reprinted in Cox); Rebecca Harding Davis "A Story of a Shadow" (1872) *Galaxy* 13 (1872): 541-52. George Eliot also produced a supernatural story, "The Lifted Veil" (reprinted in Haining). This is, however, more a novella than a short story and does not show Eliot at her best.

empowered by death. It is hardly surprising that so many women found the supernatural such a congenial form in which to work.

The ghost story also has links with the sensation fiction which became popular during the 1860s and remained so for much of the century. Mary Elizabeth Braddon and Ellen Wood, best known for the novels *Lady Audley's Secret* and *East Lynne* respectively, produced numerous short stories in a similar vein. This type of fiction, as popular in America and Canada as it was in Britain, is represented in this anthology by Braddon's "Good Lady Ducayne," Louisa May Alcott's "A Whisper in the Dark," and L.M. Montgomery's "The Red Room."

In dealing quite openly with issues of power, these three sensation stories are representative of a general movement in women's literature during the last two decades of the century. With the emergence of the "New Woman," who rejected conventional female roles and claimed her right to a career, the female narrative voice became more assertive, and willing to address women's problems directly and openly. Elizabeth Ammons's astute summary of the change she identifies in American women writers of the time is equally applicable to their counterparts in Britain: these women, she observes, address

> a network of recurrent, complicated themes which, though constantly shifting and even at times conflicting, finally interlock in their shared focus on issues of power; the will to break silence by exposing the connection among institutionalized violence, the sexual exploitation of women, and female muteness; preoccupation with the figure of the woman artist; the need to find union and reunion with the world of one's mother, particularly as one journeyed farther and farther from that world into territory marked off as forbidden. (Ammons, 5)

In America, Charlotte Perkins Gilman's "The Yellow Wallpaper" and Alice Dunbar-Nelson's lesser known "Sister Josepha" provide clear examples of this trend. And in Britain the two most influential writers of the "New Woman" school, Ella D'Arcy and George Egerton, address similar issues in "The Pleasure Pilgrim" and "Gone Under."

There is little trace remaining of the frequently convention-bound fiction of the early annuals in these often stark and sometimes painful stories. Female sexuality can be either openly celebrated, as in Kate Chopin's "The Storm," or turned into a violent instrument of vengeance, as in Vernon Lee's "Dionea." And while women's problems may still be much the same, there is a new angry directness in the manner in which they are faced and exposed, particularly in the case of sexual exploitation. This is particularly evident in the manner in which the Cinderella motif, used by a striking number of women in this anthology, develops throughout the century. The nineteenth-century Cinderella begins as the "untaught, lowborn, portionless girl" loved by Lord Reginald in Shelley's "The Parvenue." As good and dutiful as her prototype, this cast-off Cinderella finds some comfort in her familial devotion and the knowledge that her death will soon free the man she loves to marry another. By century's end she is the victimized prostitute "Mrs. Grey" in George Egerton's "Gone Under," a story of promiscuity, child-murder, abortion, and female alcoholism. There is no comfort for this exploited and discarded woman; abandoned to despair, she runs not only from her Prince turned Beast, but even from the compassion of the female narrator. What she leaves behind is no dainty glass slipper, but a "frayed, mud-soaked, satin shoe" and a cry "like the fancied echo of the laughter of hell."

A Note on Selection and Format

The preparation of an anthology of this kind inevitably calls for difficult choices, and no doubt each reader will regret the omission of at least one favorite author or text. Readers who are familiar with nineteenth-century literature and yet perhaps not specifically familiar with the short stories of the time may be puzzled not to find some of the better-known women writers. I have wanted to give an accurate sense of the work short story genre, and to focus on stories that deal particularly with women's issues and that allow for the exploration of the woman's voice. And so I have tried to avoid falling into the trap of including women writers simply because of their achievements as novelists or poets. I could have included stories by George Eliot, Augusta Ward, even, by stretching the point, by Elizabeth Barrett Browning and Christina Rossetti but my aim was not to focus on novelists or poets who only incidentally wrote an occasional story. Even within these boundaries, many short story writers eventually had to be omitted; a few, like Ellen Wood, because I found their stories to be flatly conventional, unnecessarily long, and even tedious: their stories simply did not live up to the promise of their better known novels. Some, like Edith Wharton, I omitted because, although they started writing during the last part of the nineteenth century, they are more generally associated with the twentieth century and their works are readily available elsewhere. Others had to be omitted quite simply because of limitations of space: this book could quite easily have been four times its present size.

Each story is followed by a discussion of the author's personal and professional life. To facilitate further exploration of the author's other short fiction, whenever possible I have also followed each story with a list of modern reprints or collections. I also provide a list of secondary sources which necessarily vary in their scope: for those authors who have received much critical attention, I have limited the list to the major general works and some articles on the specific story included; for those authors upon whom very little has as yet been written, I include criticism less specific to the particular story and issues at hand. A more general guide to further reading may be found in the bibliography at the back of this book. This is divided into three parts. First, there is a list of short story collections by some of the many other women who, although not represented in this anthology, are deserving of further study: I have focused when possible on reprinted works that are easily available. Second is list of various anthologies of women's short stories (primarily those published within the last fifty years) that will allow the reader to focus on a particular aspect of nineteenth-century women's short stories. And finally, there is a selection of secondary sources. All of these lists are intended only as guides to further reading and are necessarily selective.

Works Cited

Carpenter, Lynette and Wendy K. Kolmar. *Haunting the House of Fiction: Feminist Perspectives on Ghost Stories by American Women*. Knoxville: U of Tennessee P, 1991.

Cox, Michael, and R.A. Gilbert, intro. *Victorian Ghost Stories: An Oxford Anthology*. Oxford: Oxford UP, 1991.

Dalby, Richard, ed. *The Virago Book of Victorian Ghost Stories*. London: Virago, 1992.

Donovan, Josephine. *New England Local Color Literature: A Women's Tradition*. New York: Ungar, 1983.

Douglas, Ann. "The 'Scribbling Women' and Fanny Fern: Why Women Wrote." *American Quarterly* 23 (1971): 3-24.

Duyckinck, Evert S, and George L. Duyckinck. *Cyclopedia of American Literature*. 2 vols. Philadelphia: Rutter, 1855.

Fetterley, Judith, ed. *Provisions. A Reader from Nineteenth-Century American Women*. Bloomington: Indiana UP, 1985.

Gilbert, Sandra, and Susan Gubar. *The Madwoman in the Attic: The Woman Writer and the Nineteenth-Century Literary Imagination*. New Haven: Yale UP, 1979.

Haining, Peter. ed. *The Gentlewomen of Evil: An Anthology of Rare Supernatural Stories from the Pens of Victorian Ladies*. London: Hale, 1967.

Kelley, Mary. *Private Women, Public Stage: Literary Domesticity in Nineteenth Century America*. New York: Oxford UP, 1984.

McMullen, Lorraine. *Re(Dis)covering Our Foremothers: Nineteenth-Century Canadian Women Writers*. Ottawa: U of Ottawa P, 1990.

Moodie, Susanna. *Voyages. Short Narratives of Susanna Moodie*. Ed. John Thurston. Ottawa: U of Ottawa P, 1991.

Salmonson, Jessica Amanda, ed. *What Did Miss Darrington See? An Anthology of Feminist Supernatural Fiction*. Intro. Rosemary Jackson. New York: Feminist P, 1989.

Scudder, Horace, ed. *Masterpieces of American Literature*. 1891. New York: Books for Libraries P, 1970.

LOUISA MAY ALCOTT.

22   LOUISA MAY ALCOTT (1832-1888)

Louisa May Alcott (1832-1888)

A Whisper in the Dark

AS WE ROLLED ALONG, I SCANNED MY COMPANION COVERTLY, and saw much to interest a girl of seventeen. My uncle was a handsome man, with all the polish of foreign life fresh upon him; yet it was neither comeliness nor graceful ease which most attracted me; for even my inexperienced eye caught glimpses of something stern and sombre below those external charms, and my long scrutiny showed me the keenest eye, the hardest mouth, the subtlest smile I ever saw, – a face which in repose wore the look which comes to those who have led lives of pleasure and learned their emptiness. He seemed intent on some thought that absorbed him, and for a time rendered him forgetful of my presence, as he sat with folded arms, fixed eyes, and restless lips. While I looked, my own mind was full of deeper thought than it had ever been before; for I was recalling, word for word, a paragraph in that half-read letter: —

"At eighteen Sybil is to marry her cousin, the compact having been made between my brother and myself in their childhood. My son is with me now, and I wish them to be together during the next few months, therefore my niece must leave you sooner than I at first intended. Oblige me by preparing her for an immediate and final separation, but leave all disclosures to me, as I prefer the girl to remain ignorant of the matter for the present."

That displeased me. Why was I to remain ignorant of so important an affair? Then I smiled to myself, remembering that I did know, thanks to the wilful curiosity that prompted me to steal a peep into the letter that Madame Bernard had pored over with such an anxious face. I saw only a single paragraph, for my own name arrested my eye; and, though wild to read all, I had scarcely time to whisk the paper back into the reticule the forgetful old soul had left hanging on the arm of her chair. It was enough, however, to set my girlish brain in a ferment, and keep me gazing wistfully at my uncle, conscious that my future now lay in his hands; for I was an orphan and he my guardian, though I had seen him but seldom since I was confided to madame a six years' child. Presently my uncle became cognizant of my steady stare, and returned it with one as steady for a moment, then said, in a low, smooth tone that ill accorded with the satirical smile that touched his lips, —

"I am a dull companion for my little niece. How shall I provide her with pleasanter amusement than counting my wrinkles or guessing my thoughts?"

I was a frank, fearless creature, quick to feel, speak, and act, so I answered readily, —

"Tell me about my cousin Guy. Is he as handsome, brave, and clever as madame says his father was when a boy?"

My uncle laughed a short laugh, touched with scorn, whether for madame, himself, or me I could not tell, for his countenance was hard to read.

"A girl's question and artfully put; nevertheless I shall not answer it, but let you judge for yourself."

"But, sir, it will amuse me and beguile the way. I feel a little strange and forlorn at leaving madame, and talking of my new home and friends will help me to know and love them sooner. Please tell me, for I've had my own way all my life, and can't bear to be crossed."

My petulance seemed to amuse him, and I became aware that he was observing me with a scrutiny as keen as my own had been; but I smilingly sustained it, for my vanity was pleased by the approbation his eye betrayed. The evident interest he now took in all I said and did was sufficient flattery for a young thing, who felt her charms and longed to try their power.

"I, too, have had my own way all my life; and as the life is double the length, the will is double the strength of yours, and again I say no. What next, mademoiselle?"

He was blander than ever as he spoke, but I was

piqued, and resolved to try coaxing, eager to gain my point, lest a too early submission now should mar my freedom in the future.

"But that is ungallant, uncle, and I still have hopes of a kinder answer, both because you are too generous to refuse so small a favour to your 'little niece,' and because she can be charmingly wheedlesome when she likes. Won't you say yes now, uncle?" and, pleased with the daring of the thing, I put my arm about his neck, kissed him daintily, and perched myself upon his knee with most audacious ease.

He regarded me mutely for an instant, then holding me fast deliberately returned my salute on lips, cheeks, and forehead, with such warmth that I turned scarlet and struggled to free myself, while he laughed that mirthless laugh of his till my shame turned to anger, and I imperiously commanded him to let me go.

"Not yet, young lady. You came here for your own pleasure, but shall stay for mine, till I tame you as I see you must be tamed. It is a short process with me, and I possess experience in the work; for Guy, though by nature as wild as a hawk, has learned to come at my call as meekly as a dove. Chut! What a little fury it is."

I was just then; for exasperated at his coolness, and quite beside myself, I had suddenly stooped and bitten the shapely white hand that held both my own. I had better have submitted; for slight as the foolish action was, it had an influence on my after life as many another such has had. My uncle stopped laughing, his hand tightened its grasp, for a moment his cold eye glittered and a grim look settled round the mouth, giving to his whole face a ruthless expression that entirely altered it. I felt perfectly powerless. All my little arts had failed, and for the first time I was mastered. Yet only physically; my spirit was rebellious still. He saw it in the glance that met his own, as I sat erect and pale, with something more than childish anger. I think it pleased him, for swiftly as it had come the dark look passed, and quietly, as if we were the best of friends, he began to relate certain exciting adventures he had known abroad, lending to the picturesque narration the charm of that particularly melodious voice, which soothed and won me in spite of myself, holding me intent till I forgot the past; and when he paused I found that I was leaning confidentially on his shoulder, asking for more, yet conscious of an instinctive distrust of this man whom I had so soon learned to fear yet fancy.

As I was recalled to myself, I endeavored to leave him; but he still detained me, and, with a curious expression, produced a case so quaintly fashioned that I cried out in admiration, while he selected two cigarettes, mildly aromatic with the herbs they were composed of, lit them, offered me one, dropped the window, and leaning back surveyed me with an air of extreme enjoyment, as I sat meekly puffing and wondering what prank I should play a part in next. Slowly the narcotic influence of the herbs diffused itself like a pleasant haze over all my senses; sleep, the most grateful, fell upon my eyelids, and the last thing I remember was my uncle's face dreamily regarding me through a cloud of fragrant smoke. Twilight wrapped us in its shadows when I woke, with the night wind blowing on my forehead, the muffled roll of wheels sounding in my ear, and my cheek pillowed upon my uncle's arm. He was humming a French *chanson*[1] about "Love and Wine, and the Seine to-morrow!" I listened till I caught the air, and presently joined him, mingling my girlish treble with his flute-like tenor. He stopped at once, and, in the coolly courteous tone I had always heard in our few interviews, asked if I was ready for lights and home.

"Are we there?" I cried; and looking out saw that we were ascending an avenue which swept up to a pile of buildings that rose tall and dark against the sky, with here and there a gleam along its gray front.

"Home at last, thank Heaven!" And springing out with the agility of a young man, my uncle led me over a terrace into a long hall, light and warm, and odorous with the breath of flowers blossoming here and there in graceful groups. A civil, middle-aged maid received and took me to my room, a bijou of a place, which increased my wonder when told that my uncle had chosen all its decorations and superintended their arrangement. "He understands women," I thought, handling the toilet ornaments, trying luxurious chair and lounge, and ending by slipping my feet into the scarlet and white Turkish slippers, coquettishly turning up their toes before the fire. A few moments I gave to examination, and, having expressed my satisfaction, was asked by my maid if I would be pleased to dress, as "the master" never allowed dinner to wait for any one. This recalled to me the fact that I was doubtless to meet my future husband at that meal, and in a moment every faculty was intent upon achieving a grand toilette for this first interview. The maid possessed skill and taste, and I a wardrobe lately embellished with Parisian gifts from my uncle which I was eager to display in his honor.

When ready, I surveyed myself in the long mirror as I had never done before, and saw there a little figure, slender, yet stately, in a dress of foreign fashion, ornamented with lace and carnation ribbons which enhanced the fairness of neck and arms, while blonde hair, wavy and golden, was gathered into an antique knot of curls behind, with a carnation fillet, and below a blooming dark-eyed face, just then radiant with girlish vanity and eagerness and hope.

"I'm glad I'm pretty!"

"So am I, Sybil."

I had unconsciously spoken aloud, and the echo came from the doorway where stood my uncle, carefully dressed, looking comelier and cooler than ever. The disagreeable smile flitted over his lips as he spoke, and I started, then stood abashed, till beckoning, he added in his most courtly manner, —

"You were so absorbed in the contemplation of your charming self, that Janet answered my tap and took herself away unheard. You are mistress of my table now; it waits; will you come down?"

With a last touch to that unruly hair of mine, a last, comprehensive glance and shake, I took the offered arm and rustled down the wide staircase, feeling that the romance of my life was about to begin. Three covers were laid, three chairs set, but only two were occupied, for no Guy appeared. I asked no questions, showed no surprise, but tried to devour my chagrin with my dinner, and exerted myself to charm my uncle into the belief that I had forgotten my cousin. It was a failure, however, for that empty seat had an irresistible fascination for me, and more than once, as my eye returned from its furtive scrutiny of napkin, plate, and trio of colored glasses, it met my uncle's and fell before his penetrative glance. When I gladly rose to leave him to his wine, – for he did not ask me to remain, – he also rose, and, as he held the door for me, he said, –

"You asked me to describe your cousin: you have seen one trait of his character to-night; does it please you?"

I knew he was as much vexed as I at Guy's absence, so quoting his own words I answered saucily, –

"Yes; for I'd rather see the hawk free than coming tamely at your call, uncle."

He frowned slightly, as if unused to such liberty of speech, yet bowed when I swept him a stately little curtsey and sailed away to the drawing-room, wondering if my uncle was as angry with me as I was with my cousin. In solitary grandeur I amused myself by strolling through the suite of handsome rooms henceforth to be my realm, looked at myself in the long mirrors, as every woman is apt to do when alone and in costume, danced over the mossy carpets, touched the grand piano, smelt the flowers, fingered the ornaments on *étagère*[2] and table, and was just giving my handkerchief a second drench of some refreshing perfume from a filigree flask that had captivated me, when the hall door was flung wide, a quick step went running upstairs, boots tramped overhead, drawers seemed hastily opened and shut, and a bold, blithe voice broke out into a hunting song in a tone so like my uncle's that I involuntarily flew to the door, crying, –

"Guy is come!"

Fortunately for my dignity, no one heard me, and hurrying back I stood ready to skim into a chair and assume propriety at a minute's notice, conscious, meanwhile, of the new influence which seemed suddenly to gift the silent house with vitality, and add the one charm it needed, – that of cheerful companionship. "How will he meet me?

and how shall I meet him?" I thought, looking up at the bright-faced boy, whose portrait looked back at me with a mirthful light in the painted eyes and a trace of his father's disdainful smile in the curves of the firm-set lips. Presently the quick steps came flying down again, past the door, straight to the dining-room opposite, and, as I stood listening with a strange flutter at my heart, I heard an imperious young voice say rapidly, —

"Beg pardon, sir, unavoidably detained. Has she come? Is she bearable?"

"I find her so. Dinner is over, and I can offer you nothing but a glass of wine."

My uncle's voice was frostily polite, making a curious contrast to the other, so impetuous and frank, as if used to command or win all but one.

"Never mind the dinner! I'm glad to be rid of it; so I'll drink your health, father, and then inspect our new ornament."

"Impertinent boy!" I muttered, yet at the same moment resolved to deserve his appellation, and immediately regrouped myself as effectively as possible, laughing at my folly as I did so. I possessed a pretty foot, therefore one little slipper appeared quite naturally below the last flounce of my dress; a bracelet glittered on my arm as it emerged from among the lace and carnation knots; that arm supported my head. My profile was well cut, my eyelashes long, therefore I read with face half averted from the door. The light showered down, turning my hair to gold; so I smoothed my curls, retied my snood, and, after a satisfied survey, composed myself with an absorbed aspect and a quickened pulse to await the arrival of the gentlemen.

Soon they came. I knew they paused on the threshold, but never stirred till an irrepressible, "You are right, sir!" escaped the younger. Then I rose prepared to give him the coldest greeting, yet I did not. I had almost expected to meet the boyish face and figure of the picture; I saw, instead, a man comely and tall. A dark moustache half hid the proud mouth; the vivacious eyes were far kinder, though quite as keen as his father's, and the freshness of unspoiled youth lent a charm which the older man had lost for ever. Guy's glance of pleased surprise was flatteringly frank, his smile so cordial, his "Welcome, cousin!" such a hearty sound, that my coldness melted in a breath, my dignity was all forgotten, and before I could restrain myself I had offered both hands with the impulsive exclamation, —

"Cousin Guy, I know I shall be very happy here! Are you glad I have come?"

"Glad as I am to see the sun after a November fog."

And, bending his tall head, he kissed my hand in the graceful foreign fashion he had learned abroad. It pleased me mightily, for it was both affectionate and respectful. Involuntarily I contrasted it with my uncle's manner, and flashed a significant glance at him as I did so. He understood it, but only nodded with the satirical look I hated, shook out his paper and began to read. I sat down again, careless of myself now; and Guy stood on the rug, surveying me with an expression of surprise that rather nettled my pride.

"He is only a boy after all; so I need not be daunted by his inches or his airs. I wonder if he knows I am to be his wife, and likes it."

The thought sent the color to my forehead, my eyes fell, and despite my valiant resolution, I sat like any bashful child before my handsome cousin. Guy laughed a boyish laugh as he sat down on his father's footstool, saying, while he warmed his slender brown hands, —

"I beg your pardon, Sybil. (We won't be formal, will we?) But I haven't seen a lady for a month, so I stare like a boor at sight of a silk gown and high-bred face. Are those people coming, sir?"

"If Sybil likes, ask her."

"Shall we have a flock of people here to make it gay for you, cousin, or do you prefer our quiet style better; just riding, driving, lounging, and enjoying life, each in his own way? Henceforth it is to be as you command in such matters."

"Let things go on as they have done, then. I don't care for society, and strangers wouldn't make it gay to me, for I like freedom; so do you, I think."

"Ah, don't I!"

A cloud flitted over his smiling face, and he punched the fire, as if some vent were necessary for the sudden gust of petulance that knit his black brows into a frown, and caused his father to tap him on the shoulder with the bland request, as he rose to leave the room, —

"Bring the portfolios and entertain your cousin; I have letters to write, and Sybil is too tired to care for music to-night."

Guy obeyed with a shrug of the shoulder his father touched, but lingered in the recess till my uncle, having made his apologies to me, had left the room; then my cousin rejoined me, wearing the same cordial aspect I first beheld. Some restraint was evidently removed, and his natural self appeared. A very winsome self it was, courteous, gay, and frank, with an undertone of deeper feeling than I had hoped to find. I watched him covertly, and soon owned to myself that he was all I most admired in the ideal hero every girl creates in her romantic fancy; for I no longer looked upon this young man as my cousin, but my lover, and through all our future intercourse this thought was always uppermost, full of a charm that never lost its power.

Before the evening ended Guy was kneeling on the rug beside me, our two heads close together, while he turned the contents of the great portfolio spread before us, looking each other freely in the face, as I listened and he described, both breaking into frequent peals of laughter at some odd adventure or comical mishap in his own travels, suggested by the pictured scenes before us. Guy was very charming, I my blithest, sweetest self, and when we parted late, my cousin watched me up the stairs with still another, "Good night, Sybil," as if both sight and sound were pleasant to him.

"Is that your horse Sultan?" I called from my window next morning, as I looked down upon my cousin, who was coming up the drive from an early gallop on the moors.

"Yes, bonny Sybil; come and admire him," he called

back, hat in hand, and a quick smile rippling over his face.

I went, and, standing on the terrace, caressed the handsome creature, while Guy said, glancing up at his father's undrawn curtains, —

"If your saddle had come, we would take a turn before 'my lord' is ready for breakfast. This autumn air is the wine you women need."

I yearned to go, and when I willed the way soon appeared; so careless of bonnetless head and cambric gown, I stretched my hands to him, saying boldly, —

"Play young Lochinvar,[3] Guy; I am little and light; take me up before you and show me the sea."

He liked the daring feat, held out his hand, I stepped on his boot toe, sprang up, and away we went over the wide moor, where the sun shone in a cloudless heaven, the lark soared singing from the green grass at our feet, and the September wind blew freshly from the sea. As we paused on the upland slope, that gave us a free view of the country for miles, Guy dismounted, and, standing with his arm about the saddle to steady me in my precarious seat, began to talk.

"Do you like your new home, cousin?"

"More than I can tell you!"

"And my father, Sybil?"

"Both yes and no to that question, Guy; I hardly know him yet."

"True, but you must not expect to find him as indulgent and fond as many guardians would be to such as you. It's not his nature. Yet you can win his heart by obedience, and soon grow quite at ease with him."

"Bless you! I'm that already, for I fear no one. Why, I sat on his knee yesterday and smoked a cigarette of his own offering, though madame would have fainted if she had seen me; then I slept on his arm an hour, and he was fatherly kind, though I teased him like a gnat."

"The deuce he was!" with which energetic expression Guy frowned at the landscape and harshly checked Sultan's attempt to browse, while I wondered what was amiss between father and son, and resolved to discover; but, finding the conversation at an end, started it afresh, by asking, —

"Is any of my property in this part of the country, Guy? Do you know I am as ignorant as a baby about my own affairs; for, as long as every whim was gratified and my purse full, I left the rest to madame and uncle, though the first hadn't a bit of judgment, and the last I scarcely knew. I never cared to ask questions before, but now I am intensely curious to know how matters stand."

"All you see is yours, Sybil," was the brief answer.

"What, that great house, the lovely gardens, these moors, and the forest stretching to the sea? I'm glad! I'm glad! But where, then, is your home, Guy?"

"Nowhere."

At this I looked so amazed, that his gloom vanished in a laugh, as he explained, but briefly, as if this subject were no pleasanter than the first —

"By your father's will you were desired to take possession of the old place at eighteen. You will be that soon; therefore, as your guardian, my father has prepared things for you, and is to share your home until you marry."

"When will that be, I wonder?" and I stole a glance from under my lashes, wild to discover if Guy knew of the compact and was a willing party to it. His face was half averted, but over his dark cheek I saw a deep flush rise, as he answered, stooping to pull a bit of heather, —

"Soon, I hope, or the gentleman sleeping there below will be tempted to remain a fixture with you on his knee as 'madame my wife.' He is not your own uncle, you know."

I smiled at the idea, but Guy did not see it; and seized with a whim to try my skill with the hawk that seemed inclined to peck at its master, I said demurely, —

"Well, why not? I might be very happy if I learned to love him, as I should, if he were always in that kindest mood of his. Would you like me for a little mamma, Guy?"

"No!" short and sharp as a pistol shot.

"Then you must marry and have a home of your own, my son."

"Don't, Sybil! I'd rather you didn't see me in a rage, for I'm not a pleasant sight, I assure you; and I'm afraid

I shall be in one if you go on. I early lost my mother, but I love her tenderly, because my father is not much to me, and I know if she had lived I should not be what I am."

Bitter was his voice, moody his mien, and all the sunshine gone at once. I looked down and touched his black hair with a shy caress, feeling both penitent and pitiful.

"Dear Guy, forgive me if I pained you. I'm a thoughtless creature, but I'm not malicious, and a word will restrain me if kindly spoken. My home is always yours, and when my fortune is mine you shall never want, if you are not too proud to accept help from your own kin. You are a little proud, aren't you?"

"As Lucifer, to most people. I think I should not be to you, for you understand me, Sybil, and with you I hope to grow a better man."

He turned then, and through the lineaments his father had bequeathed him I saw a look that must have been his mother's, for it was womanly, sweet, and soft, and lent new beauty to the dark eyes, always kind, and just then very tender. He had checked his words suddenly, like one who has gone too far, and with that hasty look into my face had bent his own upon the ground, as if to hide the unwonted feeling that had mastered him. It lasted but a moment, then his old manner returned, as he said gayly, —

"There drops your slipper. I've been wondering what kept it on. Pretty thing! They say it is a foot like this that oftenest tramples on men's hearts. Are you cruel to your lovers, Sybil?"

"I never had one, for madame guarded me like a dragon, and I led the life of a nun; but when I do find one I shall try his mettle well before I give up my liberty."

"Poets say it is sweet to give up liberty for love, and they ought to know," answered Guy, with a sidelong glance.

I liked that little speech, and recollecting the wistful look he had given me, the significant words that had escaped him, and the variations of tone and manner constantly succeeding one another, I felt assured that my cousin was cognizant of the family league, and accepted it, yet, with the shyness of a young lover, knew not how to woo. This pleased me, and, quite satisfied with my morning's work, I mentally resolved to charm my cousin slowly, and enjoy the romance of a genuine wooing, without which no woman's life seems complete, – in her own eyes, at least. He had gathered me a knot of purple heather, and as he gave it I smiled my sweetest on him, saying, –

"I commission you to supply me with nosegays, for you have taste, and I love wild-flowers. I shall wear this at dinner in honor of its giver. Now take me home; for my moors, though beautiful, are chilly, and I have no wrapper but this microscopic handkerchief."

Off went his riding-jacket, and I was half smothered in it. The hat followed next, and as he sprung up behind I took the reins, and felt a thrill of delight in sweeping down the slope with that mettlesome creature tugging at the bit, that strong arm round me, and the happy hope that the heart I leaned on might yet learn to love me.

The day so began passed pleasantly, spent in roving over house and grounds with my cousin, setting my possessions in order, and writing to dear old madame. Twilight found me in my bravest attire, with Guy's heather in my hair, listening for his step, and longing to run and meet him when he came. Punctual to the instant he appeared, and this dinner was a far different one from that of yesterday, for both father and son seemed in their gayest and most gallant mood, and I enjoyed the hour heartily. The world seemed all in tune now, and when I went to the drawing-room I was moved to play my most stirring marches, sing my blithest songs, hoping to bring one at least of the gentlemen to join me. It brought both, and my first glance showed me a curious change in each. My uncle looked harassed and yet amused, Guy looked sullen and eyed his father with covert glances.

The morning's case flashed into my mind, and I asked myself, "Is Guy jealous so soon?" It looked a little like it, for he threw himself upon a couch and lay there silent and morose; while my uncle paced to and fro, thinking deeply, while apparently listening to the song he bade me finish. I did so, then followed the whim that now possessed me, for I wanted to try my power over them both, to see if I could restore that gentler mood of my uncle's, and assure myself that Guy cared whether I was friendliest with him or not.

"Uncle, come and sing with me; I like that voice of yours."

"Tut, I am too old for that; take this indolent lad instead, his voice is fresh and young, and will chord well with yours."

"Do you know that pretty *chanson* about 'Love and Wine, and the Seine to-morrow,' cousin Guy?" I asked, stealing a sly glance at my uncle.

"Who taught you that?" and Guy eyed me over the top of the couch with an astonished expression which greatly amused me.

"No one; uncle sang a bit of it in the carriage yesterday. I like the air, so come and teach me the rest."

"It is no song for you, Sybil. You choose strange entertainment for a lady, sir."

A look of unmistakable contempt was in the son's eye, of momentary annoyance in the father's, yet his voice betrayed none as he answered, still pacing placidly along the room, —

"I thought she was asleep, and unconsciously began it to beguile a silent drive. Sing on, Sybil; that Bacchanalian[4] snatch will do you no harm."

But I was tired of music now they had come, so I went to him, and, passing my arm through his, walked beside him, saying with my most persuasive aspect, —

"Tell me about Paris, uncle; I intend to go there as soon as I'm of age, if you will let me. Does your guardianship extend beyond that time?"

"Only till you marry."

"I shall be in no haste, then, for I begin to feel quite homelike and happy here with you, and shall be content without other society; only you'll soon tire of me, and leave me to some dismal governess, while you and Guy go pleasuring."

"No fear of that, Sybil; I shall hold you fast till some

younger guardian comes to rob me of my merry ward."

As he spoke, he took the hand that lay upon his arm into a grasp so firm, and turned on me a look so keen, that I involuntarily dropped my eyes lest he should read my secret there. Eager to turn the conversation, I asked, pointing to a little miniature hanging underneath the portrait of his son, before which he had paused, —

"Was that Guy's mother, sir?"

"No, your own."

I looked again, and saw a face delicate yet spirited, with dark eyes, a passionate mouth, and a head crowned with hair as plenteous and golden as my own; but the whole seemed dimmed by age, the ivory was stained, the glass cracked, and a faded ribbon fastened it. My eyes filled as I looked, and a strong desire seized me to know what had defaced this little picture of the mother whom I never knew.

"Tell me about her, uncle; I know so little, and often long for her so much. Am I like her, sir?"

Why did my uncle avert his eyes as he answered, —

"You are a youthful image of her, Sybil."

"Go on please, tell me more; tell me why this is so stained and worn; you know all, and surely I am old enough now to hear any history of pain and loss."

Something caused my uncle to knit his brows, but his bland voice never varied a tone as he placed the picture in my hand and gave me this brief explanation: —

"Just before your birth your father was obliged to cross the Channel, to receive the last wishes of a dying friend; there was an accident; the vessel foundered, and many lives were lost. He escaped, but by some mistake his name appeared in the list of missing passengers; your mother saw it, the shock destroyed her, and when your father returned he found only a motherless little daughter to welcome him. This miniature, which he always carried with him, was saved with his papers at the last moment; but though the sea-water ruined it he would never have it copied or retouched, and gave it to me when he died in memory of the woman I had loved for his sake. It is yours now, my child; keep it, and never feel that you are fatherless or motherless while I remain."

Kind as was both act and speech, neither touched me, for something seemed wanting. I felt, yet could not define it, for then I believed in the sincerity of all I met.

"Where was she buried, uncle? It may be foolish, but I should like to see my mother's grave."

"You shall some day, Sybil," and a curious change came over my uncle's face as he averted it.

"I have made him melancholy, talking of Guy's mother and my own; now I'll make him gay again if possible, and pique that negligent boy," I thought, and drew my uncle to a lounging-chair, established myself on the arm thereof, and kept him laughing with my merriest gossip, both of us apparently unconscious of the long dark figure stretched just opposite, feigning sleep, but watching us through half-closed lids, and never stirring except to bow silently to my careless "Good-night."

As I reached the stairhead, I remembered that my letter to madame, full of frankest criticisms upon people and things, was lying unsealed on the table in the little room my uncle had set apart for my boudoir; fearing servants' eyes and tongues, I slipped down again to get it. The room adjoined the parlors, and just then was lit only by a ray from the hall lamp. I had secured the letter, and was turning to retreat, when I heard Guy say petulantly, as if thwarted yet submissive, —

"I *am* civil when you leave me alone; I *do* agree to marry her, but I won't be hurried or go a-wooing except in my own way. You know I never liked the bargain, for it's nothing else; yet I can reconcile myself to being sold, if it relieves you and gives us both a home. But, father, mind this, if you tie me to that girl's sash too tightly I shall break away entirely, and then where are we?"

"I should be in prison and you a homeless vagabond. Trust me, my boy, and take the good fortune which I secured for you in your cradle. Look in pretty Sybil's face, and resignation will grow easy; but remember time presses, that this is our forlorn hope, and for God's sake be cautious, for she is a headstrong creature, and may refuse to fulfil her part if she learns that the contract is not binding against her will."

"I think she'll not refuse, sir; she likes me already. I see it in her eyes; she has never had a lover, she says, and according to your account a girl's first sweetheart is apt to fare the best. Besides, she likes the place, for I told her it was hers, and she said she could be very happy here, if my father was always kind."

"She said that, did she? little hypocrite! For your father, read yourself, and tell me what else she babbled about in that early *tête-à-tête* of yours."

"You are as curious as a woman, sir, and always make me tell you all I do and say, yet never tell me any thing in return, except this business, which I hate, because my liberty is the price, and my poor little cousin is kept in the dark. I'll tell her all, before I marry her, father."

"As you please, hot-head. I am waiting for an account of the first love passage, so leave blushing to Sybil and begin."

I knew what was coming and stayed no longer, but caught one glimpse of the pair. Guy in his favorite place, erect upon the rug, half-laughing, half-frowning as he delayed to speak, my uncle serenely smoking on the couch; then I sped away to my own room, thinking, as I sat down in a towering passion, —

"So he does know of the baby betrothal and hates it, yet submits to it to please his father, who covets my fortune, – mercenary creatures! I can annul the contract, can I? I'm glad to know that, for it makes me mistress of them both. I like you already, do I? and you see it in my eyes. Coxcomb! I'll be the thornier for that. Yet I do like him; I do wish he cared for me, I'm so lonely in the world, and he can be so kind."

So I cried a little, brushed my hair a good deal, and went to bed, resolving to learn all I could when, where, and how I pleased, to render myself as charming and valuable as possible, to make Guy love me in spite of himself, and then say yes or no, as my heart prompted me.

That day was a sample of those that followed, for my cousin was by turns attracted or repelled by the capricious moods that ruled me. Though conscious of a secret distrust of my uncle, I could not resist the fascination of his manner when he chose to exert its influence over me; this made my little plot easier of execution, for jealousy seemed the most effectual means to bring my wayward cousin to subjection. Full of this fancy, I seemed to tire of his society, grew thorny as a briar rose to him, affectionate as a daughter to my uncle, who surveyed us both with that inscrutable glance of his, and slowly yielded to my dominion as if he had divined my purpose and desired to aid it. Guy turned cold and gloomy, yet still lingered near me as if ready for a relenting look or word. I liked that, and took a wanton pleasure in prolonging the humiliation of the warm heart I had learned to love, yet not to value as I ought, until it was too late.

One dull November evening as I went wandering up and down the hall, pretending to enjoy the flowers, yet in reality waiting for Guy, who had left me alone all day, my uncle came from his room, where he had sat for many hours with the harassed and anxious look he always wore when certain foreign letters came.

"Sybil, I have something to show and tell you," he said, as I garnished his button-hole with a spray of heliotrope,[5] meant for the laggard, who would understand its significance, I hoped. Leading me to the drawing-room, my uncle put a paper into my hands, with the request, —

"This is a copy of your father's will; oblige me by reading it."

He stood watching my face as I read, no doubt wondering at my composure while I waded through the dry details of the will, curbing my impatience to reach the one important passage. There it was, but no word concerning my power to dissolve the engagement if I pleased; and, as I realized the fact, a sudden bewilderment and sense of helplessness came over me, for the strange law terms seemed to make inexorable the paternal decree which I had not seen before. I forgot my studied calmness, and asked several questions eagerly.

"Uncle, did my father really command that I should marry Guy, whether we loved each other or not?"

"You see what he there set down as his desire; and I

have taken measures that you *should* love one another, knowing that few cousins, young, comely, and congenial, would live three months together without finding themselves ready to mate for their own sakes, if not for the sake of the dead and living fathers to whom they owe obedience."

"You said I need not, if I didn't choose; why is it not here?"

"I said that? Never, Sybil!" and I met a look of such entire surprise and incredulity it staggered my belief in my own senses, yet also roused my spirit, and, careless of consequences, I spoke out at once, —

"I heard you say it myself the night after I came, when you told Guy to be cautious, because I could refuse to fulfil the engagement, if I knew that it was not binding against my will."

This discovery evidently destroyed some plan, and for a moment threw him off his guard; for, crumpling the paper in his hand, he sternly demanded, —

"You turned eavesdropper early; how often since?"

"Never, uncle; I did not mean it then, but, going for a letter in the dark, I heard your voices, and listened for an instant. It was dishonorable, but irresistible; and, if you force Guy's confidence, why should not I steal yours? All is fair in war, sir, and I forgive as I hope to be forgiven."

"You have a quick wit and a reticence I did not expect to find under that frank manner. So you have known your future destiny all these months, then, and have a purpose in your treatment of your cousin and myself?"

"Yes, uncle."

"May I ask what?"

I was ashamed to tell; and, in the little pause before my answer came, my pique at Guy's desertion was augmented by anger at my uncle's denial of his own words the ungenerous hopes he cherished, and a strong desire to perplex and thwart him took possession of me, for I saw his anxiety concerning the success of this interview, though he endeavored to repress and conceal it. Assuming my coldest mien, I said, —

"No, sir, I think not; only I can assure you that my

little plot has succeeded better than your own."

"But you intend to obey your father's wish, I hope, and fulfil your part of the compact, Sybil?"

"Why should I? It is not binding, you know, and I'm too young to lose my liberty just yet; besides, such compacts are unjust, unwise. What right had my father to mate me in my cradle? how did he know what I should become, or Guy? how could he tell that I should not love some one else better? No! I'll not be bargained away like a piece of merchandise, but love and marry when I please!"

At this declaration of independence my uncle's face darkened ominously, some new suspicion lurked in his eye, some new anxiety beset him; but his manner was calm, his voice blander than ever as he asked, —

"Is there then, some one whom you love? Confide in me, my girl."

"And if there were, what then?"

"All would be changed at once, Sybil. But who is it? Some young lover left behind at madame's?"

"No, sir."

"Who, then? You have led a recluse life here. Guy has no friends who visit him, and mine are all old, yet you say you love."

"With all my heart, uncle."

"Is this affection returned, Sybil?"

"I think so."

"And it is not Guy?"

I was wicked enough to enjoy the bitter disappointment he could not conceal at my decided words, for I thought he deserved that momentary pang; but I could not as decidedly answer that last question, for I would not lie, neither would I confess just yet; so, with a little gesture of impatience, I silently turned away, lest he should see the tell-tale color in my cheeks. My uncle stood an instant in deep thought, a slow smile crept to his lips, content returned to his mien, and something like a flash of triumph glittered for a moment in his eye, then vanished, leaving his countenance earnestly expectant. Much as this change surprised me, his words did more, for, taking both my hands in his, he gravely said, —

"Do you know that I am your uncle by adoption and not blood, Sybil?"

"Yes, sir; I heard so, but forgot about it," and I looked up at him, my anger quite lost in astonishment.

"Let me tell you, then. Your grandfather was childless for many years, my mother was an early friend, and when her death left me an orphan, he took me for his son and heir. But two years from that time your father was born. I was too young to realize the entire change this might make in my life. The old man was too just and generous to let me feel it, and the two lads grew up together like brothers. Both married young, and when you were born a few years later than my son, your father said to me, 'Your boy shall have my girl, and the fortune I have innocently robbed you of shall make us happy in our children.' Then the family league was made, renewed at his death, and now destroyed by his daughter, unless – Sybil, I am forty-five, you not eighteen, yet you once said you could be very happy with me, if I were always kind to you. I can promise that I will be, for I love you. My darling, you reject the son, will you accept the father?"

If he had struck me, it would have scarcely dismayed me more. I started up, and snatching away my hands hid my face in them, for after the first tingle of surprise an almost irresistible desire to laugh came over me, but I dared not, and gravely, gently, he went on, —

"I am a bold man to say this, yet I mean it most sincerely. I never meant to betray the affection I believed you could never return, and would only laugh at as a weakness; but your past acts, your present words, give me courage to confess that I desire to keep my ward for ever. Shall it be so?"

He evidently mistook my surprise for maidenly emotion, and the suddenness of this unforeseen catastrophe seemed to deprive me of words. All thought of merriment or ridicule was forgotten in a sense of guilt, for if he feigned the love he offered it was well done, and I believed it then. I saw at once the natural impression conveyed by my conduct; my half confession and the folly of it all oppressed me with a regret and shame I could not master.

My mind was in dire confusion, yet a decided "No" was rapidly emerging from the chaos, but was not uttered; for just at this crisis, as I stood with my uncle's arm about me, my hand again in his, and his head bent down to catch my answer, Guy swung himself gayly into the room. A glance seemed to explain all, and in an instant his face assumed that expression of pale wrath so much more terrible to witness than the fiercest outbreak; his eye grew fiery, his voice bitterly sarcastic, as he said, —

"Ah, I see; the play goes on, but the actors change parts. I congratulate you, sir, on your success, and Sybil on her choice. Henceforth I am *de trop*,[6] but before I go allow me to offer my wedding gift. You have taken the bride, let me supply the ring."

He threw a jewel-box upon the table, adding, in that unnaturally calm tone that made my heart stand still:

"A little candor would have spared me much pain, Sybil; yet I hope you will enjoy your bonds as heartily as I shall my escape from them. A little confidence would have made me your ally, not your rival, father. I have not your address; therefore I lose, you win. Let it be so. I had rather be the vagabond this makes me than sell myself, that you may gamble away that girl's fortune as you have your own and mine. You need not ask me to the wedding, I will not come. Oh, Sybil, I so loved, so trusted you!"

And with that broken exclamation he was gone.

The stormy scene had passed so rapidly, been so strange and sudden, Guy's anger so scornful and abrupt, I could not understand it, and felt like a puppet in the grasp of some power I could not resist; but as my lover left the room I broke out of the bewilderment that held me, imploring him to stay and hear me.

It was too late, he was gone, and Sultan's tramp was already tearing down the avenue. I listened till the sound died, then my hot temper rose past control, and woman-like asserted itself in vehement and voluble speech: I was angry with my uncle, my cousin, and myself, and for several minutes poured forth a torrent of explanations, reproaches, and regrets, such as only a passionate girl could utter.

My uncle stood where I had left him when I flew to the door with my vain cry; he now looked baffled, yet sternly resolved, and as I paused for breath his only answer was, —

"Sybil, you ask me to bring back that headstrong boy; I cannot; he will never come. This marriage was distasteful to him, yet he submitted for my sake, because I have been unfortunate, and we are poor. Let him go, forget the past, and be to me what I desire, for I loved your father and will be a faithful guardian to his daughter all my life. Child, it must be, — come, I implore, I command you."

He beckoned imperiously as if to awe me, and held up the glittering betrothal ring as if to tempt me. The tone, the act, the look put me quite beside myself. I did go to him, did take the ring, but said as resolutely as himself, —

"Guy rejects me, and I have done with love. Uncle, you would have deceived me, used me as a means to your own selfish ends. I will accept neither yourself nor your gifts, for now I despise both you and your commands;" and, as the most energetic emphasis I could give to my defiance, I flung the ring, case and all, across the room; it struck the great mirror, shivered it just in the middle, and sent several loosened fragments crashing to the floor.

"Great heavens! is the young lady mad?" exclaimed a voice behind us. Both turned and saw Dr. Karnac, a stealthy, sallow-faced Spaniard, for whom I had an invincible aversion. He was my uncle's physician, had been visiting a sick servant in the upper regions, and my adverse fate sent him to the door just at that moment with that unfortunate exclamation on his lips.

"What do you say?"

My uncle wheeled about and eyed the new-comer intently as he repeated his words. I have no doubt I looked like one demented, for I was desperately angry, pale and trembling with excitement, and as they fronted me with a curious expression of alarm on their faces, a sudden sense of the absurdity of the spectacle came over me; I laughed hysterically a moment, then broke into a passion of regretful tears, remembering that Guy was gone. As I sobbed behind my hands, I knew the gentlemen were whispering together and of me, but I never heeded them, for as I wept myself calmer a comforting thought occurred to me; Guy could not have gone far, for Sultan had been out all day, and though reckless of himself he was not of his horse, which he loved like a human being; therefore he was doubtless at the house of a humble friend near by. If I could slip away unseen, I might undo my miserable work, or at least see him again before he went away into the world, perhaps never to return. This hope gave me courage for any thing, and dashing away my tears I took a covert survey. Dr. Karnac and my uncle still stood before the fire, deep in their low-toned conversation; their backs were toward me, and, hushing the rustle of my dress, I stole away with noiseless steps into the hall, seized Guy's plaid, and, opening the great door unseen, darted down the avenue.

Not far, however; the wind buffeted me to and fro, the rain blinded me, the mud clogged my feet and soon robbed me of a slipper; groping for it in despair, I saw a light flash into the outer darkness; heard voices calling, and soon the swift tramp of steps behind me. Feeling like a hunted doe, I ran on, but before I had gained a dozen yards my shoeless foot struck a sharp stone, and I fell half-stunned upon the wet grass of the wayside bank. Dr. Karnac reached me first, took me up as if I were a naughty child, and carried me back through a group of staring servants to the drawing-room, my uncle following with breathless entreaties that I would be calm, and a most uncharacteristic display of bustle.

I was horribly ashamed; my head ached with the shock of the fall, my foot bled, my heart fluttered, and when the doctor put me down the crisis came, for as my uncle bent over me with the strange question, "My poor girl, do you know me?" an irresistible impulse impelled me to push him from me, crying passionately, —

"Yes, I know and hate you; let me go! let me go, or it will be too late!" then, quite spent with the varying emotions of the last hour, for the first time in my life I swooned away.

Coming to myself, I found I was in my own room, with my uncle, the doctor, Janet, and Mrs. Best, the housekeeper, gathered about me, the latter saying, as she bathed my temples, —

"She's a sad sight, poor thing, so young, so bonny, and so unfortunate. Did you ever see her so before, Janet?"

"Bless you, no, ma'am; there was no signs of such a tantrum when I dressed her for dinner."

"What do they mean? did they never see any one angry before?" I dimly wondered, and presently, through the fast disappearing stupor that had held me, Dr. Karnac's deep voice came distinctly, saying, —

"If it continues, you are perfectly justified in doing so."

"Doing what?" I demanded sharply, for the sound both roused me and irritated me, I disliked the man so intensely.

"Nothing, my dear, nothing," purred Mrs. Best, supporting me as I sat up, feeling weak and dazed, yet resolved to know what was going on. I was "a sad sight" indeed; my drenched hair hung about my shoulders, my dress was streaked with mud, one shoeless foot was red with blood, the other splashed and stained, and a white, wild-eyed face completed the ruinous image the opposite mirror showed me. Every thing looked blurred and strange, and a feverish unrest possessed me, for I was not one to subside easily after such a mental storm. Leaning on my arm, I scanned the room and its occupants with all the composure I could collect. The two women eyed me curiously yet pitifully; Dr. Karnac stood glancing at me furtively as he listened to my uncle, who spoke rapidly in Spanish as he showed the little scar upon his hand. That sight did more to restore me than the cordial just administered, and I rose erect, saying abruptly, —

"Please, everybody, go away; my head aches, and I want to be alone."

"Let Janet stay and help you, dear; you are not fit," began Mrs. Best; but I peremptorily stopped her.

"No, go yourself, and take her with you; I'm tired of so much stir about such foolish things as a broken glass and a girl in a pet."

"You will be good enough to take this quieting draught before I go, Miss Sybil."

"I shall do nothing of the sort, for I need only solitude and sleep to be perfectly well," and I emptied the glass the doctor offered into the fire. He shrugged his shoulders with a disagreeable smile, and quietly began to prepare another draught, saying, —

"You are mistaken, my dear young lady; you need much care, and should obey, that your uncle may be spared further apprehension and anxiety."

My patience gave out at this assumption of authority; and I determined to carry matters with a high hand, for they all stood watching me in a way which seemed the height of impertinent curiosity.

"He is not my uncle! never has been, and deserves neither respect nor obedience from me! I am the best judge of my own health, and you are not bettering it by contradiction and unnecessary fuss. This is my house, and you will oblige me by leaving it, Dr. Karnac; this is my room, and I insist on being left in peace immediately."

I pointed to the door as I spoke; the women hurried out with scared faces; the doctor bowed and followed, but paused on the threshold, while my uncle approached me, asking in a tone inaudible to those still hovering round the door, —

"Do you still persist in your refusal, Sybil?"

"How dare you ask me that again? I tell you I had rather die than marry you!"

"The Lord be merciful to us! just hear how she's going on now about marrying master. Ain't it awful, Jane?" ejaculated Mrs. Best, bobbing her head in for a last look.

"Hold your tongue, you impertinent creature!" I called out; and the fat old soul bundled away in such comical haste I laughed, in spite of languor and vexation.

My uncle left me, and I heard him say as he passed the doctor, —

"You see how it is."

"Nothing uncommon; but that virulence is a bad symptom," answered the Spaniard, and closing the door locked it, having dexterously removed the key from within.

I had never been subjected to restraint of any kind; it made me reckless at once, for this last indignity was not to be endured.

"Open this instantly!" I commanded, shaking the door. No one answered, and after a few ineffectual attempts to break the lock I left it, threw up the window for a look out; the ground was too far off for a leap, but the trellis where summer-vines had clung was strong and high, a step would place me on it, a moment's agility bring me to the terrace below. I was now in just the state to attempt any rash exploit, for the cordial had both strengthened and excited me; my foot was bandaged, my clothes still wet; I could suffer no new damage, and have my own way at small cost. Out I crept, climbed safely down, and made my way to the lodge as I had at first intended. But Guy was not there; and, returning, I boldly went in at the great door, straight to the room where my uncle and the doctor were still talking.

"I wish the key of my room," was my brief command. Both started as if I had been a ghost, and my uncle exclaimed, —

"You here! how in Heaven's name came you out?"

"By the window. I am no child to be confined for a fit of anger. I will not submit to it; to-morrow I shall go to madame; till then I will be mistress in my own house. Give me the key, sir."

"Shall I?" asked the doctor of my uncle, who nodded with a whispered, —

"Yes, yes; don't excite her again."

It was restored, and without another word I went loftily up to my room, locked myself in, and spent a restless, miserable night. When morning came, I breakfasted above stairs, and then busied myself packing trunks, burning papers, and collecting every trifle Guy had ever given me. No one annoyed me, and I saw only Janet, who had evidently received some order that kept her silent and respectful, though her face still betrayed the same curiosity and pitiful interest as the night before. Lunch was brought up, but I could not eat, and began to feel that the exposure, the fall, and excitement of the evening had left me weak and nervous, so I gave up the idea of going to madame till the morrow; and, as the afternoon waned, tried to sleep, yet could not, for I had sent a note to several of Guy's haunts, imploring him to see me; but my messenger brought word that he was not to be found, and my heart was too heavy to rest.

When summoned to dinner, I still refused to go down; for I heard Dr. Karnac's voice, and would not meet him, so I sent word that I wished the carriage early the following morning, and to be left alone till then. In a few minutes, back came Janet, with a glass of wine set forth on a silver salver, and a card with these words, —

"Forgive, forget, for your father's sake, and drink with me, 'Oblivion to the past.'"

It touched and softened me. I knew my uncle's pride, and saw in this an entire relinquishment of the hopes I had so thoughtlessly fostered in his mind. I was passionate, but not vindictive. He had been kind, I very wilful. His mistake was natural, my resentment ungenerous. Though my resolution to go remained unchanged, I was sorry for my part in the affair; and remembering that through me his son was lost to him, I accepted his apology, drank his toast, and sent him back a dutiful "Good-night."

I was unused to wine. The draught I had taken was powerful with age, and, though warm and racy to the palate, proved too potent for me. Still sitting before my fire, I slowly fell into a restless drowse, haunted by a dim dream that I was seeking Guy in a ship, whose motion gradually lulled me into perfect unconsciousness.

Waking at length, I was surprised to find myself in bed, with the shimmer of daylight peeping through the curtains. Recollecting that I was to leave early, I sprang up, took one step and remained transfixed with dismay, for the room was not my own! Utterly unfamiliar was every object on which my eyes fell. The place was small, plainly furnished, and close, as if long unused. My trunks stood against the wall, my clothes lay on a chair, and on the bed I had left trailed a fur-lined cloak I had often seen on my uncle's shoulders. A moment I stared about me bewildered, then hurried to the window – it was grated!

A lawn, sere and sodden, lay without, and a line of firs hid the landscape beyond the high wall which encompassed the dreary plot. More and more alarmed, I flew to the door and found it locked. No bell was visible, no sound audible, no human presence near me, and an ominous foreboding thrilled cold through nerves and blood, as, for the first time, I felt the paralyzing touch of fear. Not long, however. My native courage soon returned, indignation took the place of terror, and excitement gave me strength. My temples throbbed with a dull pain, my eyes were heavy, my limbs weighed down by an unwonted lassitude, and my memory seemed strangely confused; but one thing was clear to me. I must see somebody, ask questions, demand explanations, and get away to madame without delay.

With trembling hands I dressed, stopping suddenly, with a cry; for, lifting my hands to my head, I discovered that my hair, my beautiful, abundant hair, was gone! There was no mirror in the room, but I could feel that it had been shorn away close about face and neck. This outrage was more than I could bear, and the first tears I shed fell for my lost charm. It was weak, perhaps, but I felt better for it, clearer in mind and readier to confront whatever lay before me. I knocked and called. Then, losing patience, shook and screamed; but no one came or answered me, and, wearied out at last, I sat down and cried again in impotent despair.

An hour passed, then a step approached, the key turned, and a hard-faced woman entered with a tray in her hand. I had resolved to be patient, if possible, and controlled myself to ask quietly, though my eyes kindled, and my voice trembled with resentment, —

"Where am I, and why am I here against my will?"

"This is your breakfast, miss; you must be sadly hungry," was the only reply I got.

"I will never eat till you tell me what I ask."

"Will you be quiet, and mind me if I do, miss?"

"You have no right to exact obedience from me, but

I'll try."

"That's right. Now all I know is that you are twenty miles from the Moors, and came because you are ill. Do you like sugar in your coffee?"

"When did I come? I don't remember it."

"Early this morning; you don't remember because you were put to sleep before being fetched, to save trouble."

"Ah, that wine! Who brought me here?"

"Dr. Karnac, miss."

"Alone?"

"Yes, miss; you were easier to manage asleep than awake, he said."

I shook with anger, yet still restrained myself, hoping to fathom the mystery of this nocturnal journey.

"What is your name, please?" I meekly asked.

"You can call me Hannah."

"Well, Hannah, there is a strange mistake somewhere. I am not ill – you see I am not – and I wish to go away at once to the friend I was to meet to-day. Get me a carriage and have my baggage taken out."

"It can't be done, miss. We are a mile from town, and have no carriages here; besides, you couldn't go if I had a dozen. I have my orders, and shall obey 'em."

"But Dr. Karnac has no right to bring or keep me here."

"Your uncle sent you. The doctor has the care of you, and that is all I know about it. Now I have kept my promise, do you keep yours, miss, and eat your breakfast, else I can't trust you again."

"But what is the matter with me? How can I be ill and not know or feel it?" I demanded, more and more bewildered.

"You look it, and that's enough for them as is wise in such matters. You'd have had a fever, if it hadn't been seen to in time."

"Who cut my hair off?"

"I did; the doctor ordered it."

"How dared he? I hate that man, and never will obey him."

"Hush, miss, don't clench your hands and look in that

way, for I shall have to report every thing you say and do to him, and it won't be pleasant to tell that sort of thing."

The woman was civil, but grim and cool. Her eye was unsympathetic, her manner business-like, her tone such as one uses to a refractory child, half-soothing, half-commanding. I conceived a dislike to her at once, and resolved to escape at all hazards, for my uncle's inexplicable movements filled me with alarm. Hannah had left my door open, a quick glance showed me another door also ajar at the end of a wide hall, a glimpse of green, and a gate. My plan was desperately simple, and I executed it without delay. Affecting to eat, I presently asked the woman for my handkerchief from the bed. She crossed the room to get it. I darted out, down the passage, along the walk, and tugged vigorously at the great bolt of the gate, but it was also locked. In despair I flew into the garden, but a high wall enclosed it on every side; and as I ran round and round, vainly looking for some outlet, I saw Hannah, accompanied by a man as gray and grim as herself, coming leisurely toward me, with no appearance of excitement or displeasure. Back I would not go; and, inspired with a sudden hope, swung myself into one of the firs that grew close against the wall. The branches snapped under me, the slender tree swayed perilously, but up I struggled, till the wide coping of the wall was gained. There I paused and looked back. The woman was hurrying through the gate to intercept my descent on the other side, and close behind me the man, sternly calling me to stop. I looked down; a stony ditch was below, but I would rather risk my life than tamely lose my liberty, and with a flying leap tried to reach the bank; failed, fell heavily among the stones, felt an awful crash, and then came an utter blank.

For many weeks I lay burning in a fever, fitfully conscious of Dr. Karnac and the woman's presence; once I fancied I saw my uncle, but was never sure, and rose at last a shadow of my former self, feeling pitifully broken, both mentally and physically. I was in a better room now, wintry winds howled without, but a generous fire glowed behind the high closed fender, and books lay on my table.

I saw no one but Hannah, yet could wring no intelligence from her beyond what she had already told, and no sign of interest reached me from the outer world. I seemed utterly deserted and forlorn, my spirit was crushed, my strength gone, my freedom lost, and for a time I succumbed to despair, letting one day follow another without energy or hope. It is hard to live with no object to give zest to life, especially for those still blest with youth, and even in my prison-house I soon found one quite in keeping with the mystery that surrounded me.

As I sat reading by day or lay awake at night, I became aware that the room above my own was occupied by some inmate whom I never saw. A peculiar person it seemed to be; for I heard steps going to and fro, hour after hour, in a tireless march, that wore upon my nerves, as many a harsher sound would not have done. I could neither tease nor surprise Hannah into any explanation of the thing, and day after day I listened to it, till I longed to cover up my ears and implore the unknown walker to stop, for Heaven's sake. Other sounds I heard and fretted over: a low monotonous murmur, as of some one singing a lullaby; a fitful tapping, like a cradle rocking on a carpetless floor; and at rare intervals cries of suffering, sharp but brief, as if forcibly suppressed. These sounds, combined with the solitude, the confinement, and the books I read, a collection of ghostly tales and weird fancies, soon wrought my nerves to a state of terrible irritability, and wore upon my health so visibly that I was allowed at last to leave my room.

The house was so well guarded that I soon relinquished all hope of escape, and listlessly amused myself by roaming through the unfurnished rooms and echoing halls, seldom venturing into Hannah's domain; for there her husband sat, surrounded by chemical apparatus, poring over crucibles and retorts. He never spoke to me, and I dreaded the glance of his cold eye, for it looked unsoftened by a ray of pity at the little figure that sometimes paused a moment on his threshold, wan and wasted as the ghost of departed hope.

The chief interest of these dreary walks centred in the

door of the room above my own, for a great hound lay before it, eying me savagely as he rejected all advances, and uttering his deep bay if I approached too near. To me this room possessed an irresistible fascination. I could not keep away from it by day, I dreamed of it by night, it haunted me continually, and soon became a sort of monomania, which I condemned, yet could not control, till at length I found myself pacing to and fro as those invisible feet paced over head. Hannah came and stopped me, and a few hours later Dr. Karnac appeared. I was so changed that I feared him with a deadly fear. He seemed to enjoy it; for in the pride of youth and beauty I had shown him contempt and defiance at my uncle's, and he took an ungenerous satisfaction in annoying me by a display of power. He never answered my questions or entreaties, regarded me as being without sense or will, insisted on my trying various mixtures and experiments in diet, gave me strange books to read, and weekly received Hannah's report of all that passed. That day he came, looked at me, said, "Let her walk," and went away, smiling that hateful smile of his.

Soon after this I took to walking in my sleep, and more than once woke to find myself roving lampless through that haunted house in the dead of night. I concealed these unconscious wanderings for a time, but an ominous event broke them up at last, and betrayed them to Hannah.

I had followed the steps one day for several hours, walking below as they walked above; had peopled that mysterious room with every mournful shape my disordered fancy could conjure up; had woven tragical romances about it, and brooded over the one subject of interest my unnatural life possessed with the intensity of a mind upon which its uncanny influence was telling with perilous rapidity. At midnight I woke to find myself standing in a streak of moonlight, opposite the door whose threshold I had never crossed. The April night was warm, a single pane of glass high up in that closed door was drawn aside, as if for air; and, as I stood dreamily collecting my sleep-drunken senses, I saw a ghostly hand emerge and beckon,

as if to me. It startled me broad awake, with a faint exclamation and a shudder from head to foot. A cloud swept
over the moon, and when it passed the hand was gone,
but shrill through the keyhole came a whisper that chilled
me to the marrow of my bones, so terribly distinct and
imploring was it.

"Find it! for God's sake find it before it is too late!"

The hound sprang up with an angry growl; I heard
Hannah leave her bed near by, and, with an inspiration
strange as the moment, I paced slowly on with open eyes
and lips apart, as I had seen "Amina" in the happy days
when kind old madame took me to the theatre, whose
mimic horrors I had never thought to equal with such
veritable ones. Hannah appeared at her door with a light,
but on I went in a trance of fear; for I was only kept from
dropping in a swoon by the blind longing to fly from that
spectral voice and hand. Past Hannah I went, she following; and, as I slowly laid myself in bed, I heard her say to
her husband, who just then came up, —

"Sleep-walking, John; it's getting worse and worse, as
the doctor foretold; she'll settle down like the other presently, but she must be locked up at night, else the dog
will do her a mischief."

The man yawned and grumbled; then they went, leaving me to spend hours of unspeakable suffering, which
aged me more than years. What was I to find? where was
I to look? and when would it be too late? These questions
tormented me; for I could find no answers to them, divine
no meaning, see no course to pursue. Why was I here?
what motive induced my uncle to commit such an act?
and when would I be liberated? were equally unanswer-
able, equally tormenting, and they haunted me like ghosts.
I had no power to exorcise or forget. After that I walked
no more, because I slept no more; sleep seemed scared
away, and waking dreams harassed me with their terrors.
Night after night I paced my room in utter darkness, –
for I was allowed no lamp, – night after night I wept bitter
tears wrung from me by anguish, for which I had no
name; and night after night the steps kept time to mine,
and the faint lullaby came down to me as if to soothe and

comfort my distress. I felt that my health was going, my mind growing confused and weak, my thoughts wandered vaguely, memory began to fail, and idiocy or madness seemed my inevitable fate; but through it all my heart clung to Guy, yearning for him with a hunger that would not be appeased.

At rare intervals I was allowed to walk in the neglected garden, where no flowers bloomed, no birds sang, no companion came to me but surly John, who followed with his book or pipe, stopping when I stopped, walking when I walked, keeping a vigilant eye upon me, yet seldom speaking except to decline answering my questions. These walks did me no good, for the air was damp and heavy with vapors from the marsh: for the house stood near a half-dried lake, and hills shut it in on every side. No fresh winds from upland moor or distant ocean ever blew across the narrow valley; no human creature visited the place, and nothing but a vague hope that my birthday might bring some change, some help, sustained me. It did bring help, but of such an unexpected sort that its effects remained through all my after-life. My birthday came, and with it my uncle. I was in my room, walking restlessly, – for the habit was a confirmed one now, – when the door opened, and Hannah, Dr. Karnac, my uncle, and a gentleman whom I knew to be his lawyer, entered, and surveyed me as if I were a spectacle. I saw my uncle start and turn pale; I had never seen myself since I came, but, if I had not suspected that I was a melancholy wreck of my former self, I should have known it then, such sudden pain and pity softened his ruthless countenance for a single instant. Dr. Karnac's eye had a magnetic power over me; I had always felt it, but in my present feeble state I dreaded, yet submitted to it with a helpless fear that should have touched his heart, – it was on me then, I could not resist it, and paused fixed and fascinated by that repellent yet potent glance. Hannah pointed to the carpet worn to shreds by my weary march, to the walls which I had covered with weird, grotesque, or tragic figures to while away the heavy hours, lastly to myself, mute, motionless, and scared, saying, as if in confirmation of some previous assertion, —

"You see, gentlemen, she is, as I said, quiet, but quite hopeless."

I thought she was interceding for me; and, breaking from the bewilderment and fear that held me, I stretched my hands to them, crying with an imploring cry, —

"Yes, I *am* quiet! I *am* hopeless! Oh, have pity on me before this dreadful life kills me or drives me mad!"

Dr. Karnac came to me at once with a black frown, which I alone could see; I evaded him, and clung to Hannah, still crying frantically, – for this seemed my last hope, —

"Uncle, let me go! I will give you all I have, will never ask for Guy, will be obedient and meek if I may only go to madame and never hear the feet again, or see the sights that terrify me in this dreadful room. Take me out! for God's sake take me out!"

My uncle did not answer me, but covered up his face with a despairing gesture, and hurried from the room; the lawyer followed, muttering pitifully, "Poor thing! poor thing!" and Dr. Karnac laughed the first laugh I had ever heard him utter as he wrenched Hannah from my grasp and locked me in alone. My one hope died then, and I resolved to kill myself rather than endure this life another month; for now it grew clear to me that they believed me mad, and death of the body was far more preferable than that of the mind. I think I *was* a little mad just then, but remember well the sense of peace that came to me as I tore strips from my clothing, braided them into a cord, hid it beneath my mattress, and serenely waited for the night. Sitting in the last twilight I thought to see in this unhappy world, I recollected that I had not heard the feet all day, and fell to pondering over the unusual omission. But, if the steps had been silent in that room, voices had not, for I heard a continuous murmur at one time: the tones of one voice were abrupt and broken, the other low, yet resonant, and that, I felt assured, belonged to my uncle. Who was he speaking to? what were they saying? should I ever know? and even then, with death before me, the intense desire to possess the secret filled me with its old unrest.

Night came at last; I heard the clock strike one, and, listening to discover if John still lingered up, I heard through the deep hush a soft grating in the room above, a stealthy sound that would have escaped ears less preternaturally alert than mine. Like a flash came the thought, "Some one is filing bars or picking locks: will the unknown remember me and let me share her flight?" The fatal noose hung ready, but I no longer cared to use it, for hope had come to nerve me with the strength and courage I had lost. Breathlessly I listened; the sound went on, stopped, a dead silence reigned; then something brushed against my door, and, with a suddenness that made me tingle from head to foot like an electric shock, through the keyhole came again that whisper, urgent, imploring, and mysterious, —

"Find it! for God's sake find it before it is too late!" then fainter, as if breath failed, came the broken words, "The dog – a lock of hair – there is yet time."

Eagerness rendered me forgetful of the secrecy I should preserve, and I cried aloud, "What shall I find? where shall I look?" My voice, sharpened by fear, rang shrilly through the house, Hannah's quick tread rushed down the hall, something fell, then loud and long rose a cry that made my heart stand still, so helpless, so hopeless was its wild lament. I had betrayed and I could not save or comfort the kind soul who had lost liberty through me. I was frantic to get out, and beat upon my door in a paroxysm of impatience, but no one came; and all night long those awful cries went on above, cries of mortal anguish, as if soul and body were being torn asunder. Till dawn I listened, pent in that room which now possessed an added terror; till dawn I called, wept, and prayed, with mingled pity, fear, and penitence, and till dawn the agony of that unknown sufferer continued unabated. I heard John hurry to and fro, heard Hannah issue orders with an accent of human sympathy in her hard voice; heard Dr. Karnac pass and repass my door, and all the sounds of confusion and alarm in that once quiet house. With daylight all was still, a stillness more terrible than the stir;

for it fell so suddenly, remained so utterly unbroken, that there seemed no explanation of it but the dread word death.

At noon Hannah, a shade paler, but grim as ever, brought me some food, saying she forgot my breakfast, and when I refused to eat, yet asked me no questions, she bade me go into the garden and not fret myself over last night's flurry. I went, and, passing down the corridor, glanced furtively at the door I never saw without a thrill; but I experienced a new sensation then, for the hound was gone, the door was open, and, with an impulse past control, I crept in and looked about me. It was a room like mine, the carpet worn like mine, the windows barred like mine; there the resemblance ended, for an empty cradle stood beside the bed, and on that bed, below a sweeping cover, stark and still a lifeless body lay. I was inured to fear now, and an unwholesome craving for new terrors seemed to have grown by what it fed on: an irresistible desire led me close, nerved me to lift the cover and look below, – a single glance, – then, with a cry as panic-stricken as that which rent the silence of the night, I fled away, for the face I saw was a pale image of my own. Sharpened by suffering, pallid with death, the features were familiar as those I used to see; the hair, beautiful and blonde as mine had been, streamed long over the pulseless breast, and on the hand, still clenched in that last struggle, shone the likeness of a ring I wore, a ring bequeathed to me by my father. An awesome fancy that it was myself assailed me; I had plotted death, and, with the waywardness of a shattered mind, I recalled legends of spirits returning to behold the bodies they had left.

Glad now to seek the garden, I hurried down, but on the threshold of the great hall-door was arrested by the sharp crack of a pistol; and, as a little cloud of smoke dispersed, I saw John drop the weapon and approach the hound, who lay writhing on the bloody grass. Moved by compassion for the faithful brute whose long vigilance was so cruelly repaid, I went to him, and, kneeling there, caressed the great head that never yielded to my touch before. John assumed his watch at once, and leaning against a tree cleaned the pistol, content that I should amuse myself with the dying creature, who looked into my face with eyes of almost human pathos and reproach. The brass collar seemed to choke him as he gasped for breath, and, leaning nearer to undo it, I saw, half hidden in his own black hair, a golden lock wound tightly round the collar, and so near its color as to be unobservable, except upon a close inspection. No accident could have placed it there; no head but mine in that house wore hair of that sunny hue, – yes, one other, and my heart gave a sudden leap as I remembered the shining locks just seen on that still bosom.

"Find it – the dog – the lock of hair," rung in my ears, and swift as light came the conviction that the unknown help was found at last. The little band was woven close, I had no knife, delay was fatal, I bent my head as if lamenting over the poor beast and bit the knot apart, drew out a folded paper, hid it in my hand, and rising strolled leisurely back to my own room, saying I did not care to walk till it was warmer. With eager eyes I examined my strange treasure-trove; it consisted of two strips of thinnest paper, without address or signature, one almost illegible, worn at the edges and stained with the green rust of the collar; the other fresher, yet more feebly written, both abrupt and disjointed, but terribly significant to me. This was the first, —

"I have never seen you, never heard your name, yet I know that you are young, that you are suffering, and I try to help you in my poor way. I think you are not crazed yet, as I often am: for your voice is sane, your plaintive singing not like mine, your walking only caught from me, I hope. I sing to lull the baby whom I never saw; I walk to lessen the long journey that will bring me to the husband I have lost, – stop! I must not think of those things or I shall forget. If you are not already mad, you will be; I suspect you were sent here to be made so; for the air is poison, the solitude is fatal, and Karnac remorseless in his mania for prying into the mysteries of human minds. What devil sent you I may never know, but I long to warn you. I can devise no way to do this; the dog comes into my room sometimes, you sometimes pause at my door and talk to him; you may find the paper I shall hide about his collar. Read, destroy, but obey it. I implore you to leave this house before it is too late."

The other paper was as follows: —

"I have watched you, tried to tell you where to look, for you have not found my warning yet, though I often tie it there and hope. You fear the dog, perhaps, and my plot fails; yet I know by your altered step and voice that you are fast reaching my unhappy state; for I am fitfully mad, and shall be till I die. To-day I have seen a familiar face; it seems to have calmed and strengthened me, and, though he would not help you, I shall make one desperate attempt. I may not find you, so leave my warning to the hound, yet hope to breathe a word into your sleepless ear that shall send you back into the world the happy thing you should be. Child! woman! whatever you are, leave this accursed house, while you have power to do it."

That was all; I did not destroy the papers, but I obeyed them, and for a week watched and waited till the propitious instant came. I saw my uncle, the doctor, and two others, follow the poor body to its grave beside the lake, saw all depart but Dr. Karnac, and felt redoubled hatred and contempt for the men who could repay my girlish slights with such a horrible revenge. On the seventh day, as I went down for my daily walk, I saw John and Dr. Karnac so deep in some uncanny experiment that I passed out unguarded. Hoping to profit by this unexpected chance, I sprang down the steps, but the next moment dropped half-stunned upon the grass; for behind me rose a crash, a shriek, a sudden blaze that flashed up and spread, sending a noisome vapor rolling out with clouds of smoke and flame. Aghast, I was just gathering myself up, when Hannah fled out of the house, dragging her husband senseless and bleeding, while her own face was ashy with affright. She dropped her burden beside me, saying, with white lips and a vain look for help where help was not, —

"Something they were at has burst, killed the doctor,

and fired the house! Watch John till I get help, and leave him at your peril!" then flinging open the gate she sped away.

"Now is my time," I thought, and only waiting till she vanished, I boldly followed her example, running rapidly along the road in an opposite direction, careless of bonnetless head and trembling limbs, intent only upon leaving that prison-house far behind me. For several hours I hurried along that solitary road; the spring sun shone, birds sang in the blooming hedges, green nooks invited me to pause and rest, but I heeded none of them, steadily continuing my flight, till spent and footsore I was forced to stop a moment by a wayside spring. As I stooped to drink, I saw my face for the first time in many months, and started to see how like that dead one it had grown, in all but the eternal peace which made that beautiful in spite of suffering and age. Standing thus and wondering if Guy would know me, should we ever meet, the sound of wheels disturbed me. Believing them to be coming from the place I had left, I ran desperately down the hill, turned a sharp corner, and before I could check myself passed a carriage slowly ascending. A face sprang to the window, a voice cried "Stop!" but on I flew, hoping the traveller would let me go unpursued. Not so, however; soon I heard fleet steps following, gaining rapidly, then a hand seized me, a voice rang in my ears, and with a vain struggle I lay panting in my captor's hold, fearing to look up and meet a brutal glance. But the hand that had seized me tenderly drew me close, the voice that had alarmed cried joyfully, —

"Sybil, it is Guy! lie still, poor child, you are safe at last."

Then I knew that my surest refuge was gained, and, too weak for words, clung to him in an agony of happiness, which brought to his kind eyes the tears I could not shed.

The carriage returned; Guy took me in, and for a time cared only to soothe and sustain my worn soul and body with the cordial of his presence, as we rolled homeward through a blooming world, whose beauty I had never truly felt before. When the first tumult of emotion had subsided, I told the story of my captivity and my escape, ending with a passionate entreaty not to be returned to my uncle's keeping, for henceforth there could be neither affection nor respect between us.

"Fear nothing, Sybil; madame is waiting for you at the Moors, and my father's unfaithful guardianship has ended with his life."

Then with averted face and broken voice Guy went on to tell his father's purposes, and what had caused this unexpected meeting. The facts were briefly these: The knowledge that my father had come between him and a princely fortune had always rankled in my uncle's heart, chilling the ambitious hopes he cherished even in his boyhood, and making life an eager search for pleasure in which to drown his vain regrets. This secret was suspected by my father, and the household league was formed as some atonement for the innocent offence. It seemed to soothe my uncle's resentful nature, and as years went on he lived freely, assured that ample means would be his through his son. Luxurious, self-indulgent, fond of all excitements, and reckless in their pursuit, he took no thought for the morrow till a few months before his return. A gay winter in Paris reduced him to those straits of which women know so little; creditors were oppressive, summer friends failed him, gambling debts harassed him, his son reproached him, and but one resource remained, Guy's speedy marriage with the half-forgotten heiress. The boy had been educated to regard this fate as a fixed fact, and submitted, believing the time to be far distant; but the sudden summons came, and he rebelled against it, preferring liberty to love. My uncle pacified the claimants by promises to be fulfilled at my expense, and hurried home to press on the marriage, which now seemed imperative. I was taken to my future home, approved by my uncle, beloved of my cousin, and, but for my own folly, might have been a happy wife on that May morning when I listened to this unveiling of the past. My mother had been melancholy mad since that unhappy rumor of my father's death; this affliction had been well concealed from me, lest the knowledge should prey upon my excitable nature and perhaps induce a like misfortune. I believed her dead, yet I had seen her, knew where her solitary grave was made, and still carried in my bosom the warning she had sent me, prompted by the unerring instinct of a mother's heart. In my father's will a clause was added just below the one confirming my betrothal, a clause decreeing that, if it should appear that I inherited my mother's malady, the fortune should revert to my cousin, with myself a mournful legacy, to be cherished by him whether his wife or not. This passage, and that relating to my freedom of choice, had been omitted in the copy shown me on the night when my seeming refusal of Guy had induced his father to believe that I loved him, to make a last attempt to keep the prize by offering himself, and, when that failed, to harbor a design that changed my little comedy into the tragical experience I have told.

Dr. Karnac's exclamation had caused the recollection of that clause respecting my insanity to flash into my uncle's mind, – a mind as quick to conceive as fearless to execute. I unconsciously abetted the strategem, and Dr. Karnac was an unscrupulous ally, for love of gain was as strong as love of science; both were amply gratified, and I, poor victim, was given up to be experimented upon, till by subtle means I was driven to the insanity which would give my uncle full control of my fortune and my fate. How the black plot prospered has been told; but retribution speedily overtook them both, for Dr. Karnac paid his penalty by the sudden death that left his ashes among the blackened ruins of that house of horrors, and my uncle had preceded him. For before the change of heirs could be effected my mother died, and the hours spent in that unhealthful spot insinuated the subtle poison of the marsh into his blood; years of pleasure left little vigor to withstand the fever, and a week of suffering ended a life of generous impulses perverted, fine endowments wasted, and opportunities for ever lost. When death drew near, he sent for Guy (who, through the hard discipline of poverty and honest labor, was becoming a manlier man), confessed all, and implored him to save me before it was too late. He did, and when all was told, when each saw the other by the light of this strange and sad experience, – Guy poor again, I free, the old bond still existing, the barrier of misunderstanding gone, – it was easy to see our way, easy to submit, to forgive, forget, and begin anew the life these clouds had darkened for a time.

Home received me, kind madame welcomed me, Guy married me, and I was happy; but over all these years, serenely prosperous, still hangs for me the shadow of the past, still rises that dead image of my mother, still echoes that spectral whisper in the dark.

Notes

1 Song.
2 Shelf with various levels.
3 The hero of a popular ballad. Ellen is about to be married to another man when Lochinvar arrives at the bridal feast, swings his lady on his horse, and rides off with her.
4 In Roman mythology, Bacchus is the god of wine; he is generally associated with anything riotous.
5 In classical mythology, Clytie, an ocean nymph in love with Apollo, is deserted by the god and changed into the heliotrope, or sunflower, which supposedly still turns to the sun and follows its daily course. In the language of flowers, heliotrope signifies eternal attachment.
6 One too many.

Source: *A Modern Mephistopheles and A Whisper in the Dark*, Boston: Roberts Brothers, 1889.

Biographical Note

Louisa May Alcott, born on November 29, 1832, in German-town, Pennsylvania, was the second of four daughters of the Transcendentalist and educator, Amos Bronson Alcott. She was given little formal schooling; during her early years in Concord, Massachusetts, her father tutored her at home according to his own educational theories. Idealistic and impractical, Bronson was quite incapable of earning a living, and his family consequently lived in relative poverty. Alcott helped by working at a variety of jobs, including teacher, seamstress, and governess; she also began to publish. She wrote in a variety of genres for the periodicals—poetry, fairy-tales, sketches, and thrillers, published under the pseudonym of "A.M. Barnard." Her first book, a collection of fantasies for children called *Flower Fables*, appeared in 1855. In 1862 she volunteered as a nurse in a Civil War army hospital, but after only six weeks contracted typhoid fever and had to return home. The experience formed the basis for *Hospital Sketches* (1863), her first major literary success. She spent some time in Europe as companion to a wealthy invalid, Anna Weld, during 1865-1866, and returned home to find the family's financial situation critical.

In 1868 Alcott joined the New England Woman's Suffrage Association and became editor of a Boston children's magazine, *Merry's Museum*, contributing many of the stories and poems under the pseudonym of "Aunty Wee." That same year Thomas Niles, of the Boston publisher Roberts Brothers, asked her to write a girls' story; although she was not enthusiastic about the project, she accepted in the hope that it would help pay off some of her parents' continuing debts. The result was *Little Women* (1868). Between 1869 and 1888, in response to the demands of her readers and the continuing financial needs of her family, Alcott produced a series of wholesome and somewhat sentimentalized domestic narratives for children in a similar vein. At the same time she continued to write a number of novels for adults, including *Work* (1873), which can be seen as a feminist rewriting of *Little*

Women, and the unfinished *Diana and Persis* (1879), a study of the woman artist. In addition, she wrote a comic memoir based on her father's failed attempt, in 1843, to establish a self-supporting utopian commune, run on vegetarian principles, *Transcendental Wild Oats* (1872), and a variety of historical and feminist essays. Plagued by ill-health for much of her life, the result of mercury poisoning from the calomel treatment for her typhoid, she died on March 6, 1888, two days after her father. At the joint funeral, the minister supposed "that Bronson had needed his dutiful daughter's help even in heaven" (Showalter xxvi).

In such stories as "A Modern Cinderella" (1860), "A Marble Woman" (1865), and "Psyche's Art" (1868), Alcott frequently returned to the subject of the problems faced by the woman artist. The story reprinted here, first published in *Frank Leslie's Illustrated Newspaper* in 1863, may be read at least in part as a commentary on the particular pressures that resulted in her dual existence as the well-known author of domestic narratives and the anonymous author of sensation fiction. With its Gothic treatment of rage, madness, and excess, and its echoes of such key nineteenth-century texts as Charlotte Brontë's *Jane Eyre* (1847), "A Whisper in the Dark" provides a telling analysis of society's insistence on women's self-repression and self-control.

Selected Modern Reprints:

Alternative Alcott. Ed. Elaine Showalter. New Brunswick: Rutgers UP, 1988.
Behind a Mask: The Unknown Thrillers of Louisa May Alcott. Ed. Madeleine Stern. New York: Morrow, 1975.
Flower Fables. 1855. New York: Reprint Services, 1989.
Hospital Sketches and the Memoir of Emily E. Parsons. New York: Garland, 1992.
The Journals of Louisa May Alcott. Ed. Joel Myerson. Denver, CO: Little, 1989.
On Picket Duty and Other Tales. New York: Reprint Services, 1988.

Plots and Counterplots: More Unknown Thrillers of Louisa May Alcott. Ed. Madeleine Stern. New York: Morrow, 1976.
Selected Letters of L.M. Alcott. 2 vols. Intro. Madeleine B. Stern. Ed. Joel Myerson and Daniel Shealy. Toronto: Little, Brown, 1989.

Selected Secondary Sources:

Burke, Kathleen. *Louisa May Alcott.* New York: Chelsea House, 1988.
Carpenter, Lynette. "'Did They Never See Anyone Angry Before?': The Sexual Politics of Self-Control in Alcott's 'A Whisper in the Dark.'" *Legacy: A Journal of Nineteenth Century American Women Writers* 3.2 (1986): 31-41.
Elbert, Sarah. *A Hunger for Home: Louisa May Alcott's Place in American Culture.* New Brunswick: Rutgers UP, 1987.
Macdonald, Ruth K. *Louisa May Alcott.* Boston: Twayne, 1983.
Marsalla, Joy A. *The Promise of Destiny: Children and Women in the Short Stories of Louisa May Alcott.* Boston: Greenwood, 1983.
Stern, Madeleine B. *Critical Essays on Louisa May Alcott.* Boston: Hall, 1984.
—. *Louisa May Alcott.* Norman: U of Oklahoma P, 1950.

70   MARY ELIZABETH BRADDON (1835-1915)

Mary Elizabeth Braddon (1835-1915)

Good Lady Ducayne

I

BELLA ROLLESTON HAD MADE UP HER MIND THAT HER ONLY chance of earning her bread and helping her mother to an occasional crust was by going out into the great unknown world as companion to a lady. She was willing to go to any lady rich enough to pay her a salary and so eccentric as to wish for a hired companion. Five shillings told off reluctantly from one of those sovereigns which were so rare with the mother and daughter, and which melted away so quickly, five solid shillings, had been handed to a smartly-dressed lady in an office in Harbeck Street, W., in the hope that this very Superior Person would find a situation and a salary for Miss Rolleston.

The Superior Person glanced at the two half-crowns as they lay on the table where Bella's hand had placed them, to make sure they were neither of them florins, before she wrote a description of Bella's qualifications and requirements in a formidable-looking ledger.

"Age?" she asked, curtly.

"Eighteen, last July."

"Any accomplishments?"

"No; I am not at all accomplished. If I ever were I should want to be a governess – a companion seems the lowest stage."

"We have some highly accomplished ladies on our books as companions, or chaperon companions."

"Oh, I know!" babbled Bella, loquacious in her youthful candour. "But that is quite a different thing. Mother hasn't been able to afford a piano since I was twelve years old, so I'm afraid I've forgotten how to play. And I have had to help mother with her needlework, so there hasn't been much time to study.

"Please don't waste time upon explaining what you can't do, but kindly tell me anything you can do," said the Superior Person, crushingly, with her pen poised between delicate fingers waiting to write. "Can you read aloud for two or three hours at a stretch? Are you active and handy, an early riser, a good walker, sweet tempered, and obliging?"

"I can say yes to all those questions except about the sweetness. I think I have a pretty good temper, and I should be anxious to oblige anybody who paid for my services. I should want them to feel that I was really earning my salary."

"The kind of ladies who come to me would not care for a talkative companion," said the Person, severely, having finished writing in her book. "My connection lies chiefly among the aristocracy, and in that class considerable deference is expected."

"Oh, of course," said Bella; "but it's quite different when I'm talking to you. I want to tell you about myself once and for ever."

"I am glad that it is to be only once!" said the Person, with the edges of her lips.

The Person was of uncertain age, tightly laced in a black silk gown. She had a powdery complexion and a handsome clump of somebody else's hair on the top of her head. It may be that Bella's girlish freshness and vivacity had an irritating effect upon nerves weakened by an eight hours day in that over-heated second floor in Harbeck Street. To Bella the official apartment, with its Brussels carpet, velvet curtains and velvet chairs, and French clock, ticking loud on the marble chimney-piece, suggested the luxury of a palace, as compared with another second floor in Walworth where Mrs. Rolleston and her daughter had managed to exist for the last six years.

"Do you think you have anything on your books that

would suit me?" faltered Bella, after a pause.

"Oh, dear no; I have nothing in view at present," answered the Person, who had swept Bella's half-crowns into a drawer, absent-mindedly, with the tips of her fingers. "You see, you are so very unformed – so much too young to be a companion to a lady of position. It is a pity you have not enough education for a nursery governess; that would be more in your line."

"And do you think it will be very long before you can get me a situation?" asked Bella, doubtfully.

"I really cannot say. Have you any particular reason for being so impatient – not a love affair, I hope?"

"A love affair!" cried Bella, with flaming cheeks. "What utter nonsense. I want a situation because mother is poor, and I hate being a burden to her. I want a salary that I can share with her."

"There won't be much margin for sharing in the salary you are likely to get at your age – and with your – very – unformed manners," said the Person, who found Bella's peony cheeks, bright eyes, and unbridled vivacity more and more oppressive.

"Perhaps if you'd be kind enough to give me back the fee I could take it to an agency where the connection isn't quite so aristocratic," said Bella, who – as she told her mother in her recital of the interview – was determined not to be sat upon.

"You will find no agency that can do more for you than mine," replied the Person, whose harpy[1] fingers never relinquished coin. "You will have to wait for your opportunity. Yours is an exceptional case: but I will bear you in mind, and if anything suitable offers I will write to you. I cannot say more than that."

The half-contemptuous bend of the stately head, weighted with borrowed hair, indicated the end of the interview. Bella went back to Walworth – tramped sturdily every inch of the way in the September afternoon – and "took off" the Superior Person for the amusement of her mother and the landlady, who lingered in the shabby little sitting-room after bringing in the tea-tray, to applaud Miss Rolleston's "taking off."

"Dear, dear, what a mimic she is!" said the landlady. "You ought to have let her go on the stage, mum. She might have made her fortune as a hactress."

II

Bella waited and hoped, and listened for the postman's knocks, which brought such store of letters for the parlours and the first floor, and so few for that humble second floor, where mother and daughter sat sewing with hand and with wheel and treadle, for the greater part of the day. Mrs. Rolleston was a lady by birth and education; but it had been her bad fortune to marry a scoundrel; for the last half-dozen years she had been that worst of widows, a wife whose husband had deserted her. Happily, she was courageous, industrious, and a clever needlewoman; and she had been able just to earn a living for herself and her only child, by making mantles and cloaks for a West-end house. It was not a luxurious living. Cheap lodgings in a shabby street off the Walworth Road, scanty dinners, homely food, well-worn raiment, had been the portion of mother and daughter; but they loved each other so dearly, and Nature had made them both so light-hearted, that they had contrived somehow to be happy.

But now this idea of going out into the world as companion to some fine lady had rooted itself into Bella's mind, and although she idolized her mother, and although the parting of mother and daughter must needs tear two loving hearts into shreds, the girl longed for enterprise and change and excitement, as the pages of old longed to be knights, and to start for the Holy Land to break a lance with the infidel.

She grew tired of racing downstairs every time the postman knocked, only to be told "nothing for you, miss," by the smudgy-faced drudge who picked up the letters from the passage floor. "Nothing for you, miss," grinned the lodging-house drudge, till at last Bella took heart of grace and walked up to Harbeck Street, and asked the

Superior Person how it was that no situation had been found for her.

"You are too young," said the Person, "and you want a salary."

"Of course I do," answered Bella; "don't other people want salaries?"

"Young ladies of your age generally want a comfortable home."

"I don't," snapped Bella; "I want to help mother."

"You can call again this day week," said the Person; "or, if I hear of anything in the meantime, I will write to you."

No letter came from the Person, and in exactly a week Bella put on her neatest hat, the one that had been seldomest caught in the rain, and trudged off to Harbeck Street.

It was a dull October afternoon, and there was a greyness in the air which might turn to fog before night. The Walworth Road shops gleamed brightly through that grey atmosphere, and though to a young lady reared in Mayfair or Belgravia such shop-windows would have been unworthy of a glance, they were a snare and temptation for Bella. There were so many things that she longed for, and would never be able to pay.

Harbeck Street is apt to be empty at this dead season of the year, a long, long street, an endless perspective of eminently respectable houses. The Person's office was at the further end, and Bella looked down that long, grey vista almost despairingly, more tired than usual with the trudge from Walworth. As she looked, a carriage passed her, an old-fashioned, yellow chariot, on cee springs,[2] drawn by a pair of high grey horses, with the stateliest of coachmen driving them, and a tall footman sitting by his side.

"It looks like the fairy god-mother's coach," thought Bella. "I shouldn't wonder if it began by being a pumpkin."

It was a surprise when she reached the Person's door to find the yellow chariot standing before it, and the tall footman waiting near the doorstep. She was almost afraid to go in and meet the owner of that splendid carriage. She had caught only a glimpse of its occupant as the chariot rolled by, a plumed bonnet, a patch of ermine.

The Person's smart page ushered her upstairs and knocked at the official door. "Miss Rolleston," he announced, apologetically, while Bella waited outside.

"Show her in," said the Person, quickly; and then Bella heard her murmuring something in a low voice to her client.

Bella went in fresh, blooming, a living image of youth and hope, and before she looked at the Person her gaze was riveted by the owner of the chariot.

Never had she seen anyone as old as the old lady sitting by the Person's fire: a little old figure, wrapped from chin to feet in an ermine mantle; a withered, old face under a plumed bonnet – a face so wasted by age that it seemed only a pair of eyes and a peaked chin. The nose was peaked, too, but between the sharply pointed chin and the great, shining eyes, the small, aquiline nose was hardly visible.

"This is Miss Rolleston, Lady Ducayne."

Claw-like fingers, flashing with jewels, lifted a double eyeglass to Lady Ducayne's shining black eyes, and through the glasses Bella saw those unnaturally bright eyes magnified to a gigantic size, and glaring at her awfully.

"Miss Torpinter has told me all about you," said the old voice that belonged to the eyes. "Have you good health? Are you strong and active, able to eat well, sleep well, walk well, able to enjoy all there is good in life?"

"I have never known what it is to be ill, or idle," answered Bella.

"Then I think you will do for me."

"Of course, in the event of references being perfectly satisfactory," put in the Person.

"I don't want references. The young woman looks frank and innocent. I'll take her on trust."

"So like you, dear Lady Ducayne," murmured Miss Torpinter.

"I want a strong young woman whose health will give me no trouble."

"You have been so unfortunate in that respect," cooed the Person, whose voice and manner were subdued to a melting sweetness by the old woman's presence.

"Yes. I've been rather unlucky," grunted Lady Ducayne.

"But I am sure Miss Rolleston will not disappoint you, though certainly after your unpleasant experience with Miss Tomson, who looked the picture of health – and Miss Blandy, who said she had never seen a doctor since she was vaccinated –"

"Lies, no doubt," muttered Lady Ducayne, and then turning to Bella, she asked, curtly, "You don't mind spending the winter in Italy, I suppose?"

In Italy! The very word was magical. Bella's fair young face flushed crimson.

"It has been the dream of my life to see Italy," she gasped.

From Walworth to Italy! How far, how impossible such a journey had seemed to that romantic dreamer.

"Well, your dream will be realized. Get yourself ready to leave Charing Cross by the train deluxe this day week at eleven. Be sure you are at the station a quarter before the hour. My people will look after you and your luggage."

Lady Ducayne rose from her chair, assisted by her crutch-stick, and Miss Torpinter escorted her to the door.

"And with regard to salary?" questioned the Person on the way.

"Salary, oh, the same as usual – and if the young woman wants a quarter's pay in advance you can write me for a cheque," Lady Ducayne answered, carelessly.

Miss Torpinter went all the way downstairs with her client, and waited to see her seated in the yellow chariot. When she came upstairs again, she was slightly out of breath, and she had resumed that superior manner which Bella had found so crushing.

"You may think yourself uncommonly lucky, Miss Rolleston," she said. "I have dozens of young ladies on my books whom I might have recommended for this situation – but I remembered having told you to call this afternoon – and I thought I would give you a chance. Old

Lady Ducayne is one of the best people on my books. She gives her companion a hundred a year, and pays all travelling expenses. You will live in the lap of luxury."

"A hundred a year! How too lovely! Shall I have to dress very grandly? Does Lady Ducayne keep much company?"

"At her age! No, she lives in seclusion – in her own apartments – her French maid, her footman, her medical attendant, her courier."

"Why did those other companions leave her?" asked Bella.

"Their health broke down!"

"Poor things, and so they had to leave?"

"Yes, they had to leave. I suppose you would like a quarter's salary in advance?"

"Oh, yes, please. I shall have things to buy."

"Very well, I will write for Lady Ducayne's cheque, and I will send you the balance – after deducting my commission for the year."

"To be sure, I had forgotten the commission."

"You don't suppose I keep this office for pleasure."

"Of course not," murmured Bella, remembering the five shillings entrance fee; but nobody could expect a hundred a year and a winter in Italy for five shillings.

III

"From Miss Rolleston, at Cap Ferino, to Mrs. Rolleston, in Beresford Street, Walworth."

"How I wish you could see this place, dearest; the blue sky, the olive woods, the orange and lemon orchards between the cliffs and the sea – sheltering in the hollow of the great hills – and with summer waves dancing up to the narrow ridge of pebbles and weeds which is the Italian idea of a beach! Oh, how I wish you could see it all, mother dear, and bask in this sunshine, that makes it so difficult to believe the date at the head of this paper. November! The air is like an English June – the sun is so hot that I can't walk a few yards without an umbrella. And to think of you at Walworth while I am here! I could cry at the thought that perhaps you will never see this lovely coast, this wonderful sea, these summer flowers that bloom in winter. There is a hedge of pink geraniums under my window, mother – a thick, rank hedge, as if the flowers grew wild – and there are Dijon roses climbing over arches and palisades all along the terrace – a rose garden full of bloom in November! Just picture it all! You could never imagine the luxury of this hotel. It is nearly new, and has been built and decorated regardless of expense. Our rooms are upholstered in pale blue satin, which shows up Lady Ducayne's parchment complexion; but as she sits all day in a corner of the balcony basking in the sun, except when she is in her carriage, and all the evening in her armchair close to the fire, and never sees anyone but her own people, her complexion matters very little.

"She has the handsomest suite of rooms in the hotel. My bedroom is inside hers, the sweetest room – all blue satin and white lace – white enamelled furniture, looking-glasses on every wall, till I know my pert little profile as I never knew it before. The room was really meant for Lady Ducayne's dressing-room, but she ordered one of the blue satin couches to be arranged as a bed for me – the prettiest little bed, which I can wheel near the window on sunny mornings, as it is on castors and easily moved about. I feel as if Lady Ducayne were a funny old grandmother, who had suddenly appeared in my life, very, very rich, and very, very kind.

"She is not at all exacting. I read aloud to her a good deal, and she dozes and nods while I read. Sometimes I hear her moaning in her sleep – as if she had troublesome dreams. When she is tired of my reading she orders Francine, her maid, to read a French novel[3] to her, and I hear her chuckle and groan now and then, as if she were more interested in those books than in Dickens or Scott. My French is not good enough to follow Francine, who reads very quickly. I have a great deal of liberty, for Lady Ducayne often tells me to run away and amuse myself; I roam about the hills for hours. Everything is so lovely. I lose myself in olive woods, always climbing up and up towards the pine woods above – and above the pines there are the snow mountains that just show their white peaks above the dark hills. Oh, you poor dear, how can I ever make you understand what this place is like – you, whose poor, tired eyes have only the opposite side of Beresford Street? Sometimes I go no farther than the terrace in front of the hotel, which is a favourite lounging-place with everybody. The gardens lie below, and the tennis courts where I sometimes play with a very nice girl, the only person in the hotel with whom I have made friends. She is a year older than I, and has come to Cap Ferrino with her brother, a doctor – or a medical student, who is going to be a doctor. He passed his M.B. exam at Edinburgh just before they left home, Lotta told me. He came to Italy entirely on his sister's account. She had a troublesome chest attack last summer and was ordered to winter abroad. They are orphans, quite alone in the world, and so fond of each other. It is very nice for me to have such a friend as Lotta. She is so thoroughly respectable. I can't help using that word, for some of the girls in the hotel go on in a way that I know you would shudder at. Lotta was brought up by an aunt, deep down in the country, and knows hardly anything about life. Her brother won't allow her to read a novel, French or English, that he has not read and approved.

"'He treats me like a child,' she told me, 'but I don't mind, for it's nice to know somebody loves me, and cares about what I do, and even about my thoughts.'

"Perhaps this is what makes some girls so eager to marry – the want of someone strong and brave and honest and true to care for them and order them about. I want no one, mother darling, for I have you, and you are all the world to me. No husband could ever come between us two. If I were ever to marry he would have only the second place in my heart. But I don't suppose I ever shall marry, or even know what it is like to have an offer of marriage. No young man can afford to marry a penniless girl nowadays. Life is too expensive.

"Mr. Stafford, Lotta's brother, is very clever, and very kind. He thinks it is rather hard for me to have to live with such an old woman as Lady Ducayne, but then he does not know how poor we are – you and I – and what a wonderful life this seems to me in this lovely place. I feel a selfish wretch for enjoying all my luxuries, while you, who want them so much more than I, have none of them – hardly know what they are like – do you, dearest? – for my scamp of a father began to go to the dogs soon after you were married, and since then life has been all trouble and care and struggle for you."

This letter was written when Bella had been less than a month at Cap Ferrino, before the novelty had worn off the landscape, and before the pleasure of luxurious surroundings had begun to cloy. She wrote to her mother every week, such long letters as girls who have lived in closest companionship with a mother, alone can write; letters that are like a diary of heart and mind. She wrote gaily always; but when the new year began Mrs. Rolleston thought she detected a note of melancholy under all those lively details about the place and the people.

"My poor girl is getting home-sick," she thought. "Her heart is in Beresford Street."

It might be that she missed her new friend, Lotta Stafford, who had gone with her brother for a little tour to Genoa and Spezzia, and as far as Pisa. They were to return before February; but in the meantime Bella might naturally feel very solitary among all those strangers, whose manners and doings she described so well.

The mother's instinct had been true. Bella was not so happy as she had been in that first flush of wonder and delight which followed the change from Walworth to the Riviera. Somehow, she knew not how, lassitude had crept upon her. She no longer loved to climb the hills, no longer flourished her orange stick in sheer gladness of heart as her light feet skipped over the rough ground and the coarse grass on the mountain side. The odour of rosemary and thyme, the fresh breath of the sea, no longer filled her with rapture. She thought of Beresford Street and her mother's face with a sick longing. They were so far – so far away! And then she thought of Lady Ducayne, sitting by the heaped-up olive logs in the over-heated salon – thought of that wizened nut-cracker profile, and those gleaming eyes, with an invincible horror.

Visitors at the hotel had told her that the air of Cap Ferrino was relaxing – better suited to age than to youth, to sickness than to health. No doubt it was so. She was not so well as she had been at Walworth; but she told herself that she was suffering only from the pain of separation from the dear companion of her girlhood, the mother who had been nurse, sister, friend, flatterer, all things in this world to her. She had shed many tears over that parting, had spent many a melancholy hour on the marble terrace with yearning eyes looking westward, and with her heart's desire a thousand miles away.

She was sitting in her favourite spot, an angle at the eastern end of the terrace, a quiet little nook sheltered by orange trees, when she heard a couple of Riviera habi-tués talking in the garden below. They were sitting on a bench against the terrace wall.

She had no idea of listening to their talk, till the sound of Lady Ducayne's name attracted her, and then she listened without any thought of wrong-doing. They were talking no secrets – just casually discussing an hotel acquaintance.

They were two elderly people whom Bella only knew by sight. An English clergyman who had wintered abroad for half his life-time; a stout, comfortable, well-to-do spinster, whose chronic bronchitis obliged her to migrate an-nually.

"I have met her about Italy for the last ten years," said the lady; "but have never found out her real age."

"I put her down at a hundred – not a year less," replied the parson. "Her reminiscences all go back to the Regency.[4] She was evidently then in her zenith; and I have heard her say things that showed she was in Parisian society when the First Empire was at its best – before Josephine was divorced."[5]

"She doesn't talk much now."

"No; there's not much life left in her. She is wise in

keeping herself secluded. I only wonder that wicked old quack, her Italian doctor, didn't finish her off years ago."

"I should think it must be the other way, and that he keeps her alive."

"My dear Miss Manders, do you think foreign quackery ever kept anybody alive?"

"Well, there she is – and she never goes anywhere without him. He certainly has an unpleasant countenance."

"Unpleasant," echoed the parson, "I don't believe the foul fiend himself can beat him in ugliness. I pity that poor young woman who has to live between old Lady Ducayne and Dr. Parravicini."

"But the old lady is very good to her companions."

"No doubt. She is very free with her cash; the servants call her good Lady Ducayne. She is a withered old female Croesus,[6] and knows she'll never be able to get through her money, and doesn't relish the idea of other people enjoying it when she's in her coffin. People who live to be as old as she is become slavishly attached to life. I daresay she's generous to those poor girls – but she can't make them happy. They die in her service."

"Don't say they, Mr. Carton; I know that one poor girl died at Mentone last spring."

"Yes, and another poor girl died in Rome three years ago. I was there at the time. Good Lady Ducayne left her there in an English family. The girl had every comfort. The old woman was very liberal to her – but she died. I tell you, Miss Manders, it is not good for any young woman to live with two such horrors as Lady Ducayne and Parravicini."

They talked of other things – but Bella hardly heard them. She sat motionless, and a cold wind seemed to come down upon her from the mountains and to creep up to her from the sea, till she shivered as she sat there in the sunshine, in the shelter of the orange trees in the midst of all that beauty and brightness.

Yes, they were uncanny, certainly, the pair of them – she so like an aristocratic witch in her withered old age; he of no particular age, with a face that was more like a waxen mask than any human countenance Bella had ever seen. What did it matter? Old age is venerable, and worthy of all reverence; and Lady Ducayne had been very kind to her. Dr. Parravicini was a harmless, inoffensive student, who seldom looked up from the book he was reading. He had his private sitting-room, where he made experiments in chemistry and natural science – perhaps in alchemy.[7] What could it matter to Bella? He had always been polite to her, in his far-off way. She could not be more happily placed than she was – in this palatial hotel, with this rich old lady.

No doubt she missed the young English girl who had been so friendly, and it might be that she missed the girl's brother, for Mr. Stafford had talked to her a good deal – had interested himself in the books she was reading, and her manner of amusing herself when she was not on duty.

"You must come to our little salon when you are 'off,' as the hospital nurses call it, and we can have some music. No doubt you play and sing?" upon which Bella had to own with a blush of shame that she had forgotten how to play the piano ages ago.

"Mother and I used to sing duets sometimes between the lights, without accompaniment," she said, and the tears came into her eyes as she thought of the humble room, the half-hour's respite from work, the sewing-machine standing where a piano ought to have been, and her mother's plaintive voice, so sweet, so true, so dear.

Sometimes she found herself wondering whether she would ever see that beloved mother again. Strange forebodings came into her mind. She was angry with herself for giving way to melancholy thoughts.

One day she questioned Lady Ducayne's French maid about those two companions who had died within three years.

"They were poor, feeble creatures," Francine told her. "They looked fresh and bright enough when they came to Miladi: but they ate too much, and they were lazy. They died of luxury and idleness. Miladi was too kind to them. They had nothing to do; and so they took to fancying things; fancying the air didn't suit them, that they couldn't sleep."

"I sleep well enough, but I have had a strange dream several times since I have been to Italy."

"Ah, you had better not begin to think about dreams, or you will be like those other girls. They were dreamers – and they dreamt themselves into the cemetery."

The dream troubled her a little, not because it was a ghastly or frightening dream, but on account of sensations which she had never felt before in sleep – a whirring of wheels that went round in her brain, a great noise like a whirlwind, but rhythmical like the ticking of a gigantic clock: and then in the midst of this uproar as of winds and waves she seemed to sink into a gulf of unconsciousness, out of sleep into far deeper sleep – total extinction. And then, after that blank interval, there had come the sound of voices, and then again the whirr of wheels, louder and louder – and again the blank – and then she knew no more till morning, when she awoke, feeling languid and oppressed.

She told Dr. Parravicini of her dream one day, on the only occasion when she wanted his professional advice. She had suffered rather severely from the mosquitoes before Christmas – and had been almost frightened at finding a wound upon her arm which she could only attribute to the venomous sting of one of these torturers. Parravicini put on his glasses, and scrutinized the angry mark on the round, white arm, as Bella stood before him and Lady Ducayne with her sleeve rolled up above her elbow.

"Yes, that's rather more than a joke," he said; "he has caught you on the top of a vein. What a vampire! But there's no harm done, signorina, nothing that a little dressing of mine won't heal. You must always show me any bite of this nature. It might be dangerous if neglected. These creatures feed on poison and disseminate it."

"And to think that such tiny creatures can bite like this," said Bella; "my arm looks as if it had been cut by a knife."

"If I were to show you a mosquito's sting under my microscope you wouldn't be surprised at that," replied Parravicini.

Bella had to put up with the mosquito bites, even

when they came on the top of a vein, and produced that ugly wound. The wound recurred now and then at longish intervals, and Bella found Dr. Parravicini's dressing a speedy cure. If he were the quack his enemies called him, he had at least a light hand and a delicate touch in performing this small operation.

"Bella Rolleston to Mrs. Rolleston. – April 14th.

"EVER DEAREST, – Behold the cheque for my second quarter's salary – five and twenty pounds. There is no one to pinch off a whole tenner for a year's commission as there was last time, so it is all for you, mother, dear. I have plenty of pocket-money in hand from the cash I brought away with me, when you insisted on my keeping more than I wanted. It isn't possible to spend money here – except on occasional tips to servants, or sous[8] to beggars and children – unless one had lots to spend, for everything one would like to buy – tortoise-shell, coral, lace – is so ridiculously dear that only a millionaire ought to look at it. Italy is a dream of beauty: but for shopping, give me Newington Causeway.

"You ask me so earnestly if I am quite well that I fear my letters must have been very dull lately. Yes, dear, I am well – but I am not quite as strong as I was when I used to trudge to the West-end to buy half a pound of tea – just for a constitutional walk – or to Dulwich to look at the pictures. Italy is relaxing; and I feel what the people here call 'slack.' But I fancy I can see your dear face looking worried as you read this. Indeed, and indeed, I am not ill. I am only a little tired of this lovely scene – as I suppose one might get tired of looking at one of Turner's[9] pictures if it hung on a wall that was always opposite one. I think of you every hour in every day – think of you and our homely little room – our dear little shabby parlour, with the arm-chairs from the wreck of your old home, and Dick singing in his cage over the sewing-machine. Dear, shrill, maddening Dick, who, we flattered ourselves, was so passionately fond of us. Do tell me in your next that he is well.

"My friend Lotta and her brother never came back after all. They went from Pisa to Rome. Happy mortals!

And they are to be on the Italian lakes in May; which lake was not decided when Lotta last wrote to me. She has been a charming correspondent, and has confided all her little flirtations to me. We are all to go to Bellaggio next week – by Genoa and Milan. Isn't that lovely? Lady Ducayne travels by the easiest stages – except when she is bottled up in the train de luxe. We shall stop two days at Genoa and one at Milan. What a bore I shall be to you with my talk about Italy when I come home.

"Love and love – and ever more love from your adoring, BELLA."

IV

Herbert Stafford and his sister had often talked of the pretty English girl with her fresh complexion, which made such a pleasant touch of rosy colour among all those sallow faces at the Grand Hotel. The young doctor thought of her with a compassionate tenderness – her utter loneliness in that great hotel where there were so many people, her bondage to that old, old woman, where everybody else was free to think of nothing but enjoying life. It was a hard fate; and the poor child was evidently devoted to her mother, and felt the pain of separation – "only two of them, and very poor, and all the world to each other," he thought.

Lotta told him one morning that they were to meet again at Bellaggio. "The old thing and her court are to be there before we are," she said. "I shall be charmed to have Bella again. She is so bright and gay – in spite of an occasional touch of home-sickness. I never took to a girl on a short acquaintance as I did to her."

"I like her best when she is home-sick," said Herbert; "for then I am sure she has a heart."

"What have you to do with hearts, except for dissection? Don't forget that Bella is an absolute pauper. She told me in confidence that her mother makes mantles for a West-end shop. You can hardly have a lower depth than that."

"I shouldn't think any less of her if her mother made match-boxes."

"Not in the abstract – of course not. Match-boxes are honest labour. But you couldn't marry a girl whose mother makes mantles."

"We haven't come to the consideration of that question yet," answered Herbert, who liked to provoke his sister.

In two years' hospital practice he had seen too much of the grim realities of life to retain any prejudices about rank. Cancer, phthisis,[10] gangrene, leave a man with little respect for the outward differences which vary the husk of humanity. The kernel is always the same – fearfully and wonderfully made – a subject for pity and terror.

Mr. Stafford and his sister arrived at Bellaggio in a fair May evening. The sun was going down as the steamer approached the pier; and all the glory of purple bloom which curtains every wall at this season of the year flushed and deepened in the glowing light. A group of ladies were standing on the pier watching the arrivals, and among them Herbert saw a pale face that startled him out of his wonted composure.

"There she is," murmured Lotta, at his elbow, "but how dreadfully changed. She looks a wreck."

They were shaking hands with her a few minutes later, and a flush had lighted up her poor pinched face in the pleasure of meeting.

"I thought you might come this evening," she said. "We have been here a week."

She did not add that she had been there every evening to watch the boat in, and a good many times during the day. The Grand Bretagne was close by, and it had been easy for her to creep to the pier when the boat bell rang. She felt a joy in meeting these people again: a sense of being with friends; a confidence which Lady Ducayne's goodness had never inspired in her.

"Oh, you poor darling, how awfully ill you must have been," exclaimed Lotta, as the two girls embraced.

Bella tried to answer, but her voice was choked with tears.

"What has been the matter, dear? That horrid influenza, I suppose?"

"No, no, I have not been ill – I have only felt a little weaker than I used to be. I don't think the air of Cap Ferrino quite agreed with me."

"It must have disagreed with you abominably. I never saw such a change in anyone. Do let Herbert doctor you. He is fully qualified, you know. He prescribed for ever so many influenza patients at the Londres. They were glad to get advice from an English doctor in a friendly way."

"I am sure he must be very clever!" faltered Bella, "but there is really nothing the matter. I am not ill, and if I were ill, Lady Ducayne's physician —"

"That dreadful man with the yellow face? I would as soon one of the Borgias[11] prescribed for me. I hope you haven't been taking any of his medicines."

"No, dear, I have taken nothing. I have never complained of being ill."

This was said while they were all three walking to the hotel. The Staffords' rooms had been secured in advance, pretty ground-floor rooms, opening into the garden. Lady Ducayne's statelier apartments were on the floor above.

"I believe these rooms are just under ours," said Bella.

"Then it will be all the easier for you to run down to us," replied Lotta, which was not really the case, as the grand staircase was in the centre of the hotel.

"Oh, I shall find it easy enough," said Bella. "I'm afraid you'll have too much of my society. Lady Ducayne sleeps away half the day in this warm weather, so I have a good deal of idle time; and I get awfully moped thinking of mother and home."

Her voice broke upon the last word. She could not have thought of that poor lodging which went by the name of home more tenderly had it been the most beautiful that art and wealth ever created. She moped and pined in this lovely garden, with the sunlit lake and the romantic hills spreading out their beauty before her. She was homesick and she had dreams: or, rather, an occasional recurrence of that one bad dream with all its strange sensations – it was more like a hallucination than dreaming – the

– it was more like a hallucination than dreaming – the whirring of wheels; the sinking into an abyss; the struggling back to consciousness. She had the dream shortly before she left Cap Ferrino, but not since she had come to Bellaggio, and she began to hope the air in this lake district suited her better, and that those strange sensations would never return.

Mr. Stafford wrote a prescription and had it made up at a chemist's near the hotel. It was a powerful tonic, and after two bottles, and a row or two on the lake, and some rambling over the hills and in the meadows where the spring flowers made earth seem paradise, Bella's spirits and looks improved as if by magic.

"It is a wonderful tonic," she said, but perhaps in her heart of hearts she knew that the doctor's kind voice, and the friendly hand that helped her in and out of the boat, and the watchful care that went with her by land and lake, had something to do with her cure.

"I hope you don't forget that her mother makes mantles," Lotta said, warningly.

"Or match-boxes: it is just the same thing, so far as I am concerned."

"You mean that in no circumstances could you think of marrying her?"

"I mean that if ever I love a woman well enough to think of marrying her, riches or rank will count for nothing with me. But I fear – I fear your poor friend may not live to be any man's wife."

"Do you think her so very ill?"

He sighed, and left the question unanswered.

One day, while they were gathering wild hyacinths in an upland meadow, Bella told Mr. Stafford about her bad dream.

"It is curious only because it is hardly like a dream," she said. "I daresay you could find some common-sense reason for it. The position of my head on my pillow, or the atmosphere, or something."

And then she described her sensations; how in the midst of sleep there came a sudden sense of suffocation; and then those whirring wheels, so loud, so terrible; and ness.

"Have you ever had chloroform given you – by a dentist, for instance?"

"Never – Dr. Parravicini asked me that question one day."

"Lately?"

"No, long ago, when we were in the train de luxe."

"Has Dr. Parravicini prescribed for you since you began to feel weak and ill?"

"Oh, he has given me a little tonic from time to time, but I hate medicine, and took very little of the stuff. And then I am not ill, only weaker than I used to be. I was ridiculously strong and well when I lived at Walworth, and used to take long walks every day. Mother made me take those tramps to Dulwich or Norwood, for fear I should suffer from too much sewing-machine; sometimes – but very seldom – she went with me. She was generally toiling at home while I was enjoying fresh air and exercise. And she was very careful about our food – that, however plain it was, it should be always nourishing and ample. I owe it to her care that I grew up such a great, strong creature."

"You don't look great or strong, now, you poor dear," said Lotta.

"I'm afraid Italy doesn't agree with me."

"Perhaps it is not Italy, but being cooped up with Lady Ducayne that has made you ill."

"But I am never cooped up. Lady Ducayne is absurdly kind, and lets me roam about or sit in the balcony all day if I like. I have read more novels since I have been with her than in all the rest of my life."

"Then she is very different from the average old lady, who is usually a slave-driver," said Stafford. "I wonder why she carries a companion about with her if she has so little need of society."

"Oh, I am only part of her state. She is inordinately rich – and the salary she gives me doesn't count. Apropos of Dr. Parravicini, I know he is a clever doctor, for he cures my horrid mosquito bites."

"A little ammonia would do that, in the early stage of the mischief. But there are no mosquitoes to trouble you now."

"Oh, yes, there are; I had a bite just before we left Cap Ferrino."

She pushed up her loose lawn sleeve, and exhibited a scar, which he scrutinized intently, with a surprised and puzzled look.

"This is no mosquito bite," he said.

"Oh, yes it is – unless there are snakes or adders at Cap Ferrino."

"It is not a bite at all. You are trifling with me. Miss Rolleston – you have allowed that wretched Italian quack to bleed you. They killed the greatest man in modern Europe that way, remember. How very foolish of you."

"I was never bled in my life, Mr. Stafford."

"Nonsense! Let me look at your other arm. Are there any more mosquito bites?"

"Yes; Dr. Parravicini says I have a bad skin for healing, and that the poison acts more virulently with me than with most people."

Stafford examined both her arms in the broad sunlight, scars new and old.

"You have been very badly bitten, Miss Rolleston," he said, "and if ever I find the mosquito I shall make him smart. But, now tell me, my dear girl, on your word of honour, tell me as you would tell a friend who is sincerely anxious for your health and happiness – as you would tell your mother if she were here to question you – have you no knowledge of any cause for these scars except mosquito bites – no suspicion even?"

"No, indeed! No, upon my honour! I have never seen a mosquito biting my arm. One never does see the horrid little fiends. But I have heard them trumpeting under the curtains, and I know that I have often had one of the pestilent wretches buzzing about me."

Later in the day Bella and her friends were sitting at tea in the garden, while Lady Ducayne took her afternoon drive with her doctor.

"How long do you mean to stop with Lady Ducayne, Miss Rolleston?" Herbert Stafford asked, after a thoughtful silence, breaking suddenly upon the trivial talk of the two girls.

"As long as she will go on paying me twenty-five pounds a quarter."

"Even if you feel your health breaking down in her service?"

"It is not the service that has injured my health. You can see that I have really nothing to do – to read aloud for an hour or so once or twice a week; to write a letter once in a way to a London tradesman. I shall never have such an easy time with anybody else. And nobody else would give me a hundred a year.

"Then you mean to go on till you break down; to die at your post?"

"Like the other two companions? No! If ever I feel seriously ill – really ill – I shall put myself in a train and go back to Walworth without stopping."

"What about the other two companions?"

"They both died. It was very unlucky for Lady Ducayne. That's why she engaged me; she chose me because I was ruddy and robust. She must feel rather disgusted at my having grown white and weak. By-the-bye, when I told her about the good your tonic had done me, she said she would like to see you and have a little talk with you about her own case."

"And I should like to see Lady Ducayne. When did she say this?"

"The day before yesterday."

"Will you ask her if she will see me this evening?"

"With pleasure! I wonder what you will think of her? She looks rather terrible to a stranger; but Dr. Parravicini says she was once a famous beauty."

It was nearly ten o'clock when Mr. Stafford was summoned by message from Lady Ducayne, whose courier came to conduct him to her ladyship's salon. Bella was reading aloud when the visitor was admitted; and he noticed the languor in the low, sweet tones, the evident effort.

"Shut up the book," said the querulous old voice. "You are beginning to drawl like Miss Blandy."

Stafford saw a small, bent figure crouching over the

piled-up olive logs; a shrunken old figure in a gorgeous garment of black and crimson brocade, a skinny throat emerging from a mass of old Venetian lace, clasped with diamonds that flashed like fire-flies as the trembling old head turned towards him.

The eyes that looked at him out of the face were almost as bright as the diamonds – the only living feature in that narrow parchment mask. He had seen terrible faces in the hospital – faces on which disease had set dreadful marks – but he had never seen a face that impressed him so painfully as this withered countenance, with its indescribable horror of death outlived, a face that should have been hidden under a coffin-lid years and years ago.

The Italian physician was standing on the other side of the fireplace, smoking a cigarette, and looking down at the little old woman brooding over the hearth as if he were proud of her.

"Good evening, Mr. Stafford; you can go to your room, Bella, and write your everlasting letter to your mother at Walworth," said Lady Ducayne. "I believe she writes a page about every wild flower she discovers in the woods and meadows. I don't know what else she can find to write about," she added, as Bella quietly withdrew to the pretty little bedroom opening out of Lady Ducayne's spacious apartment. Here, as at Cap Ferrino, she slept in a room adjoining the old lady's.

"You are a medical man, I understand, Mr. Stafford."

"I am a qualified practitioner, but I have not begun to practise."

"You have begun upon my companion, she tells me."

"I have prescribed for her, certainly, and I am happy to find my prescription has done her good; but I look upon that improvement as temporary. Her case will require more drastic treatment."

"Never mind her case. There is nothing the matter with the girl – absolutely nothing – except girlish nonsense; too much liberty and not enough work."

"I understand that two of your ladyship's previous companions died of the same disease," said Stafford, looking first at Lady Ducayne, who gave her tremulous old head an impatient jerk, and then at Parravicini, whose yellow complexion had paled a little under Stafford's scrutiny.

"Don't bother me about my companions, sir," said Lady Ducayne. "I sent for you to consult you about myself – not about a parcel of anaemic girls. You are young, and medicine is a progressive science, the newspapers tell me. Where have you studied?"

"In Edinburgh – and in Paris."

"Two good schools. And you know all the new-fangled theories, the modern discoveries – that remind one of the mediaeval witchcraft, of Albertus Magnus,[12] and George Ripley;[13] you have studied hypnotism – electricity?"

"And the transfusion of blood," said Stafford, very slowly, looking at Parravicini.

"Have you made any discovery that teaches you to prolong human life – any elixir – any mode of treatment? I want my life prolonged, young man. That man there has been my physician for thirty years. He does all he can to keep me alive – after his lights. He studies all the new theories of all the scientists – but he is old; he gets older every day – his brain-power is going – he is bigoted – prejudiced – can't receive new ideas – can't grapple with new systems. He will let me die if I am not on my guard against him."

"You are of an unbelievable ingratitude, Ecclenza," said Parravicini.

"Oh, you needn't complain. I have paid you thousands to keep me alive. Every year of my life has swollen your hoards; you know there is nothing to come to you when I am gone. My whole fortune is left to endow a home for indigent women of quality who have reached their ninetieth year. Come, Mr. Stafford, I am a rich woman. Give me a few years more above ground, and I will give you the price of a fashionable London practice — I will set you up at the West-end."

"How old are you, Lady Ducayne?"

"I was born the day Louis XVI was guillotined."[14]

"Then I think you have had your share of the sunshine and the pleasures of the earth, and that you should spend your few remaining days in repenting your sins and trying to make atonement for the young lives that have been sacrificed to your love of life."

"What do you mean by that, sir?"

"Oh, Lady Ducayne, need I put your wickedness and your physician's still greater wickedness in plain words? The poor girl who is now in your employment has been reduced from robust health to a condition of absolute danger by Dr. Parravicini's experimental surgery; and I have no doubt those other two young women who broke down in your service were treated by him in the same manner. I could take upon myself to demonstrate – by most convincing evidence, to a jury of medical men – that Dr. Parravicini has been bleeding Miss Rolleston, after putting her under chloroform, at intervals, ever since she has been in your service. The deterioration in the girl's health speaks for itself; the lancet marks upon the girl's arms are unmistakable; and her description of a series of sensations, which she calls a dream, points unmistakably to the administration of chloroform while she was sleeping. A practice so nefarious, so murderous, must, if exposed, result in a sentence only less severe than the punishment of murder."

"I laugh," said Parravicini, with an airy motion of his skinny fingers; "I laugh at once at your theories and at your threats. I, Parravicini Leopold, have no fear that the law can question anything I have done."

"Take the girl away, and let me hear no more of her," cried Lady Ducayne, in the thin, old voice, which so poorly matched the energy and fire of the wicked old brain that guided its utterances. "Let her go back to her mother – I want no more girls to die in my service. There are girls enough and to spare in the world, God knows."

"If you ever engage another companion – or take another English girl into your service, Lady Ducayne, I will make all England ring with the story of your wickedness."

"I want no more girls. I don't believe in his experiments. They have been full of danger for me as well as for the girl – an air bubble, and I should be gone. I'll have no more of his dangerous quackery. I'll find some new man – a better man than you, sir, a discoverer like Pasteur,[15] or Virchow,[16] a genius – to keep me alive. Take your girl away, young man. Marry her if you like. I'll write her a cheque for a thousand pounds, and let her go and live on beef and beer, and get strong and plump again. I'll have no more such experiments. Do you hear, Parravicini?" she screamed, vindictively, the yellow, wrinkled face distorted with fury, the eyes glaring at him.

The Staffords carried Bella Rolleston off to Varese next day, she very loth to leave Lady Ducayne, whose liberal salary afforded such help for the dear mother. Herbert Stafford insisted, however, treating Bella as coolly as if he had been the family physician, and she had been given over wholly to his care.

"Do you suppose your mother would let you stop here to die?" he asked. "If Mrs. Rolleston knew how ill you are, she would come post haste to fetch you."

"I shall never be well again till I get back to Walworth," answered Bella, who was low-spirited and inclined to tears this morning, a reaction after her good spirits of yesterday.

"We'll try a week or two at Varese first," said Stafford. "When you can walk half-way up Monte Generoso without palpitation of the heart, you shall go back to Walworth."

"Poor mother, how glad she will be to see me, and how sorry that I've lost such a good place."

This conversation took place on the boat when they were leaving Bellaggio. Lotta had gone to her friend's room at seven o'clock that morning, long before Lady Ducayne's withered eyelids had opened to the daylight, before even Francine, the French maid, was astir, and had helped to pack a Gladstone bag[17] with essentials, and hustled Bella downstairs and out of doors before she could make any strenuous resistance.

"It's all right," Lotta assured her. "Herbert had a good talk with Lady Ducayne last night, and it was settled for you to leave this morning. She doesn't like invalids, you see."

"No," sighed Bella, "she doesn't like invalids. It was very unlucky that I should break down, just like Miss Tomson and Miss Blandy."

"At any rate, you are not dead, like them," answered Lotta, "and my brother says you are not going to die."

It seemed rather a dreadful thing to be dismissed in that off-hand way, without a word of farewell from her employer.

"I wonder what Miss Torpinter will say when I go to her for another situation," Bella speculated, ruefully, while she and her friends were breakfasting on board the steamer.

"Perhaps you may never want another situation," said Stafford.

"You mean that I may never be well enough to be useful to anybody?"

"No, I don't mean anything of the kind."

It was after dinner at Varese, when Bella had been induced to take a whole glass of Chianti, and quite sparkled after that unaccustomed stimulant, that Mr. Stafford produced a letter from his pocket.

"I forgot to give you Lady Ducayne's letter of adieu!" he said.

"What, did she write to me? I am so glad – I hated to leave her in such a cool way: for after all she was very kind to me, and if I didn't like her it was only because she was too dreadfully old."

She tore open the envelope. The letter was short and to the point: —

"Good-bye, child. Go and marry your doctor. I inclose a farewell gift for your trousseau. – ADELINE DUCAYNE."

"A hundred pounds, a whole year's salary – no – why, it's for a – 'A cheque for a thousand!'" cried Bella. "What a generous old soul! She really is the dearest old thing."

"She just missed being very dear to you, Bella," said Stafford.

He had dropped into the use of her Christian name while they were on board the boat. It seemed natural now that she was to be in his charge till they all three went back to England.

"I shall take upon myself the privileges of an elder brother till we land at Dover," he said; "after that – well, it must be as you please."

The question of their future relations must have been satisfactorily settled before they crossed the Channel, for Bella's next letter to her mother communicated three startling facts.

First, that the inclosed cheque for £1,000 was to be invested in debenture stock in Mrs. Rolleston's name, and was to be her very own, income and principal, for the rest of her life.

Next, that Bella was going home to Walworth immediately.

And last, that she was going to be married to Mr. Herbert Stafford in the following autumn.

"And I am sure you will adore him, mother, as much as I do," wrote Bella. "It is all good Lady Ducayne's doing. I never could have married if I had not secured that little nest-egg for you. Herbert says we shall be able to add to it as the years go by, and that wherever we live there shall be always a room in our house for you. The word 'mother-in-law' has no terrors for him."

Notes

1   In classical mythology, a harpy is a winged monster with the head and breasts of a woman.
2   Springs, shaped like the letter C, used to support the body of a carriage.
3   French novels were considered somewhat racy reading.
4   The years 1811-1820, during which George IV, then Prince of Wales, acted as Regent for his father George III.
5   Napoleon's empire was established on May 28, 1804. He married Josephine in 1796 and divorced her in 1810 on the grounds that she had produced no children.
6   The last king of Lydia, Croesus reigned from 560-546 BC. He was so rich and powerful that his name became proverbial for wealth.
7   Medieval chemistry, especially the pursuit of the transformation of base metals into gold.

8   Coins.

9   Joseph Turner (1775-1851). British landscape artist.

10 Progressive wasting disease, especially pulmonary tuberculosis.

11 Cesare (1476-1507) and Lucretia (1430-1519) Borgia were the illegitimate children of Pope Alexander VI. The ruthless Borgia family were reputed to be particularly adept at poisoning their enemies.

12 Albertus Magnus (1206-1280). Scholastic philosopher of the Dominican order known as "doctor universalis" because of the breadth of his knowledge; he gained a reputation as a wizard.

13 George Ripley (1802-1880). Transcendentalist whose thought was much influenced by the scientific discoveries of the age.

14 Louis XVI was guillotined on January 21, 1793.

15 Louis Pasteur (1822-1895). French chemist whose experiments in fermentation led to the science of microbiology. He is also renowned for developing a vaccine for rabies.

16 Rudolph Virchow (1821-1902). German pathologist whose *Cellular Pathology* (1858) was highly influential.

17 Portmanteau named after the Victorian statesman, W.E. Gladstone.

Source: *Strand Magazine*, February 1896.

Biographical Note

Braddon, one of the foremost nineteenth-century writers of sensation fiction, was born in London on October 4, 1835. Her father deserted the family while she was still a child, and so to help support the family, Braddon, at the age of nineteen and in defiance of all Victorian notions about what constituted acceptable behavior for middle-class women, went on the stage under the name of "Mary Seyton." The financial help of a Yorkshire admirer named Gilby eventually allowed her to leave the stage and focus on writing. Her first novel was *Three Times Dead* (1860), revised and then re-released by the publisher John Maxwell in 1861 as *The Trail of the Serpent*. Braddon began to write sensational thrillers for such penny-dreadfuls as the *Halfpenny Journal* and *Reynold's Miscellany*, produced an average of two three-decker novels each year, and founded the periodical *Belgravia*. In 1861 she moved in with her publisher. Maxwell already had a wife confined to a Dublin insane asylum, so they were unable to marry until his wife died thirteen years later. By this time Braddon had five illegitimate children by Maxwell and had raised five more from his first marriage. In 1862 she published *Lady Audley's Secret*, the story of a deceptively angelic woman who turns bigamist in order to marry advantageously and then murders to protect what she subsequently gains: it was a spectacular best-seller. Two more popular works, *Aurora Floyd* and *John Marchmont's Legacy*, appeared in 1863, and were followed in 1864 by *The Doctor's Wife*, an impressive reworking of Flaubert's *Madame Bovary* (1856), in which Braddon moves away from her usual focus on sensational plot to an interest in character.

Braddon's own position in society had much to do with the constant juxtaposition in her female characters of a superficial social respectability with wild rebellion and a refusal to conform to convention. She was continually attacked by such critics as Margaret Oliphant for her immorality—both in her life and in her work—but her sales nevertheless steadily soared, and her influence extended to much of nineteenth-century "main-stream" fiction: her admirers included Dickens, Thackeray, and Tennyson. When her mother died in 1868, Braddon suffered a complete nervous collapse and produced nothing for two years. In the next two decades, she worked on children's stories, thrillers, plays, and condensations of Scott's novels for the penny press. She remained busy and active all her life, producing over seventy novels in all and numerous short stories.

"Good Lady Ducayne," which reveals Braddon's fascination with theories about blood transfusion, is typical of much of her work with the detached and ironic narrative voice forming a striking contrast with the sensational subject of the story. The best of her other short fiction can be found in the collections entitled *Ralph the Bailiff, and Other Tales* (1862), *Milly Darrell, and Other Tales* (1873), and *Weavers and Weft, and Other Tales* (1877). Braddon lived to see a silent film production of her best-seller *Aurora Floyd*, and died at eighty while revising *Mary*, a partly autobiographical work that appeared post-humously.

Selected Modern Reprints:

Lady Audley's Secret. Ed. David Skilton. Oxford: Oxford UP, 1987.

Selected Secondary Sources:

Hughes, Winifred. *The Maniac in the Cellar: Sensation Novels of the 1860s*. Princeton, NJ: Princeton UP, 1980.
Peterson, Audrey. *Victorian Masters of Mystery: From Wilkie Collins to Conan Doyle*. New York: Ungar, 1984.
Wolff, Robert Lee. *Sensational Victorian: The Life and Fiction of Mary Elizabeth Braddon*. New York: Garland, 1979.

104   KATE CHOPIN (1851-1904)

Kate Chopin (1851-1904)

The Storm

I

THE LEAVES WERE SO STILL THAT EVEN BIBI THOUGHT IT WAS
going to rain. Bobinôt, who was accustomed to converse on
terms of perfect equality with his little son, called the child's
attention to certain sombre clouds that were rolling with sinister intention from the west, accompanied by a sullen,
threatening roar. They were at Friedheimer's store and decided to remain there till the storm had passed. They sat
within the door on two empty kegs. Bibi was four years old
and looked very wise.

"Mama'll be 'fraid, yes," he suggested with blinking
eyes.

"She'll shut the house. Maybe she got Sylvie helpin'
her this evenin'," Bobinôt responded reassuringly.

"No; she ent got Sylvie. Sylvie was helpin' her yisti-
day," piped Bibi. Bobinôt arose and going across to the
counter purchased a can of shrimps, of which Calixta was
very fond. Then he returned to his perch on the keg and
sat stolidly holding the can of shrimps while the storm
burst. It shook the wooden store and seemed to be ripping
great furrows in the distant field. Bibi laid his little hand
on his father's knee and was not afraid.

II

Calixta, at home, felt no uneasiness for their safety. She sat
at a side window sewing furiously on a sewing machine. She

was greatly occupied and did not notice the approaching storm. But she felt very warm and often stopped to mop her face on which the perspiration gathered in beads. She unfastened her white sacque at the throat. It began to grow dark, and suddenly realizing the situation she got up hurriedly and went about closing windows and doors.

Out on the small front gallery she had hung Bobinôt's Sunday clothes to air and she hastened out to gather them before the rain fell. As she stepped outside, Alcée Laballière rode in at the gate. She had not seen him very often since her marriage, and never alone. She stood there with Bobinôt's coat in her hands, and the big rain drops began to fall. Alcée rode his horse under the shelter of a side projection where the chickens had huddled and there were plows and a harrow piled up in the corner.

"May I come and wait on your gallery till the storm is over, Calixta?," he asked.

"Come 'long in, M'sieur Alcée."

His voice and her own startled her as if from a trance, and she seized Bobinôt's vest. Alcée, mounting to the porch, grabbed the trousers and snatched Bibi's braided jacket that was about to be carried away by a sudden gust of wind. He expressed an intention to remain outside, but it was soon apparent that he might as well have been out in the open: the water beat in upon the boards in driving sheets, and he went inside, closing the door after him. It was even necessary to put something beneath the door to keep the water out.

"My! what a rain! It's good two years sence it rain' like that," exclaimed Calixta as she rolled up a piece of bagging and Alcée helped her to thrust it beneath the crack.

She was a little fuller of figure than five years before when she married; but she had lost nothing of her vivacity. Her blue eyes still retained their melting quality; and her yellow hair, dishevelled by the wind and rain, kinked more stubbornly than ever about her ears and temples.

The rain beat upon the low, shingled roof with a force and clatter that threatened to break an entrance and deluge them there. They were in the dining room – the sitting room – the general utility room. Adjoining was her bed room, with Bibi's couch along side her own. The door stood open, and the room with its white, monumental bed, its closed shutters, looked dim and mysterious.

Alcée flung himself into a rocker and Calixta nervously began to gather up from the floor the lengths of a cotton sheet which she had been sewing.

"If this keeps up, *Dieu sait*[1] if the levees[2] goin' to stan' it!" she exclaimed.

"What have you got to do with the levees?"

"I got enough to do! An' there's Bobinôt with Bibi out in that storm – if he only didn't left Friedheimer's!'"

"Let us hope, Calixta, that Bobinôt's got sense enough to come in out of a cyclone."

She went and stood at the window with a greatly disturbed look on her face. She wiped the frame that was clouded with moisture. It was stiflingly hot. Alcée got up and joined her at the window, looking over her shoulder. The rain was coming down in sheets obscuring the view of far-off cabins and enveloping the distant wood in a gray mist. The playing of the lightning was incessant. A bolt struck a tall chinaberry tree at the edge of the field. It filled all visible space with a blinding glare and the crash seemed to invade the very boards they stood upon.

Calixta put her hands to her eyes, and with a cry, staggered backward. Alcée's arm encircled her, and for an instant he drew her close and spasmodically to him.

"*Bonté!*"[3] she cried, releasing herself from his encircling arm and retreating from the window, "the house'll go next! If I only knew w'ere Bibi was!" She would not compose herself; she would not be seated. Alcée clasped her shoulders and looked into her face. The contact of her warm, palpitating body when he had unthinkingly drawn her into his arms, had aroused all the old-time infatuation and desire for her flesh.

"Calixta," he said, "don't be frightened. Nothing can happen. The house is too low to be struck, with so many tall trees standing about. There! aren't you going to be quiet? say, aren't you?" He pushed her hair back from her face that was warm and steaming. Her lips were as red and moist as pomegranate seed. Her white neck and a glimpse of her full, firm bosom disturbed him powerfully. As she glanced up at him the fear in her liquid blue eyes had given place to a drowsy gleam that unconsciously betrayed a sensuous desire. He looked down into her eyes and there was nothing for him to do but to gather her lips in a kiss. It reminded him of Assumption.

"Do you remember – in Assumption, Calixta?" he asked in a low voice broken by passion. Oh! she remembered; for in Assumption he had kissed her and kissed and kissed her; until his senses would well nigh fail, and to save her he would resort to a desperate flight. If she was not an immaculate dove in those days, she was still inviolate; a passionate creature whose very defenselessness had made her defense, against which his honor forbade him to prevail. Now – well, now – her lips seemed in a manner free to be tasted, as well as her round, white throat and her whiter breasts.

They did not heed the crashing torrents, and the roar of the elements made her laugh as she lay in his arms. She was a revelation in that dim, mysterious chamber; as white as the couch she lay upon. Her firm, elastic flesh that was knowing for the first time its birthright, was like a creamy lily that the sun invites to contribute its breath and perfume to the undying life of the world.

The generous abundance of her passion, without guile or trickery, was like a white flame which penetrated and found response in depths of his own sensuous nature that had never yet been reached.

When he touched her breasts they gave themselves up in quivering ecstasy, inviting his lips. Her mouth was a fountain of delight. And when he possessed her, they seemed to swoon together at the very borderland of life's mystery.

He stayed cushioned upon her, breathless, dazed, enervated, with his heart beating like a hammer upon her. With one hand she clasped his head, her lips lightly touching his forehead. The other hand stroked with a soothing rhythm his muscular shoulders.

The growl of the thunder was distant and passing

away. The rain beat softly upon the shingles, inviting them to drowsiness and sleep. But they dared not yield.

The rain was over; and the sun was turning the glistening green world into a palace of gems. Calixta, on the gallery, watched Alcée ride away. He turned and smiled at her with a beaming face; and she lifted her pretty chin in the air and laughed aloud.

III

Bobinôt and Bibi, trudging home, stopped without at the cistern to make themselves presentable.

"My! Bibi, w'at will yo' mama say! You ought to be ashame'. You oughtn' put on those good pants. Look at 'em! An' that mud on yo' collar! How you got that mud on yo' collar' Bibi? I never saw such a boy!" Bibi was the picture of pathetic resignation. Bobinôt was the embodiment of serious solicitude as he strove to remove from his own person and his son's the signs of their tramp over heavy roads and through wet fields. He scraped the mud off Bibi's bare legs and feet with a stick and carefully removed all traces from his heavy brogans.[4] Then, prepared for the worst – the meeting with an over-scrupulous housewife, they entered cautiously at the back door.

Calixta was preparing supper. She had set the table and was dripping coffee at the hearth. She sprang up as they came in.

"Oh, Bobinôt! You back! My! but I was uneasy. W'ere you been during the rain? An' Bibi? he ain't wet? he ain't hurt?" She had clasped Bibi and was kissing him effusively. Bobinôt's explanations and apologies which he had been composing all along the way, died on his lips as Calixta felt him to see if he were dry, and seemed to express nothing but satisfaction at their safe return.

"I brought you some shrimps, Calixta," offered Bobinôt hauling the can from his ample side pocket and laying it on the table.

"Shrimps! Oh, Bobinôt! you too good fo' anything!

and she gave him a smacking kiss on the cheek that re-
sounded. "*J' vous réponds,*[5] we'll have a feas' to night!
umph-umph!"

Bobinôt and Bibi began to relax and enjoy themselves,
and when the three seated themselves at table they
laughed much and so loud that anyone might have heard
them as far away as Laballière's.

IV

Alcée Laballière wrote to his wife, Clarisse, that night. It was
a loving letter, full of tender solicitude. He told her not to
hurry back, but if she and the babies liked it at Biloxi, to stay
a month longer. He was getting on nicely; and though he
missed them, he was willing to bear the separation a while
longer – realizing that their health and pleasure were the
first things to be considered.

V

As for Clarisse, she was charmed upon receiving her husband's letter. She and the babies were doing well. The society was agreeable; many of her old friends and acquaintances were at the bay. And the first free breath since her
marriage seemed to restore the pleasant liberty of her
maiden days. Devoted as she was to her husband, their in-
timate conjugal life was something which she was more than
willing to forego for a while.

So the storm passed and every one was happy.

Notes

1 God knows.
2 Built up embankment along a river.
3 Goodness!
4 Coarse stout sort of shoes.
5 I respond to you.

Source: *The Complete Works of Kate Chopin*. Ed. Per Seyersted. 2 vols. Baton Rouge: Louisiana State UP, 1969.

Biographical Note

Kate Chopin was born in St. Louis, Missouri, on February 8, 1851. After graduating from the Sacred Heart Convent, she married Oscar Chopin in 1870, and moved to the Natchitoches Parish, an area that was to serve as the setting for many of her later stories. She had five sons over the next ten years, and when her husband died in 1882, she remained in Louisiana for two more years, managing the family plantation, before returning to her mother's home in St. Louis and beginning to write. Her first poem, "If It Might Be," appeared in the *American* in 1889; during the following year, two of her stories were published in local papers. Chopin wrote three novels—one of which, *Young Doctor Gosse*, she eventually destroyed after being unable to find a publisher. In her first novel Chopin established her unconventionality with her refusal to condemn divorce: a widow insists her suitor return to remarry the weak alcoholic wife he had divorced, disaster ensues for all, and the widow is left realizing herself to be, as the title of the novel indicates, *At Fault* (1890). Two collections of stories followed, *Bayou Folk* (1894) and *A Night in Acadie* (1897). Chopin's depictions of the Creoles and Acadians of Louisiana established her reputation as a local colorist—a label that, because of its associations with quaintness, Chopin herself deplored. Like many writers of the time, she was influenced not only by the local color movement, but more importantly by the European realists: echoes of Maupassant, Flaubert, Hardy, and Zola can be found throughout her writing. In stories like "Desiree's Baby," "Wiser than a God," and "A Shameful Affair," Chopin treats such subjects as miscegenation, the conflict between love and a career, and female sexuality. The theme of women's search for self-fulfillment is most fully developed in her second novel and best known work, *The Awakening* (1899). The protagonist, Edna Pontellier, whose self-awakening is prompted by her contact with Creole society and the attentions of Robert Le Brun, leaves her husband and children and attempts to make a new life for herself outside the traditional woman's sphere. Eventually recognizing the impossibility of her task, she chooses suicide over capitulation to the demands of her old life. The outrage that greeted the amoral treatment of adultery and suicide in *The Awakening* badly damaged Chopin's reputation and effectively put an end to her literary career. She died in 1904 of a brain hemorrhage.

Although the story reprinted here can stand alone, it forms a telling comparison with its precursor, "At the 'Cadian Ball." In this story the simple farmer Bobinôt and the more favored gentleman planter Alcée compete for the attentions of Calixta. But when Alcée's kinswoman Clarisse calls him home, the planter responds like one awakening from a dream, leaving the disappointed Calixta to settle for the farmer. If sexual desire must give way to social convention in the first story, it nevertheless emerges triumphant in the sequel. Written in the same year as *The Awakening* was published, "The Storm" is striking for its frank and exultant depiction of woman's sensuality, and after the response to the novel, it is hardly surprising that Chopin made no attempt to publish the story.

Selected Modern Reprints:

The Awakening and Selected Stories. Ed. and Intro. Sandra M. Gilbert. New York: Penguin, 1984.
Kate Chopin: Portraits. Intro. Helen Taylor. London: Women's P, 1979.

Kate Chopin. A Vocation and a Voice: Stories. Ed. and Intro.
   Emily Toth. Toronto: Viking Penguin, 1991.
*"The Storm" and Other Stories by Kate Chopin: With The Awak-
   ening.* Intro. Per Seyersted. Old Westbury, NY: Feminist
   P, 1974.

Selected Secondary Sources:

Arner, Robert D. "Kate Chopin's Realism: 'At the 'Cadian
   Ball' and 'The Storm.'" *Markham Review.* 2.2 (1970): 1-4.
Bloom, Harold, ed. *Kate Chopin.* Philadelphia: Chelsea
   House, 1987.
Bonner, Thomas, ed. *The Kate Chopin Companion: with
   Chopin's Translations from French Fiction.* New York:
   Greenwood P, 1988.
Ewell, Barbara C. *Kate Chopin.* New York: Ungar, 1986.
Gaude, Pamela. "Kate Chopin's 'The Storm': A Study of
   Maupassant's Influence." *Kate Chopin Newsletter* 1
   (1975): 1-6.
Seyersted, Per. *Kate Chopin: A Critical Biography.* Baton
   Rouge: Louisiana State UP, 1969.
Skaggs, Peggy. *Kate Chopin.* Boston: Twayne, 1985.

114   ISABELLA VALANCY CRAWFORD (1850-1887)

Isabella Valancy Crawford (1850-1887)

Extradited

"OH, SAM! BACK SO SOON? WELL, I'M GLAD."

She had her arms round his neck. She curved serpent-wise in his clasp to get her eyes on his eye.

"How's mammy?" she asked, in a slight panic, "not worse, is she?" "Better," returned Sam; he pushed her away mechanically, and glanced round the rude room with its touches of refinement: the stop organ against the wall of unplastered logs, the primitive hearth, its floor of hewn planks.

"Oh yes! Baby!" she exclaimed, "you missed him; he's asleep on our bed; I'll fetch him."

He caught her apron string, still staring round the apartment.

"Where's Joe, Bess? I don't see him round,"

Bessie crimsoned petulantly.

"You can think of the hired man first before me and Baby!"

"Baby's a sort of fixed fact. A hired man, ain't," said Sam, slowly. "Mebbe Joe's at the barn!"

"Maybe he is, and maybe he isn't," retorted Bessie sharply. "I didn't marry Samuel O'Dwyer to have a hired man set before me and my child, and I won't stand it—so there!"

"You needn't to," said Sam, smiling. He was an Irish Canadian: a rich smack of brogue adorned his tongue; a kindly graciousness of eye made a plain face almost captivating, while the proud and melancholy Celtic fire and intentness of his glance gave dignity to his expression. The lips were curved in a humorous smile, but round them were deeply graven heroic and Spartan lines.

"Sure, darlin', isn't it you an' the boy are the pulses

of my heart?" he said, smiling. "Sure Joe can wait. I was sort of wonderin' at not seein' him—that's all. Say, I'll un-hitch the horses. They've done fifteen miles o' mud holes an' corduroy since noon, an' then we'll have supper. I could 'most eat my boots, so hurry up, woman darlin', or maybe it's the boy I'll be aitin', or the bit of a dog your daddy sent to him. Hear the baste howlin' like a banshee out yonder."

"It's one of Cricket's last year's pups," cried Bessie, running to the waggon. "Wonder Father spared him; he thinks a sight of her pups. My! ain't he a beauty; won't baby just love him!"

She carried the yelping youngster into the house, while Sam took the horses to the barn, a primitive edifice of rough logs, standing in a bleak chaos of burned stumps, for "O'Dwyer's Clearing" was but two years old, and had the rage of its clearing fires on it yet. The uncouth eaves were fine crimson on one side, from the sunset; on the other a delicate, spiritual silver, from the moon hanging above the cedar swamp: the rude doors stood open: a vigorous purple haze, shot with heavy bars of crimson light, filled the interior; a "Whip-Poor-Will" chanted from a distant tree, like a muezzin from a minaret; the tired horses whinnied at a whiff of fresh clover, and rubbed noses in sedate congratulation. Sam looked at the ground a moment, reflectively, and then shouted:

"Hullo, Joe!"

"Hullo, Sam!"

By this time Sam was stooping over the Waggon-tongue, his rugged face in the shadow, too intent on straps and buckles to glance up.

"Back all right, you see, Joe," he remarked. "How's things gettin' along?"

"Sublimely," said Joe, coming to his assistance. "I got the south corner cut—we've only to draw it tomorrow,"

"I never seen the beat of you at hard work," remarked Sam. "A slight young chap like you, too. It's just the spirit of you! But you mustn't outdo the strength that is in you for all that. I'm no slave-driver: I don't want your heart's blood. Sure, I've had your sweat two long years—an' the place shows it—it's had your sense an' sinews, so it had. I'll never forget it to you, Joe."

Joe's tanned, nervous face was shaded by the flap of his limp straw hat. He looked piercingly at Sam, as the released horses walked decorously into the barn.

"Go to your supper, Sam," he said. "I'll bed them. I venture to say you're pretty sharp-set; go in."

"I'll lend a hand first," returned Sam. He followed the other into the barn.

"It's got dark in here suddenly," remarked Sam. "I'll get the lantern."

"Don't," said Sam, slowly. "There's something to be spoke about betwixt you an' me, Joe, an' I'd as lieve say it in the dark; let the lantern be—I'd as lieve say it in the dark."

* * *

"A thousand dollars!"

Bessie rose on her elbow and looked at her sleeping husband. Slumber brought the iron to the surface instead of melting it, and his face became sterner and more resolute in its repose. Its owner was not a man to be trifled with, she admitted as she gazed, and watching him she shivered slightly in the mournful moonlight. Many of her exceedingly respectable virtues were composed mainly of two or three minor vices: her conjugal love was a compound of vanity and jealousy: her maternal affection an agreement of rapacity and animal instinct. In giving her a child, nature had developed the she eagle in her breast. She was full of impotent, unrecognized impulses to prey on all things in her child's behalf. By training and habit she was honest, but her mind was becoming active with the ingenuity of self-cheatry. She held a quiet contempt for her husband, the unlearned man who had won the pretty schoolmistress: and, hedged in by the prim fence of routine knowledge and imperfect education, she despised the large crude movements of the untrained intellect, and the primitive power of the strong and lofty soul. He muttered uneasily as she slipped out of bed. The electric chill of the moonlight did not affect her spirit—she was not vulnerable to these hints and petitions of nature. She crept carefully into the great rude room, which was hall, parlor, and kitchen. The back log, which never died out, smouldered on the hearth. A block of moonlight fell like a slab of marble on the floor of loose planks which rattled faintly under her firm, bare foot. The wooden benches, the coarse table, the log walls, started through the gloom like bleak sentinels of the great Army of Privation. She looked at them without disgust, as she stole to the corner where her organ stood. She sang a silent little hymn of self-laudation.

"Some women would spend it on fine fallals for their backs or houses," she thought. "I won't. I'll bank every cent of it for baby. Money doubles in ten years. A thousand dollars will grow nicely in twenty — or I'll get Daddy to loan it out on farm mortgages. I guess Sam will stare twenty years hence when he finds how rich I've got to be. I'm glad I know my duty as a parent — Sam would never see things as I do — and a thousand dollars is a sight of money."

She groped on the organ for her paper portefolio, an elegant trifle Joe had sent to the city for, to delicately grace her last birthday; its scent of violets guided her. She took from it a paper and pencil, and standing in the moonlight scribbled a few lines. She dotted her "i's" and crossed her "t's" with particularity, and was finnickin in her nice folding of the written sheet. Her cool cheeks kept their steady pink; her round eyes their untroubled calm; her chin bridled a little with spiritual pride, as she cautiously opened the outer door.

"It's my clear duty as a parent and a citizen," she thought, with self-approval, "the thousand dollars would not tempt me if my duty were not so plainly set before me: and the money will be in good hands. I'm not one to spend it in vain show. Money's a great evil to a weak and worldly mind, but I'm not one for vain show."

She looked up at the sky from under the morning glories Joe had thoughtfully planted to make cool shadows for her rocker in the porch.

"It will rain to-morrow. So I'll not wash till Friday; I wonder will that pink print Sam fetched home turn out a fast color; I'll make it up for Baby; he'll look too cunning for anything in it, with those coral sleeve links Joe gave him. I hope he won't cry, and wake Sam before I get back."

He did not. As she had left him she found him on her return, a little snowy ball, curled up against his father's massive shoulder, the beautiful, black, baby head, thrust against the starting sinews of the man's bare and massive throat. When choice was possible Baby scrambled into the aura of the father — not of the mother. Sam stirred, started, and yawned.

"What's up, Bess?" he asked sleepily.

"I went to the well to draw fresh water," she replied, folding her shawl neatly on the back of a chair. "I was wakeful and thirsty — the night is so hot."

"Guess that consarned pup worried you with his howlen'," he said. "I don't hear him now — hope he won't get out of the barn — but that ain't probable — Joe shut him in, right enough; you should have sent me to the well, girl darlin', so you should."

Bessie picked out a burr which she felt in the fringes of her shawl, and said nothing. She was strictly truthful, so far as the letter of truth went; she had gone to the well and had drawn a bucket of cool water from that shaft of solid shadow. What else she had accomplished she decidedly had no intention of confiding to Sam. She slipped into bed, took the baby on her arm, and kissed his pouting lips.

"God bless the darling," she said with her pretty smile.

"Amen," said Sam earnestly. "God come betwixt every man's child an' harm." Bessie dosed off placidly, the child on her arm. Sam lay staring at the moonlight, listening, thinking, and grandly sorrowing.

There was the unceasing sound of someone tossing feverishly on a creaking bedstead, the eternal sound of heavy sighs resolutely smothered.

"He ain't sleepin' well, ain't Joe," thought Sam. "Not even though he knows Bessie an' me is his friends, true as the day. Guess he ain't sleepin' at all, poor chap!"

"The consarned pup is gone," remarked Sam, disgustedly, as he came in to breakfast. "Guess he scrambled up to the hay gap and jumped out. Too bad!"

"He's safe enough," said Joe. "He probably ran for home. You will find him at your father's on your next visit, Mrs. O'Dwyer. Dogs have the 'homing' instinct as well as pigeons."

"Yes, I guess he went back to pa," said Bessie. Her color rose, her eyes flashed. "Do put baby down, Joe," she said sharply, "I don't want — that is, you are mussing his clean frock."

Joe looked keenly at her,

"I understand," he said, gently. He placed the child tenderly on the rude lounge, which yet was pretty like all Bessie's belongings, and walked to the open door.

"I think I'll straighten things a bit at the landing," he said. "Piner's booms burst yesterday and before the drive reaches here it's as well to see to the boats—those river drivers help themselves to canoes wherever they come across them."

"Just as you say, Joe," said Sam, gravely. "I've never known your head or your heart at fault yet."

Joe gave a long, wistful look of gratitude, and went out. He did not glance at Bessie, nor she at him.

"Bess, woman," said Sam, "what ails you at Joe?"

"You know well enough," she said placidly. "He's free to stay here; I don't deny he's working well; though that was his duty, and he was paid for it, but he shan't touch my child again. No parent who understood her duty would permit it; I know mine. I'm thankful to say."

Her small rancors and spites were the 'Judas' doors' through which she most frequently betrayed herself. She had always faintly disliked Joe, before whom her shabby little school routine, her small affectations of intellectual superiority had shrivelled into siccous leaves. She would assert herself now against Sam's dearly-loved friend, she thought, jealously and with an approving conscience, and it was her plain duty to tear him out of that large and constant heart, she was pleased to feel.

Sam's face changed, in a breath, to a passionate pallor of skin; a proud and piercing gloom of anger darkened his blue eyes to black; he looked at her in wonder.

"What's all this, woman?" he demanded, slowly. "But it's never your heart that's said it! Him that gave the sweat of his body and the work of his mind to help me make this home for you! Him that's saved my life more nor once at risk of his own young days! Him that's as close to my heart as my own brother! Tut, woman! It's never you would press the thorn in the breast of him into his heart's core. I won't demane myself with leavin' the thought to you, Bessie O'Dwyer!"

He struck his fist on the table; he stared levelly at her, defying her to lower herself in his eyes.

She smoothly repaired her error.

"I spoke in a hurry," she said, lifting the baby's palm, and covering Sam's lips with its daintiness. "I feel hurt he had so little confidence in me. I wish him well; you know that."

Sam smiled under the fluttering of the child's palm upon his lips; he gave a sigh of relief. "Be kind to him, Bessie darlin'," he said, "Shure our own boy is born—but he isn't dead yet: the Lord stand betwixt the child an' harm! An' there is no tellin' when he, too, may need the kind word and the tender heart. Shure I'm sorry I took you up in arnest just now."

"I spoke in a pet," said Bessie gently. "I remember, of course, all we owe to Joe—how could I forget it?"

"Forgettin's about the aisiest job in life," said Sam, rising. "Guess I'll help Joe at the landin'; he's downhearted, an' I won't lave him alone to his throuble."

Bessie looked after his disapprovingly.

"Trouble indeed! I thought Sam had clearer ideas on such points. The notion of confounding trouble with rightdown sin and wickedness! Well, it's a good thing I know my duty. I wonder if Pa has any mortgage in his mind ready for that money? It must be a first mortgage: I won't risk any other—I know my responsibility as a mother better than that."

* * *

"Why, man alive!"

Sam was astonished: for the first time in his experience of Joe, the latter was idle. He sat on a fallen tree, looking vacantly into the strong current below him.

"I'm floored, Sam," he answered, without looking up, "I've no grit left in me — not a grain."

"Then it's the first time since I've known you," said Sam, regarding him with wistful gravity. "Don't let the sorrow master you, Joe."

"You call it sorrow, Sam?"

"That's the blessed an' holy name for it now," said Sam, with his lofty, simple seriousness, "what ever it may have been afore. Hearten up, Joe! Shure you're as safe at O'Dwyer's Clearin', as if you were hid unther a hill. Rouse your heart, man alive! What's to fear?"

"Not much to fear, but a great deal to feel," said Joe. "Am I not stripped of my cloak to you — that's bitter."

"The only differ is that I'm dead sure now of what I suspicioned right along," said Sam. "It's not in reason that a schollard an' a gentleman should bury himself on O'Dwyer's Clearin' for morenor two years, unless to sconce shame an' danger. Rouse your sowl, Joe! don't I owe half of all I have to your arm an' your larnin'? When this danger blows past I'll divide with you, an' you can make a fresh start in some sthrange counthry. South Americay's a grond place, they tell me; shure, I'll take Bessie an' the boy an' go with you. I've no kin nor kith of my own, an' next to her an' the child it is yourself is in the core of my heart. Kape the sorrow, Joe; it's the pardon of God on you, but lave the shame an' the fear go; you'll do the world's wonder yet, boy."

Joe was about three-and-twenty, Sam in middle age. He placed his massive hand on the other's bare and throbbing head, and both looked silently at the dark and rapid river: Joe with a faint pulse of hope in his bruised and broken soul.

"Piner's logs'll get here about to-morrow," said Sam at last, "'shure it's Bessie'll be in the twitteration, watchin' the hens an' geese from them mauraudtherin river drivers. I wish the pup hadn't got away; it's a good watch dog his mother is, an' likely he'd show her blood in him — the villain that he was to run away with himself, like that, but liberty's a swate toothful, so it is, to man or brute."

The following day, Bessie having finished her ironing and baking with triumphant exactness, stood looking from the lovely vines of the porch, down the wild farm road. She was crystal-clean and fresh, and the child in her arms was like a damask rose in his turkey red frock and white bib. A model young matron was Mrs. O'Dwyer and looked it to the fine point of perfection, Sam thought, as he glanced back at her, pride and tenderness in his eyes. She was not looking after his retreating figure, but eagerly down the farm road, and, it seemed to Sam, she was listening intently. "Mebbe she thinks the shouting of them river drivers is folks comin' up the road," he thought, as he turned the clump of cedar bushes by the landing, and found Joe at work, patching a bark canoe. As usual he was laboring fiercely as men rush in battle, the sweat on his brow, his teeth set, his eyes fixed. Sam smiled reprovingly.

"Shure, it's all smashed up: you'll have her, Joe, again she's mended," he remarked, "more power to your elbow; but take it easy, man! You'll wear out soon enough."

"I must work like the devil, or think," said Joe, feverishly. "Some day, Sam, I'll tell you all the treasures of life I threw from me, then you'll understand."

"When a man understands by the road of the heart, where's the good of larnin' by the road of the ears?" said Sam, with the tenderest compassion; "but I'll listen when it's your will to tell, never fear. Hark, now! don't I hear them rollickin' divvils of pike pole men shoutin' beyant the bend there?"

"Yes; Piner's logs must be pretty close," answered Joe, looking up the river.

"They'll come down the rapids in style," said Sam, throwing a chip on the current, "the sthrame's swift as a swallow and strong as a giant with the rains."

They worked in silence for a while, then Joe began to

whistle softly. Sam smiled.

"That's right, Joe," he said, "there's nothing so bad that it mightn't be worse — there's hope ahead for you yet, never fear."

A glimmer of some old joyous spirit sparkled in the young man's melancholy eyes, to fade instantly. "It's past all that, dear old friend," he said. As he spoke he glanced towards the cedar scrub between them and the house.

"Here comes Mrs. O'Dwyer with the boy," he said, "and Sam, there are three men, strangers, with her."

"Shanty bosses come to buy farm stuff," said Sam. He turned on Joe with an air of sudden mastery.

"Away with you down the bank," he said. "Into the bush with you, an' don't come out until you hear me fire five shots in a string. Away with you!"

"Too late, Sam," said the other, "they have seen me."

"What's all this, Bessie?"

Bessie wiped the baby's wet lips with her apron.

"These gentlemen asked to see you, Sam. I guess they want some farm stuff off us for Piner's Camp. So I brought them along."

She looked placidly at her husband; the baby sprang in her arms eager to get to his friend Joe, whose red flannel shirt he found very attractive.

"Potatoes or flour?" asked Sam curtly, turning on the strangers.

"Well, it ain't neither," said one of them — he laid his hand on Joe's wrist. "It's this young gentleman we're after; he robbed his employer two years' back, and he's wanted back by Uncle Sam. That's about the size of it."

There was nothing brutal in his look or speech; he knew he was not dealing with a hardened criminal: he even felt compassion for the wretched quarry he had in his talons.

"He's in Canada — on British soil; I dare you to touch him!" said Sam fiercely.

"We have his extradition papers right enough," said one of the other detectives. "Don't be so foolish as to resist the law, Mr. O'Dwyer."

"He shan't for me," said Joe, quietly. He stood motionless while the detective snapped one manacle of the handcuffs on his wrist; the steel glittered like a band of fire in the sun.

The child leaped strongly in Bessie's arms, crowing with delight at the pretty brightness. She was a little off her guard, somewhat faint as she watched the deathly shame on the young man's face which had never turned on her or hers but with tenderness and goodwill. Her brain reeled a little, her hands felt weak.

Suddenly there was a shriek, a flash of red, a soft plunge in the water. Joe threw his arms open, dashing aside the detectives like straws.

"Don't hold me — let me save him!" he cried.

Sam could not swim; he stood on the bank holding Bessie, who screamed and struggled in convulsions of fright as she saw her child drowning. Joe rose in the current, fighting his way superbly towards the little red bundle whirling before him. One of the detectives covered him with a revolver.

"Try to escape and I'll shoot," he called out, "understand?"

Joe smiled. Escape to the opposite shore and leave Sam's child to drown? No; he had no idea of it. It was a terrible fight between the man and the river — and the man subdued it unto him. He turned back to shore, the child in his teeth, both arms — one with the shining handcuff on it — beating the hostile current with fine, steady strokes.

Another moment and he would be safe on shore, a captive and ashamed.

He spurned the yellow fringes of the current; he felt ground under his feet; he half rose to step on the bank. Then there rose a bewildering cry from Sam and the men watching him; he turned and saw his danger.

With one sublime effort he flung the child on the bank, and then with the force of a battering ram the first of Piner's logs crashed upon him. It reared against him like a living thing instinct with rage, and wallowing monster-like led its barky hordes down the rushing stream, rolling triumphantly over a bruised and shattered pigmy of creation, a man.

"Extradited, by ginger," said one of the detectives, as the groaning logs rolled compactly together over the spot where Joe had gone down.

Before the men departed, Bessie, with the baby on her arm, in a nice clean frock, found opportunity to ask one of them a momentous question. "Do you think, he being dead, that I shall get any of the reward promised for his arrest? Only for me sending that note to Pa tied round the pup's neck, you would never have found him away back here, you know."

"I guess not," replied the detective eyeing her thoughtfully. "You're a smart woman, you are, but you won't get no reward all the same; pity, ain't it?"

"It's a shame," she said, bursting into a passion of tears. "It don't seem that there's any reward for doing one's duty; oh, it's a downright shame."

"Best keep all this tol'ble shady from that man of yours," said the detective, meditatively. "He ain't got no idee of dooty to speak of, he ain't, and seein' he was powerful fond of that poor, brave, young chap as saved that remarkably fine infant in your arms, he might cut up rough. Some folks ain't got no notion of dooty, they ain't. You best keep dark, ma'am, on the inspiritin' subject of havin' done your dooty an' lost a thousand dollars reward."

And Bessie followed his advice very carefully indeed, though she always had the private luxury of regarding herself as an unrewarded and unrecognized heroine of duty.

Source: *The Globe*, September 4, 1886.

Biographical Note

Isabella Valancy Crawford, daughter of Stephen Crawford, M.D., and Sydney Scott, was born in Dublin, Ireland on December 25, 1850 and educated at home. After unsuccessful attempts to establish a medical practice in America, Stephen Crawford left for Australia in 1855; almost immediately after his departure from Ireland a fever epidemic claimed seven of the eleven Crawford children in one week. A year later the family joined him in Paisley, a pioneer community in Canada. They left there rather suddenly, a departure probably linked to the doctor's alcoholism and his embezzlement of public funds in his position as treasurer for Elderslie Township. They next moved to Lakefield in 1862 — where Crawford met Catherine Parr Traill, who was to have a considerable influence upon her — and then to Peterborough in 1869. Crawford had certainly started writing stories by this point, but, as is the case with so many women included in this anthology, it was the family's financial problems that prompted her to start writing seriously and to submit her work for publication. In 1873 she won a short story competition, and in December of the same year the first of her many poems to be published in the local newspapers, "The Vesper Star," appeared in the Toronto *Mail*. In 1875 Crawford's father and then her younger sister died, and she moved with her mother to Toronto. She published *Old Spookses' Pass, Malcolm's Katie and Other Poems* at her own expense in 1884, and, while favorably reviewed, the book sold poorly and stirred far more interest in England than in Canada: Tennyson even wrote to offer his congratulations.

Although now known primarily as a poet, during her life Crawford was equally admired for her short stories. She was a regular contributor to Frank Leslie's New York publications and many popular Canadian journals which are now unfortunately difficult to locate; while numerous titles are recorded, very few of the actual published stories have been traced. She was, however, certainly prolific and successful enough to support herself and her mother with her writing while they lived in Toronto. Since none of

Crawford's letters, diaries, or journals survive, little is known about these years; Crawford and her mother seem to have lived in boarding houses and made few friends. "Extradited," the story reprinted here, is, as Penny Petrone has noted in her introduction to the *Selected Stories*, one of Crawford's most successful works, and of particular interest both for its insights into early Canadian life and for its demonstration of Crawford's "concern for realism at a time when Canadian subject matter was still strongly romantic" (Petrone 15). Crawford died on February 12, 1887, only five months after this story was published.

Selected Modern Reprints:

Fairy Tales of Isabella Valancy Crawford. Ed. Penny Petrone. Ottawa: Borealis P, 1977.
Selected Stories of Isabella Valancy Crawford. Ed. Penny Petrone. Ottawa: U of Ottawa P, 1975.

Selected Secondary Sources:

Farmiloe, Dorothy. *Isabella Valancy Crawford: The Life and the Legends*. Ottawa: Tecumseh P, 1983.
Livesay, Dorothy. "The Life of Isabella Valancy Crawford." *The Crawford Symposium*. Ed. Frank M. Tierney. Ottawa: U of Ottawa P, 1979.
Ross, Catherine Sheldrick. "I.V. Crawford's Prose Fiction." *Canadian Literature* 81 (1974): 47-58.

130   ELLA D'ARCY (1856[?]-1939)

Ella D'Arcy (1856[7]-1939)

The Pleasure-Pilgrim

CAMPBELL WAS ON HIS WAY TO SCHLOSS[1] ALTENAU, FOR A SEC-
ond quiet season with his work. He had spent three profitable months there a year ago, and he was hoping now for
a repetition of that good fortune. His thoughts outran the
train; and long before his arrival at the Hamelin railway station, he was enjoying his welcome by the Ritterhausens, was
revelling in the ease and comfort of the old Castle, and was
contrasting the pleasures of his home-coming – for he
looked upon Schloss Altenau as a sort of temporary home
– with his recent cheerless experiences of lodging-houses in
London, hotels in Berlin, and strange indifferent faces everywhere. He thought with especial satisfaction of the
Maynes, and of the good talks Mayne and he would have together, late at night, before the great fire in the hall, after
the rest of the household had gone to bed. He blessed the
adverse circumstances which had turned Schloss Altenau
into a boarding-house, and had reduced the Freiherr Ritterhausen to eke out his shrunken revenues by the reception,
as paying guests, of English and American pleasure-pilgrims.

He rubbed the blurred window-pane with the fringed
end of the strap hanging from it, and, in the snow-covered
landscape reeling towards him, began to recognise objects
that were familiar. Hamelin could not be far off....In another ten minutes the train came to a standstill.

He stepped down with a sense of relief from the over-
heated atmosphere of his compartment into the cold,
bright February afternoon, and saw through the open station doors one of the Ritterhausen carriages awaiting him,
with Gottlieb in his second-best livery on the box. Gottlieb
showed every reasonable consideration for the Baron's
boarders, but had various methods of marking his sense

of the immense abyss separating them from the family. The use of his second-best livery was one of these methods. Nevertheless, he turned a friendly German eye up to Campbell, and in response to his cordial "Guten Tag, Gottlieb. Wie geht's? Und die Herrschaften?"[2] expressed his pleasure at seeing the young man back again.

While Campbell stood at the top of the steps that led down to the carriage and the Platz, looking after the collection of his luggage and its bestowal by Gottlieb's side, he became aware of two persons, ladies, advancing towards him from the direction of the Wartsaal.[3] It was surprising to see any one at any time in Hamelin Station. It was still more surprising when one of these ladies addressed him by name.

"You are Mr Campbell, are you not?" she said. "We have been waiting for you to go back in the carriage together. When we found this morning that there was only half-an-hour between your train and ours, I told the Baroness it would be perfectly absurd to send to the station twice. I hope you won't mind our company?"

The first impression Campbell received was of the magnificent apparel of the lady before him; it would have been noticeable in Paris or Vienna – it was extravagant here. Next, he perceived that the face beneath the upstanding feathers and the curving hat-brim was that of so very young a girl, as to make the furs and velvets seem more incongruous still. But the sense of incongruity vanished with the intonation of her first phrase, which told him she was an American. He had no standards for American conduct. It was clear that the speaker and her companion were inmates of the Schloss.

He bowed, and murmured the pleasure he did not feel. A true Briton, he was intolerably shy; and his heart sank at the prospect of a three-mile drive with two strangers who evidently had the advantage of knowing all about him, while he was in ignorance of their very names. As he took his place opposite to them in the carriage, he unconsciously assumed a cold, blank stare, pulling nervously at his moustache, as was his habit in moments of discomposure. Had his companions been British also, the ordeal of the drive must have been a terrible one; but these young American ladies showed no sense of embarrassment whatever.

"We've just come back from Hanover," said the girl who had already spoken to him. "I go over once a week for a singing lesson, and my little sister comes along to take care of me."

She turned a narrow, smiling glance from Campbell to her little sister, and then back to Campbell again. She had red hair; freckles on her nose, and the most singular eyes he had ever seen; slit-like eyes, set obliquely in her head, Chinese fashion.

"Yes, Lulie requires a great deal of taking care of," assented the little sister sedately, though the way in which she said this seemed to imply something less simple than the words themselves. The speaker bore no resemblance to Lulie. She was smaller, thinner, paler. Her features were straight, a trifle peaked; her skin sallow; her hair of a nondescript brown. She was much less gorgeously dressed. There was even a suggestion of shabbiness in her attire, though sundry isolated details of it were handsome too. She was also much less young; or so, at any rate, Campbell began by pronouncing her. Yet presently he wavered. She had a face that defied you to fix her age. Campbell never fixed it to his own satisfaction, but veered in the course of that drive (as he was destined to do during the next few weeks) from point to point up and down the scale from eighteen to thirty-five. She wore a spotted veil, and beneath it a pince-nez, the lenses of which did something to temper the immense amount of humorous meaning which lurked in her gaze. When her pale prominent eyes met Campbell's, it seemed to the young man that they were full of eagerness to add something at his expense to the stores of information they had already garnered up. They chilled him with misgivings; there was more comfort to be found in her sister's shifting, red-brown glances.

"Hanover is a long way to go for lessons," he observed, forcing himself to be conversational. "I used to go there myself about once a week, when I first came to Schloss Altenau, for tobacco, or notepaper, or to get my hair cut.

But later on I did without, or contented myself with what Hamelin, or even the village, could offer me."

"Nannie and I," said the young girl, "meant to stay only a week at Altenau, on our way to Hanover, where we were going to pass the winter; but the Castle is just too lovely for anything." She raised her eyelids the least little bit as she looked at him, and such a warm and friendly gaze shot out, that Campbell was suddenly thrilled. Was she pretty, after all? He glanced at Nannie; she, at least, was indubitably plain. "It's the very first time we've ever stayed in a castle," Lulie went on; "and we're going to remain right along now, until we go home in the spring. Just imagine living in a house with a real moat, and a drawbridge, and a Rittersaal,[4] and suits of armour that have been actually worn in battle! And oh, that delightful iron collar and chain! You remember it, Mr Campbell? It hangs right close to the gateway on the courtyard side. And you know, in old days the Ritterhausens used it for the punishment of their serfs. There are horrible stories connected with it. Mr Mayne can tell you them. But just think of being chained up there like a dog! So wonderfully picturesque."

"For the spectator perhaps," said Campbell, smiling. "I doubt if the victim appreciated the picturesque aspect of the case."

With this Lulie disagreed. "Oh, I think he must have been interested," she said. "It must have made him feel so absolutely part and parcel of the Middle Ages. I persuaded Mr Mayne to fix the collar round my neck the other day; and though it was very uncomfortable, and I had to stand on tiptoe, it seemed to me that all at once the courtyard was filled with knights in armour, and crusaders, and palmers, and things; and there were flags flying and trumpets sounding; and all the dead and gone Ritterhausens had come down from their picture-frames, and were walking about in brocaded gowns and lace ruffles."

"It seemed to require a good deal of persuasion to get Mr Mayne to unfix the collar again," said the little sister. "How at last did you manage it?"

But Lulie replied irrelevantly: "And the Ritterhausens are such perfectly lovely people, aren't they, Mr Campbell? The old Baron is a perfect dear. He has such a grand manner. When he kisses my hand I feel nothing less than a princess. And the Baroness is such a funny, busy, delicious little round ball of a thing. And she's always playing bagatelle,[5] isn't she? Or else cutting up skeins of wool for carpet-making." She meditated a moment. "Some people always *are* cutting things up in order to join them together again," she announced, in her fresh drawling young voice.

"And some people cut things up, and leave other people to do the reparation," commented the little sister enigmatically.

And meantime the carriage had been rattling over the cobble-paved streets of the quaint mediaeval town, where the houses stand so near together that you may shake hands with your opposite neighbour; where allegorical figures, strange birds and beasts, are carved and painted over the windows and doors; and where to every distant sound you lean your ear to catch the fairy music of the Pied Piper,[6] and at every street corner you look to see his tatterdemalion[7] form with the frolicking children at his heels.

Then the Weser bridge was crossed, beneath which the ice-floes jostled and ground themselves together, as they forced their way down the river; and the carriage was rolling smoothly along country roads, between vacant snow-decked fields.

Campbell's embarrassment began to wear off. Now that he was getting accustomed to the girls, he found neither of them awe-inspiring. The red-haired one had a simple child-like manner that was charming. Her strange little face, with its piquant irregularity of line, its warmth of colour, began to please him. What though her hair was red, the uncurled wisp which strayed across her white forehead was soft and alluring; he could see soft masses of it tucked up beneath her hat-brim as she turned her head. When she suddenly lifted her red-brown lashes, those queer eyes of hers had a velvety softness too. Decidedly, she struck him as being pretty – in a peculiar way. He felt an immense accession of interest in her. It seemed to him that he was the discoverer of her possibilities. He did not doubt that the rest of the world called her plain; or at least odd-looking. He, at first, had only seen the freckles on her nose, her oblique-set eyes. He wondered now what she thought of herself, how she appeared to Nannie. Probably as a very ordinary little girl; sisters stand too close to see each other's qualities. She was too young to have had much opportunity of hearing flattering truths from strangers; and besides, the average stranger would see nothing in her to call for flattering truths. Her charm was something subtle, out-of-the-common, in defiance of all known rules of beauty. Campbell saw superiority in him self for recognising it, for formulating it; and he was not displeased to be aware that it would always remain caviare to the multitude.

The carriage had driven through the squalid village of Durrendorf, had passed the great Ritterhausen barns and farm-buildings, on the tie-beams of which are carved Bible texts in old German; had turned in at the wide open gates of Schloss Altenau, where Gottlieb always whipped up his horses to a fast trot. Full of feeling both for the pocket and the dignity of the Ritterhausens, he would not use up his beasts in unnecessary fast driving. But it was to the credit of the family that he should reach the Castle in fine style. And so he thundered across the drawbridge, and through the great archway pierced in the north wing, and over the stones of the cobbled courtyard, to pull up before the door of the hall, with much clattering of hoofs and a final elaborate whip-flourish.

II

"I'm jolly glad to have you back," Mayne said, that same evening, when, the rest of the boarders having retired to their rooms, he and Campbell were lingering over the hall-fire for a talk and smoke. "I've missed you awfully, old chap, and the good times we used to have here. I've often meant to write to you, but you know how one shoves off letter-writing day after day, till at last one is too ashamed of one's indolence to write at all. But tell me – you had a pleasant drive from Hamelin? What do you think of our young ladies?"

"Those American girls? But they're charming," said Campbell, with enthusiasm. "The red-haired one is particularly charming."

At this Mayne laughed so strangely that Campbell, questioned him in surprise. "Isn't she charming?"

"My dear chap," Mayne told him, "the red-haired one, as you call her, is the most remarkably charming young person I've ever met or read of. We've had a good many American girls here before now – you remember the good old Choate family, of course – they were here in your time, I think? – but we've never had anything like this Miss Lulie Thayer. She is something altogether unique."

Campbell was struck with the name. "Lulie – Lulie Thayer," he repeated. "How pretty it is!" And, full of his great discovery, he felt he must confide it to Mayne, at least. "Do you know," he went on, "she is really very pretty too? I didn't think so at first, but after a bit I discovered that she is positively quite pretty – in an odd sort of way."

Mayne laughed again. "Pretty, pretty!" he echoed in derision. "Why, *Lieber Gott im Himmel*,[8] where are your eyes? Pretty! The girl is beautiful, gorgeously beautiful; every trait, every tint, is in complete, in absolute harmony with the whole. But the truth is, of course, we've all grown accustomed to the obvious, the commonplace; to violent contrasts; blue eyes, black eyebrows, yellow hair; the things that shout for recognition. You speak of Miss Thayer's hair as red. What other colour would you have, with that warm, creamy skin? And then, what a red it is! It looks as though it had been steeped in red wine."

"Ah, what a good description," said Campbell, appreciatively. "That's just it – steeped in red wine."

"Though it's not so much her beauty," Mayne continued. "After all, one has met beautiful women before now. It's her wonderful generosity, her complaisance. She doesn't keep her good things to herself. She doesn't condemn you to admire from a distance."

"How do you mean?" Campbell asked, surprised again.

"Why, she's the most egregious little flirt I've ever met. And yet, she's not exactly a flirt, either. I mean she doesn't flirt in the ordinary way. She doesn't talk much, or laugh, or apparently make the least claims on masculine attention. And so all the women like her. I don't believe there's one, except my wife, who has an inkling as to her true character. The Baroness, as you know, never observes anything. *Seigneur Dieu!*[9] if she knew the things I could tell her about Miss Lulie! For I've had opportunities of studying her. You see, I'm a married man, and not in my first youth, and the looker-on generally gets the best view of the game. But you, who are young and charming and already famous – we've had your book here, by-the-by, and there's good stuff in it – you're going to have no end of pleasant experiences. I can see she means to add you to her ninety-and-nine[10] other spoils; I saw it from the way she looked at you at dinner. She always begins with those velvety red-brown glances. She began that way with March and Prendergast and Willie Anson, and all the men we've had here since her arrival. The next thing she'll do will be to press your hand under the tablecloth."

"Oh come, Mayne, you're joking," cried Campbell a little brusquely. He thought such jokes in bad taste. He had a high ideal of Woman, an immense respect for her; he could not endure to hear her belittled, even in jest. "Miss Thayer is refined and charming. No girl of her class would do such things."

"But what is her class? Who knows anything about her? All we know is that she and her uncanny little friend – her little sister, as she calls her, though they're no more sisters than you and I are – they're not even related – all we know is, that she and Miss Dodge (that's the little sister's name) arrived here one memorable day last October from the Kronprinz Hotel at Waldeck-Pyrmont. By-the-by, it was the Choates, I believe, who told her of the Castle – hotel acquaintances – you know how travelling Americans always cotton to each other. And we've picked up a few little auto and biographical notes from her and Miss Dodge since. *Zum Beispiel*[11], she's got a rich father somewhere away back in Michigan, who supplies her with all the money she wants. And she's been travelling about since last May: Paris, Vienna, the Rhine, Dusseldorf, and so on here. She must have had some rich experiences, by Jove, for she's done everything. Cycled in Paris; you should see her in her cycling costume, she wears it when the Baron takes her out shooting – she's an admirable shot by the way, an accomplishment learned, I suppose, from some American cow-boy – then in Berlin she did a month's hospital nursing; and now she's studying the higher branches of the Terpsichorean[12] art. You know she was in Hanover to-day. Did she tell you what she went for?"

"To take a singing lesson," said Campbell, remembering the reason she had given.

"A singing lesson! Do you sing with your legs? A dancing lesson, *mein lieber*.[13] A dancing lesson from the ballet-master of the Hof Theater. She could deposit a kiss on your forehead with her foot, I don't doubt. I must ask her if she can do the *grand écart*[14] yet." And when Campbell, in astonishment, wondered why on earth she should wish to learn such things, "Oh, to extend her opportunities," Mayne explained, "and to acquire fresh sensations. She's an adventuress. Yes, an adventuress, but an end-of-the-century one. She doesn't travel for profit, but for pleasure. She has no desire to swindle her neighbour, but to amuse herself. And she's clever; she's read a good deal; she knows how to apply her reading to practical life., Thus, she's learned from Herrick not to be coy[15] and from Shakespeare that sweet-and-twenty is the time for kissing and being kissed.[16] She honours her masters in the observance. She was not in the least abashed when, one day, I suddenly came upon her teaching that damned idiot, young Anson, two new ways of kissing."

Campbell's impressions of the girl were readjusting themselves completely, but for the moment he was unconscious of the change. He only knew that he was partly angry, partly incredulous, and inclined to believe that Mayne was chaffing him.

"But, Miss Dodge," he objected, "the little sister, she

is older; old enough to look after her friend. Surely she could not allow a young girl placed in her charge to behave in such a way ——— ."

"Oh, that little Dodge girl," said Mayne contemptuously; "Miss Thayer pays the whole shot, I understand, and Miss Dodge plays gooseberry, sheep-dog, jackal, what you will. She finds her reward in the other's cast-off finery. The silk blouse she was wearing to-night, I've good reason for remembering, belonged to Miss Lulie. For, during a brief season, I must tell you, my young lady had the caprice to show attentions to your humble servant. I suppose my being a married man lent me a factitious fascination. But I didn't see it. That kind of girl doesn't appeal to me. So she employed Miss Dodge to do a little active canvassing. It was really too funny; I was coming in one day after a walk in the woods; my wife was trimming bonnets, or had neuralgia, or something. Anyhow, I was alone, and Miss Dodge contrived to waylay me in the middle of the courtyard. 'Don't you find it vurry dull walking all by yourself?' she asked me; and then blinking up in her strange little short-sighted way – she's really the weirdest little creature – 'Why don't you make love to Lulie?' she said; 'you'd find her vurry charming.' It took me a minute or two to recover presence of mind enough to ask her whether Miss Thayer had commissioned her to tell me so. She looked at me with that cryptic smile of hers; 'She'd like you to do so, I'm sure,' she finally remarked, and pirouetted away. Though it didn't come off, owing to my bashfulness, it was then that Miss Dodge appropriated the silk 'waist'; and Providence, taking pity on Miss Thayer's forced inactivity, sent along March, a young fellow reading for the army, with whom she had great doings. She fooled him to the top of his bent; sat on his knee; gave him a lock of her hair, which, having no scissors handy, she burned off with a cigarette taken from his mouth; and got him to offer her marriage. Then she turned round and laughed in his face, and took up with a Dr Weber, a cousin of the Baron's, under the other man's very eyes. You never saw anything like the unblushing coolness with which she would permit March to catch her in Weber's arms."

"Come," Campbell protested again, "aren't you drawing it rather strong?"

"On the contrary, I'm drawing it mild, as you'll discover presently for yourself; and then you'll thank me for forewarning you. For she makes love – desperate love, mind you – to every man she meets. And goodness knows how many she hasn't met in the course of her career, which began presumably at the age of ten, in some 'Amur'can' hotel or watering-place. Look at this." Mayne fetched an alpenstock[17] from a corner of the hall; it was decorated with a long succession of names, which, ribbon-like, were twisted round and round it, carved in the wood. "Read them," insisted Mayne, putting the stick in Campbell's hands. "You'll see they're not the names of the peaks she has climbed, or the towns she has passed through; they're the names of the men she has fooled. And there's room for more; there's still a good deal of space, as you see. There's room for yours."

Campbell glanced down the alpenstock – reading here a name, there an initial, or just a date – and jerked it impatiently from him on to a couch. He wished with all his heart that Mayne would stop, would talk of something else, would let him get away. The young girl had interested him so much; he had felt himself so drawn towards her; he had thought her so fresh, so innocent. But Mayne, on the contrary, was warming to his subject, was enchanted to have some one to listen to his stories, to discuss his theories, to share his cynical amusement.

"I don't think, mind you," he said, "that she is a bit interested herself in the men she flirts with. I don't think she gets any of the usual sensations from it, you know. My theory is, she does it for mere devilry, for a laugh. Or, and this is another theory, she is actuated by some idea of retribution. Perhaps some woman she was fond of—her mother even – who knows? – was badly treated at the hands of a man. Perhaps this girl has constituted herself the Nemesis[18] for her sex, and goes about seeing how many masculine hearts, she can break, by way of revenge. Or can it be that she is simply the newest development of the New Woman – she who in England preaches and bores you, and in America practises and pleases? Yes, I believe she's the American edition, and so new that she hasn't yet found her way into fiction. She's the pioneer of the army coming out of the West, that's going to destroy the existing scheme of things, and rebuild it nearer to the heart's desire."

"Oh, damn-it all, Mayne," cried Campbell, rising abruptly, "why not say at once that she's a wanton, and have done with it? Who wants to hear your rotten theories?" And he lighted his candle without another word, and went off to bed.

III

It was four o'clock, and the Baron's boarders were drinking their afternoon coffee, drawn up in a semicircle round the hall fire. All but Campbell, who had carried his cup away to a side-table, and, with a book open beside him, appeared to be reading assiduously. In reality he could not follow a line of what he read; he could not keep his thoughts from Miss Thayer. What Mayne had told him was germinating in his mind. Knowing his friend as he did, he could not on reflection doubt his word. In spite of much superficial cynicism, Mayne was incapable of speaking lightly of any young girl without good cause. It now seemed to Campbell that, instead of exaggerating the case, Mayne had probably understated it. He asked himself with horror, what had this girl not already known, seen, permitted? When now and again his eyes travelled over, perforce, to where she sat, her red head leaning against Miss Dodge's knee, and seeming to attract to, and concentrate upon itself all the glow of the fire, his forehead set itself in frowns, and he returned to his book with an increased sense of irritation.

"I'm just sizzling up, Nannie," Miss Thayer presently complained, in her child-like, drawling little way; "this fire is too hot for anything." She rose and shook straight her loose tea-gown, a marvellous plush and lace garment created in Paris, which would have accused a duchess of wilful extravagance. She stood smiling round a moment, pulling on and off with her right hand a big diamond ring which decorated the left. At the sound of her voice Campbell had looked up, and his cold, unfriendly eyes encountered hers. He glanced rapidly past her, then back to his book. But she, undeterred, with a charming sinuous movement and a frou-frou of trailing silks, crossed over towards him. She slipped into an empty chair next his.

"I'm going to do you the honour of sitting beside you, Mr Campbell," she said sweetly.

"It's an honour I've done nothing whatever to merit," he answered, without looking at her, and turned a page.

"The right retort," she approved; "but you might have said it a little more cordially."

"I don't feel cordial."

"But why not? What has happened? Yesterday you were so nice."

"Ah, a good deal of water has run under the bridge since yesterday."

"But still the river remains as full," she told him, smiling, "and still the sky is as blue. The thermometer has even risen six degrees."

"What did you go into Hanover for yesterday?" Campbell suddenly asked her.

She flashed him a comprehending glance from half-shut eyes. "I think men gossip a great deal more than women," she observed, "and they don't understand things either. They try to make all life suit their own pre-conceived theories. And why, after all, should I not wish to learn dancing thoroughly? There's no harm in that."

"Only, why call it singing?" Campbell enquired.

Miss Thayer smiled. "Truth is so uninteresting!" she said, and paused. "Except in books. One likes it there. And I wanted to tell you, I think your books perfectly lovely. I know them, most all. I've read them away home. They're very much thought of in America. Only last night I was saying to Nannie how glad I am to have met you, for I think we're going to be great friends, aren't we, Mr Campbell? At least, I hope so, for you can do me so much good, if you will. Your books always make me feel real good; but you yourself can help me much more."

She looked up at him with one of her warm, narrow, red-brown glances, which yesterday would have thrilled his blood, and to-day merely stirred it to anger.

"You over-estimate my abilities," he said coldly; "and, on the whole, I fear you will find writers a very disappointing race. You see, they put their best into their books. So not to disillusion you too rapidly" – he rose – "will you excuse me? I have some work to do." And he left her sitting there alone.

But he did no work when he got to his room. Whether Lulie Thayer was actually present or not, it seemed that her influence was equally disturbing to him. His mind was full of her: of her singular eyes, her quaint intonation, her sweet, seductive praise. Twenty-four hours ago such praise would have been delightful to him: what young author is proof against appreciation of his books? Now, Campbell simply told himself that she laid the butter on too thick; that it was in some analogous manner she had flattered up March, Anson, and all the rest of the men that Mayne had spoken of. He supposed it was the first step in the process by which he was to be fooled, twisted round her finger, added to the list of victims who strewed her conquering path. He had a special fear of being fooled. For beneath a somewhat supercilious exterior, the dominant note of his character was timidity, distrust of his own merits; and he knew he was single-minded – one-idea'd almost – if he were to let himself go, to get to care very much for a woman, for such a girl as this girl, for instance, he would lose himself completely, be at her mercy absolutely. Fortunately, Mayne had let him know her character. He could feel nothing but dislike for her — disgust, even; and yet he was conscious how pleasant it would be to believe in her innocence, in her candour. For she was so adorably pretty; her flower-like beauty grew upon him; her head, drooping a little on one side when she looked up, was so like a flower bent by its own weight. The texture of her cheeks, her lips, was delicious as the petals of a flower. He found he could recall with perfect accuracy every detail of her appearance: the manner in which the red hair grew round her temples; the way in which it was loosely and gracefully fastened up behind with just a single tortoise-shell pin. He recollected the suspicion of a dimple that shadowed itself in her cheek when she spoke, and deepened into a delicious reality every time she smiled. He remembered her throat; her hands, of a beautiful whiteness, with pink palms and pointed fingers. It was impossible to write. He speculated long on the ring she wore on her engaged finger. He mentioned this ring to Mayne the next time he saw him.

"Engaged? very much so, I should say. Has got a *fiance* in every capital of Europe probably. But the ring-man is the *fiancé en titre*.[19] He writes to her by every mail, and is tremendously in love with her. She shows me his letters. When she's had her fling, I suppose she'll go back and marry him. That's what these little American girls do, I'm told; sow their wild oats here with us, and settle down into *bonnes ménagères*[20] over yonder. Meanwhile, are you having any fun with her? Aha, she presses your hand? The 'gesegnete Mahlzeit'[21] business after dinner is an excellent institution, isn't it? She'll tell you how much she loves you soon; that's the next move in the game."

But so far she had done neither of these things, for Campbell gave her no opportunities. He was guarded in the extreme, ungenial; avoiding her even at the cost of civility. Sometimes he was downright rude. That especially occurred when he felt himself inclined to yield to her advances. For she made him all sorts of silent advances, speaking with her eyes, her sad little mouth, her beseeching attitude. And then one evening she went further still. It occurred after dinner in the little green drawing-room. The rest of the company were gathered together in the big drawing-room beyond. The small room has deep embrasures to the windows. Each embrasure holds two old faded green velvet sofas in black oaken frames, and an oaken oblong table stands between them. Campbell had flung himself down on one of these sofas in the corner nearest the window. Miss Thayer, passing through the room, saw him, and sat down opposite. She leaned her elbows on the table, the laces of her sleeves falling away from her round white arms, and clasped her hands.

"Mr Campbell, tell me, what have I done? How have I vexed you? You have hardly spoken two words to me all day. You always try to avoid me." And when he began to utter evasive banalities, she stopped him with an imploring "Ah, don't! I love you. You know I love you. I love you so much I can't bear you to put me off with mere phrases."

Campbell admired the well-simulated passion in her voice, remembered Mayne's prediction, and laughed aloud.

"Oh, you may laugh," she said, "but I'm serious. I love you, I love you with my whole soul." She slipped round the end of the table, and came close beside him. His first impulse was to rise; then he resigned himself to stay. But it was not so much resignation that was required, as self-mastery, cool-headedness. Her close proximity, her fragrance, those wonderful eyes raised so beseechingly to his, made his heart beat.

"Why are you so cold?" she said. "I love you so, can't you love me a little too?"

"My dear young lady," said Campbell, gently repelling her, "what do you take me for? A foolish boy like your friends Anson and March? What you are saying is monstrous, preposterous. Ten days ago you'd never even seen me."

"What has length of time to do with it?" she said. "I loved you at first sight."

"I wonder," he observed judicially, and again gently removed her hand from his, "to how many men you have not already said the same thing?"

"I've never meant it before," she said quite earnestly, and nestled closer to him, and kissed the breast of his coat, and held her mouth up towards his. But he kept his chin resolutely high, and looked over her head.

"How many men have you not already kissed, even since you've been here?"

"But there've not been many here to kiss!" she exclaimed naively.

"Well, there was March; you kissed him?"

"No, I'm quite sure I didn't."

"And young Anson; what about him? Ah, you don't answer! And then the other fellow – what's his name – Prendergast – you've kissed him?"

"But, after all, what is there in a kiss?" she cried ingenuously. "It means nothing, absolutely nothing. Why, one has to kiss all sorts of people one doesn't care about."

Campbell remembered how Mayne had said she had probably known strange kisses since the age of ten; and a wave of anger with her, of righteous indignation, rose within him.

"To me," said he, "to all right-thinking people, a young girl's kisses are something pure, something sacred, not to be offered indiscriminately to every fellow she meets. Ah, you don't know what you have lost! You have seen a fruit that has been handled, that has lost its bloom? You have seen primroses, spring flowers gathered and thrown away in the dust? And who enjoys the one, or picks up the others? And this is what you remind me of – only you have deliberately, of your own perverse will, tarnished your beauty, and thrown away all the modesty, the reticence, the delicacy, which make a young girl so infinitely dear. You revolt me, you disgust me. I want nothing from you but to be let alone. Kindly take your hands away, and let me go."

He shook her roughly off and got up, then felt a moment's curiosity to see how she would take the repulse. Miss Thayer never blushed: had never, he imagined, in her life done so. No faintest trace of colour now stained the warm pallor of her rose leaf skin; but her eyes filled up with tears, two drops gathered on the under lashes, grew large, trembled an instant, and then rolled unchecked down her cheeks. Those tears somehow put him in the wrong, and he felt he had behaved brutally to her, for the rest of the night. He began to seek excuses for her: after all, she meant no harm: it was her upbringing, her *genre*: it was a *genre* he loathed; but perhaps he need not have spoken so harshly. He thought he would find a more friendly word for her next morning; and he loitered

about the Mahlsaal, where the boarders come in to breakfast as in an hotel just when it suits them, till past eleven;
but she did not come. Then, when he was almost tired
of waiting, Miss Dodge put in an appearance, in a flannel
wrapper, and her front hair twisted up in steel pins.

Campbell judged Miss Dodge with even more severity
than he did Miss Thayer; there was nothing in this weird
little creature's appearance to temper justice with mercy.
It was with difficulty that he brought himself to inquire
after her friend.

"Lulie is sick this morning," she told him. "I've come
down to order her some broth. She couldn't sleep any last
night, because of your unkindness to her. She's vurry,
vurry unhappy about it."

"Yes, I'm sorry for what I said. I had no right to speak
so strongly, I suppose. But I spoke strongly because I feel
strongly. However, there's no reason why my bad manners
should make her unhappy."

"Oh, yes, there's vurry good reason," said Miss Dodge.
"She's vurry much in love with you."

Campbell looked at the speaker long and earnestly to
try and read her mind; but the prominent blinking eyes,
the cryptic physiognomy, told him nothing.

"Look here," he said brusquely, "what's your object in
trying to fool me like this? I know all about your friend.
Mayne has told me. She has cried 'Wolf' too often before
to expect to be believed now."

"But, after all," argued Miss Dodge, blinking more
than ever behind her glasses, "the wolf did really come at
last, you know; didn't he? Lulie is really in love this time.
We've all made mistakes in our lives, haven't we? But that's
no reason for not being right at last. And Lulie has cried
herself sick."

Campbell was a little shaken. He went and repeated
the conversation to Mayne, who laughed derisively.

"Capital, capital!" he cried; "excellently contrived. It
quite supports my latest theory about our young friend.
She's an actress, a born comedienne. She acts always, and
to every one: to you, to me, to the Ritterhausens, to the
Dodge girl – even to herself when she is quite alone. And

she has a great respect for her art; she'll carry out her role, *coûte que coûte*,[22] to the bitter end. She chooses to pose as in love with you; you don't respond; the part now requires that she should sicken and pine. Consequently, she takes to her bed, and sends her confidante to tell you so. Oh, it's colossal, it's *famos!* [23]"

IV

"If you can't really love me," said Lulie Thayer — and I know I've been a bad girl and don't deserve that you should - at least, will you allow me to go on loving you?"

She walked by Campbell's side, through the solitary, uncared-for park of Schloss Altenau. It was three weeks later in the year, and the spring feeling in the air stirred the blood. All round were signs and tokens of spring; in the busy gaiety of bird and insect life; in the purple flower-tufts which thickened the boughs of the ash trees; in the young green things pushing up pointed heads from amidst last season's dead leaves and grasses. The snow-wreaths, that had for so long decorated the distant hills, were shrinking perceptibly away beneath the strong March sunshine.

There was every invitation to spend one's time out of doors, and Campbell passed long mornings in the park, or wandering through the woods and the surrounding villages. Miss Thayer often accompanied him. He never invited her to do so, but when she offered him her company, he could not, or at least did not, refuse it.

"May I love you? Say," she entreated.

"'Wenn ich Dich liebe, was geht's Dich an?'"[24] he quoted lightly. "Oh, no, it's nothing to me, of course. Only don't expect me to believe you – that's all."

This disbelief of his was the recurring decimal of their conversation. No matter on what subject they began, they always ended thus. And the more sceptical he showed himself, the more eager she became. She exhausted herself in endeavours to convince him.

They had reached the corner in the park where the road to the Castle turns off at right angles from the road to Dürrendorf. The ground rises gently on the park-side to within three feet of the top of the boundary wall, although on the other side there is a drop of at least twenty feet. The broad wall-top makes a convenient seat. Campbell and the girl sat down on it. At his last words she wrung her hands together in her lap.

"But how can you disbelieve me?" she cried, "when I tell you I love you, I adore you? when 1 swear it to you? And can't you see for yourself? Why, every one at the Castle sees it."

"Yes, you afford the Castle a good deal of unnecessary amusement; and that shows you don't understand what love really is. Real love is full of delicacy, of reticences, and would feel itself profaned if it became the jest of the servants' hall."

"It's not so much my love for you, as your rejection of it, which has made me talked about."

"Isn't it rather on account of the favours you've lavished on all my predecessors?"

She sprang to her feet, and walked up and down in agitation. "But, after all, surely, mistakes of that sort are not to be counted against us? I did really think I was in love with Mr March. Willie Anson doesn't count. He's an American too, and he understands things. Besides, he is only a boy. And how could I know I should love you before I had met you? And how can I help loving you now I have? You're so different from other men. You're good, you're honourable, you treat women with respect. Oh, I do love you so, I do love you! Ask Nannie if I don't."

The way in which Campbell shrugged his shoulders clearly expressed the amount of reliance he would place on any testimony from Miss Dodge. He could not forget her "Why don't you make love to Lulie?" addressed to a married man. Such a want of principle argued an equal want of truth.

Lulie seemed on the brink of weeping.

"I wish I were dead," she struggled to say; "life's impossible if you won't believe me. I don't ask you any longer to love me. I know I've been a bad girl, and I don't deserve that you should; but if you won't believe that I love you, I don't want to live any longer."

Campbell confessed to himself that she acted admirably, but that the damnable iteration of the one idea become monotonous. He sought a change of subject. "Look there," he said, "close by the wall, what's that jolly little blue flower? It's the first I've seen this year."

He showed her where, at the base of the wall, a solitary blossom rose above a creeping stem and glossy dark green leaves.

Lulie, all smiles again, picked it with childlike pleasure. "Oh, if that's the first you've seen," she cried, "you can take a wish. Only you mustn't speak until some one asks you a question."

She began to fasten it in his coat. "It's just as blue as your eyes," she said. "You have such blue and boyish eyes, you know. Stop, stop, that's not a question," and seeing that he was about to speak, she laid her finger across his mouth. "You'll spoil the charm."

She stepped back, folded her arms, and seemed to dedicate herself to eternal silence; then relenting suddenly:

"Do you believe me?" she entreated.

"What's become of your ring?" Campbell answered beside the mark. He had noticed its absence from her finger while she had been fixing in the flower.

"Oh, my engagement's broken."

Campbell asked how the fiancé would like that.

"Oh, he won't mind. He knows I only got engaged because he worried so. And it was always understood between us that I was to be free if I ever met any one I liked better."

Campbell asked her what sort of fellow this accommodating fiancé was.

"Oh, he's all right. And he's very good too. But he's not a bit clever, and don't let us talk about him. He makes me tired."

"But you're wrong," Campbell told her, "to throw away a good, a sincere affection. If you really want to reform and turn over a new leaf, as you are always telling me you do, I should advise you to go home and marry him."

"What, when I'm in love with you?" she cried reproachfully. "Would that be right?"

"It's going to rain," said Campbell. "Didn't you feel a drop just then? And it's getting near lunch-time. Shall we go in?"

Their shortest way led through the little cemetery in which the departed Ritterhausens lay at peace, in the shadow of their sometime home.

"When I die the Baron has promised I shall be buried here," said Lulie pensively; "just here, next to his first wife. Don't you think it would be lovely to be buried in a beautiful, peaceful, baronial graveyard instead of in some horrid, crowded city cemetery?"

Mayne met them as they entered the hall. He noticed the flower in his friend's coat. "Ah, my dear chap, been treading the – periwinkle path of dalliance, I see? How many desirable young men have I not witnessed, led down the same broad way by the same seductive lady ! Always the same thing; nothing changes but the flower according to the season."

When Campbell reached his room he took the poor periwinkle out of his coat, and threw it away into the stove.

And yet, had it not been for Mayne, Miss Thayer might have triumphed after all; might have convinced Campbell of her passion, or have added another victim to her long list. But Mayne had set himself as determinedly to spoil her game, as she was bent on winning it. He had always the cynical word, the apt reminiscence ready, whenever he saw signs on Campbell's part of surrender. He was very fond of Campbell. He did not wish him to fall a prey to the wiles of this little American siren. He had watched her conduct in the past with a dozen different men; he genuinely believed she was only acting in the present.

Campbell, for his part, began to experience an ever-increasing exasperation in the girl's presence. Yet he did not avoid it; he could not well avoid it, she followed him about so persistently: but his speech would overflow with bitterness towards her. He would say the cruellest things; then remembering them when alone, be ashamed of his brutalities. But nothing he said ever altered her sweetness of temper or weakened the tenacity of her purpose. His rebuffs made her beautiful eyes run over with tears, but the harshest of them never elicited the least sign of resentment. There would have been something touching as well as comic in this dog-like humility, which accepted everything as welcome at his hands, had he not been imbued with Mayne's conviction that it was all an admirable piece of acting. Or when for a moment he forgot the histrionic theory, then invariably there would come a chance word in her conversation which would fill him with cold rage. They would be talking of books, travels, sport, what not, and she would drop a reference to this man or to that. So-and-so had taken her to Bullier's, she had learned skating with this other; Duroy, the *prix de Rome* man, had painted her as Hebe, Franz Weber had tried to teach her German by means of Heine's poems.[25] And he got glimpses of long vistas of amourettes played in every state in America, in every country of Europe, since the very beginning, when, as a mere child, elderly men, friends of her father's, had held her on their knee and fed her on sweetmeats and kisses. It was sickening to think of; it was pitiable. So much youth and beauty tarnished; the possibility for so much good thrown away. For if one could only blot out her record, forget it, accept her for what she chose to appear, a more endearing companion no man could desire.

V

It was a wet afternoon; the rain had set in at midday, with a gray determination, which gave no hopes of clearing. Nevertheless, Mayne had accompanied his wife and the Baroness into Hamelin. "To take up a servant's character, and expostulate with a recalcitrant dressmaker," he explained to

Campbell, and wondered what women would do to fill up their days were it not for the perennial crimes of dressmakers and domestic servants. He himself was going to look in at the English Club; wouldn't Campbell come too? There was a fourth seat in the carriage. But Campbell was in no social mood; he felt his temper going all to pieces; a quarter of an hour of Mrs Mayne's society would have brought on an explosion. He thought he must be alone; and yet when he had read for half an hour in his room he wondered vaguely what Lulie was doing; he had not seen her since luncheon. She always gave him her society when he could very well dispense with it, but on a wet day like this, when a little conversation would be tolerable, of course she stayed away. Then there came down the long Rittersaal the tapping of high heels, and a well-known knock at his door.

He went over and opened it. Miss Thayer, in the plush and lace tea-gown, fronted him serenely.

"Am I disturbing you?" she asked; and his mood was so capricious that, now she was standing there on his threshold, he thought he was annoyed at it. "It's so dull," she said persuasively: "Nannie's got a sick headache, and I daren't go downstairs, or the Baron will annex me to play Halma.[26] He always wants to play Halma on wet days."

"And what do you want to do?" said Campbell, leaning against the doorpost, and letting his eyes rest on the strange piquant face in its setting of red hair.

"To be with you, of course."

"Well," said he, coming out and closing the door, "I'm at your service. What next?"

They strolled together through the room and listened to the falling rain. The Rittersaal occupies all the space on the first floor that the hall and four drawing-rooms do below. Wooden pillars support the ceiling, dividing the apartment lengthwise into a nave and two aisles. Down the middle are long tables, used for ceremonial banquets. Six windows look into the courtyard, and six out over the open country. The centre pane of each window is emblazoned with a Ritterhausen shield. Between the windows hang family portraits, and the sills are broad and low and cushioned in faded velvet.

"How it rains!" said Lulie, stopping before one of the south windows; "why, you can't see anything for the rain, and there's no sound at all but the rain either. I like it. It makes me feel as though we had the whole world to ourselves."

Then, "Say, what would you like to do" she asked him. "Shall I fetch over my pistols, and we'll practise with them? You've no notion how well I can shoot. We couldn't hurt anything here, could we?"

Campbell thought they might practise there without inconvenience, and Lulie, bundling up the duchess tea-gown over one arm, danced off in very unduchess-like fashion to fetch the case. It was a charming little box of cedar-wood and mother-o'pearl, lined with violet velvet; and two tiny revolvers lay inside, hardly more than six inches long, with silver engraved handles.

"I won them in a bet," she observed complacently, "with the Hon. Billie Thornton. He's an Englishman, you know, the son of Lord Thornton. I knew him in Washington two years ago last fall. He bet I couldn't hit a three-cent piece at twenty yards and I did. Aren't they perfectly sweet? Now, can't you contrive a target?"

Campbell went back to his room, drew out a rough diagram, and pasted it down on to a piece of cardboard. Then this was fixed up by means of a penknife driven into the wood of one of the pillars, and Campbell, with his walking-stick laid down six successive times, measured off the distance required, and set a chalk mark across the floor. Lulie took the first shot. She held the little weapon up at arm's length above her head, the first finger stretched out along the barrel; then dropping her hand sharply so that the finger pointed straight at the butt, she pulled the trigger with the third. There was the sharp report, the tiny smoke film – and when Campbell went up to examine results, he found she had only missed the very centre by a quarter of an inch.

Lulie was exultant. "I don't seem to have got out of practice any," she remarked. "I'm so glad, for I used to be a very good shot. It was Hiram P. Ladd who taught me. He's the crack shot of Montana. What! you don't know Hiram P.? Why, I should have supposed every one must have heard of him. He had the next ranche to my Uncle Samuel's, where I used to go summers, and he made me do an hour's pistol practice every morning after bathing. It was he who taught me swimming too – in the river."

"Damnation," said Campbell under his breath, then shot in his turn, and shot wide. Lulie made another bull's-eye, and after that a white. She urged Campbell to continue, which he sullenly did, and again missed.

"You see I don't come up to your Hiram P. Ladd," he remarked savagely, and put the pistol down, and walked over to the window. He stood with one foot on the cushioned seat, staring out at the rain, and pulling moodily at his moustache.

Lulie followed him, nestled up to him, lifted the hand that hung passive by his side, put it round her waist and held it there. Campbell lost in thought, let it remain so for a second; then remembered how she had doubtless done this very same thing with other men in this very room. All her apparently spontaneous movements, he told himself, were but the oft-used pieces in the game she played so skilfully.

"Let go," he said, and flung himself down on the window-seat, looking up at her with darkening eyes.

She sitting meekly in the other corner folded her offending hands in her lap.

"Do you know, your eyes are not a bit nice when you're cross?" she said; "they seem to become quite black."

He maintained a discouraging silence.

She looked over at him meditatively.

"I never cared a bit for Hiram P., if that's what you mean," she remarked presently.

"Do you suppose I care a button if you did?"

"Then why did you leave off shooting, and why won't you talk to me?"

He vouchsafed no reply.

Lulie spent some moments immersed in thought. Then she sighed deeply, and recommenced on a note of pensive regret.

"Ah, if I'd only met you sooner in life, I should be a

very different girl."

The freshness which her quaint, drawling enunciation lent to this time-dishonoured formula, made Campbell smile, till, remembering all its implications, his forehead set in frowns again.

Lulie continued her discourse. "You see," said she, "I never had any one to teach me what was right. My mother died when I was quite a child, and my father has always let me do exactly as I pleased, so long as I didn't bother him. Then I've never had a home, but have always lived around in hotels and places: all winter in New York or Washington, and summers out at Longbranch or Saratoga. It's true we own a house in Detroit, on Lafayette Avenue, that we reckon as home, but we don't ever go there. It's a bad sort of life for a girl, isn't it?" she pleaded.

"Horrible," he said mechanically. His mind was at work. The loose threads of his angers, his irritations, his desires, were knitting themselves together, weaving themselves into something overmastering and definite.

The young girl meanwhile was moving up towards him along the seat, for the effect which his sharpest rebuke produced on her never lasted more than four minutes. She now again possessed herself of his hand, and holding it between her own, began to caress it in childlike fashion, pulling the fingers apart and closing them again, spreading it palm downwards on her lap, and laying her own little hand over it, to exemplify the differences between them. He let her be; he seemed unconscious of her proceedings.

"And then," she continued, "I've always known a lot of young fellows who've liked to take me round; and no one ever objected to my going with them, and so I went. And I enjoyed it, and there wasn't any harm in it, just kissing and making believe, and nonsense. But I never really cared for one of them – I can see that now, when I compare them with you; when I compare what I felt for them with what I feel for you. Oh, I do love you so much," she murmured; "don't you believe me?" She lifted his hand to her lips and covered it with kisses.

He pulled it roughly from her. "I wish you'd give over

such fool's play," he told her, got up, walked to the table, came back again, stood looking at her with sombre eyes and dilating pupils.

"But I do love you," she repeated, rising and advancing towards him.

"For God's sake, drop that damned rot," he cried out with sudden fury. "It wearies me, do you hear? it sickens me. Love, love – my God, what do you know about it? Why, if you really loved me, really loved any man – if you had any conception of what the passion of love is, how beautiful, how fine, how sacred – the mere idea that you could not come to your lover fresh, pure, untouched, as a young girl should – that you had been handled, fondled, and God knows what besides, by this man and the other – would fill you with such horror for yourself, with such supreme disgust – you would feel yourself so unworthy, so polluted .... that .... that .... by God! you would take up that pistol there, and blow your brains out!"

Lulie seemed to find the idea quite entertaining. She picked the pistol up from where it lay in the window, examined it critically, with her pretty head drooping on one side, and then sent one of her long red-brown caressing glances up towards him.

"And suppose I were to," she asked lightly, "would you believe me then?"

"Oh, ... well .. . . then, perhaps! If you showed sufficient decency to kill yourself, perhaps I might," said he, with ironical laughter. His ebullition had relieved him; his nerves were calmed again. "But nothing short of that would ever make me."

With her little tragic air, which seemed to him so like a smile disguised, she raised the weapon to the bosom of her gown. There came a sudden, sharp crack, a tiny smoke film. She stood an instant swaying slightly, smiling certainly, distinctly outlined against the background of rain-washed window, of gray falling rain, the top of her head cutting in two the Ritterhausen escutcheon.[27] Then all at once there was nothing at all between him and the window – he saw the coat of arms entire – but a motionless, inert heap of plush and lace, and fallen wine-red hair, lay at his feet upon the floor.

"Child, child, what have you done?" he cried with anguish, and kneeling beside her, lifted her up, and looked into her face.

When from a distance of time and place Campbell was at last able to look back with some degree of calmness on the catastrophe, the element in it which stung him most keenly was this: he could never convince himself that Lulie had really loved him after all. And the only two persons who had known them both, and the circumstances of the case, sufficiently well to have resolved his doubts one way or the other, held diametrically opposite views. "Well, listen, then, and I'll tell you how it was," Miss Nannie Dodge had said to him impressively, the day before he left Schloss Altenau for ever. "Lulie was tremendously, terribly in love with you. And when she found that you wouldn't care about her, she didn't want to live any more. As to the way in which it happened, you don't need to reproach yourself for that. She'd have done it, anyhow. If not then, why later. But it's all the rest of your conduct to her that was so mean. Your cold, cruel, complacent British unresponsiveness. I guess you'll never find another woman to love you as Lulie did. She was just the darlingest, the sweetest, the most loving girl in the world."

Mayne, on the other hand, summed it up in this way: "Of course, old chap, it's horrible to think of: horrible, horrible, horrible! I can't tell you how badly I feel about it. For she was a gorgeously beautiful creature. That red hair of hers! Good Lord! You won't come across such hair as that again in a lifetime. But, believe me, she was only fooling with you. Once she had you in her hunting-noose, once her buccaneering instincts satisfied, and she'd have chucked you as she did all the rest. As to her death, I've got three theories – no, two – for the first being that she compassed it in a moment of genuine emotion, we may dismiss, I think, as quite untenable. The second is, that it arose from pure misadventure. You had both been shooting, hadn't you? Well, she took up the pistol and pulled the trigger from mere mischief, to frighten you, and quite forgetting one barrel was still loaded. And the third is, it was just her histrionic sense of the fitness of things. The role she had played so long and so well now demanded a sensational finale in the centre of the stage. And it's the third theory I give the preference to. She was the most consummate little actress I ever met."

Notes:

1. Castle.
2. Good day, Gottlieb, How are you? and your master and mistress?
3. Waiting room.
4. Hall where knights assembled.
5. Game similar to billiards.
6. In medieval legend, a piper rid the town of Hamelin of its rats by leading them to the river. When not paid for his services as promised, he led the town's children to a hill where they disappeared.
7. Person wearing ragged clothes.
8. Dear God in Heaven.
9. Lord God.
10. "He rejoiceth more of that sheep, than of the ninety-and-nine which went not astray" Matthew 18:13
11. For example.
12. Relating to dancing; Terpsichore is the muse of dancing.
13. My dear.
14. The splits.
15. Robert Herrick: (1591-1674), best known for the carpe diem poem "To the Virgins to Make Much of Time" ("Gather ye rosebuds while ye may . . .").
16. William Shakespeare: (1564-1616). "Then come and kiss me, sweet and twenty, / Youth's a stuff will not endure." *Twelfth-Night* 2.3:54-55.
17. Long iron-pointed staff used by mountain climbers.
18. Nemesis is the Greek goddess of vengeance, and the personification of retributive justice generally.
19. A fiancé in name only.

20. Good housekeepers.
21. Good appetite.
22. At all costs.
23. Grand, on a large scale.
24. Johanne Wolfgang von Goethe (1749-1832): "Meister" 4.9. "If I love you, what business is that of yours?"
25. The *prix de Rome* is a prize awarded annually since 1803 by Institut de France to a student at the Paris Conservatory. Hebe is the Greek goddess of youth and spring, and cupbearer to the gods. Henrich Heine (1797-1856), German poet, is best known for his lyrics which combine self-indulgent Ramanticism with a sharp, deflating irony.
26. Game on a board of 26 squares.
27. The shield shaped surface bearing armorial bearings on the window.

Source: *Monochromes.* London: John Lane, 1895.

Biographical Note

Born in London of Irish parents, probably in either 1856 or 1857, D'Arcy was educated in France and Germany and lived for a time in the Channel Islands. She trained as an artist at the Slade School in London, but deteriorating eyesight led her to abandon her artistic ambitions and turn to writing. Her first major literary success came with the publication of "Irremediable," a scathing treatment of marriage, in the *Yellow Book* (1894). She was, unofficially at least, assistant editor of this periodical and continued to contribute many stories, both to the *Yellow Book* and to *All the Year Round, Blackwood's Magazine,* and *Temple Bar;* these were eventually collected into *Monochromes* (1895) and *Modern Instances* (1898). Under the pseudonym of "Gilbert H. Page," she also published stories in the popular London *Argosy.* D'Arcy completed one novel, *The Bishop's Dilemma* (1898), and worked on several others, including one based on Shelley and his circle, that have not been recovered. Very little is known about her life; she is one of the most elusive of all the women writers represented here. Contemporaries, such as Netta Syrett, in her autobiography, *Sheltering Tree*, believed that D'Arcy never filled her potential because she was incurably idle. Henry Harland of the *Yellow Book* is said to have locked her in a room on one occasion, and refused to let her out until a story was completed. Although she probably had affairs with both John Lane of the Bodley Head and Harland, she seems to have had little interest in a more permanent relationship. She spent most of her later years in Paris, and, after the end of the nineteenth century, produced only one book, a translation of André Maurois's fictional biography of Shelley, *Ariel* (1924).

D'Arcy's stories repeatedly focus on lonely, isolated characters, often women, who are shown to be victims of social institutions. Marriage is always bleakly depicted, inflicting misery on both partners. People suffer through the selfishness and heartlessness of others—as in the pyschologically acute "The Elegie" in which the young woman dies for love and the young man happily adapts his experience to enhance his music. "The Pleasure-Pilgrim," first published in *The Yellow Book* in 1895 and then almost immediately reprinted in *Monochromes*, was a favorite with the critics for what they saw as its masterly characterization of a peculiarly American—and particularly puzzling—type, and was celebrated by the novelist Israel Zangwill as the "cleverest" story in "the cleverest volume of short stories that the year has given us" (*Pall Mall Magazine* 7 [1895]: 158). One of the most challenging and disillusioned of the New Women writers, D'Arcy has been unaccountably neglected by critics for most of the twentieth century.

Selected Modern Reprints:

Ella D'Arcy: Some Letters to John Lane. Ed. Alan Anderson.
    Edinburgh: Tragara P, 1990.
Modern Instances. 1898. New York: Garland, 1984.
Monochromes. 1895. New York: Garland, 1977.

Selected Secondary Sources:

Beckson, Karl. *Henry Harland: His Life and Work.* London:
    Eighteen Nineties Society, 1978.
Fisher, Benjamin Franklin. "Ella D'Arcy: A Commentary
    with a Primary and Annotated Secondary Bibliography."
    English Literature in Transition 35.2 (1992): 179-211.
Mix, Katherine. *A Study in Yellow: The Yellow Book and Its*
    Contributors. New York: Greenwood P, 1960.
Stetz, Margaret. "Turning Points: Ella D'Arcy." *Turn of the*
    Century Women 3 (1986): 2-3.

164   REBECCA HARDING DAVIS (1831-1910)

Rebecca Harding Davis (1831-1910)

Anne

IT WAS A STRANGE THING, THE LIKE OF WHICH HAD NEVER BE-
fore happened to Anne. In her matter-of-fact, orderly life
mysterious impressions were rare. She tried to account for
it afterward by remembering that she had fallen asleep out-
of-doors. And out-of-doors, where there is the hot sun and
the sea and the teeming earth and tireless winds, there are
perhaps great forces at work, both good and evil, mighty
creatures of God going to and fro, who do not enter into
the little wooden or brick boxes in which we cage ourselves.
One of these, it may be, had made her its sport for the time.

Anne, when she fell asleep, was sitting in a hammock
on a veranda of the house nearest to the water. The wet
bright sea-air blew about her. She had some red roses in
her hands, and she crushed them up under her cheek to
catch the perfume, thinking drowsily that the colors of
the roses and cheek were the same. For she had had great
beauty ever since she was a baby, and felt it, as she did
her blood, from her feet to her head, and triumphed and
was happy in it. She had a wonderful voice too. She was
silent now, being nearly asleep. But the air was so cold
and pure, and the scent of the roses so strong in the
sunshine, and she was so alive and throbbing with youth
and beauty, that it seemed to her that she was singing so
that all the world could hear, and that her voice rose –
rose up and up into the very sky.

Was that George whom she saw through her half-shut
eyes coming across the lawn? And Theresa with him? She
started, with a sharp wrench at her heart.

But what was Theresa to George? Ugly, stupid, and
older than he, a woman who had nothing to win him –
but money. *She* had not cheeks like rose leaves, nor youth,

nor a voice that could sing at heaven's gate. Anne curled herself, smiling, down to sleep again. A soft warm touch fell on her lips.

"George!"

The blood stopped in her veins; she trembled even in her sleep. A hand was laid on her arm.

"Bless grashus, Mrs. Palmer! hyah's dat coal man wants he's money. I's been huntin' you low an' high, an' you a-sleepin' out'n dohs!"

Anne staggered to her feet.

"Mother," called a stout young man from the tan-bark path below, "I must catch this train. Jenny will bring baby over for tea. I wish you would explain the dampers in that kitchen range to her."

The wet air still blew in straight from the hazy sea horizon; the crushed red roses lay on the floor.

But she —

There was a pier-glass[1] in the room beside her. Going up to it, she saw a stout woman of fifty with grizzled hair and a big nose. Her cheeks were yellow.

She began to sing. Nothing came from her mouth but a discordant yawp. She remembered that her voice left her at eighteen, after she had that trouble with her larynx. She put her trembling hand up to her lips.

George had never kissed them. He had married Theresa more than thirty years ago. George Forbes was now a famous author.

Her fingers still lay upon her lips. "I thought that he —" she whispered, with a shudder of shame through all of her stout old body.

But below, underneath that, her soul flamed with rapture. Something within her cried out, "*I* am here – Anne! I am beautiful and young. If this old throat were different, my voice would ring through earth and heaven."

"Mrs. Palmer, de coal man —"

"Yes, I am coming, Jane." She took her account-book from her orderly work-basket and went down to the kitchen.

When she came back she found her daughter Susan at work at the sewing-machine. Mrs. Palmer stopped beside her, a wistful smile on her face. Susan was so young: she would certainly take an interest in this thing which had moved her so deeply. Surely some force outside of nature had been thrust into her life just now, and turned it back to its beginnings!

"I fell asleep out on the porch awhile ago, Susy," she said, "and I dreamed that I was sixteen again. It was very vivid. I cannot even now shake off the impression that I am young and beautiful and in love."

"Ah, yes! poor dear papa!" Susy said, with a sigh, snipping her thread. She wished to say something more, something appropriate and sympathetic, about this ancient love of her parents; but it really seemed a little ridiculous, and besides, she was in a hurry to finish the ruffle. Jasper was coming up for tea.

Mrs. Palmer hesitated, and then went on into her own room. She felt chilled and defeated. She had thought Susy would take an interest, but — Of course she could not explain to her that it was not of her poor dear papa that she had dreamed. After all, was it quite decent in a middle-aged respectable woman to have such a dream? Her sallow jaws reddened as she shut herself in. She had been very foolish to tell Susy about it at all.

Mrs. Nancy Palmer was always uncomfortably in awe of the hard common-sense of her children. They were both Palmers. When James was a baby he had looked up one day from her breast with his calm attentive eyes, and she had quailed before them. "I never shall be as old as he is already," she had thought. But as they grew up they loved their mother dearly. Her passionate devotion to them would have touched hearts of stone, and the Palmers were not at all stony-hearted, but kindly, good-humored folk, like their father.

The neighborhood respected Mrs. Palmer as a woman of masculine intellect because, after her husband's death, she had managed the plantation with remarkable energy and success. She had followed his exact, methodical habits in peach-growing and in the management of house, had cleared the property of debt, and then had invested in Western lands so shrewdly as to make herself and the children rich.

But James and Susan were always secretly amused at the deference paid to their mother by the good Delaware planters. She was the dearest woman in the world, but as to a business head —

All her peach crops, her Dakota speculations, and the bank stock which was the solid fruit thereof went for nothing as proofs to them of adult good sense. They were only dear mamma's lucky hits. How could a woman have a practical head who grew so bored with the pleasant church sociables, and refused absolutely to go to the delightful Literary Circle? who would listen to a hand-organ with tears in her eyes, and who had once actually gone all the way up to Philadelphia to hear an Italian stroller named Salvini?[2]

Neither of them could understand such childish outbreaks. Give a Palmer a good peach farm, a comfortable house, and half a dozen servants to worry him, and his lines of life were full. Why should their mother be uneasy inside of these lines?

That she was uneasy to-day, Susy soon perceived. A letter came from Pierce and Wall, her consignees in Philadelphia; but Mrs. Palmer threw it down unopened, although she had shipped three hundred crates of Morris Whites last Monday.

She was usually a most careful house-keeper, keeping a sharp eye on the careless negroes, but she disappeared for hours this afternoon, although Jasper Tyrrell was coming for tea, and Jane was sure to make a greasy mess of the terrapin[3] if left to herself.

Jasper certainly had paid marked attention to Susy lately, but she knew that he was a cool, prudent young fellow, who would look at the matter on every side before he committed himself. The Tyrrells were an old, exclusive family, who would expect perfection from a bride coming among them, from her theology to her tea biscuit.

"A trifle of less importance than messy terrapin has often disgusted a man," thought Susy, her blue eyes dim with impatience.

Just before sunset Mrs. Palmer came up the road, her

hands full of brilliant maple leaves. Susy hurried to meet and kiss her; for the Palmers were a demonstrative family, who expressed their affection by a perpetual petting and buzzing about each other. The entire household would shudder with anxiety if a draught blew on mamma's neck, and fall into an agony of apprehension if the baby had a cold in its head. Mrs. Palmer, for some reason, found that this habit of incessant watchfulness bored her just now.

"No, my shoes are *not* damp, Susy. No, I did not need a shawl. I am not in my dotage, child, that I cannot walk out without being wrapped up like an Esquimau.[4] One would think I was on the verge of the grave."

"Oh, no, but you are not young, darling mamma. You are just at the age when rheumatisms and lumbagoes and such things set in if one is not careful. Where have you been?"

"I took a walk in the woods."

"Woods! No wonder your shoulders are damp. Come in directly, dear. Four grains of quinine and a hot lemonade going to bed. Walking in the woods! Really, now, that is something I cannot understand," – smiling at her mother as though she were a very small child indeed. "Now I can walk any distance to church, or to shop, or for any reasonable motive, but to go wandering about in the swampy woods for no earthly purpose – I'll press those leaves for you," checking herself.

"No; I do not like to see pressed leaves and grasses about in vases. It is like making ornaments of hair cut from a dead body. When summer is dead, let it die." She threw down the leaves impatiently, and the wind whirled them away.

"How queer mamma and the people of that generation are – so little self-control!" thought Susy. "It is nearly time for Mr. Tyrrell to be here," she said aloud. "Can Jane season the terrapin?"

"Oh, I suppose so," said Mrs. Palmer, indifferently, taking up a book.

She was indifferent and abstracted all evening. Peter clattered the dishes as he waited at the supper-table, and the tea was lukewarm. Jasper was lukewarm too, silent and critical.

James's wife, Jenny, had come over for supper, and finding her mother-in-law so absent and inattentive, poured forth her anecdotes of baby to Mr. Tyrrell. Jenny, like most young mothers, gave forth inexhaustibly theories concerning the sleep, diet, and digestion of infants. Jasper, bored and uneasy, shuffled in his chair. He had always thought Mrs. Palmer was charming as a hostess, full of tact, in fine rapport with every one. Couldn't she see how this woman was bedevilling him with her croup and her flannels? She was apparently blind and deaf to it all.

Mrs. Palmer's vacant eyes were turned out of the window. Susy glanced at her with indignation. Was mamma deranged?

How petty the pursuits of these children were! thought the older woman, regarding them as from a height. How cautious and finical Tyrrell was in his love-making! Susy too – six months ago she had carefully inquired into Jasper's income.

Tea biscuit and flannels and condensed milk! At seventeen *her* horizon had not been so cramped and shut in. How wide and beautiful the world had been! Nature had known her and talked to her, and in all music there had been a word for her, alone and apart. How true she had been to her friends! how she had hated her enemies! how, when love came to her – Mrs. Palmer felt a sudden chill shiver through her limbs. She sat silent until they rose from table. Then she hurried to her own room. She did not make a light. She told herself that she was absurdly nervous, and bathed her face and wrists in cold water. But she could not strike a light. This creature within her, this Anne, vivid and beautiful and loving, was she to face the glass and see the old yellow-skinned woman?

She ought to think of that old long-ago self as dead.

But it was not dead.

"If I had married the man I loved," this something within her cried, "I should have had my true life. He would have understood me."

How ridiculous and wicked it all was!

"I was a loyal, loving wife to Job Palmer," she told

herself, resolutely lighting the lamp and facing the stout figure in the glass with its puffy black silk gown. "My life went down with his into the grave."

But there was a flash in the gray pleading eyes which met her in the glass that gave her the lie.

They were Anne's eyes, and Anne had never been Job Palmer's wife.

Mrs. Palmer did not go down again that night. A wood fire blazed on her hearth, and she put on her wrapper and drew her easy-chair in front of it, with the little table beside her on which lay her Bible and prayer-book and à Kempis.[5] This quiet hour was usually the happiest of the day. James and Jenny always came in to kiss her good-bye, and Susy regularly crept in when the house was quiet to read a chapter with her mother and to tuck her snugly into bed.

But to-night she locked the door. She wanted to be alone. She tried to read, but pushed the books away, and turning out the light, threw herself upon the bed. Not à Kempis nor any holy saint could follow her into the solitudes into which her soul had gone. Could God Himself understand how intolerable this old clumsy body had grown to her?

She remembered that when she had been ill with nervous prostration two years ago she had in an hour suddenly grown eighty years old. Now the blood of sixteen was in her veins. Why should this soul within her thus dash her poor brain from verge to verge of its narrow range of life?

The morbid fancies of the night brought her by morning to an odd resolution. She would go away. Why should she not go away? She had done her full duty to husband, children, and property. Why should she not begin somewhere else, live out her own life? Why should she not have her chance for the few years left? Music and art and the companionship of thinkers and scholars. Mrs. Palmer's face grew pale as she named these things so long forbidden to her.

It was now dawn. She hastily put on a travelling dress, and placed a few necessary articles and her check-book in a satchel.

"Carry this to the station," she said to Peter, who, half asleep, was making up the fires.

"Gwine to Philadelphy, Mis' Palmer? Does Miss Susy know?"

"No. Tell her I have been suddenly called away."

As she walked to the station she smiled to think how Susy would explain her sudden journey by the letter from Pierce and Wall, and would look to find whether she had taken her overshoes and chamois jacket. "I hate overshoes, and I would like to tear that jacket into bits!" she thought as she took her seat in the car. She was going to escape from it all. She would no longer be happed and dosed and watched like a decrepit old crone. She was an affectionate mother, but it actually did not occur to her that she was leaving Susy and James and the baby. She was possessed with a frenzy of delight in escaping. The train moved. She was free! She could be herself now at last!

It could be easily arranged. She would withdraw her certificates and government bonds from the vaults of the trust company in Philadelphia. The children had their own property secure.

Where should she go? To Rome? Venice? No. There were so many Americans trotting about Europe. She must be rid of them all. Now there was Egypt and the Nile. Or if another expedition were going to Iceland? Up there in the awful North among the glaciers and geysers, and sagas and Runic relics,[6] one would be in another world, and forget Morris Whites and church sociables and the wiggling village gossip.

"There are people in this country who live in a high pure atmosphere of thought, who never descend to gossip or money-making," she thought, remembering the lofty strains of George Forbes's last poem. "If I had been his wife I too might have thought great thoughts and lived a noble life."

She tried angrily to thrust away this idea. She did not mean to be a traitor to her husband, whom she had loved well and long.

But the passion of her youth maddened her. Job had

been a good commonplace man. But this other was a Seer, a Dictator of thought to the world.

The train rolled into Broad Street station. Mrs. Palmer went to the Trust company and withdrew her bonds. She never before had come up to the city alone; Susy always accompanied her to "take care of dear mamma." Susy, who had provincial ideas as to "what people in our position should do," always took her to the most fashionable hotel, and ordered a dinner the cost of which weighed on her conscience for months afterward. Mrs. Palmer now went to a cheap little café in a back street, and ate a chop with the keen delight of a runaway dog gnawing a stolen bone. A cold rain began to fall, and she was damp and chilled when she returned to the station.

Where should she go? Italy – the Nile – Heavens! there were the Crotons from Dover getting out of the train! She must go somewhere at once to hide herself; afterward she could decide on her course. A queue of people were at the ticket window. She placed herself in line.

"Boston?" said the agent.

She nodded. In five minutes she was seated in a parlor car, and thundering across the bridge above the great abattoir. She looked down on the cattle in their sheds. "I do wonder if Peter will give Rosy her warm mash to-night?" she thought, uneasily.

There were but three seats occupied in the car. Two men and a lady entered together and sat near to Mrs. Palmer, so that she could not but hear their talk, which at first ran upon draughts.

"You might open your window, Corvill," said one of the men, "if Mrs. Ames is not afraid of neuralgia."

Corvill? Ames? Mrs. Palmer half rose from her seat. She had an etching of his "Hagar."[7] She never looked into that woman's face without a wrench at her heart. All human pain and longing spoke in it as they did in George Forbes's poems. Mrs. Ames, she had heard, was chairman of the Woman's National Society for the Examination of Prisons. Mrs. Palmer had read her exposé of the abominations of the lessee system – words burning with a fiery zeal for humanity. There had been a symposium in Philadelphia, she remembered, of noted authors and artists this week.

No doubt these were two of those famous folk. Mrs. Palmer drew nearer, feeling as if she were creeping up to the base of Mount Olympus.[8] This was what happened when one cut loose from Morris Whites and terrapin and that weary Jane and Peter! The Immortals were outside, and she had come into their company.

"Oh, open the window!" said Mrs. Ames, who had a hoarse voice which came in bass gusts and snorts out of a mouth mustached like a man's. "Let's have some air! The sight of those emigrants huddled in the station nauseated me. Women and babies all skin and bone and rags."

Now Mrs. Palmer had just emptied her purse and almost cried over that wretched group. That sick baby's cry would wring any woman's heart, she thought. Could it be that this great philanthropist had pity only for the misery of the masses? But the man who painted "Hagar" surely would be pitiful and tender?

"Sorry they annoyed you," he was saying. "Some very good subjects among them. I made two sketches," pulling out a note-book. "That half-starved woman near the door – see? – eh? Fine slope in the chin and jaw. I wanted a dying baby for my 'Exiles,' too. I caught the very effect I wanted. Sick child."

Mrs. Palmer turned her revolving chair away. It was a trifling disappointment, but it hurt her. She was in that strained, feverish mood when trifles hurt sharply. These were mere hucksters of art and humanity. They did not belong to the high pure level on which stood great interpreters of the truth – such, for instance, as George Forbes. The little quake which always passed through her at this man's name was increased by a shiver from the damp wind blowing upon her. She sneezed twice.

Mrs. Ames stared at her insolently, and turned her back, fearing that she might be asked to put down the window.

Mr. Corvill was talking about the decoration of the car. "Not bad at all," he said. "There is great tenderness in the color of that ceiling, and just look at the lines of the chairs! They are full of feeling."

Mrs. Palmer listened, bewildered. But now they were looking at the landscape. If he found feeling in the legs of a chair, what new meaning would he not discover in that vast stretch of lonely marsh with the narrow black lagoons creeping across it?

"Nice effect," said Mr. Corvill – "the lichen on that barn against the green. I find little worth using in the fall this year, however. Too much umber in the coloring."

Could it be, she thought, that these people had made a trade of art and humanity until they had lost the perception of their highest meanings?

"I should think," continued Corvill, turning to the other man, "you could find *matériel* for some verses in these flats. Ulalume, or The Land of Dolor. Something in that line. Eh, Forbes?"

Forbes! Her breath stopped. That fat hunched man with the greasy black whispers and gaudy chain! Yes, that was his voice; but had it always that tone of vulgar swagger?

"I've stopped verse-writing," he said. "Poetry's a drug in the market. My infernal publishers shut down on it five years ago."

He turned, and she then saw his face – the thin hard lips, the calculating eye.

Was this man "George"? Or had that George ever lived except in her fancy?

"Mr. Forbes." She rose. The very life in her seemed to stop; her knees shook. But habit is strong. She bowed as she named him, and stood there, smiling, the courteous, thorough-bred old lady whose charm young Tyrrell had recognized. Some power in the pathetic gray eyes startled Forbes and brought him to his feet.

"I think I knew you long ago," she said. "If it is you – ?"

"Forbes is my name, ma'am. Lord bless me! you can't be — Something familiar in your eyes. You remind me of Judge Sinclair's daughter Fanny."

"Anne was my name."

"Anne. To be sure. I knew it was Nanny or Fanny. I

ought to remember, for I was spoons on you myself for a week or two. You know you were reckoned the best catch in the county, eh? Sit down, ma'am, sit down; people of our weight aren't built for standing."

"Is – your wife with you?"

"You refer to the first Mrs. Forbes – Theresa Stone? I have been married twice since her decease. I am now a widower." He put his hand to his mouth and coughed, glancing at the crape on his hat. His breath crossed her face. It reeked of heavy feeding and night orgies; for Forbes, though avaricious, had gross appetites.

Suddenly Job Palmer stood before her, with his fine clear-cut face and reasonable eyes. He knew little outside of his farm perhaps; but how clean was his soul! How he had loved her!

The car at that moment swayed violently from side to side; the lamps went out. "Hello!" shouted Forbes. "Something wrong! We must get out of this!" rushing to the door. She braced herself against her chair.

In the outside darkness the rushing of steam was heard, and shrieks of women in mortal agony. A huge weight fell on the car, crushing in the roof. Mrs. Palmer was jammed between two beams, but unhurt. A heavy rain was falling.

"I shall not be burned to death, at any rate," she thought, and then fortunately became insensible.

In half an hour she was cut out and laid on the bank, wet and half frozen, but with whole bones. She tried to rise, but could not; every joint ached with rheumatism; her gown was in tatters, the mud was deep under her, and the rain pelted down. She saw the fire burning on her hearth at home, and the easy-chair in front of it, and the Bible and à Kempis.

Some men with lanterns came up and bent over her.

"Great God, mother!" one of them cried. It was James, who had been on the same train, going to New York.

The next day she was safely laid in her own bed. The fire was burning brightly, and Susy was keeping guard that she might sleep. Jenny had just brought a delicious bowl of soup and fed it to her, and baby had climbed up on the bed, and fallen asleep there. She held him in her arm. James came in on tiptoe, and bent anxiously over her. She saw them all through her half-shut eyes.

"My own – flesh of my flesh!" she thought, and thanked God from her soul for the love that held her warm and safe.

As she dozed, Susy and James bent over her. "Where could she have been going?" said Susy.

"To New York; no doubt to make a better contract than the one she has with Pierce and Wall – to make a few more dollars for us. Or, an investment: her bonds were all in her satchel. Poor dear unselfish soul! Don't worry her with questions, Susy – don't speak of it."

"No, I will not, Jim," said Susy, wiping her eyes. "But if she only had taken her chamois jacket!"

James himself, when his mother was quite well, remarked one day, "We had a famous fellow-traveller in that train to New York – Forbes, the author."

"A most disagreeable, underbred person!" said Mrs. Palmer, vehemently. "I would not have you notice such people, James – a mere shopman of literature!"

*   *   *   *   *   *   *

Susy married Jasper Tyrrell that winter. They live in the homestead now, and Mrs. Palmer has four or five grandchildren about her, whom she spoils to her heart's content. She still dabbles a little in mining speculations; but since her accident on the cars she is troubled with rheumatism, and leaves the management of the farm and house to Jasper and Susy. She has a quiet, luxurious, happy life, being petted like a baby by all of the Palmers. Yet sometimes in the midst of all this comfort and sunshine a chance note of music or the sound of the restless wind will bring an expression into her eyes which her children do not understand, as if some creature unknown to them looked out of them.

At such times Mrs. Palmer will say to herself, "Poor Anne!" as of somebody whom she once knew that is dead.

Is she dead? she feebly wonders; and if she is dead here, will she ever live again?

Notes

1   Large mirror.

2   Tommasso Salvini (1829-1916). Italian actor, well-known all over Europe and North America. He visited the U.S.A. five times and was renowned for his interpretation of Othello.

3   North American freshwater edible tortoise.

4   Eskimo.

5   Thomas à Kempis (1380-1471). Augustinian monk and author of many Christian mystical works; the *Imitations of Christ*, which is probably what Mrs. Palmer is reading, is generally attributed to him.

6   Runes are letters of the earliest Germanic alphabet used by Scandinavians and Anglo-Saxons during the third century.

7   Abraham's concubine, mother of Ishmael. Hagar was forced to flee into the wilderness when Sarah, Abraham's wife, eventually gave birth to Isaac. Genesis 16, 21, 25.

8   In Greek mythology, Mount Olympus is home of the gods.

Source: *Silhouettes of American Life*. Scribner's, 1892.

Biographical Note

Rebecca Harding Davis, best known as the author of *Life in the Iron Mills*, an early example of American realism, was born on June 24, 1831, in Washington, Pennsylvania. She spent her early years in Wheeling, Virginia, where she was educated at home. At fourteen, she entered the Washington Female Seminary in Pennsylvania and, upon graduating, returned to help her mother at home in Virginia. Little is known about her life from this time until she published *Life in the Iron Mills* in the *Atlantic* in 1861. Considered the first American proletarian novel, it is the realistic story of Hugh Wolfe, a sensitive artist restricted by his harsh life as a furnace tender in a Virginia mill. James T. Fields, editor of the *Atlantic Monthly*, asked for more of her work. Davis followed with *A Story of Today*, serialized from October 1861 to March 1862 after she made revisions to eradicate the gloom of which Fields initially complained, and then published in book form as *Margret Howth* later in 1862. In that same year Davis visited Fields and his wife, Annie, with whom she became lifelong friends. On the journey home she stopped in Philadelphia to meet Lemuel Clarke Davis, a part-time journalist and law clerk with whom she had been corresponding since the publication of *Life in the Iron Mills*. They married in 1863 and subsequently had three children, a daughter, Nora, and two sons, Richard and Charles, who also became writers.

Davis was a prolific author, producing children's stories, historical essays, travel sketches, and gothic thrillers for many of the magazines of the time. The overall quality of her work is generally considered to have declined after her marriage, partly because of her need to supplement her husband's meagre income by the production of "potboilers." One of her more interesting works is *Waiting For the Verdict* (1868), an examination of the problems faced by a prominent surgeon after he reveals that he is part black. In 1869 Davis joined the staff on the *New York Tribune* as contributing editor, and a year later her husband bought a house in Philadelphia where she stayed, devoting most of her energy first to supporting her husband in his new role as managing editor of the Philadelphia *Inquirer* and then to supporting the career of her more famous son, Richard Harding Davis. Although Davis was continually overshadowed by her husband and son, it is likely that she never became as conservative in her views as is suggested by the continuing misattribution to Davis of *Pro Aris et Focis* (1870), which argues that motherhood is a woman's true destiny and that only women with absolutely no chance for such fulfillment should consider a career. "Anne," the story chosen for inclusion here, appeared in *Silhouettes of American Life* (1892), and is interesting for its poignant questioning of those very notions about women's fulfillment; Anne's final inability to accept her loss of vitality and self-sufficiency suggests Davis would be less than delighted to know that after her death in Philadelphia at the age of seventy-nine, she would be buried in the same grave as her husband under a stone that reads "L. Clarke Davis . . . And His Wife."

Selected Modern Reprints:

Life in the Iron Mills and Other Stories. Ed. and Intro. Tillie Olsen. New York: Feminist P, 1985.
Margret Howth: A Story of Today. 1862. New York: Feminist P, 1990.
Silhouettes of American Life. 1892. New York: Garrett P, 1968.
Waiting for the Verdict. 1868. New York: Irvington, 1986.

Selected Secondary Sources:

Harris, Sharon M. *Rebecca Harding Davis and American Realism*. Philadelphia: U of Pennsylvania P, 1991.
—. "Rebecca Harding Davis (1831-1910); A Bibliography of Secondary Criticism, 1958-1986." *Bulletin of Bibliography* 45.4 (1988): 233-46.
Langford, Gerald. *The Richard Harding Davis Years: A Biography of Mother and Son*. New York: Rinehart, Winston, 1961.

Pfaelzer, Jean. "Rebecca Harding Davis: Domesticity, Social Order and the Industrial Novel." *International Journal of Women's Studies* 4 (1981): 234-44.

182   ALICE DUNBAR-NELSON (1875-1935)

Alice Dunbar-Nelson (1875-1935)

Sister Josepha

SISTER JOSEPHA TOLD HER BEADS MECHANICALLY, HER FINGERS numb with the accustomed exercise. The little organ creaked a dismal, "O Salutaris,"[1] and she still knelt on the floor, her white-bonneted head nodding suspiciously. The Mother Superior gave a sharp glance at the tired figure; then, as a sudden lurch forward brought the little sister back to consciousness, Mother's eyes relaxed into a genuine smile.

The bell tolled the end of vespers, and the sombre-robed nuns filed out of the chapel to go about their evening duties. Little Sister Josepha's work was to attend to the household lamps, but there must have been as much oil spilled upon the table to-night as was put in the vessels. The small brown hands trembled so that most of the wicks were trimmed with points at one corner which caused them to smoke that night.

"Oh, cher Seigneur,"[2] she sighed, giving an impatient polish to a refractory chimney, "it is wicked and sinful, I know, but I am so tired. I can't be happy and sing any more. It doesn't seem right for le bon Dieu[3] to have me all cooped up here with nothing to see but stray visitors, and always the same old work, teaching those mean little girls to sew, and washing and filling the same old lamps. Pah!" And she polished the chimney with a sudden vigorous jerk which threatened destruction.

They were rebellious prayers that the red mouth murmured that night, and a restless figure that tossed on the hard dormitory bed. Sister Dominica called from her couch to know if Sister Josepha were ill.

"No," was the somewhat short response; then a muttered, "Why can't they let me alone for a minute? That pale-eyed Sister Dominica never sleeps; that's why she is so ugly."

About fifteen years before this night some one had brought to the orphan asylum connected with this convent, du Sacré Coeur,[4] a round, dimpled bit of three-year-old humanity, who regarded the world from a pair of gravely twinkling black eyes, and only took a chubby thumb out of a rosy mouth long enough to answer in monosyllabic French. It was a child without an identity; there was but one name that any one seemed to know, and that, too, was vague, – Camille.

She grew up with the rest of the waifs; scraps of French and American civilization thrown together to develop a seemingly inconsistent miniature world. Mademoiselle Camille was a queen among them, a pretty little tyrant who ruled the children and dominated the more timid sisters in charge.

One day an awakening came. When she was fifteen, and almost fully ripened into a glorious tropical beauty of the type that matures early, some visitors to the convent were fascinated by her and asked the Mother Superior to give the girl into their keeping.

Camille fled like a frightened fawn into the yard, and was only unearthed with some difficulty from behind a group of palms. Sulky and pouting, she was led into the parlour, picking at her blue pinafore like a spoiled infant.

"The lady and the gentleman wish you to go home with them, Camille," said the Mother Superior, in the language of the convent. Her voice was kind and gentle apparently; but the child, accustomed to its various inflections, detected a steely ring behind its softness, like the proverbial iron hand in the velvet glove.

"You must understand, madame," continued Mother, in stilted English, "that we never force children from us. We are ever glad to place them in comfortable – how you say that? – quarters – maisons – homes – bien![5] But we will not make them go if they do not wish."

Camille stole a glance at her would-be guardians, and decided instantly, impulsively, finally. The woman suited her; but the man! It was doubtless intuition of the quick, vivacious sort which belonged to her blood that served her. Untutored in worldly knowledge, she could not divine the meaning of the pronounced leers and admiration of her physical charms which gleamed in the man's face, but she knew it made her feel creepy, and stoutly refused to go.

Next day Camille was summoned from a task to the Mother Superior's parlour. The other girls gazed with envy upon her as she dashed down the courtyard with impetuous movement. Camille, they decided crossly, received too much notice. It was Camille this, Camille that; she was pretty, it was to be expected. Even Father Ray lingered longer in his blessing when his hands pressed her silky black hair.

As she entered the parlour, a strange chill swept over the girl. The room was not an unaccustomed one, for she had swept it many times, but to-day the stiff black chairs, the dismal crucifixes, the gleaming whiteness of the walls, even the cheap lithograph of the Madonna which Camille had always regarded as a perfect specimen of art, seemed cold and mean.

"Camille, ma chère,"[6] said Mother, "I am extremely displeased with you. Why did you not wish to go with Monsieur and Madame Lafayé yesterday?"

The girl uncrossed her hands from her bosom, and spread them out in a deprecating gesture.

"Mais, ma mère,[7] I was afraid."

Mother's face grew stern. "No foolishness now," she exclaimed.

"It is not foolishness, ma mère; I could not help it, but that man looked at me so funny, I felt all cold chills down my back. Oh, dear Mother, I love the convent and the sisters so, I just want to stay and be a sister too, may I?"

And thus it was that Camille took the white veil at sixteen years. Now that the period of novitiate was over, it was just beginning to dawn upon her that she had made a mistake.

"Maybe it would have been better had I gone with the funny-looking lady and gentleman," she mused bitterly one night. "Oh, Seigneur, I'm so tired and impatient; it's so dull here, and, dear God, I'm so young."

There was no help for it. One must arise early in the morning, and help in the refectory with the stupid Sister Francesca, and go about one's duties with a prayerful mien, and not even let a sigh escape when one's head ached with the eternal telling of beads.

A great fête[8] day was coming, and an atmosphere of preparation and mild excitement pervaded the brown walls of the convent like a delicate aroma. The old Cathedral around the corner had stood a hundred years, and all the city was rising to do honour to its age and time-softened beauty. There would be a service, oh, but such a one! with two Cardinals, and Archbishops and Bishops, and all the accompanying glitter of soldiers and orchestras. The little sisters of the Convent du Sacré Coeur clasped their hands in anticipation of the holy joy. Sister Josepha curled her lip, she was so tired of churchly pleasures.

The day came, a gold and blue spring day, when the air hung heavy with the scent of roses and magnolias, and the sunbeams fairly laughed as they kissed the houses. The old Cathedral stood gray and solemn, and the flowers in Jackson Square smiled birthday greetings across the way. The crowd around the door surged and pressed and pushed in its eagerness to get within. Ribbons stretched across the banquette were of no avail to repress it, and important ushers with cardinal colours could do little more.

The Sacred Heart sisters filed slowly in at the side door, creating a momentary flutter as they paced reverently to their seats, guarding the blue-bonneted orphans. Sister Josepha, determined to see as much of the world as she could, kept her big black eyes opened wide, as the church rapidly filled with the fashionably dressed, perfumed, rustling, and self-conscious throng.

Her heart beat quickly. The rebellious thoughts that will arise in the most philosophical of us surged in her small heavily gowned bosom. For her were the gray things, the neutral tinted skies, the ugly garb, the coarse meats;

for them the rainbow, the ethereal airiness of earthly joys, the bonbons and glacés[9] of the world. Sister Josepha did not know that the rainbow is elusive, and its colours but the illumination of tears; she had never been told that earthly ethereality is necessarily ephemeral, nor that bonbons and glacés, whether of the palate or the soul, nauseate and pall upon the taste. Dear God, forgive her, for she bent with contrite tears over her worn rosary, and glanced no more at the worldly glitter of femininity.

The sunbeams streamed through the high windows in purple and crimson lights upon a veritable fugue of colour. Within the seats, crush upon crush of spring millinery; within the aisles erect lines of gold-braided, gold-buttoned military. Upon the altar, broad sweeps of golden robes, great dashes of crimson skirts, mitres and gleaming crosses, the soft neutral hue of rich lace vestments; the tender heads of childhood in picturesque attire; the proud, golden magnificence of the domed altar with its weighting mass of lilies and wide-eyed roses, and the long candles that sparkled their yellow star points above the reverent throng within the altar rails.

The soft baritone of the Cardinal intoned a single phrase in the suspended silence. The censer took up the note in its delicate clink clink, as it swung to and fro in the hands of a fair-haired child. Then the organ, pausing an instant in a deep, mellow, long-drawn note, burst suddenly into a magnificent strain, and the choir sang forth, "Kyrie Eleïson, Christe Eleïson."[10] One voice, flute-like, piercing, sweet, rang high over the rest. Sister Josepha heard and trembled, as she buried her face in her hands, and let her tears fall, like other beads, through her rosary.

It was when the final word of the service had been intoned, the last peal of the exit march had died away, that she looked up meekly, to encounter a pair of youthful brown eyes gazing pityingly upon her. That was all she remembered for a moment, that the eyes were youthful and handsome and tender. Later, she saw that they were placed in a rather beautiful boyish face, surmounted by waves of brown hair, curling and soft, and that the head was set on a pair of shoulders decked in military uniform.

Then the brown eyes marched away with the rest of the rear guard, and the white-bonneted sisters filed out the side door, through the narrow court, back into the brown convent.

That night Sister Josepha tossed more than usual on her hard bed, and clasped her fingers often in prayer to quell the wickedness in her heart. Turn where she would, pray as she might, there was ever a pair of tender, pitying brown eyes, haunting her persistently. The squeaky organ at vespers intoned the clank of military accoutrements to her ears, the white bonnets of the sisters about her faded into mists of curling brown hair. Briefly, Sister Josepha was in love.

The days went on pretty much as before, save for the one little heart that beat rebelliously now and then, though it tried so hard to be submissive. There was the morning work in the refectory, the stupid little girls to teach sewing, and the insatiable lamps that were so greedy for oil. And always the tender, boyish brown eyes, that looked so sorrowfully at the fragile, beautiful little sister, haunting, following, pleading.

Perchance, had Sister Josepha been in the world, the eyes would have been an incident. But in this home of self-repression and retrospection, it was a life-story. The eyes had gone their way, doubtless forgetting the little sister they pitied; but the little sister?

The days glided into weeks, the weeks into months. Thoughts of escape had come to Sister Josepha, to flee into the world, to merge in the great city where recognition was impossible, and, working her way like the rest of humanity, perchance encounter the eyes again.

It was all planned and ready. She would wait until some morning when the little band of black-robed sisters wended their way to mass at the Cathedral. When it was time to file out the side-door into the courtway, she would linger at prayers, then slip out another door, and unseen glide up Chartres Street to Canal, and once there, mingle in the throng that filled the wide thoroughfare. Beyond this first plan she could think no further. Penniless, garbed, and shaven though she would be, other difficulties never presented themselves to her. She would rely on the mercies of the world to help her escape from this torturing life of inertia. It seemed easy now that the first step of decision had been taken.

The Saturday night before the final day had come, and she lay feverishly nervous in her narrow little bed, wondering with wide-eyed fear at the morrow. Pale-eyed Sister Dominica and Sister Francesca were whispering together in the dark silence, and Sister Josepha's ears pricked up as she heard her name.

"She is not well, poor child," said Francesca. "I fear the life is too confining."

"It is best for her," was the reply. "You know, sister, how hard it would be for her in the world, with no name but Camille, no friends, and her beauty; and then —"

Sister Josepha heard no more, for her heart beating tumultuously in her bosom drowned the rest. Like the rush of the bitter salt tide over a drowning man clinging to a spar, came the complete submerging of her hopes of another life. No name but Camille, that was true; no nationality, for she could never tell from whom or whence she came; no friends, and a beauty that not even an ungainly bonnet and shaven head could hide. In a flash she realised the deception of the life she would lead, and the cruel self-torture of wonder at her own identity. Already, as if in anticipation of the world's questionings, she was asking herself, "Who am I? What am I?"

The next morning the sisters du Sacré Coeur filed into the Cathedral at High Mass, and bent devout knees at the general confession. "Confiteor Deo omnipotenti,"[11] murmured the priest; and tremblingly one little sister followed the words, "Je confesse à Dieu, tout puissant – que j'ai beaucoup péché par pensées – c'est ma faute – c'est ma faute – c'est ma très grande faute."[12]

The organ pealed forth as mass ended, the throng slowly filed out, and the sisters paced through the courtway back into the brown convent walls. One paused at the entrance, and gazed with swift longing eyes in the direction of narrow, squalid Chartres Street, then, with a gulping sob, followed the rest, and vanished behind the heavy door.

Notes

1 From the opening line of "O Salutaris Hostia" (O saving Host).
2 Dear Lord.
3 The good God.
4 Of the Sacred Heart.
5 Good.
6 My dear.
7 But my mother.
8 Feast day.
9 Sweets and ices.
10 "Lord have mercy, Christ have mercy." Ancient liturgical petition.
11 Roman Catholic prayer in which confession of sins is made.
12 "I confess to almighty God that I have sinned many times in thought – it's my fault – it's my fault – it's so very much my fault."
Source: *The Goodness of St. Rocque and Other Stories*. New York: Dodd, Mead, 1899.

Biographical Note

Alice Dunbar-Nelson, the daughter of Patricia Wright, a seamstress, and Joseph Moore, a Merchant marine, was born in New Orleans, where she lived for the first twenty years of her life. She began a teacher-training program at Straight University at the age of fifteen. Her first book, *Violets and Other Tales* (1895), was a collection of short stories, essays, and poems, many of which had been previously published in newspapers and magazines. In 1895 the poet Paul Laurence Dunbar fell in love with her after seeing her photograph in the *Boston Monthly Review* and began an epistolary courtship in the Browning manner; it was only after she accepted a teaching post in Brooklyn in 1897—a post which allowed her to continue her studies both at Cornell, where she received an M.A., and at the University of Pennsylvania—that she finally met Dunbar; they were married in 1898. A collection of short stories focusing on New Orleans Creole culture, *The Goodness of St. Rocque*, appeared in 1899, and established her as a significant local colorist. In 1902, when the Dunbars' stormy marriage came to an end, she moved to Wilmington, Delaware, where she was Head of the English department at Howard High School until 1920. She remarried twice: first, briefly, to a teacher, Henry Callis, in 1910, and then to a journalist, Robert Nelson, with whom she remained until she died on September 18, 1935.

Dunbar Nelson is one of the most multi-talented of all the women represented in this anthology. She edited the *Wilmington Advocate*, and was a regular contributor and a respected reviewer for a variety of other newspapers and magazines. She played an important role in Delaware politics, and, as a member of the Women's Committee on the Council of Defense, helped to organize Southern black women for the war effort. She was a historian and in great demand as a lecturer, and she was a suffragist and feminist who advocated the independence that could be achieved by working women. While Dunbar Nelson, unlike her contemporary Pauline Hopkins, rarely writes about black characters or addresses the problems of racism directly in her stories, her work in exposing and combatting discrimination, in bringing black history to light, and in helping to make the voice of black writers heard was ongoing. For the fiftieth anniversary of the Emancipation Proclamation, she compiled *Masterpieces of Negro Eloquence* (1914); later she edited *The Dunbar Speaker and Entertainer* (1920), a collection of literature by and about black men and women; and she produced numerous monographs on black history and traditions. While Dunbar Nelson's work, with the possible exception of the frequently anthologized and powerful poem, "I Sit and Sew," has been forgotten for most of this century, she had a significant influence on the writers of the Harlem Renaissance. The importance of her work is once again gradually being acknowledged.

Selected Modern Reprints:

An Alice Dunbar-Nelson Reader. Ed. R. Ora Williams. Washington: UP of America, 1979.
Give Us Each Day: The Diary of Alice Dunbar-Nelson. Ed. Gloria T. Hull. New York: Norton, 1984.
The Goodness of St. Roque and Other Stories. 1899. NY: AMS P, 1975.
Violets and Other Tales. 1895. Boston: Monthly Review, 1985.
The Works of Alice Dunbar-Nelson. 3 vols. Ed. Gloria T. Hull. New York: Oxford UP, 1988.

Selected Secondary Sources:

Ammons, Elizabeth. *Conflicting Stories: American Women Writers at the Turn into the Twentieth Century.* New York: Oxford UP, 1991.
Hull, Gloria T. "Alice Dunbar-Nelson: Delaware Writer and Woman of Affairs." *Delaware History* 17 (1976): 87-103.
—. *Color, Sex, and Poetry: Three Women Writers of the Harlem Renaissance.* Bloomington: Indiana UP, 1987.
—. "Two-Facing Life: The Duality of Alice Nelson-Dunbar." *Collections* 4 (1989): 19-35.
Williams, Ora. "Works by and About Alice Ruth (Moore) Dunbar-Nelson: A Bibliography." *CLA Journal* 19 (1976): 322-26.

194   GEORGE EGERTON (1859-1945)

George Egerton

(Mary Chavelita Dunne Bright)

(1859-1945)

Gone Under

ONE FORENOON IN LATE AUTUMN AN OUTWARD-BOUND steamer lay close to a wharf in New York. She lay quietly waiting for the signal of her departure, in which few seemed to take an interest. There was a lonely note in her waiting. No telegraph boys bearing God-speeds to much-initialled citizens, no loquacious interviewers, no crowd of friends and relatives with floral offerings boarded the gangway of the *Portugal*, for she was only a third-rate steamer carrying a live freight of cattle to London, and her score of passengers either studied economy, absence of scrutiny, or a longer spell of sea.

The last of the weary, harassed beasts was packed closely under decks, but their presence was betrayed by uneasy lowing and a warm smell that made an Irish dock-labourer think, with tears in his eyes, of a thatched cabin on a Kerry hillside, and his old mother, with the rent coming due; made him brace his back to the work anew and croon an old Irish melody, because of the ten dollars saved to send her.

A girl leaning over the side smiles as she hears him; she has a grave, tender face, plain at a first look; but her eyes are the changeful hazel that lighten with mirth or darken with thought, as when cloud-rifts or sun-slants flit across a turf-fringed tarn.

She has no 'style,' and her clothes are plainly made and rather shabby; she is going home on a free pass.

She has been working for two years in New York, and

is glad to go back, even if it be only to seek fresh work amongst her own people. She has read much, thought much, worked hard, and lived clean – been necessarily lonely. She has observed closely during her stay in this polyglot city of striking paradoxes, this monster dollar-mint, this gigantic sieve through which the surplus of the old world is silted over the new; city of many sects and blatant atheism; narrow prudery, and naked vice; where foreign literature is emasculated, and native newspapers are as broad as the Bible, and filthy as Sterne.[1]

She has suffered physically under the mighty throb and high pressure hustle of a life that rolls on like a mighty steam-roller, crushing the sap out of the men before their prime, making the women the most consciously sexless, and unconsciously selfish, on the face of the globe.

She has learnt strange lessons in social economy; understands how sealskin 'saques' and imported hats can be bought on a salary of six dollars a week; has lost most of her illusions.

She is watching idly a man and a woman who have driven up in a closed carriage. They have seated themselves on a bench on the wharf and are talking earnestly. The woman has her back turned to the boat; she is very tall, her figure is superb, her waist too round and too small. The sunlight mates with the golden knot of hair under her crimson toque. She wears a plaid woollen gown in which cream predominates, and a red satin bodice, and carries a useless silk parasol to match. She is dressed for a garden-party, and, save for the new travelling-bag, ulster,[2] and rug lying next to her on the wharf, shows no signs of fitness for a perhaps rough voyage.

The man seems to be trying to reassure or convince her, but she shakes her head as she listens, and her shoulders heave, and she wipes her eyes impatiently.

The girl wonders vaguely in what relationship they stand to one another, and if she will be a passenger, and why in that gown.

A laughing party troop up the gangway and divert her attention. Most of them are members of a stranded burlesque company, and they have come to say good-bye to the leading girl.

The doctor joins them, and the quiet girl, who takes life too seriously, listens with a touch of wistfulness to their chaff and quaint slang. She even admires the effect of their smartly cut clothes, and is not feminine enough to see how cheaply it is gained.

She is a great child in spite of her knowledge, and she envies these girls their gift of repartee and the ease with which they turn aside foolish compliments. She has had little experience of men – she does not get on with them very well. She has started with old-fashioned ideas as to their superiority; she is so desperately in earnest that she takes them too seriously, she fails to see how comic they are, and they find her a bore. She is having a lesson now, and she tells herself musingly: 'This is the secret: look pretty, laugh *à pleine gorge*,[3] if you have white teeth or dimples; smile up through your lashes if they are long; don't tax them, don't ask them to take you seriously; just amuse them, that must be the great thing, to amuse them.'

Meanwhile the bustle has increased; the odd people that crowd the deck of outward-bound vessels troop down the gangways. The cattle-jobbers laugh lustily and bandy jokes with friends on the wharf; the steam falls in feathery spray, with a suspicion of oil in it; and ear-splitting whistles call responsive bellows from the penned beasts below, and echo through the creak of grain-elevators and giant cranes, and the thousand vagrant sounds of the harbour.

The woman with the red bodice comes on deck; she steps to the girl's side and waves her hand to the man below. He raises his hat and goes, looking back as the carriage turns.

She is younger than a back view alone would lead one to think; she cannot be more than five and twenty; but there are fine lines about her eyes, they are circled with heavy indigo stains, and her lids are swollen with tears. She is dazzlingly fair, and the blue veins show in delicate tracery at her temples, her lips are crimson, and the under one is full, but her chin runs softly into her white throat.

The girl, endowed as she is with the passionate worship of beauty and the imagination that belong to Celtic ancestry, feels attracted to her, and yet repelled.

Off at last! She has watched the scene too often during her luncheon hour from the top of the great building in which she has worked to see any novelty in it; she goes down to find her cabin. It is dark, small, near the pantry, as befits a shabby girl who travels free. She arranges her few belongings and goes on deck. The smell of the cattle, for it is hot down there, and the hatch-ways are open, oozes forth and mingles with the briny smell of the sea, recalling childhood scenes – stretches of sandy dune melting into the grey-green sea, red-tiled homesteads, and lowing kine going home to be milked; and she realises that she has been home-sick unawares; that the old world has a glamour for her in its reverend age, far beyond the crude green youth of the new – the witchery of its great past, its dead in some of whom she has a share, who still live in her, making her what she is.

The first days pass as usual on a steamer of the kind; she sees nothing of the fair woman, but notices that the stewardess brings many empty bottles out of her cabin. It amuses her to watch people, it is almost like a play in which she is sole audience. Two maiden sisters take a fancy to her and have a daily talk. The little actress sings and plays, and the men cluster around her, but the doctor is first in favour.

Then the wind changed, places got vacant, and the 'fiddles'[4] appeared on the table, and early one morning they ran into the boisterous clutches of an autumn gale. Her cabin became unsupportable, the nauseous smell of paint and bilge-water made her sick; all the plate and crockery in the pantry next her seemed to shiver into atoms, and wash about her very ears; and sometimes the little silvery thread of light in the pear-shaped globe would dwindle to a red thread to plunge her suddenly into total darkness. She fought through her dressing, and the fresher air of the saloon revived her, and she crept up on to one of the lounges.

Stifled cries from the state-rooms mingle with the rattle of chains and howl of the wind. The steamer strains and groans like a huge beast in labour, and the screw rises and falls with a desperate thud. A second of suspensive quiet, and they sink into darkness with a sickening dive that turns her hot and cold with a feeling of melting; and the screw pops out of the water, and the steamer shudders, until they float up again, and it is struck by a giant wave with a crash like the deafening report of mighty cannon, terrific after the ghastly silence. A rush of hurried steps mingled with confused hoarse shouts overhead, and the trickle of water finding its way out again adds to the feeling of excitement.

The doctor passed through, and paused to give her a word of praise for her pluck, but a shout down the companion-way hurried him off to a man crushed in the cattle-pens. Sometimes in a lull in the tumult of wind and waves she fancied that she could hear terrified groans from the prisoned beasts. Then the stewardess disappeared, and the second steward answered the bells instead, and crept along the floor balancing brandy and biscuits. She fell into a troubled sleep to wake with a start, as if some one had called her. She sat up and listened; it is colder, darker, and the steamer labours more; the electric light is out, and a few lamps swing dismally to and fro. A stifled groan reaches her, and a voice moans in a cabin near her:

'O God, will no one come to me, I guess I'll die, my God, my God!' She got down and managed by waiting for the uprising swell to creep on her hands and knees towards it.

She pushed aside the curtain and went in; the golden-haired woman lay moaning in the lower berth; the bedclothes had fallen into a confused heap upon the floor, and she was uncovered, shivering with cold, her hair streaming out like amber drift-weed at every lurch; a trickle of blood ran from one of her white wrists. A diminutive pair of boots, an empty champagne bottle, fragments of glass and china, and an upturned tray slid noisily to and fro on the floor; an unopened bottle is propped with towels in the basin. The girl caught the empty one as it rolled towards her, and thrust it, with the other loose things, into the empty berth.

The woman is utterly helpless with terror and sickness, and the girl had to exert all her strength to lift her into a better position; she bound up her wrist and tucked the bedclothes and rug about her, and knelt down, holding fast to keep herself from slipping; but the smell of stale champagne and the closeness of the air made her feel faint, and she touched the bell.

The second steward answered it, muttering angrily as he pushed aside the curtain, but checked himself on seeing her there:

'Can you tidy up a little?' she asks hesitatingly, 'mop up the floor and straighten things?'

'I'll have a try, miss; the stewardess has sprained her wrist, and every one's ill. You just leave her to me, I'll fix her up, she's boozed' – with contempt – 'that's wot she is.'

'Don't leave me; O God, don't leave me!' whimpers the woman in terror, and her blue eyes stare wildly; and the girl, who has flushed at his words, pauses irresolutely and then goes back and kneels again.

'It can't matter,' she says to the youth; 'the poor thing is frightened, and perhaps I can do her some good.'

He tidies in silence, and later he brings her some sandwiches and tells her that the galley fires are out, and some men hurt, and one man washed overboard, and that the night promises to be no better than the day. He fixes her some cushions for her to kneel upon, and fetches a striped blanket and tucks it respectfully round her, with a look of ill-concealed disgust at the woman and resentment for her own sake. For her face reminds him of a little girl with whom he kept company down Wapping way, one whole glorious summer, until she got 'saved' and joined the 'army,'[5] and gave him up as unregenerate.

The woman moaned and cowered in terror, and once when there was a crash, and they were plunged in darkness, she put out her hand, and clutching the girl, besought her to pray.

The night passed slowly, but towards morning the gale abated, and the steamer rolled with long steady swings, and the woman fell asleep holding the girl's hand. The latter is cramped by her crouching position and nods wearily, but it never occurs to her to leave her post. At length she dozes and has a dream, in which dragons and leviathans[6] fight bloody battles, churning red-stained foam as they hurl islets at one another in their rage, whilst a mermaid with streaming golden tresses urges them on with a shrill voice like the scream of sea-mews.

The lad comes in the early dawn with some coffee, and tells her that the worst is over. She forces the woman to eat a little, and then finds a hair-brush; it is silver-backed, and brand new, as everything is, even the night things she is wearing, as if bought for the journey. She brushes the wonderful hair into a long shining braid, parts the fringe, and the uncurled hair, soft as raw silk, frames the temples chastely; the head and forehead and drooping white lids and pencilled brows have the delicacy of a Madonna by Ary Scheffer;[7] but the mouth cannot lie – the pout of the wine-red lips, the soft receding chin, and the strange indefinable expression that lurks about them rather fits a priestess of passion.

'I would paint her as Helen,'[8] thinks the girl, 'I wonder who she is, and why she sets out on a journey with a satin bodice and lace-flounced petticoats, and how old she is?' Her forehead is a child-girl's; her mouth a courtesan's of forty. She unclasps the hand that prisons hers, and considers it: hands tell age better than faces. It is white, pink-palmed, and satin-soft, the nails are manicured and polished as agates – twenty-five. She has been so alone that she has acquired a habit of observing closely things that happier women barely understand. She speculates and weaves stories about the people she meets; they strike her fancy as the characters in a book or a picture, and interest her always. She is saved, not knowing them, from finding their limitations.

The forenoon has dragged through before the woman awakens from her long restful sleep; she smiles up at the girl, and then a burning flush stains her face, and she turns it aside, and when it has ebbed away she looks back searchingly into the girl's grave eyes, and taking her hand kisses it closely and holds it to her cheek.

'You are better now, I can leave you, I am very tired,' says the girl.

'Yes,' letting go her hand; then with an impulse: 'Will you — ?'

'Yes?' a silence.

'Will I — ?'

'Will you? – ah, no matter – thank you – I guess you'd best go —,' and she turns her face to the wall.

The girl creeps to the top of the companion-way for a breath of fresh air. The sea still washes the after-deck, and sometimes a sheet of spray dashes over the bridge. A dismantled barque rides erratically on the right, and a piece of wreckage dances on the waves. Deep groans and a pained lowing rise from the hold, and a smell of steaming beasts blows with the wind; some sailors, in shining oilskins, are tipping a dead ox overboard. Her vivid imagination calls up horrid scenes of broken limbs under heavy swaying bodies, gored sides, and gouged eyes amongst the penned beasts below; and she descends with a shudder. She visits most of the cabins, and in an unobtrusive way shortens the time for the other women, but she does not go near the only one that really awakens her interest.

Two days pass, and then the little actress appears in a fascinating tea-gown; she is better, for she has curled her fringe and koholed her lashes, and the doctor is radiant. The maiden sisters come out with knitting-bags and Testaments, and the woman who travels in embroidery silks follows, and the man who quoted 'Rocked in the Cradle of the Deep'[9] the first evening, and sang nautical songs (in which 'yeo-ho' was the only intelligible word) in a brave manner, and collapsed at the first roll. They congratulate her as the only passenger with 'sea-legs,' and are very friendly, but when she speaks of the sufferings of the other woman, they purse their lips, look virtuous, and change the subject.

The girl is sitting in her favourite corner, and presently the woman, Mrs. Grey on the passenger-list, comes out with a novel and seats herself near her. In reply to the girl's shy query she flushes a little, says she is well, and begins to read; her eyelids are pink and swollen, her whole face is puffed as with much weeping.

The little actress plays for them, enthralls them with the spirit of music that is so often a birth-right of the children of Israel, witches, and warms, and saddens them, as Miriam[10] in olden days. They beg for their favourite songs, and once in a pause the woman, it is the first time she has spoken to any of them, asks for a serenade of Kjerulf.[11] There is a dead silence, every one looks round – the little actress very slowly – then, drawing herself up to her full height, she lets her black eyes travel coldly from the woman's head to her feet and up again, with the well-known air of affronted scorn with which she is wont to annihilate the villain in her best part, and turns away without replying.

The woman winces, the girl has winced more; she moves nearer and speaks to her, but the woman makes no reply; keeps her eyes on her book, and tries to brave it out. When a few minutes have passed, in which every one talks together, she goes back to her cabin; the bell rings sharply, and the steward answering it comes out calling to the second steward:

'A bottle of fizz for Mrs. Grey!'

She is seen no more that day.

Late the following evening the girl is up on deck watching the phosphor froth in the steamer's wake, and the moon playing hide-and-seek through a feathery maze of clouds. She is roused by *her* voice beside her:

'Have you heard when we arrive?'

'Yes, Saturday, if all goes well.'

'And this is Wednesday, oh, my God, my God, pity me!' (under her breath). 'If I were not such a coward' – with passionate emphasis – 'I'd just jump over right here into the middle of that shining streak. It would make a lovely shroud wouldn't it?' (with a laugh). She rests her hand on the girl's shoulder, and then her head, and rocks her shoulders as if in pain. The girl smoothes her hair silently.

'Why are you so good to me?' she asks suddenly.

'I don't know, because you are a woman, I suppose,

as I am —'

'I believe I'll go mad,' she cries, ruffling her hair back from her lovely wretched face. 'I must tell some one, my head is bursting; come down to my cabin later on, will you?'

'Yes, if it will help you in any way, yes.'

The head steward has been standing near them. He saunters up to the girl as the woman leaves her, and makes some remark about the fineness of the night; but he keeps his cap on, and has a cheap cigar stuck between his teeth; there is a familiar note, too, in his voice. Her look of grave surprise disconcerts him, and he moves off with a swagger. She has been conscious of a difference in her treatment for some days, a shrinking on the part of the women, a touch of insolence in the glance of the men. It hurts her a little.

It is late when she seeks the woman. She finds her crouched on the floor, with her head resting on her arms, that are crossed on the plush seat. She looks up as the girl enters.

'I don't know why I asked you to come,' she cries, 'except that I am so wretched, and you seem so sure of yourself. I am very miserable.'

'Poor woman' – with tenderness – 'don't tell me anything on impulse. Can't I help you without? Aren't you going to friends?'

She groans and buries her face in her hands.

'Is your husband in London, don't you want to go to him?'

'O, no, no,' she writhes, 'I am afraid. O God, what *will* I do?'

'But why? Listen to me, Mrs. Grey,' she says persuasively.

The woman lifts her head, her breath smells of brandy, and says:

'My name is Edith.'

'Isn't it Grey as well though – I thought —'

'No, I am called so, I am not really married —' There is a pause.

'Well, no matter. He looked upon you as his wife,

didn't he? He was good to you or you wouldn't be going to him.'

'He cabled for me, I have to go.'

'And you don't want to?' with a puzzled look. 'Don't you care about him?'

'I did when I was with him, but he left me. He shouldn't have, I implored him not,' with a wild gesture. 'Now he is angry, and I am afraid,' sobbing.

'But why, dear woman, what have you done? Tell me' – with hesitation – 'is it because of this?' pointing to a bottle.

The question seems to strike the woman in some ludicrous way, for she stifles an hysterical inclination to laughter, and replies shamefacedly:

'No, oh no, he docs not know I take anything, it isn't that.'

'Why do you? It shows so plainly, and people notice it, and it spoils you – you are so beautiful, it's such a pity –'

'I can't help myself – I want to forget – I used to nearly go mad, and so I began it, and now I can't do without it. I wasn't meant to be what I am, do believe me,' – with a pleading in her voice. 'I am not bad at heart, I don't care about it really, but I can't help it. I was only sixteen when he took me, I was a silly fool of a girl, and I had no one belonging to me. I thought it was a grand thing. Even his relatives didn't know I wasn't married to him. He petted and spoiled me, and dressed me like a doll, and whenever I wanted to learn anything he laughed at me. There were times when I wanted something better, I used to tire of it all: but I was always a little afraid of him; the set we mixed in was a fast one, and I learnt no good; and the women I met were worse than the men –'

'But he was really fond of you?'

'Yes, in a way. He loved my beauty, he was proud of my figure, and the admiration other men had for me. I had a very good time, and I enjoyed life, except sometimes when a fit came over me. I suppose I should have gone on like that for ever, only – I don't know why I should tell you this – there is something in you draws it out of

me – well, one day' – there is a sharper note in her voice
– 'I found I was going to have a little child. He was away
when I discovered it, and I was just crazy with delight –
I played with dolls until I was fifteen, you know. I used
to sit and think about it, and I wished he would come
home. I never was so glad. They're such cunning little
things, with such cute little ways, and,' – there is a touching pathos in her tear-stained face – 'when he did come
I flew to tell him —'

'Yes?'

'He was as angry as ever he could be; it was as if he
struck me sharply in the face. He said it would spoil me;
he didn't want it; it would make complications; he had no
intention of marrying me, we were quite well as we were
– we had a dreadful scene – he – well – I defied him for
the first time – I could have killed him, I hated him so –
I was almost mad, I wanted to run away, to be safe. Then
he pretended to be sorry, and I let him fool me' – clench-
ing her hands – 'fool me into thinking it was all right. He
took me to a quiet place in the country, asked me not to
write to any one about it, and I was to stay there till the
time came. I was quite content, I used to go into the woods
and listen to the birds, I was just as happy as I ever could
be. Then the time drew near, and we went up to town.
He took me to Madame Rachelle's. I thought it a little
strange, I had heard so many stories about her establishment; but he said I should be well taken care of, and
I was a fool in his hands, and too happy to trouble —'

Her face is set and her voice is bitter.

'They gave me some anaesthetic, and when I came
back to myself, as it seemed to me out of a rush of swirling
waters, I was lying, too weak to lift my hand, too confused
to call. But suddenly I did; it all came back to me in a
flash of consciousness, and I sat up and screamed, for I
had a presentiment of what it meant; and I beat with my
hands and called for my baby, – and that she-devil, curse
her! rushed in and held me down, and put a handkerchief
over my face, and I lost myself again, and I pretended to
be unconscious. My brain was in a whirl, and I fancied'
– her voice has sunk to a whisper, it is as if she is mut-

tering to herself – 'I could hear *it* cry, and that it wanted me so; I felt its tears on my breast, it was only my milk had come, and *that* made me think of the little baby head; and I felt as if my brain and heart would burst. I nearly went crazy. I got cunning, and when she bent over the bed I lay quite still and held my breath. She thought I was unconscious, and I watched her; she went into the dressing-room, and then a nurse called her hurriedly. She had many patients,' – with a laugh, – 'and she went away with her. I got up quickly, and by holding to things I managed to crawl to that room. I *had a feeling it was there.*' There is such a frenzy of passion in her voice, such a seal of despairing remembrance on her face, that the girl holds her breath in suspense.

'I got there and crawled in,...there was a bundle there —.' She chokes down a sob and her eyes flash fire. 'I felt my heart stop.... I snatched it up and unrolled it, and God curse them! it was my little one. I couldn't believe it was dead. I kissed it and tried to warm it, and I put it inside my nightgown between my breasts; and then I heard voices, and I rushed out and down the stairs. A nurse met me and tried to stop me, but I screamed and bit her hand. Then more came, and I felt everything grow black around me, and my little one melted like a lump of ice on my heart, and I knew no more.' There is a silence, both women are pale. 'When I came to my senses I was back in the country, and they told me I had been ill for months, and that I could never endure him to come near me.'

'You poor thing, you poor woman,' cries the girl; 'the brutes! I would have had them up for murder. I would never have rested —'

'So you think, but I guess you wouldn't. Money can do everything; the certificate of death said it was stillborn, and it was signed by a medical man. It was only last year the death of a schoolgirl of good family caused such scandal that the place was closed; but too many big people were implicated to make a fuss, and Madame Rachelle escaped. I went back to town and threw myself into every dissipation. He was glad; I *seemed* reconciled, but it haunted me. I could feel it at night groping about for me, and the chill of its poor little hands clung to me, and I used to drink to get warm again and forget it. I used to wonder if it cried when it came into the world, and if they hurt it. Can you think' – with piteous, hiccoughing sobs – 'how any one could hurt a little thing like that? or can you wonder I drink? I would have loved it so – I wanted something better than I had. I wasn't meant to be bad; you don't think I was – say you don't' – gazing eagerly into the girl's face, that is blanched by intense feeling.

'No, you poor woman, you were not meant to be bad. I think you were meant to be *very good*. I have known many women, and I think the *only divine* fibre in a woman is her maternal instinct. Every good quality she has is consequent or co-existent with that. Suppress it, and it turns to a fibroid, sapping all that is healthful and good in her nature, for I have seen it – we had many girls in the office.... Every woman ought to have a little child, if only as a moral educator. I have often thought that a woman who mothers a bastard, and endeavours bravely to rear it decently, is more to be commended than the society wife who contrives to shirk her motherhood. *She* is at heart loyal to the finest fibre of her being, the deep, underlying generic instinct, the "mutterdrang,"[12] that lifts her above and beyond all animalism, and fosters the sublimest qualities of unselfishness and devotion. No, indeed, you poor woman, you are not bad; you are, perhaps, just as God intended you!'

Her cheeks burn with the vehemence of her words, and a tear hangs on her lashes.

'But drink will not help you, believe me; work might –'

'But what could I do? I can't put a stitch in my clothes. I haven't learnt a single useful thing. I know how to attract men' – with bitterness – 'that is all.'

'Have you ever told him how you felt, spoken to him frankly? After all, he was good to you in a way; he must be touched by it. Try it when you meet him, dear! Let him see the real woman, as you have let me!'

Her words have a startling effect; the woman's face changes, a look of terror and the remembrance of something momentarily forgotten gathers upon it; she hides her face, and rocks impatiently with moaning cries.

'It's no use, no use; it's too late. My God, what is to become of me? You don't know all; you never could understand; you are strong, you don't know what reckless passion means – if you only knew you would go away, you wouldn't touch me. O God! O God!'

She has slid on to the floor, and kneels, wringing her hands and crying, the girl looking helplessly down at her.

'Try me,' she says, 'I promise you I won't go away. What are you afraid to tell him? what else is there?'

'What else?' she groans, stretching out her hands, 'the worst that could be. He had to go to Europe a year ago. I begged him to take me with him. I knew how it would be if I were left; I had no occupation, and the child haunted me! I drank to kill it; it made me reckless, and he was the only check. But he said he couldn't take me; he wouldn't. I tried to tell him what I felt, but I was afraid. And now a letter was written to him about me, and he cabled to me to sail by this steamer – my passage was taken – or never see him again. I was not at home; the cable was sent after me; I had only time to catch the train for the boat, without clothes or anything. I wired for my things to be sent, but they did not come in time, and I had to get some before I came on board. I know him so well; he will never forgive me, and I am afraid to face him, and I have hardly any money.'

'But I don't understand. What was written to him? Who wrote?'

'Oh, a woman, of course. She got to know things; she likes him.'

'Well, but can't you explain? isn't it something you can tell him?'

The golden head shakes a dismal denial; and a tortured moan is the only reply.

'Tell *me*, then; two heads are better than one.'

'You saw' – the girl has to stoop to catch the words – 'that man who came with me?'

'Yes.'

'He is my husband's cousin; he owes everything to

him. Well, it...it...*was with him* – he used to come to see me; he didn't admire me...not a bit...I was lonely and wretched, and I don't know what madness possessed me – you can't understand. One just gets insane, and lets oneself be carried away. I think the devil gets hold of one. I tried to attract him; there was a kind of excitement in it,...and...well, we let ourselves drift...' – she has grown calmer as she speaks – 'and afterwards, when we thought of him, we felt like shooting ourselves. He cried like a child and cursed me, and I hated him; but that soon passed over – we grew reckless, and sometimes we quarrelled and said good-bye; then we felt miserable, and sought one another again, and' – with a musing air – 'all through there was a kind of fascination in the danger, though we didn't really care a bit for one another.'

The girl is dumb with pained realisation; it is her first actual contact with a problem of such a nature, and so little does she grasp it that she says:

'It's dreadful, but you must tell him the truth. You see he sends for you in spite of all, and, besides, he first taught you to...to...be as you are; he must remember that. He shouldn't have left you to yourself; you were beautiful and wretched; you must tell him —'

The woman cowers lower; her hair has come undone and covers her shoulders like a tawny golden garment.

'I can't,' she groans hoarsely; '*that was a year ago...since*...Oh, I can't tell you – I can't! Better go, far better go! you can't help me – no one can —'

'*Since?*' repeats the girl, with stark-white lips and horror-filled eyes, '*since?*'

'*There was some one else.* You don't know what it is to have nothing to hold one back. I had no control over myself, something used to possess me; it is always like that, *one stifles the memory of the first with the excitement of the second.* Afterwards I wanted to kill myself straight away, that is God's truth, but I was afraid.'

There is a long silence, only the woman cries with stifled groans of crushing misery; and the girl listens as if in a confused, horrible dream to the sobs that shake the bowed figure at her feet, for she has risen, and is standing at the door, holding the curtain with one hand. Something in the crouching figure, with the rippling waves of hair falling about her in a glory of colour, recall to her the beautiful story of tender pity for such another;[13] and the simple great words of it repeat themselves in her inner soul, and the lesson comes home to her, and she goes back, and, stooping, clasps her arms about the heaving shoulders of the woman at her feet, and says, with her heart breaking her voice:

'Hush, hush, Edith, sister! look at me!'

The woman obeys with incredulous look, and then buries her face in the girl's lap, saying:

'I am not worth it, indeed I am not. I am sure you —'

'Think nothing. I have no right to sit in judgment; I have never been tempted. I simply can't understand it. I am as ready to help you now as before, if I only can —'

'You say that, but' – lifting her head and searching the grave white face – 'would you kiss me?'

The girl bends her head, but the woman drops to the floor with a sharp 'No, no,' and hides her face in the girl's gown, with the tears streaming down her cheeks.

They talk late, and the girl soothes her. She promises not to drink for the remaining days, and a spark of hope flickers up in her weak soul, and the girl, to whom no one any longer speaks, spends most of her time with her.

Saturday morning early they go up on deck and watch the fleet of fishing smacks, with their ochre-red sails, and the low land, shrouded in silver mists, that looks as if a big wave might wash it away. And the sound of bells floats out to them, and further up the river the blast of foghorns, and the shriek of whistles, and the rumbling hum of the city mingle in a great symphony. The beasts below divine the nearness of the land in some subtle way; perhaps they scent the brackish grass, for they low deeply; and the steamer creeps steadily up the Thames with the warehouses looming at its waters' side, as the spectre buildings in a land of shadow.

They watch it together. Her long travelling cloak barely covers her light gown, though the girl has pinned it up. Tears and emotions have chastened her face and effaced the traces of passion and debauch. She is filled with good intentions and the hope of a chance to do better. She trembles a little as they near the dock, and scans the crowd that awaits them.

'No,' she says, 'he is not there!'

A youth, a typical London clerk, with knowing eyes and assured manner, is one of the first to come on deck. He inquires for Mrs. Grey, hands her a letter, and waits. She turns her back to the inquisitive gaze of the stewardess and women, opens it and reads; and the girl watches her with a feeling of trouble. It crosses her mind as she watches her, that she has often scoffed at novelists, when they spoke of people turning to stone, but that now she realises this meaning; for there is a curious change in the woman's face; it is grey, and hard, as if every atom of life and feeling are being killed by the action of some petrifying fluid, working from inside; and the gold of her hair seems to stand out from it as a wig on a stone face, and her flesh changes to what children call 'goose skin.'

She folds the letter carefully; turns, grips the girl's arm, and says thickly:

'It's no good, I can't do it – I know myself too well, it is impossible – I am lost. This letter, this simple written thing, has damned me as surely as if I were already in hell. If,' – with a sudden gust of passion shaking her from head to foot – 'if I knew the address of a good fast house, I'd drive straight to it; you are a good, good woman, but say good-bye to me now, and God, if there be such a being' – with a little laugh – 'bless you! But if ever you meet me, if ever you see me in the street or elsewhere, never speak to me, or try to stop me, for if you do, by Christ, I'll throw myself under the first horse's feet.'

'Come downstairs, Edith, I can't let you go so,' pleads the girl, and she leads her by the hand. They pass through the crowd that scans their stricken faces curiously, and the girl takes the letter and reads it. It is cold, pitiless, the letter of a man with iron will, wounded in his pride. She is to go with bearer to his lawyer's, he will tell her what she is to do. She need not write to him, for he will be on his way to China when this reaches her. All her future good treatment will depend on her implicit obedience. She will be driven to rooms and supplied with all necessities; but, she is not to write to any one, or see any one, neither must she go out except under the escort of the woman in charge of her; and if she require money she must state in writing to his solicitor for what purpose. If at the end of three months, her behaviour has been satisfactory, he will consider what steps to take for her future.

No fanatical inquisitor of the middle ages, acquainted with the secret recesses of the human soul, knowing where to touch the most sensitive place, could have calculated more fiendishly.

The girl's heart burns as she reads; she knows it is the death of the woman standing with the hardness of despair on her set face. She has probed into the depths of her nature, and she sees the impossibility of it. Yet she says, feeling the want of conviction in her own words:

'You must try to do it – it is hard – cruelly hard, but you must try to endure it.'

And for answer the woman laughs, and at that the girl breaks down and pats her cold hands, only to drop them and throw her arms round her, pleading:

'When you have seen this man, if you can't do it, wire to me, won't you promise me, Edith dear? Promise to send for me, I'll come, indeed I will, no matter where you are. I'll wait all day and Monday too for a message, only promise!'

The woman takes her face, and framing it with her hands says:

'Forget me, little sister, good, kind, little sister, except when you pray. And now kiss me good-bye.'

They kiss one another, the girl with tears drenching her face, and the woman goes up, and she and the youth walk down the gangway and she never looks back once, though the girl strains her eyes to see the last of her. And when the weary customs have been gone through, the women, seeing the girl had bidden her good-bye, come and advise her for her own good to be careful. She repulses them savagely, for she is unstrung and her heart burns hotly; but when the little maiden ladies come timidly, with chaste tears in their eyes, perhaps for the sake of these she says more gently to them:

'She is a lost soul, *I* tried to do what I could for her. You are old, the others were married, you had nothing to lose, and yet you held back. It is good, untempted women like you, whose virtue makes you selfish, who help to keep women like her as they are.'

*   *   *   *   *

She waited anxiously for a message; none came. Gradually her new work engrossed her thoughts, only sometimes when the bus that carried her home after a late day's work pulled up in Leicester Square, that rendez-vous of leering, silk-hatted satyrs and flaunting nymphs of the pavement, where the frou-frou of silk mingles with the ring of artificial laughter, the glitter of paste with the hec-tic of paint, where the very air is tainted with patchouli, and souls sensitive to the psychometry of things shiver with the feel of passional atoms vibrating through the at-mosphere of the great pairing ground of this city of smug outer propriety; sometimes there, where the foot-walk is crowded with the 'fallen leaves' of fairest and frailest wom-anhood, like wild rose leaves blown by a wanton wind into a sty, she would think of her again; then she would scan fearsomely the faces of the women who thronged there with dreadful asking eyes; and every gleam of golden hair would set her heart throbbing, to recognise with relief it is not *hers*. The dreadful problem of her fate, and the ultimate fate of all these others would weigh on the soul of the girl; and the question of the justice of the arrange-ment beat insistently in her tired brain, and the hateful query force itself, With how many of them is this life just selection?

And so three years passed on and brought her a meas-ure of success, and the content patient work sometimes brings. People said she was better looking – she was simply better dressed. She was not the less lonely, not the less sad, for her sympathy with human suffering was no wise blunted, her sense of its inevitability perhaps increased. Fanciful folk who met her in the streets, such as poets and painters and Irishmen, drew inspiration from her sombre gaze and tender mouth.

Then one bitter winter's day as she stands waiting for her bus in Cornhill, a novelty vendor, a man with a strident voice, shrieks in her ear: "Ave you seen the larfin' baiby? Only one penny! See the larfin' baiby! They *all* larf! 'ow to maike the baiby larf! Wot a baiby!'

She boards her bus with the words ringing in her brain, and out of the jangled echoes a memory rises, bringing *her* face. 'Perhaps I shall see her,' she muses, for it is odd that when a person one has forgotten completely crops up in one's mind, and one wonders why one thinks of them on this particular day, a turn of a street corner sometimes brings an answer in person.

Late that night she says good-bye to a friend at the door of the College of Medicine for women, and turns her steps towards her lodgings. It has been raining, and the streets are encrusted with glass-like particles of frozen snow, a searching north-east wind rattles the blackened branches of the skeleton trees, and chills the thinly clad to the marrow. A fit of desperate coughing draws her attention to a woman holding on to the railings opposite; the abject misery of the shaken figure awakes her keenest pity. As the last hollow cough dies out in a moan, the woman clutches her breast and groans out a curse on her misery and shuffles on. Her rain-soaked skirt clings to her legs, a piece of torn frill at the back drabbles in the mud, and slops round her feet at every step. The tattered remains of a smartly cut summer jacket is her only wrap, except a dishevelled rag of a feather boa that flutters futilely in the wind, and yet there is a trace of the peculiar grace that accompanies perfect proportion of limbs.

Obeying an uncontrollable impulse, the girl turns back and follows her. As the woman passes the gates of the old graveyard where a daughter of Cromwell sleeps under a conical stone, and children peg tops[14] round forgotten graves, the hanging lamp of the Baptist Chapel next the entrance flickers over her, and the glint of golden hair under a ragged old toque catches the girl's eye and sends her heart fluttering to her throat. She hurries on, determined to pass her, to make sure, and then wait for her; she is breathless with suspense, she sees her plainly as she pauses under the lamp at the corner of Compton Street, and a stifled cry of horror bursts through the girl's lips.

What a wreck! What a face! What a mask of the tragedy of passion, and sin, and the anguish of despair! Phthisis[15] and drink have run riot together; have wasted her frame, hollowed her cheeks, puffed her eyelids, dried the dreadful purple lips and soddened the soul within. The girl follows the shambling steps with dry wide eyes and painful heart thud. A loafer at the corner says something to the woman as she passes, she answers him with a toss of head, and a peal of ribald laughter, that is worse to hear than a tortured cry; it brings on another fit of coughing, and the pity of it stirs the girl's heart again, and the feeling of sudden loathing that has possessed her gives way to a diviner impulse of compassion.

She hurries on, crosses over, and, turning back, meets her; there is barely a yard between them, her face is alight with tender feeling; the woman looks up and sees her; she pauses for the space of a second with a vivid brightening of her dull eyes, as when one strikes a light in a darkened room; then, as the eager 'Edith, sister!' reaches her, she flings up one arm wildly to hide her face, thrusts out the other to ward the girl off and sobs out, 'Oh, oh, no not that!' with a wailing moan. Then she swerves quickly into the street, still shielding her face, and breaks into a mad run; her wet skirt impedes her wavering steps and her poor rags flutter in the sharp wind, and, maddened by memory perhaps, she utters a shriek that startles the passers-by and brings faces to the upper windows, and cuts into the girl's soul to haunt it ever more like the fancied echo of the laughter of hell.

A policeman at the turn to Harrison Street walks towards her as he hears it; she screams hoarsely at him with the defiance of reckless despair, twice, thrice, never slackening her speed; further on, at a turning near Gray's Inn

Road, she stumbles, and falls heavily, but she picks herself up with lightning speed and scuds on again with a cough-broken curse; the girl halts when she reaches the corner where the woman fell in her flight, and peers down the dark street. It seems to her that it yawns like a long narrow grave or the passage to a charnel house. The only sign of life in it is a famished cat scraping at something in a rubbish heap. She has disappeared into the night as she came, into the night of despair that leads to death; and as the girl stepped back her foot struck against something, and stooping she picked it up – a frayed, mud-soaked, satin shoe – it is small, and once was a delicate rose.

To her to whom life had brought a deep under-standing of its misery and makeshifts, it is a mute epitome of a tragedy of want; and through her great agony of dis-tress the narrow practical question forced itself in a comi-cally persistent way: Had the poor weary foot without this frail covering even the sorry shelter of a stocking to pro-tect it? And facing homewards through the biting wind, with the lamp gleams shining through the dusky mists of the London night, like gorse blooms when the valley is in shadow, she holds it to her breast. What fell upon it as she turned? A raindrop or a tear?

Notes

1   Laurence Sterne (1713-68), novelist, best known for *Tristram Shandy* (1759-67).
2   Long loose overcoat of rough cloth.
3   Literally full-throated, used in the sense of shouting at the top of one's lungs.
4   Contrivances for stopping things rolling off the tables in bad weather.
5   Salvation Army.
6   Sea monsters.
7   Ary Scheffer (1795-1858). Court painter at Amsterdam best known for his religious paintings and his illustrations of scenes from Goethe, Byron, and Dante.

8   In Greek legend, Helen is the daughter of Zeus and Leda and the wife of Menelaus. Renowned for her beauty, she eloped with Paris and this precipitated the Trojan war.

9   Emma Willard (1787-1870). Teacher and writer. The title poem of her 1831 collection, *The Cradle of the Deep*, was set to music by Joseph P. Knight.

10   Miriam, sister of Moses and Aaron, was known as "the prophetess." Exodus 15:20-21.

11   Halfdan Kjerulf. (1815-1868). Norwegian composer who wrote many nationalistic songs.

12   Maternal instinct.

13   She is recalling the story of the unnamed penitent woman, popularly associated with Mary Magdalene, whose sins Christ pardoned when she anointed his feet and wiped them with her hair. Luke 7:37-48.

14   Toy, usually conical or spherical, which rotates on sharp point at bottom when set in motion by hand or by pulling a string.

15   Progressive wasting disease, especially pulmonary tuberculosis.

Source: *Discords*. London: John Lane, 1894.

Biographical Note

Daughter of an Australian sea captain, Egerton was born in Melbourne in December 1859. Privately educated, she worked at a variety of occupations before eloping to Norway with her father's friend, Henry Higginson, in 1887. Higginson, who was violent, a drunkard, and a bigamist, died two years later. The Scandinavian realists with whom she associated during this period—Ola Hansson, Knut Hamsun and others—were to have a great influence on her writing. In 1890, in London and translating Hamsun's *Hunger*, she entered into another disastrous liaison, this time with a Newfoundlander, George Egerton Clairmonte, and moved to Ireland. To support her idle husband, Egerton began writing short stories. John Lane of the Bodley Head was planning a series of short works by new writers and her *Keynotes*

(1893) came at an opportune moment. The book was so successful that Lane appropriated the title as the name for his series. Both *Keynotes* and *Discords*, which followed in 1894, drew extensively upon Egerton's own relationships, and created a sensation in the late Victorian literary world for their frank exploration of female sexuality. In 1895, Egerton had a son; soon after Clairmonte left her and went to America. After their divorce, Egerton met and married Reginald Golding Bright, a journalist and theatrical agent fifteen years younger than she. The quality of her work—and her reputation—soon declined as she tried her hand at drama. Her later collections of stories, *Symphonies* (1897) and *Fantasias* (1898), moved towards the allegorical and utopian. Three novels followed: *The Wheel of God* (1898), *Rosa Amorosa: The Love Letters of a Woman* (1901), and *Flies in Amber* (1905).

Egerton's stories are particularly notable for their frank discussions of women's sexuality and women's desire for power and freedom. Like many of the New Women writers of the time, she reacted strongly against the social conditioning that left women so constrained by an artificial morality. In such stories as "A Crossline" she celebrated instead "the eternal wildness, the untamed primitive savage temperament that lurks in the mildest, best woman. Deep in through ages of convention," she wrote, "this primeval trait burns—an untamable quantity that may be concealed but is never eradicated by culture, the keynote of women's witchcraft and woman's strength" (*Keynotes* 22). Female psychology was Egerton's main interest, and in stories like "Gone Under" she dealt openly with such subjects as alcoholism, prostitution, and promiscuity. Other stories of particular interest include "Wedlock," for its devastating portrait of marriage, and "Virgin Soil" for its bitter protest against the overly protective attitude that left women so totally unprepared for sexual life. As the satirical skits published in *Punch*—"She-Notes" by "Borgia Smudgiton"—suggest, Egerton's style of writing was as shocking and innovative as her subject matter; *Punch* made little effort to change the style—it was considered already comic enough. As an early female modernist,

Egerton used many of the techniques later to be developed in the twentieth century. Her short stories are particularly notable for their episodic, impressionistic presentation, and almost complete lack of interest in causality.

Selected Modern Reprints:

"A Keynote to *Keynotes.*" *Ten Contemporaries: Notes Toward Their Definitive Bibliography.* Ed. John Gawsworth. London, Benn, 1932.

A Leaf from the Yellow Book: The Correspondence of George Egerton. Ed. Terence de Vere White. London: Richards P, 1958.

Keynotes. 1893. New York: Garland, 1992.

Keynotes and Discords Ed. Martha Vicinus. London: Virago, 1983.

The Wheel of God. 1898. New York: AMS P, 1992.

Selected Secondary Sources:

Bjorhovde, Gerd. *Rebellious Structures: Women Writers and the Crisis of the Novel. 1880-1900.* Oslo: Norwegian UP, 1987.

Cunningham, A.R. "The 'New Woman Fiction' of the 1890s." *Victorian Studies* 18.2 (1973): 177-86.

Harris, Wendell V. "Egerton: Forgotten Realist." *Victorian Newsletter* 33 (1968): 31-35.

—. "John Lane's Keynotes Series and the Fiction of the 1890s." *PMLA* 83.5 (1968): 1407-13.

Stetz, Margaret D. "Turning Points: 'George Egerton.'" *Turn of the Century Women* 1.1 (1984): 2-3.

Vicinus, Martha. "Rediscovering the 'New Woman' of the 1890s: The Stories of 'George Egerton.'" *Feminist Re-Visions: What Has Been and Might Be.* Ed. Vivian Patraka and Louise A. Tilly. Ann Arbor, MI: U of Michigan P, 1983.

222   ANNIE HOWELLS FRÉCHETTE (1844-1938)

Annie Howells Fréchette (1844-1938)

A Widow in the
Wilderness

TWO MEN WERE STANDING UPON THE SHORE OF A FAR WESTERN lake, which, stretching away for many a mile, is lost in the dimness of late afternoon. Its surface was unbroken by any sign of human life, save a tiny canoe which glided silently across the sinking sun.

One of the two men was the factor of the Hudson Bay post which was just at hand; the other had in charge the exploring party whose canoes were drawn up on the beach for the night. More than half of his life had been spent in the wilds of Canada, and his trained eye never missed an unusual sight or sound.

"Whose canoe is that?" he asked of the factor as he let fall the hand under which he had been focusing his gaze.

The factor watched the canoe till it slid past the sun's disc into the shadows. "It must belong to the widow of Pierre. You remember, don't you, the one-eyed Indian who worked for you last summer? He died last winter, and that must be his widow. They had their camp near the end of the lake, and she often fishes there. She'll have a hard time this winter — poor thing. As you go past her camp to-morrow you had better stop and see how she is off — and advise her to go nearer her people."

The next day the party broke camp and paddled across the lake. On the western shore lay an old bark canoe, scarcely holding together, yet evidently trusted as sea-worthy, as its damp sides showed that it had just been drawn from the water. On the brow of the low bluff overlooking the lake stood a tent, brown and weather-stained. Its ragged sides flapped in the breeze, which already had the chill of autumn in it as it came over the thousand miles of wilderness and rippled the lake in long lines upon the narrow beach.

In front of the tent sat an Indian woman holding a baby to her breast, and grouped around her stood four tiny dusky children watching the canoes as they rounded in to shore. The chief engineer went up the slope to the woman. She lifted her eyes when he stood beside her, and said "Goo'-day," copying, as she had caught it, the Englishman's usual salutation. Then she was silent. The nursing baby turned from the brown breast and looked up with listless eyes which seemed to fill the wan little face. Then it stretched out its thin clawlike hand and clutched his finger.

"Your baby is sick," he said, in the woman's own language.

"Yes; it has been sick all its life."

"It is not nourished," he went on, taking the starved child into his arms. Years before, he had been a physician, and the healing instinct had never left him. "You have no food for it."

"We have fish."

"Do you remember me?"

"Yes; you were here last year."

"And your husband is dead?"

"Yes; he died last winter."

"Were you alone with him?"

"Yes; I buried him."

She had not spoken to any one but her children for weeks; but now, when suddenly one stood before her who belonged to happier days, she showed neither surprise nor pleasure nor pain.

"And what are you going to do?"

"I will stay. I fish."

"But you cannot live in that tent; your children will die this winter if you stay."

She turned and looked at the dingy mass of rags, but made no answer.

"Have you any food?"

"We have fish."

"But for the winter?"

"I will trap rabbits."

The nibbled bark and branches of the stunted trees of the surrounding country had shown the surveyors how the rabbits gathered their food, four or five feet from the ground, from the snow's surface.

"You must go to your own people or to one of the posts. What would become of your children if you were to die?"

Her sombre eyes wandered over her children.

"Yes," she answered, stolidly.

The sick baby had sunk to sleep, and was drawing the long, peaceful breaths of that perfect rest which a weak creature enjoys when held in strong arms. The good man looked at the shadowy face against his arm, and thought of his children at home.

"I will leave you food. We are starting back east, and I have more supplies than we need. I will bring some things tomorrow, enough for the present, but you must not stay here alone this winter."

He laid the baby in her arms and went back to his men. She watched the canoes as long as she could see them, then she and her children went into their tent.

The next morning the men began to pack their canoes in preparation for their homeward journey. Into one they put a strong new tent, a pair of warm blankets, bags of flour, sugar, tea, and coffee, sides of savory bacon, and numerous cans of food.

"She'll need clothes too," said their chief. "We'll throw in any coats and trousers we can spare. She'll need them this winter if she has to struggle through the snow to set her traps."

Each man contributed some unfeminine garment, and they started. As they neared the widow's camp they could see her fishing, with her gaunt children crouched about her in her old canoe. She received them with her stolid greeting of "goo'-day," and watched them as they set up her tent and stored her provisions. And when her good friend recalled his doctor's lore and left some simple remedies for the sick child, she promised to use them faithfully. But if she felt any gratitude, none showed itself through the taciturn training of her race; yet the hardy fellows worked with willing hands and aching hearts.

The short day was well advanced when they once more struck their paddles into the cold water of the lake and slipped away from the shore toward civilization. As they looked back they could see Pierre's widow with the sick baby in her arms, and the children squatting upon the edge of the cliff, with the pale yellow leaves drifting from the sparse wood about them.

Source: *Harper's Magazine* 100. Dec-May 1899-1900

Biographical Note

Annie Howells Fréchette was born in Hamilton, Ontario on March 29, 1844, the daughter of William Cooper Howells, a struggling newspaper publisher. When she was five, the family moved to America, eventually settling in Jefferson, Ohio. Here she attended school and, inspired by the example of her brother William, assistant editor for *Atlantic Monthly*, began to establish herself as a journalist with feature articles in the *Sentinel*. In January 1867 she visited her brother and his wife in Cambridge, Massachusetts; here she met Longfellow and Henry James, and had her first children's story, "Frightened Eyes," accepted for publication in *Our Young Folks*. In 1868 she started to produce a series of travel letters concerning Lake Erie ports for the *Cincinnati Chronicle* and also began travelling in Canada. She became a book reviewer, first in Chicago and then in Boston, and began having more success with short stories for adults. When her father obtained the position of American consul at Quebec City, however, she moved with him back to Canada where she could live more economically while continuing her freelance writing. Her only novel, *Reuben Dale*, serialized in *The Galaxy* from December 1875 to April 1876, is the story of an American girl who marries a widower twenty years her senior and then falls in love with a handsome young army officer. It was not a success, and the publishers declined to bring it out in book form. At the end of 1875, she met Achille Fréchette, a translator for the Canadian House of Commons and the brother of the French-Canadian poet Louis Fréchette; two years later they married and settled in Ottawa. In 1877 she began collaborating with the Spanish consul, Count Premio-Real, on a book of *Popular Sayings from Old Iberia*, and one of her short stories, "A Visit to a Country House," appeared in the September issue of *Harper's*. After her marriage, Fréchette gave up her newspaper work and concentrated on magazine fiction. She had two children, Marie-Marguérite, in 1878, and Howells, in 1879. Over the next few years, she wrote six stories about children, based on her own experiences; two collections, *On Grandfather's Farm* and *The Farm's Little People* appeared in 1897. The books were not well distributed and consequently failed to achieve much success, but Fréchette continued to draw an audience for her newspaper and magazine writings. "McDonald and Company, Builders," the story of a contractor devastated by the death of his son and then brought out of his depression by his assertive young daughter, appeared in *Harper's* in 1888, while, "How Cassie Saved the Spoons" and "The Jones's Telephone" appeared in *McClure's* magazine in September and October of 1893 respectively. Fréchette became a familiar figure in Ottawa literary circles, and her visitors included Pauline Johnson, the part-Mohawk princess and nature poet, and Sara Jeannette Duncan, at this time a journalist for the Toronto *Star*; she was also acquainted with Archibald Lampman and Duncan Campbell Scott. "A Widow in the Wilderness" reveals the influence of Scott's vignettes of Indian life. In 1910, the Fréchettes retired and settled in Lausanne, Switzerland. In 1919 they returned to Canada and spent the next two years in Ottawa; Achille's declining health eventually prompted them to move to Victoria, British Columbia, and then to San Diego, California, where he died. Fréchette remained in San Diego where she lived with her sister and her daughter until her death eleven years later at the age of ninety four.

Selected Secondary Sources:

Doyle, James. *Annie Howells and Achille Fréchette*. Toronto: U of Toronto P, 1979.

Mary E. Wilkins.

Mary Wilkins Freeman (1852-1930)

A New England Nun

IT WAS LATE IN THE AFTERNOON, AND THE LIGHT WAS WANING. There was a difference in the look of the tree shadows out in the yard. Somewhere in the distance cows were lowing and a little bell was tinkling; now and then a farm-wagon tilted by, and the dust flew; some blue-shirted laborers with shovels over their shoulders plodded past; little swarms of flies were dancing up and down before the peoples' faces in the soft air. There seemed to be a gentle stir arising over everything for the mere sake of subsidence – a very premonition of rest and hush and night.

This soft diurnal commotion was over Louisa Ellis also. She had been peacefully sewing at her sitting-room window all the afternoon. Now she quilted her needle carefully into her work, which she folded precisely, and laid in a basket with her thimble and thread and scissors. Louisa Ellis could not remember that ever in her life she had mislaid one of these little feminine appurtenances, which had become, from long use and constant association, a very part of her personality.

Louisa tied a green apron round her waist, and got out a flat straw hat with a green ribbon. Then she went into the garden with a little blue crockery bowl, to pick some currants for her tea. After the currants were picked she sat on the back door-step and stemmed them, collecting the stems carefully in her apron, and afterwards throwing them into the hen-coop. She looked sharply at the grass beside the step to see if any had fallen there.

Louisa was slow and still in her movements; it took her a long time to prepare her tea; but when ready it was set forth with as much grace as if she had been a veritable guest to her own self. The little square table stood exactly in the centre of the kitchen, and was covered with a starched linen cloth whose border pattern of flowers glistened. Louisa had a damask napkin on her tea-tray, where were arranged a cut-glass tumbler full of teaspoons, a silver cream-pitcher, a china sugar-bowl, and one pink china cup and saucer. Louisa used china every day – something which none of her neighbors did. They whispered about it among themselves. Their daily tables were laid with common crockery, their sets of best china stayed in the parlor closet, and Louisa Ellis was no richer nor better bred than they. Still she would use the china. She had for her supper a glass dish full of sugared currants, a plate of little cakes, and one of light white biscuits. Also a leaf or two of lettuce, which she cut up daintily. Louisa was very fond of lettuce, which she raised to perfection in her little garden. She ate quite heartily, though in a delicate, pecking way; it seemed almost surprising that any considerable bulk of the food should vanish.

After tea she filled a plate with nicely baked thin corn-cakes, and carried them out into the back-yard.

"Caesar!" she called. "Caesar! Caesar!"

There was a little rush, and the clank of a chain, and a large yellow-and-white dog appeared at the door of his tiny hut, which was half hidden among the tall grasses and flowers. Louisa patted him and gave him the corn-cakes. Then she returned to the house and washed the tea-things, polishing the china carefully. The twilight had deepened; the chorus of the frogs floated in at the open window wonderfully loud and shrill, and once in a while a long sharp drone from a tree-toad pierced it. Louisa took off her green gingham apron, disclosing a shorter one of pink and white print. She lighted her lamp, and sat down again with her sewing.

In about half an hour Joe Dagget came. She heard his heavy step on the walk, and rose and took off her pink-and-white apron. Under that was still another – white linen with a little cambric edging on the bottom; that was Louisa's company apron. She never wore it without her calico sewing apron over it unless she had a guest. She had barely folded the pink and white one with methodical haste and laid it in a table-drawer when the door opened and Joe Dagget entered.

He seemed to fill up the whole room. A little yellow canary that had been asleep in his green cage at the south window woke up and fluttered wildly, beating his little yellow wings against the wires. He always did so when Joe Dagget came into the room.

"Good-evening," said Louisa. She extended her hand with a kind of solemn cordiality.

"Good-evening, Louisa," returned the man, in a loud voice.

She placed a chair for him, and they sat facing each other, with the table between them. He sat bolt-upright, toeing out his heavy feet squarely, glancing with a good-humored uneasiness around the room. She sat gently erect, folding her slender hands in her white-linen lap.

"Been a pleasant day," remarked Dagget.

"Real pleasant," Louisa assented, softly. "Have you been haying?" she asked, after a little while.

"Yes, I've been haying all day, down in the ten-acre lot. Pretty hot work."

"It must be."

"Yes, it's pretty hot work in the sun."

"Is your mother well to-day?"

"Yes, mother's pretty well."

"I suppose Lily Dyer's with her now?"

Dagget colored. "Yes, she's with her," he answered, slowly.

He was not very young, but there was a boyish look about his large face. Louisa was not quite as old as he, her face was fairer and smoother, but she gave people the impression of being older.

"I suppose she's a good deal of help to your mother," she said, further.

"I guess she is; I don't know how mother'd get along without her," said Dagget, with a sort of embarrassed warmth.

"She looks like a real capable girl. She's pretty-looking too," remarked Louisa.

"Yes, she is pretty fair looking."

Presently Dagget began fingering the books on the table. There was a square red autograph album, and a Young Lady's Gift-Book which had belonged to Louisa's mother. He took them up one after the other and opened them; then laid them down again, the album on the Gift-Book.

Louisa kept eying them with mild uneasiness. Finally she rose and changed the position of the books, putting the album underneath. That was the way they had been arranged in the first place.

Dagget gave an awkward little laugh. "Now what difference did it make which book was on top?" said he.

Louisa looked at him with a deprecating smile. "I always keep them that way," murmured she.

"You do beat everything," said Dagget, trying to laugh again. His large face was flushed.

He remained about an hour longer, then rose to take leave. Going out, he stumbled over a rug, and trying to recover himself, hit Louisa's work-basket on the table, and knocked it on the floor.

He looked at Louisa, then at the rolling spools; he ducked himself awkwardly toward them, but she stopped him. "Never mind," said she; "I'll pick them up after you're gone."

She spoke with a mild stiffness. Either she was a little disturbed, or his nervousness affected her, and made her seem constrained in her effort to reassure him.

When Joe Dagget was outside he drew in the sweet evening air with a sigh, and felt much as an innocent and perfectly well-intentioned bear might feel after his exit from a china shop.

Louisa, on her part, felt much as the kind-hearted, long-suffering owner of the china shop might have done after the exit of the bear.

She tied on the pink, then the green apron, picked up all the scattered treasures and replaced them in her work-basket, and straightened the rug. Then she set the lamp on the floor, and began sharply examining the carpet. She even rubbed her fingers over it, and looked at them.

"He's tracked in a good deal of dust," she murmured. "I thought he must have."

Louisa got a dust-pan and brush, and swept Joe Dagget's track carefully.

If he could have known it, it would have increased his perplexity and uneasiness, although it would not have disturbed his loyalty in the least. He came twice a week to see Louisa Ellis, and every time, sitting there in her delicately sweet room, he felt as if surrounded by a hedge of lace. He was afraid to stir lest he should put a clumsy foot or hand through the fairy web, and he had always the consciousness that Louisa was watching fearfully lest he should.

Still the lace and Louisa commanded perforce his perfect respect and patience and loyalty. They were to be married in a month, after a singular courtship which had lasted for a matter of fifteen years. For fourteen out of those fifteen years the two had not once seen each other, and they had seldom exchanged letters. Joe had been all those years in Australia, where he had gone to make his fortune, and where he had stayed until he made it. He would have stayed fifty years if it had taken so long, and come home feeble and tottering, or never come home at all, to marry Louisa.

But the fortune had been made in the fourteen years, and he had come home now to marry the woman who had been patiently and unquestioningly waiting for him all that time.

Shortly after they were engaged he had announced to Louisa his determination to strike out into new fields, and secure a competency before they should be married. She had listened and assented with the sweet serenity which never failed her, not even when her lover set forth on that long and uncertain journey. Joe, buoyed up as he was by his sturdy determination, broke down a little at the last, but Louisa kissed him with a mild blush, and said good-by.

"It won't be for long," poor Joe had said, huskily; but it was for fourteen years.

In that length of time much had happened. Louisa's mother and brother had died, and she was all alone in the world. But greatest happening of all – a subtle happening which both were too simple to understand – Louisa's feet had turned into a path, smooth maybe under a calm, serene sky, but so straight and unswerving that it could only meet a check at her grave, and so narrow that there was no room for any one at her side.

Louisa's first emotion when Joe Dagget came home (he had not apprised her of his coming) was consternation, although she would not admit it to herself, and he never dreamed of it. Fifteen years ago she had been in love with him – at least she considered herself to be. Just at that time, gently acquiescing with and falling into the natural drift of girlhood, she had seen marriage ahead as a reasonable feature and a probable desirability of life. She had listened with calm docility to her mother's views upon the subject. Her mother was remarkable for her cool sense and sweet, even temperament. She talked wisely to her daughter when Joe Dagget presented himself, and Louisa accepted him with no hesitation. He was the first lover she had ever had.

She had been faithful to him all these years. She had never dreamed of the possibility of marrying any one else. Her life, especially for the last seven years, had been full of a pleasant peace, she had never felt discontented nor impatient over her lover's absence; still she had always looked forward to his return and their marriage as the inevitable conclusion of things. However, she had fallen into a way of placing it so far in the future that it was almost equal to placing it over the boundaries of another life.

When Joe came she had been expecting him, and expecting to be married for fourteen years, but she was as much surprised and taken aback as if she had never thought of it.

Joe's consternation came later. He eyed Louisa with an instant confirmation of his old admiration. She had changed but little. She still kept her pretty manner and soft grace, and was, he considered, every whit as attractive as ever. As for himself, his stent was done; he had turned his face away from fortune-seeking, and the old winds of romance whistled as loud and sweet as ever through his ears. All the song which he had been wont to hear in them was Louisa; he had for a long time a loyal belief that he heard it still, but finally it seemed to him that although the winds sang always that one song, it had another name. But for Louisa the wind had never more than murmured; now it had gone down, and everything was still. She listened for a while with half-wistful attention; then she turned quietly away and went to work on her wedding clothes.

Joe had made some extensive and quite magnificent alterations in his house. It was the old homestead; the newly-married couple would live there, for Joe could not desert his mother, who refused to leave her old home. So Louisa must leave hers. Every morning, rising and going about among her neat maidenly possessions, she felt as one looking her last upon the faces of dear friends. It was true that in a measure she could take them with her, but, robbed of their old environments, they would appear in such new guises that they would almost cease to be themselves. Then there were some peculiar features of her happy solitary life which she would probably be obliged to relinquish altogether. Sterner tasks than these graceful but half-needless ones would probably devolve upon her. There would be a large house to care for; there would be company to entertain; there would be Joe's rigorous and feeble old mother to wait upon; and it would be contrary to all thrifty village traditions to keep more than one servant. Louisa had a little still, and she used to occupy herself pleasantly in summer weather with distilling the sweet and aromatic essences from roses and peppermint and spearmint. By-and-by her still must be laid away. Her store of essences was already considerable, and there would be no time for her to distil for the mere pleasure of it. Then Joe's mother would think it foolishness; she had already hinted her opinion in the matter. Louisa dearly loved to sew a linen seam, not always for use, but for the simple, mild pleasure which she took in it. She would have been loath to confess how more than once she had ripped a seam for the mere delight of sewing it together again.

Sitting at her window during long sweet afternoons, drawing her needle gently through the dainty fabric, she was peace itself. But there was small chance of such foolish comfort in the future. Joe's mother, domineering, shrewd old matron that she was even in her old age, and very likely even Joe himself, with his honest masculine rudeness, would laugh and frown down all these pretty but senseless old maiden ways.

Louisa had almost the enthusiasm of an artist over the mere order and cleanliness of her solitary home. She had throbs of genuine triumph at the sight of the window-panes which she had polished until they shone like jewels. She gloated gently over her orderly bureau-drawers, with their exquisitely folded contents redolent with lavender and sweet clover and very purity. Could she be sure of the endurance of even this? She had visions, so startling that she half repudiated them as indelicate, of coarse masculine belongings strewn about in endless litter; of dust and disorder arising necessarily from a coarse masculine presence in the midst of all this delicate harmony.

Among her forebodings of disturbance, not the least was with regard to Caesar. Caesar was a veritable hermit of a dog. For the greater part of his life he had dwelt in his secluded hut, shut out from the society of his kind and all innocent canine joys. Never had Caesar since his early youth watched at a woodchuck's hole; never had he known the delights of a stray bone at a neighbor's kitchen door. And it was all on account of a sin committed when hardly out of his puppyhood. No one knew the possible depth of remorse of which this mild-visaged, altogether innocent-looking old dog might be capable; but whether or not he had encountered remorse, he had encountered a full measure of righteous retribution. Old Caesar seldom lifted up his voice in a growl or a bark; he was fat and sleepy; there were yellow rings which looked like spectacles around his dim old eyes; but there was a neighbor who bore on his hand the imprint of several of Caesar's sharp white youthful teeth, and for that he lived at the end of a chain, all alone in a little hut, for fourteen years. The neighbor, who was choleric and smarting with the pain of his wound, had demanded either Caesar's death or complete ostracism. So Louisa's brother, to whom the dog had belonged, had built him his little kennel and tied him up. It was now fourteen years since, in a flood of youthful spirits, he had inflicted that memorable bite, and with the exception of short excursions, always at the end of the chain, under the strict guardianship of his master or Louisa, the old dog had remained a close prisoner. It is doubtful if, with his limited ambition, he took much pride in the fact, but it is certain that he was possessed of considerable cheap fame. He was regarded by all the children in the village and by many adults as a very monster of ferocity. St. George's dragon[1] could hardly have surpassed in evil repute Louisa Ellis's old yellow dog. Mothers charged their children with solemn emphasis not to go too near to him, and the children listened and believed greedily, with a fascinated appetite for terror, and ran by Louisa's house stealthily, with many sidelong and backward glances at the terrible dog. If perchance he sounded a hoarse bark, there was a panic. Wayfarers chancing into Louisa's yard eyed him with respect, and inquired if the chain were stout. Caesar at large might have seemed a very ordinary dog, and excited no comment whatever; chained, his reputation overshadowed him, so that he lost his own proper outlines and looked darkly vague and enormous. Joe Dagget, however, with his good-humored sense and shrewdness, saw him as he was. He strode valiantly up to him and patted him on the head, in spite of Louisa's soft clamor of warning, and even attempted to set him loose. Louisa grew so alarmed that he desisted, but kept announcing his opinion in the matter quite forcibly at intervals. "There ain't a better-natured dog in town," he would say, "and it's downright cruel to keep him tied up there. Some day I'm going to take him out."

Louisa had very little hope that he would not, one of these days, when their interests and possessions should be more completely fused in one. She pictured to herself Caesar on the rampage through the quiet and unguarded village. She saw innocent children bleeding in his path. She was herself very fond of the old dog, because he had belonged to her dead brother, and he was always very gentle with her; still she had great faith in his ferocity. She always warned people not to go too near him. She fed him on ascetic fare of corn-mush and cakes, and never fired his dangerous temper with heating and sanguinary diet of flesh and bones. Louisa looked at the old dog munching his simple fare, and thought of her approaching marriage and trembled. Still no anticipation of disorder and confusion in lieu of sweet peace and harmony, no forebodings of Caesar on the rampage, no wild fluttering of her little yellow canary, were sufficient to turn her a hair's-breadth. Joe Dagget had been fond of her and working for her all these years. It was not for her, whatever came to pass, to prove untrue and break his heart. She put the exquisite little stitches into her wedding-garments, and the time went on until it was only a week before her wedding-day. It was a Tuesday evening, and the wedding was to be a week from Wednesday.

There was a full moon that night. About nine o'clock Louisa strolled down the road a little way. There were harvest-fields on either hand, bordered by low stone walls. Luxuriant clumps of bushes grew beside the wall, and trees – wild cherry and old apple-trees – at intervals. Presently Louisa sat down on the wall and looked about her with mildly sorrowful reflectiveness. Tall shrubs of blueberry and meadow-sweet, all woven together and tangled with blackberry vines and horsebriers, shut her in on either side. She had a little clear space between them. Opposite her, on the other side of the road, was a spreading tree; the moon shone between its boughs, and the leaves twinkled like silver. The road was bespread with a beautiful shifting dapple of silver and shadow; the air was full of a mysterious sweetness. "I wonder if it's wild grapes?" murmured Louisa. She sat there some time. She was just thinking of rising, when she heard footsteps and low voices, and remained quiet. It was a lonely place, and she felt a little timid. She thought she would keep still and let the persons, whoever they might be, pass her.

But just before they reached her the voices ceased, and the footsteps. She understood that their owners had also found seats upon the stone wall. She was wondering if she could not steal away unobserved, when the voice broke the stillness. It was Joe Dagget's. She sat still and listened.

The voice was announced by a loud sigh, which was as familiar as itself. "Well," said Dagget, "you've made up your mind, then, I suppose?"

"Yes," returned another voice; "I'm going day after to-morrow."

"That's Lily Dyer," thought Louisa to herself. The voice embodied itself in her mind. She saw a girl tall and full-figured, with a firm, fair face, looking fairer and firmer in the moonlight, her strong yellow hair braided in a close knot. A girl full of a calm rustic strength and bloom, with a masterful way which might have beseemed a princess. Lily Dyer was a favorite with the village folk; she had just the qualities to arouse the admiration. She was good and handsome and smart. Louisa had often heard her praises sounded.

"Well," said Joe Dagget, "I ain't got a word to say."

"I don't know what you could say," returned Lily Dyer.

"Not a word to say," repeated Joe, drawing out the words heavily. "I ain't sorry," he began at last, "that that happened yesterday – that we kind of let on how we felt to each other. I guess it's just as well we knew. Of course I can't do anything any different. I'm going right on an' get married next week. I ain't going back on a woman that's waited for me fourteen years, an' break her heart."

"If you should jilt her to-morrow, I wouldn't have you," spoke up the girl, with sudden vehemence.

"Well, I ain't going to give you the chance," said he; "but I don't believe you would, either."

"You'd see I wouldn't. Honor's honor, an' right's right. An' I'd never think anything of any man that went against 'em for me or any other girl; you'd find that out, Joe Dagget."

"Well, you'll find out fast enough that I ain't going against 'em for you or any other girl," returned he. Their voices sounded almost as if they were angry with each other. Louisa was listening eagerly.

"I'm sorry you feel as if you must go away," said Joe, "but I don't know but it's best."

"Of course it's best. I hope you and I have got common-sense."

"Well, I suppose you're right." Suddenly Joe's voice got an undertone of tenderness. "Say, Lily," said he, "I'll get along well enough myself, but I can't bear to think – You don't suppose you're going to fret much over it?"

"I guess you'll find out I sha'n't fret much over a married man."

"Well, I hope you won't – I hope you won't, Lily. God knows I do. And – I hope – one of these days – you'll – come across somebody else —"

"I don't see any reason why I shouldn't." Suddenly her tone changed. She spoke in a sweet, clear voice, so loud that she could have been heard across the street. "No, Joe Dagget," said she, "I'll never marry any other man as long as I live. I've got good sense, an' I ain't going to break my heart nor make a fool of myself; but I'm never going to be married, you can be sure of that. I ain't that sort of a girl to feel this way twice."

Louisa heard an exclamation and a soft commotion behind the bushes; then Lily spoke again – the voice sounded as if she had risen. "This must be a put a stop to," said she. "We've stayed here long enough. I'm going home."

Louisa sat there in a daze, listening to their retreating steps. After a while she got up and slunk softly home herself. The next day she did her housework methodically; that was as much a matter of course as breathing; but she did not sew on her wedding-clothes. She sat at her window and meditated. In the evening Joe came. Louisa Ellis had never known that she had any diplomacy in her, but when she came to look for it that night she found it, although meek of its kind, among her little feminine weapons. Even now she could hardly believe that she had heard aright, and that she would not do Joe a terrible injury should she break her troth-plight. She wanted to sound him without betraying too soon her own inclinations in the matter. She did it successfully, and they finally came to an understanding; but it was a difficult thing, for he was as afraid of betraying himself as she.

She never mentioned Lily Dyer. She simply said that while she had no cause of complaint against him, she had lived so long in one way that she shrank from making a change.

"Well, I never shrank, Louisa," said Dagget. "I'm going to be honest enough to say that I think maybe it's better this way; but if you'd wanted to keep on, I'd have stuck to you till my dying day. I hope you know that."

"Yes, I do," said she.

That night she and Joe parted more tenderly than they had done for a long time. Standing in the door, holding each other's hands, a last great wave of regretful memory swept over them.

"Well, this ain't the way we've thought it was all going to end, is it, Louisa?" said Joe.

She shook her head. There was a little quiver on her placid face.

"You let me know if there's ever anything I can do for you," said he. "I ain't never going to forget you, Louisa." Then he kissed her, and went down the path.

Louisa, all alone by herself that night, wept a little, she hardly knew why; but the next morning, on waking, she felt like a queen who, after fearing lest her domain be wrested away from her, sees it firmly insured in her possession.

Now the tall weeds and grasses might cluster around Caesar's little hermit hut, the snow might fall on its roof year in and year out, but he never would go on a rampage through the unguarded village. Now the little canary might turn itself into a peaceful yellow ball night after night, and have no need to wake and flutter with wild terror against its bars. Louisa could sew linen seams, and distil roses, and dust and polish and fold away in lavender, as long as she listed. That afternoon she sat with her nee-dle-work at the window, and felt fairly steeped in peace. Lily Dyer, tall and erect and blooming, went past; but she felt no qualm. If Louisa Ellis had sold her birthright she did not know it, the taste of the pottage was so delicious,[2] and had been her sole satisfaction for so long. Serenity and placid narrowness had become to her as to the birthright itself. She gazed ahead through a long reach of future days strung together like pearls in a rosary, every one like the others, and all smooth and flawless and innocent, and her heart went up in thankfulness. Outside was the fervid summer afternoon; the air was filled with the sounds of the busy harvest of men and birds and bees; there were halloos, metallic clatterings, sweet calls, and long hummings. Louisa sat, prayerfully numbering her days, like an uncloistered nun.

Notes

1   St. George was a Christian martyr who became Patron Saint of England. Jacob de Voragine's *Legenda Aurea* recounts the legend of his rescuing a maiden from a dragon; the story is an allegorical expression of the triumph of the Christian hero over evil.
2   Esau and Jacob were the twin sons of Isaac and Rebekah. When Esau returned hungry from an unsuccessful hunt, Jacob bought Esau's birthright – the rights due to him as eldest son – for some red pottage (soup). Genesis 25-36.

Source: *A New England Nun and Other Stories*. New York: Harper, 1891.

Biographical Note

Mary Wilkins Freeman was born on October 31, 1852, in Randolph, Massachusetts, and later moved with her family to Vermont, where she attended school, finally completing her education with a year at the Mount Holyoke Female Seminary in 1870. After the deaths of her sister, Nan, in 1876, her mother in 1880, and her father in 1883, Freeman moved back to Randolph to live with her childhood friend,

Mary Wales, and began to support herself through writing. The relationship with Wales was the most important in Freeman's life, and it is during the time spent with her friend that Freeman produced her most significant work. Her first story, "Two Old Lovers," was published by *Harper's Bazaar* in 1883. Two collections, generally considered her best, eventually followed, *A Humble Romance* in 1887 and *A New England Nun* in 1891; both focus on the darker side of New England life and pay particular attention to the problems of women. Many of Freeman's finest stories in these volumes, including "A New England Nun," "Sister Liddy," "Amanda and Love," and "The Revolt of Mother," deal either with repression and passivity or with moments of subsequent revolt; these impulses are never presented simplistically. In "A New England Nun," Louisa Ellis's decision can be interpreted as either a rejection of life or an affirmation of autonomy. Among her fourteen novels, *Jane Field* (1893), *Pembroke*, (1894), generally considered Freeman's masterpiece, and *The Portion of Labor* (1901) are most interesting for their exploration of the problems faced by the single woman during the late nineteenth century.

By 1892, Freeman was well-established as a significant local colorist. She subsequently met a New Jersey physician, Charles Freeman, and after a stormy decade of courtship, they married. Living in Metuchen, New Jersey, she complained of having nothing to write about, and indeed, after the appearance of her last collection of short fiction, *Edgewater People*, in 1918, her output was negligible: the majority of her collections of short stories date from before this time and what she subsequently produced is generally considered to be more conventional in character and plot, and overly elaborate in style. Her husband's increasing problems with alcohol strained the marriage. By 1919 Freeman had committed him to the New Jersey State Hospital for the Insane for treatment; they were legally separated in 1921.

Freeman produced twenty-two collections of short stories, fourteen novels, eight children's books, three volumes of poetry, and numerous miscellaneous essays and uncollected poems and stories. As well as achieving success as a local colorist, she became an accomplished writer of ghost stories. In 1926 she was awarded the Howells medal for distinction in fiction by the American Academy of Letters, and elected as a member in the National Institute of Arts and Letters. An inscription on the doors of the Institute still reads "Dedicated to the Memory of Mary E. Wilkins Freeman and the Women Writers of America." Freeman died of a heart attack at the age of seventy-eight.

Selected Modern Reprints:

The Best Stories of Mary E. Wilkins. Intro. H.W. Lanier. 1927. St. Clair Shores, MI: Scholarly P, 1971.

Collected Ghost Stories of Mary E. Wilkins Freeman. Intro. Edward Wagenknecht. Sauk City, WI: Arkham House, 1974.

The Infant Sphinx: Collected Letters of Mary E. Wilkins Freeman. Ed. Brent L. Kendrick. Metuchen, NJ: Scarecrow P, 1985.

The Revolt of Mother and Other Stories. Ed. with afterword by Michele Clark. Old Westbury, NY: Feminist P, 1974.

Selected Stories of Mary E. Wilkins Freeman. Ed. and Intro. Marjorie Pryse. New York: Norton, 1983.

Selected Secondary Sources:

Cutter, Martha J. "Mary E. Wilkins Freeman's Two New England Nuns." *Colby Quarterly* 26.4 (1990): 213-25.

Glasser, Leah Blatt. "Legacy Profile: Mary E. Wilkins Freeman (1852-1930)." *Legacy: A Journal of Nineteenth-Century American Women Writers* 4.1 (1987): 37-45.

Hamblen, Abigail Ann. *The New England Art of Mary E. Wilkins Freeman.* Amherst, MA: Green Knight P, 1966.

Marchalonis, Shirley, ed. *Critical Essays on Mary Wilkins Freeman.* Boston: G.K. Hall, 1991.

Pryse, Marjorie. "An Uncloistered 'New England Nun.'" *Studies in Short Fiction 20* (1983): 289-95.

Reichardt, Mary R. "Mary Wilkins Freeman: One Hundred Years of Criticism." *Legacy: A Journal of Nineteenth-Century American Women Writers* 4.2 (1987): 31-44.

Westbrook, Perry D. *Mary Wilkins Freeman*. Rev. ed. New York: Twayne, 1988.

248　ELIZABETH GASKELL (1810-1865)

Elizabeth Gaskell (1810-1865)

Lizzie Leigh

Chapter I

WHEN DEATH IS PRESENT IN A HOUSEHOLD ON A CHRISTMAS
day, the very contrast between the time as it now is, and the
day as it has often been, gives a poignancy to sorrow – a
more utter blankness to the desolation. James Leigh died
just as the far-away bells of Rochdale Church were ringing
for morning service on Christmas Day, 1836. A few minutes
before his death, he opened his already glazing eyes, and
made a sign to his wife, by the faint motion of his lips, that
he had yet something to say. She stooped close down, and
caught the broken whisper, "I forgive her, Annie! May God
forgive me!"

"Oh, my love, my dear! only get well, and I will never
cease showing my thanks for those words. May God in
heaven bless thee for saying them. Thou'rt not so restless,
my lad! may be – Oh, God!"

For even while she spoke he died.

They had been two-and-twenty years man and wife;
for nineteen of those years their life had been as calm
and happy as the most perfect uprightness on the one
side, and the most complete confidence and loving submission on the other, could make it. Milton's famous line
might have been framed and hung up as the rule of their
married life, for he was truly the interpreter, who stood
between God and her;[1] she would have considered herself
wicked if she had ever dared even to think him austere,
though as certainly as he was an upright man, so surely
was he hard, stern, and inflexible. But for three years the
moan and the murmur had never been out of her heart;

she had rebelled against her husband as against a tyrant, with a hidden, sullen rebellion, which tore up the old landmarks of wifely duty and affection, and poisoned the fountains whence gentlest love and reverence had once been for ever springing.

But those last blessed words replaced him on his throne in her heart, and called out penitent anguish for all the bitter estrangement of later years. It was this which made her refuse all the entreaties of her sons, that she would see the kind-hearted neighbours, who called on their way from church, to sympathize and condole. No! she would stay with the dead husband that had spoken tenderly at last, if for three years he had kept silence; who knew but what, if she had only been more gentle and less angrily reserved he might have relented earlier – and in time?

She sat rocking herself to and fro by the side of the bed, while the footsteps below went in and out; she had been in sorrow too long to have any violent burst of deep grief now; the furrows were well worn in her cheeks, and the tears flowed quietly, if incessantly, all the day long. But when the winter's night drew on, and the neighbours had gone away to their homes, she stole to the window, and gazed out, long and wistfully, over the dark grey moors. She did not hear her son's voice, as he spoke to her from the door, nor his footstep as he drew nearer. She started when he touched her.

"Mother! come down to us. There's no one but Will and me. Dearest mother, we do so want you." The poor lad's voice trembled, and he began to cry. It appeared to require an effort on Mrs. Leigh's part to tear herself away from the window, but with a sigh she complied with his request.

The two boys (for though Will was nearly twenty-one, she still thought of him as a lad) had done everything in their power to make the house-place comfortable for her. She herself, in the old days before her sorrow, had never made a brighter fire or a cleaner hearth, ready for her husband's return home, than now awaited her. The teathings were all put out, and the kettle was boiling; and the boys had calmed their grief down into a kind of sober cheerfulness. They paid her every attention they could think of, but received little notice on her part; she did not resist, she rather submitted to all their arrangements; but they did not seem to touch her heart.

When tea was ended – it was merely the form of tea that had been gone through – Will moved the things away to the dresser. His mother leant back languidly in her chair.

"Mother, shall Tom read you a chapter? He's a better scholar than I."

"Ay, lad!" said she, almost eagerly. "That's it. Read me the Prodigal Son.[2] Ay, ay, lad. Thank thee."

Tom found the chapter, and read it in the high-pitched voice which is customary in village schools. His mother bent forward, her lips parted, her eyes dilated; her whole body instinct with eager attention. Will sat with his head depressed and hung down. He knew why that chapter had been chosen; and to him it recalled the family's disgrace. When the reading was ended, he still hung down his head in gloomy silence. But her face was brighter than it had been before for the day. Her eyes looked dreamy, as if she saw a vision; and by-and-by she pulled the Bible towards her, and, putting her finger underneath each word, began to read them aloud in a low voice to herself; she read again the words of bitter sorrow and deep humiliation; but most of all, she paused and brightened over the father's tender reception of the prodigal.

So passed the Christmas evening in the Upclose Farm.

The snow had fallen heavily over the dark waving moorland before the day of the funeral. The black storm-laden dome of heaven lay very still and close upon the white earth, as they carried the body forth out of the house which had known his presence so long as its ruling power. Two and two the mourners followed, making a black procession, in their winding march over the unbeaten snow, to Milne Row Church; now lost in some hollow of the bleak moors, now slowly climbing the heaving ascents. There was no long tarrying after the funeral, for many of the neighbours who accompanied the body to the grave had far to go, and the great white flakes which came slowly down were the boding forerunners of a heavy storm. One old friend alone accompanied the widow and her sons to their home.

The Upclose Farm had belonged for generations to the Leighs; and yet its possession hardly raised them above the rank of labourers. There was the house and out-buildings, all of an old-fashioned kind, and about seven acres of barren unproductive land, which they had never possessed capital enough to improve; indeed, they could hardly rely upon it for subsistence; and it had been customary to bring up the sons to some trade, such as a wheelwright's or blacksmith's.

James Leigh had left a will in the possession of the old man who accompanied them home. He read it aloud. James had bequeathed the farm to his faithful wife, Anne Leigh, for her lifetime, and afterwards to his son William. The hundred and odd pounds in the savings bank was to accumulate for Thomas.

After the reading was ended, Anne Leigh sat silent for a time, and then she asked to speak to Samuel Orme alone. The sons went into the back kitchen, and thence strolled out into the fields regardless of the driving snow. The brothers were dearly fond of each other, although they were very different in character. Will, the elder, was like his father, stern, reserved and scrupulously upright. Tom (who was ten years younger) was gentle and delicate as a girl, both in appearance and character. He had always clung to his mother and dreaded his father. They did not speak as they walked, for they were only in the habit of talking about facts, and hardly knew the more sophisticated language applied to the description of feelings.

Meanwhile their mother had taken hold of Samuel Orme's arm with her trembling hand.

"Samuel, I must let the farm – I must!"

"Let the farm! What's come o'er the woman?"

"Oh, Samuel!" said she, her eyes swimming in tears, "I'm just fain to go and live in Manchester. I mun let the farm."

Samuel looked, and pondered, but did not speak for

some time. At last he said —

"If thou hast made up thy mind, there's no speaking again it; and thou must e'en go. Thou'lt be sadly pottered[3] wi' Manchester ways; but that's not my look-out. Why, thou'lt have to buy potatoes, a thing thou hast never done afore in all thy born life. Well! it's not my look-out. It's rather for me than again me. Our Jenny is going to be married to Tom Higginbotham, and he was speaking of wanting a bit of land to begin upon. His father will be dying sometime, I reckon, and then he'll step into the Croft Farm. But meanwhile" —

"Then, thou'lt let the farm," said she, still as eagerly as ever.

"Ay, ay; he'll take it fast enough, I've a notion. But I'll not drive a bargain with thee just now; it would not be right; we'll wait a bit."

"No; I cannot wait; settle it out at once."

"Well, well; I'll speak to Will about it. I see him out yonder. I'll step to him and talk it over."

Accordingly he went and joined the two lads, and, without more ado, began the subject to them.

"Will, thy mother is fain to go live in Manchester, and covets to let the farm. Now, I'm willing to take it for Tom Higginbotham; but I like to drive a keen bargain, and there would be no fun chaffering[4] with thy mother just now. Let thee and me buckle to, my lad! and try and cheat each other; it will warm us this cold day."

"Let the farm!" said both the lads at once, with infinite surprise. "Go live in Manchester!"

When Samuel Orme found that the plan had never before named to either Will or Tom, he would have nothing to do with it, he said, until they had spoken to their mother. Likely she was "dazed" by her husband's death; he would wait a day or two, and not name it to any one; not to Tom Higginbotham himself, or may be he would set his heart upon it. The lads had better go in and talk it over with their mother. He bade them good day, and left them.

Will looked very gloomy, but he did not speak till they got near the house. Then he said —

"Tom, go to th' shippon,[5] and supper the cows. I want to speak to mother alone."

When he entered the house-place, she was sitting before the fire, looking into its embers. She did not hear him come in: for some time she had lost her quick perception of outward things.

"Mother! what's this about going to Manchester?" asked he.

"Oh, lad! said she, turning round, and speaking in a beseeching tone, "I must go and seek our Lizzie. I cannot rest here for thinking on her. Many's the time I've left thy father sleeping in bed, and stole to th' window, and looked and looked my heart out towards Manchester, till I thought I must just set out and tramp over moor and moss straight away till I got there, and then lift up every downcast face till I came to our Lizzie. And often, when the south wind was blowing soft among the hollows, I've fancied (it could but be fancy, thou knowest) I heard her crying upon me; and I've thought the voice came closer and closer, till at last it was sobbing out, 'Mother!' close to the door; and I've stolen down, and undone the latch before now, and looked out into the still, black night, thinking to see her – and turned sick and sorrowful when I heard no living sound but the sough of the wind dying away. Oh, speak not to me of stopping here, when she may be perishing for hunger, like the poor lad in the parable." And now she lifted up her voice, and wept aloud.

Will was deeply grieved. He had been old enough to be told the family shame when, more than two years before, his father had had his letter to his daughter returned by her mistress in Manchester, telling him that Lizzie had left her service some time – and why. He had sympathized with his father's stern anger; though he had thought him something hard, it is true, when he had forbidden his weeping, heart-broken wife to go and try to find her poor sinning child, and declared that henceforth they would have no daughter; that she should be as one dead, and her name never more be named at market or at meal time, in blessing or in prayer. He had held his peace, with compressed lips and contracted brow, when the neighbours had noticed to him how poor Lizzie's death had aged both his father and his mother; and how they thought the bereaved couple would never hold up their heads again. He himself had felt as if that one event had made him old before his time; and had envied Tom the tears he had shed over poor, pretty, innocent, dead Lizzie. He thought about her sometimes, till he ground his teeth together, and could have struck her down in her shame. His mother had never named her to him until now.

"Mother!" said he, at last. "She may be dead. Most likely she is."

"No, Will; she is not dead," said Mrs. Leigh. "God will not let her die till I've seen her once again. Thou dost not know how I've prayed and prayed just once again to see her sweet face, and tell her I've forgiven her, though she's broken my heart – she has, Will." She could not go on for a minute or two for the choking sobs. "Thou dost not know that, or thou wouldst not say she could be dead – for God is very merciful, Will; He is; He is much more pitiful than man. I could never ha' spoken to thy father as I did to Him – and yet thy father forgave her at last. The last words he said were that he forgave her. Thou'lt not be harder than thy father, Will? Do not try and hinder me going to seek her, for it's no use."

Will sat very still for a long time before he spoke. At last he said, "I'll not hinder you. I think she's dead, but that's no matter."

"She's not dead," said her mother, with low earnestness. Will took no notice of the interruption.

"We will all go to Manchester for a twelvemonth, and let the farm to Tom Higginbotham. I'll get blacksmith's work; and Tom can have good schooling for awhile, which he's always craving for. At the end of the year you'll come back, mother, and give over fretting for Lizzie, and think with me that she is dead – and to my mind, that would be more comfort than to think of her living;" he dropped his voice as he spoke these last words. She shook her head, but made no answer. He asked again —

"Will you, mother, agree to this?"

"I'll agree to it a-this-ns," said she. "If I hear and see

nought of her for a twelvemonth, me being in Manchester looking out, I'll just ha' broken my heart fairly before the year's ended, and then I shall know neither love nor sorrow for her any more, when I'm at rest in my grave. I'll agree to that, Will."

"Well, I suppose it must be so. I shall not tell Tom, mother, why we're flitting to Manchester. Best spare him."

"As thou wilt," said she sadly; "so that we go, that's all."

Before the wild daffodils were in flower in the sheltered copses around Upclose Farm, the Leighs were settled in their Manchester home; if they could ever grow to consider that place as a home, where there was no garden or out-building, no fresh breezy outlet, no far-stretching view, over moor and hollow; no dumb animals to be tended, and, what more than all they missed, no old haunting memories, even though those remembrances told of sorrow, and the dead and gone.

Mrs. Leigh heeded the loss of all these things less than her sons. She had more spirit in her countenance than she had had for months, because now she had hope; of a sad enough kind, to be sure, but still it was hope. She performed all her household duties, strange and complicated as they were, and bewildered as she was with all the town necessities of her new manner of life; but when her house was "sided," and the boys come home from their work in the evening, she would put on her things and steal out, unnoticed, as she thought, but not without many a heavy sigh from Will, after she had closed the house-door and departed. It was often past midnight before she came back, pale and weary, with almost a guilty look upon her face; but that face so full of disappointment and hope deferred, that Will had never the heart to say what he thought of the folly and hopelessness of the search. Night after night it was renewed, till days grew to weeks, and weeks to months. All this time Will did his duty towards her as well as he could, without having sympathy with her. He stayed at home in the evenings for Tom's sake, and often wished he had Tom's pleasure in reading, for the time hung heavy on his hands as he sat up for his mother.

I need not tell you how the mother spent the weary hours. And yet I will tell you something. She used to wander out, at first as if without a purpose, till she rallied her thoughts, and brought all her energies to bear on the one point; then she went with earnest patience along the least-known ways to some new part of the town, looking wistfully with dumb entreaty into people's faces; sometimes catching a glimpse of a figure which had a kind of momentary likeness to her child's, and following that figure with never-wearying perseverance, till some light from shop or lamp showed the cold strange face which was not her daughter's. Once or twice a kind-hearted passer-by, struck by her look of yearning woe, turned back and offered help, or asked her what she wanted. When so spoken to, she answered only, "You don't know a poor girl they call Lizzie Leigh, do you?" and when they denied all knowledge, she shook her head, and went on again. I think they believed her to be crazy. But she never spoke first to any one. She sometimes took a few minutes' rest on the door-steps, and sometimes (very seldom) covered her face and cried; but she could not afford to lose time and chances in this way; while her eyes were blinded with tears, the lost one might pass by unseen.

One evening, in the rich time of shortening autumn days, Will saw an old man, who, without being absolutely drunk, could not guide himself rightly along the foot-path, and was mocked for his unsteadiness of gait by the idle boys of the neighbourhood. For his father's sake, Will regarded old age with tenderness, even when most degraded and removed from the stern virtues which dignified that father; so he took the old man home, and seemed to believe his often-repeated assertions, that he drank nothing but water. The stranger tried to stiffen himself up into steadiness as he drew nearer home, as if there were some one there for whose respect he cared even in his half-intoxicated state, or whose feelings he feared to grieve. His home was exquisitely clean and neat, even in outside appearance; threshold, window, and window-sill were outward signs of some spirit of purity within. Will was re-

warded for his attention by a bright glance of thanks, succeeded by a blush of shame, from a young woman of
twenty or thereabouts. She did not speak or second her
father's hospitable invitations to him to be seated. She
seemed unwilling that a stranger should witness her father's attempts at stately sobriety, and Will could not bear
to stay and see her distress. But when the old man, with
many a flabby shake of the hand, kept asking him to come
again some other evening, and see them, Will sought her
downcast eyes, and, though he could not read their veiled
meaning, he answered timidly, "If it's agreeable to everybody, I'll come, and thank ye." But there was no answer
from the girl, to whom this speech was in reality addressed; and Will left the house, liking her all the better
for never speaking.

He thought about her a great deal for the next day
or two; he scolded himself for being so foolish as to think
of her, and then fell to with fresh vigour, and thought of
her more than ever. He tried to depreciate her: he told
himself she was not pretty, and then made indignant answer that he liked her looks much better than any beauty
of them all. He wished he was not so country-looking, so
red-faced, so broad-shouldered; while she was like a lady,
with her smooth, colourless complexion, her bright dark
hair, and her spotless dress. Pretty or not pretty, she drew
his footsteps towards her; he could not resist the impulse
that made him wish to see her once more, and find out
some fault which should unloose his heart from her unconscious keeping. But there she was, pure and maidenly
as before. He sat and looked, answering her father at
cross-purposes, while she drew more and more into the
shadow of the chimney-corner out of sight. Then the spirit
that possessed him (it was not he himself, sure, that did
so impudent a thing!) made him get up and carry the
candle to a different place, under the pretence of giving
her more light at her sewing, but in reality to be able to
see her better. She could not stand this much longer, but
jumped up and said she must put her little niece to bed;
and surely there never was, before or since, so troublesome a child of two years old, for though Will stayed an

hour and a half hour longer, she never came down again. He won the father's heart, though, by his capacity as a listener; for some people are not at all particular, and, so that they themselves may talk on undisturbed, are not so unreasonable as to expect attention to what they say.

Will did gather this much, however, from the old man's talk. He had once been quite in a genteel line of business, but had failed for more money than any greengrocer he had heard of; at least, any who did not mix up fish and game with greengrocery proper. This grand failure seemed to have been the event of his life, and one on which he dwelt with a strange kind of pride. It appeared as if at present he rested from his past exertions (in the bankrupt line), and depended on his daughter, who kept a small school for very young children. But all these particulars Will only remembered and understood when he had left the house; at the time he heard them, he was thinking of Susan. After he had made good his footing at Mr. Palmer's, he was not long, you may be sure, without finding some reason for returning again and again. He listened to her father, he talked to his little niece, but he looked at Susan, both while he listened and while he talked. Her father kept on insisting upon his former gentility, the details of which would have appeared very questionable to Will's mind, if the sweet, delicate, modest Susan had not thrown an inexplicable air of refinement over all she came near. She never spoke much; she was generally diligent at work; but when she moved it was so noiselessly, and when she did speak, it was in so low and soft a voice, that silence, speech, motion, and stillness alike seemed to remove her high above Will's reach into some saintly and inaccessible air of glory – high above his reach, even as she knew him! And, if she were made acquainted with the dark secret behind of his sister's shame, which was kept ever present to his mind by his mother's nightly search among the outcast and forsaken, would not Susan shrink away from him with loathing, as if he were tainted by the involuntary relationship? This was his dread; and thereupon followed a resolution that he would withdraw from her sweet company before it was too late. So he resisted internal temptation, and stayed at home, and suffered and sighed. He became angry with his mother for her untiring patience in seeking for one who, he could not help hoping, was dead rather than alive. He spoke sharply to her, and received only such sad deprecatory answers as made him reproach himself, and still more lose sight of peace of mind. This struggle could not last long without affecting his health; and Tom, his sole companion through the long evenings, noticed his increasing languor, his restless irritability, with perplexed anxiety, and at last resolved to call his mother's attention to his brother's haggard, careworn looks. She listened with a startled recollection of Will's claims upon her love. She noticed his decreasing appetite and half-checked sighs.

"Will, lad! what's come o'er thee?" she said to him, as he sat listlessly gazing into the fire.

"There's nought the matter with me," said he, as if annoyed at her remark.

"Nay, lad, but there is." He did not speak again to contradict her; indeed, she did not know if he had heard her, so unmoved did he look.

"Wouldst like to go to Upclose Farm?" asked she sorrowfully.

"It's just blackberrying time," said Tom.

Will shook his head. She looked at him awhile, as if trying to read that expression of despondency, and trace it back to its source.

"Will and Tom could go," said she; "I must stay here till I've found her, thou knowest," continued she, dropping her voice.

He turned quickly around, and with the authority he at all times exercised over Tom, bade him begone to bed.

When Tom had left the room, he prepared to speak.

Chapter II

"Mother," then said Will, "why will you keep on thinking she's alive? If she were but dead, we need never name her name again. We've never heard nought on her since father wrote her that letter; we never knew whether she got it or not. She'd left her place before then. Many a one dies in" –

"Oh, my lad! dunnot speak so to me, or my heart will break outright," said his mother, with a sort of cry. Then she calmed herself, for she yearned to persuade him to her own belief. "Thou never asked, and thou'rt too like thy father for me to tell without asking – but it were all to be near Lizzie's old place that I settled down on this side o' Manchester; and the very day at after we came, I went to her old missus, and asked to speak a word wi her. I had a strong mind to cast it up to her, that she should ha' sent my poor lass away, without telling on it to us first; but she were in black, and looked so sad I could na' find in my heart to threep it up. But I did ask her a bit about our Lizzie. The master would have turned her away at a day's warning (he's gone to t'other place; I hope he'll meet wi' more mercy there than he showed our Lizzie – I do), and when the missus asked her should she write to us, she says Lizzie shook her head; and when she speered at her again, the poor lass went down on her knees, and begged her not, for she said it would break my heart (as it has done, Will – God knows it has)," said the poor mother, choking with her struggle to keep down her hard overmastering grief, "and her father would curse her – Oh, God, teach me to be patient." She could not speak for a few minutes – "and the lass threatened, and said she'd go drown herself in the canal, if the missus wrote home – and so –

"Well! I'd got a trace of my child – the missus thought she'd gone to the workhouse to be nursed; and there I went – and there, sure enough, she had been – and they'd turned her out as she were strong, and told her she were young enough to work – but whatten kind o' work would be open to her, lad, and her baby to keep?"

Will listened to his mother's tale with deep sympathy, not unmixed with the old bitter shame. But the opening of her heart had unlocked his, and after a while he spoke –

"Mother! I think I'd e'en better go home. Tom can stay wi' thee. I know I should stay too, but I cannot stay in peace so near – her – without craving to see her – Susan Palmer, I mean."

"Has the old Mr. Palmer thou telled me on a daughter?" asked Mrs. Leigh.

"Ay, he has. And I love her above a bit. And it's because I love her I want to leave Manchester. That's all."

Mrs. Leigh tried to understand this speech for some time, but found it difficult of interpretation.

"Why shouldst thou not tell her thou lov'st her? Thou'rt a likely lad, and sure o' work. Thou'lt have Upclose at my death; and as for that, I could let thee have it now, and keep mysel' by doing a bit of charing. It seems to me a very backwards sort o' way of winning her to think of leaving Manchester."

"Oh, mother, she's so gentle and so good – she's downright holy. She's never known a touch of sin; and can I ask her to marry me, knowing what we do about Lizzie, and fearing worse? I doubt if one like her could ever care for me; but if she knew about my sister, it would put a gulf between us, and she'd shudder up at the thought of crossing it. You don't know how good she is, mother!"

"Will, Will! if she's as good as thou say'st, she'll have pity on such as my Lizzie. If she has no pity for such, she's a cruel Pharisee,[6] and thou'rt best without her."

But he only shook his head and sighed; and for the time the conversation dropped.

But a new idea sprang up in Mrs. Leigh's head. She thought that she would go and see Susan Palmer, and speak up for Will, and tell her the truth about Lizzie; and according to her pity for the poor sinner, would she be worthy or unworthy of him. She resolved to go the very next afternoon, but without telling any one of her plan. Accordingly she looked out the Sunday clothes she had never before had the heart to unpack since she came to Manchester, but which she now desired to appear in, in order to do credit to Will. She put on her old-fashioned black mode bonnet, trimmed with real lace; her scarlet cloth cloak, which she had had ever since she was married; and, always spotlessly clean, she set forth on her unauthorised embassy. She knew the Palmers lived in Crown Street, though where she had heard it she could not tell; and modestly asking her way, she arrived in the street about a quarter to four o'clock. She stopped to inquire the exact number, and the woman whom she addressed told her that Susan Palmer's school would not be loosed till four, and asked her to step in and wait until then at her house.

"For," said she, smiling, "them that wants Susan Palmer wants a kind friend of ours; so we, in a manner, call cousins. Sit down, missus, sit down. I'll wipe the chair, so that it shanna dirty your cloak. My mother used to wear them bright cloaks, and they're right gradely[7] things again a green field."

"Han ye known Susan Palmer long?" asked Mrs. Leigh, pleased with the admiration of her cloak.

"Ever since they comed to live in our street. Our Sally goes to her school."

"Whatten sort of a lass is she, for I ha' never seen her?"

"Well, as for looks, I cannot say. It's so long since I first knowed her, that I've clean forgotten what I thought of her then. My master says he never saw such a smile for gladdening the heart. But may be it's not looks you're asking about. The best thing I can say of her looks is, that she's just one a stranger would stop in the street to ask help from if he needed it. All the little childer creeps as close as they can to her; she'll have as many as three or four hanging to her apron all at once."

"Is she cocket[8] at all?"

"Cocket, bless you! you never saw a creature less set up in all your life. Her father's cocket enough. No! she's not cocket any way. You've not heard much of Susan Palmer, I reckon, if you think she's cocket. She's just one to come quietly in, and do the very thing most wanted; little things, may be, that any one could do, but that few would think on, for another. She'll bring her thimble wi' her, and mend up after the childer o' nights; and she writes all Betty Harker's letters to her grandchild out at service; and she's in nobody's way, and that's a great matter, I take it. Here's the childer running past! School is loosed. You'll find her now, missus, ready to hear and to help. But we none of us frab[9] her by going near her in school-time."

Poor Mrs. Leigh's heart began to beat, and she could almost have turned round and gone home again. Her country breeding had made her shy of strangers, and this Susan Palmer appeared to her like a real born lady by all accounts. So she knocked with a timid feeling at the indicated door, and when it was opened, dropped a simple curtsey without speaking. Susan had her little niece in her arms, curled up with fond endearment against her breast; but she put her gently down to the ground, and instantly placed a chair in the best corner of the room for Mrs. Leigh, when she told her who she was. "It's not Will as has asked me to come," said the mother apologetically; "I'd wish just to speak to you myself!"

Susan coloured up to her temples, and stood to pick up the toddling girl. In a minute or two Mrs. Leigh began again.

"Will thinks you would na respect us if you knew all; but I think you could na help feeling for us in the sorrow God has put upon us; so I just put on my bonnet, and came off unknownst to the lads. Every one says you're very good, and that the Lord has keeped you from falling from His ways; but may be you've never yet been tried and tempted as some is. I'm perhaps speaking too plain, but my heart's welly broken, and I can't be choice in my words as them who are happy can. Well now! I'll tell you the truth. Will dreads you to hear it, but I'll just tell it you. You mun know" — but here the poor woman's words failed her, and she could do nothing but sit rocking herself backwards and forwards, with sad eyes, straight gazing into Susan's face, as if they tried to tell the tale of agony which the quivering lips refused to utter. Those wretched, stony eyes forced the tears down Susan's cheeks, and, as if this sympathy gave the mother strength, she went on in a low voice – "I had a daughter once, my heart's darling. Her father thought I made too much on her, and that she'd grow marred staying at home; so he said she mun go among strangers and learn to rough it. She were young, and liked the thought of seeing a bit of the world; and her father heard on a place in Manchester. Well! I'll not weary you. That poor girl were led astray; and first thing we heard on it, was when a letter of her father's was sent back by her missus, saying she'd left her place, or, to speak right, the master had turned her into the street soon as he had heard of her condition – and she not seventeen!"

She now cried aloud; and Susan wept too. The little child looked up into their faces, and, catching their sorrow, began to whimper and wail. Susan took it softly up, and hiding her face in its little neck, tried to restrain her tears, and think of comfort for the mother. At last she said –

"Where is she now?"

"Lass! I dunnot know," said Mrs. Leigh, checking her sobs to communicate this addition to her distress. "Mrs. Lomax told me she went" –

"Mrs. Lomax – what Mrs. Lomax?"

"Her as lives in Brabazon Street. She told me my poor wench went to the workhouse fra there. I'll not speak again the dead; but if her father would but ha' letten me – but he were one who had no notion – no, I'll not say that; best say nought. He forgave her on his death-bed. I dare say I did na go th' right way to work."

"Will you hold the child for me one instant?" said Susan.

"Ay, if it will come to me. Childer used to be fond on me till I got the sad look on my face that scares them, I think."

But the little girl clung to Susan; so she carried it upstairs with her. Mrs. Leigh sat all by herself – how long she did not know.

Susan came down with a bundle of far-worn baby clothes.

"You must listen to me a bit, and not think too much about what I'm going to tell you. Nanny is not my niece, nor any kin to me, that I know of. I used to go out working by the day. One night as I came home, I thought some woman was following me; I turned to look. The woman, before I could see her face (for she turned it to one side), offered me something. I held out my arms by instinct; she dropped a bundle into them, with a bursting sob that went straight to my heart. It was a baby. I looked round again; but the woman was gone. She had run away as quick as lightning. There was a little packet of clothes – very few – and as if they were made out of its mother's gowns, for they were large patterns to buy for a baby. I was always fond of babies; and I had not my wits about me, father says; for it was very cold, and when I'd seen as well as I could (for it was past ten) that there was no one in the street, I brought it in and warmed it. Father was very angry when he came, and said he'd take it to the work-house the next morning, and flyted[10] me sadly about it. But when morning came I could not bear to part with it; it had slept in my arms all night; and I've heard what workhouse bringing-up is. So I told my father I'd give up going out working, and stay at home and keep school, if I might only keep the baby; and, after a while, he said if I earned enough for him to have his comforts, he'd let me; but he's never taken to her. Now, don't tremble so – I've but a little more to tell – and may be I'm wrong in telling it; but I used to work next door to Mrs. Lomax's, in Brabazon Street, and the servants were all thick to-gether; and I heard about Bessy (they called her) being sent away. I don't know that ever I saw her; but the time would be about fitting to this child's age, and I've some-times fancied it was hers. And now, will you look at the little clothes that came with her – bless her!"

But Mrs. Leigh had fainted. The strange joy and shame, and gushing love for the little child, had overpow-ered her; it was some time before Susan could bring her round. There she was all trembling, sick with impatience to look at the little frocks. Among them was a slip of paper which Susan had forgotten to name, that had been pinned to the bundle. On it was scrawled, in a round, stiff hand —

"Call her Anne. She does not cry much, and takes a deal of notice. God bless you, and forgive me."

The writing was no clue at all; the name "Anne," common though it was, seemed something to build upon. But Mrs. Leigh recognized one of the frocks instantly, as being made out of a part of a gown that she and her daughter had bought together in Rochdale.

She stood up, and stretched out her hands in the attitude of blessing over Susan's bent head.

"God bless you, and show you His mercy in your need, as you have shown it to this little child."

She took the little creature in her arms, and smoothed away her sad looks to a smile, and kissed it fondly, saying over and over again, "Nanny, Nanny, my little Nanny." At last the child was soothed, and looked in her face and smiled back again.

"It has her eyes," said she to Susan.

"I never saw her to the best of my knowledge. I think it must be hers by the frock. But where can she be?"

"God knows," said Mrs. Leigh; "I dare not think she's dead. I'm sure she isn't."

"No; she's not dead. Every now and then a little packet is thrust in under our door, with, may be, two half-crowns in it; once it was half-a-sovereign. Altogether I've got seven-and-thirty shillings wrapped up for Nanny. I never touch it, but I've often thought the poor mother feels near to God when she brings this money. Father wanted to set the policeman to watch, but I said No; for I was afraid if she was watched she might not come, and it seemed such a holy thing to be checking her in, I could not find in my heart to do it."

"Oh, if we could but find her! I'd take her in my arms, and we'd just lie down and die together."

"Nay, don't speak so!" said Susan gently; "for all that's come and gone, she may turn right at last. Mary Magdalen[11] did, you know."

"Eh! but I were nearer right about thee than Will. He thought you would never look on him again if you knew about Lizzie. But thou'rt not a Pharisee."

"I'm sorry he thought I could be so hard," said Susan, in a low voice, and colouring up. Then Mrs. Leigh was alarmed, and, in her motherly anxiety, she began to fear lest she had injured Will in Susan's estimation.

"You see Will thinks so much of you – gold would not be good enough for you to walk on, in his eye. He said you'd never look at him as he was, let alone his being brother to my poor wench. He loves you so, it makes him think meanly on everything belonging to himself, as not fit to come near ye; but he's a good lad, and a good son. Thou'lt be a happy woman if thou'lt have him, so don't let my words go against him – don't!"

But Susan hung her head, and made no answer. She had not known until now that Will thought so earnestly and seriously about her; and even now she felt afraid that Mrs. Leigh's words promised her too much happiness, and that they could not be true. At any rate, the instinct of modesty made her shrink from saying anything which might seem like a confession of her own feelings to a third person. Accordingly she turned the conversation on the child.

"I am sure he could not help loving Nanny," said she. "There never was such a good little darling; don't you think she'd win his heart if he knew she was his niece, and perhaps bring him to think kindly on his sister?"

"I dunnot know," said Mrs. Leigh, shaking her head. "He has a turn in his eye like his father, that makes me – He's right down good though. But, you see, I've never been a good one at managing folk; one severe look turns me sick, and then I say just the wrong thing, I'm so fluttered. Now I should like nothing better than to take Nancy home with me; but Tom knows nothing but that his sister is dead, and I've not the knack of speaking rightly to Will. I dare not do it, and that's the truth. But you mun not think badly of Will. He's so good hissel, that he can't understand how any one can do wrong; and, above all, I'm sure he loves you dearly."

"I don't think I could part with Nancy," said Susan, anxious to stop this revelation of Will's attachment to herself. "He'll come around to her soon; he can't fail; and I'll keep a sharp look-out after the poor mother, and try and catch her the next time she comes with her little parcels of money."

"Ay, lass; we mun get hold of her; my Lizzie. I love thee dearly for thy kindness to her child; but if thou canst catch her for me, I'll pray for thee when I'm too near my death to speak words; and, while I live, I'll serve thee next to her – she mun come first, thou know'st. God bless thee, lass. My heart is lighter by a deal than it was when I comed in. Them lads will be looking for me home, and I mun go, and leave this little sweet one" (kissing it). "If I can take courage, I'll tell Will all that has come and gone between us two. He may come and see thee, mayn't he?"

"Father will be very glad to see him, I'm sure," replied Susan. The way in which this was spoken satisfied Mrs. Leigh's anxious heart that she had done Will no harm by what she had said; and, with many a kiss to the little one, and one more fervent tearful blessing on Susan, she went homewards.

Chapter III

That night Mrs. Leigh stopped at home – that only night for many months. Even Tom, the scholar, looked up from his books in amazement; but then he remembered that Will had not been well, and that, his mother's attention having been called to the circumstance, it was only natural she should stay to watch him. And no watching could be more tender, or more complete. Her loving eyes seemed never averted from his face – his grave, sad, careworn face. When Tom went to bed the mother left her seat, and going up to Will, where he sat looking at the fire, but not seeing it, she kissed his forehead, and said –

"Will! lad, I've been to see Susan Palmer!"

She felt the start under her hand which was placed on his shoulder, but he was silent for a minute or two. Then he said –

"What took you there, mother?"

"Why, my lad, it was likely I should wish to see one you cared for; I did not put myself forward. I put on my

Sunday clothes, and tried to behave as yo'd ha' liked me. At least, I remember trying at first; but after, I forgot all."

She rather wished that he would question her as to what made her forget all. But he only said —

"How was she looking, mother?"

"Well, thou seest I never set eyes on her before; but she's a good, gentle-looking creature; and I love her dearly, as I've reason to."

Will looked up with momentary surprise, for his mother was too shy to be usually taken with strangers. But, after all, it was natural in this case, for who could look at Susan without loving her? So still he did not ask any questions, and his poor mother had to take courage, and try again to introduce the subject near to her heart. But how?

"Will!" said she (jerking it out in sudden despair of her own powers to lead to what she wanted to say), "I telled her all."

"Mother! you've ruined me," said he, standing up, and standing opposite to her with a stern white look of affright on his face.

"No! my own dear lad; dunnot look so scared; I have not ruined you!" she exclaimed, placing her two hands on his shoulders, and looking fondly into his face. "She's not one to judge and scorn the sinner. She's too deep read in her New Testament for that. Take courage, Will; and thou may'st, for I watched her well, though it is not for one woman to let out another's secret. Sit thee down, lad, for thou look'st very white."

He sat down. His mother drew a stool towards him, and sat at his feet.

"Did you tell her about Lizzie, then?" asked he, hoarse and low.

"I did; I telled her all! and she fell a-crying over my deep sorrow, and the poor wench's sin. And then a light comed into her face, trembling and quivering with some new glad thought; and what dost thou think it was, Will, lad? Nay, I'll not misdoubt but that thy heart will give thanks as mine did, afore God and His angels, for her great goodness. That little Nanny is not her niece, she's our Lizzie's own child, my little grandchild." She could no longer restrain her tears; and they fell hot and fast, but still she looked into his face.

"Did she know it was Lizzie's child? I do not comprehend," said he, flushing red.

"She knows now; she did not at first, but took the little helpless creature in, out of her own pitiful, loving heart, guessing only that it was the child of shame; and she's worked for it, and kept it, and tended it ever sin' it were a mere baby, and loves it fondly. Will! won't you love it?" asked she beseechingly.

He was silent for an instant; then he said, "Mother, I'll try. Give me time, for all these things startle me. To think of Susan having to do with such a child!"

"Ay, Will! and to think, as may be yet, of Susan having to do with the child's mother! For she is tender and pitiful, and speaks hopefully of my lost one, and will try and find her for me, when she comes, as she does sometimes, to thrust money under the door, for her baby. Think of that, Will. Here's Susan, good and pure as the angels in heaven, yet, like them, full of hope and mercy, and one who, like them, will rejoice over her as repents. Will, my lad, I'm not afeard of you now; and I must speak, and you must listen. I am your mother, and I dare to command you, because I know I am in the right, and that God is on my side. If He should lead the poor wandering lassie to Susan's door, and she comes back, crying and sorrowful, led by that good angel to us once more, thou shalt never say a casting-up word to her about her sin, but be tender and helpful towards one 'who was lost and is found;'[12] so may God's blessing rest on thee, and so may'st thou lead Susan home as thy wife."

She stood no longer as the meek, imploring, gentle mother, but firm and dignified, as if the interpreter of God's will. Her manner was so unusual and solemn, that it overcame all Will's pride and stubbornness. He rose softly while she was speaking, and bent his head, as if in reverence at her words, and the solemn injunction which they conveyed. When she had spoken, he said, in so subdued a voice that she was almost surprised at the sound,

"Mother, I will."

"I may be dead and gone; but, all the same, thou wilt take home the wandering sinner, and heal up her sorrows, and lead her to her Father's house. My lad, I can speak no more; I'm turned very faint."

He placed her in a chair; he ran for water. She opened her eyes, and smiled.

"God bless you, Will. Oh! I am so happy. It seems as if she were found; my heart is so filled with gladness."

That night Mr. Palmer stayed out late and long. Susan was afraid that he was at his old haunts and habits – getting tipsy at some public house; and this thought oppressed her, even though she had so much to make her happy in the consciousness that Will loved her. She sat up long, and then she went to bed, leaving all arranged as well as she could for her father's return. She looked at the little rosy, sleeping girl who was her bed-fellow, with redoubled tenderness, and with many a prayerful thought. The little arms entwined her neck as she lay down, for Nanny was a light sleeper, and was conscious that she, who was loved with all the power of that sweet, childish heart, was near her, and by her, although she was too sleepy to utter any of her half-formed words.

And, by-and-by, she heard her father come home, stumbling uncertain, trying first the windows, and next the door-fastenings, with many a loud incoherent murmur. The little innocent twined around her seemed all the sweeter and more lovely, when she thought sadly of her erring father. And presently he called aloud for a light. She had left matches and all arranged as usual on the dresser; but, fearful of some accident from fire, in his unusually intoxicated state, she now got up softly, and putting on a cloak, went down to his assistance.

Alas! the little arms that were unclosed from her soft neck belonged to a light, easily-awakened sleeper. Nanny missed her darling Susy; and terrified at being left alone, in the vast mysterious darkness, which had no bounds and seemed infinite, she slipped out of bed, and tottered, in her little nightgown, towards the door. There was a light below, and there was Susy and safety! So she went onwards two steps towards the steep, abrupt stairs; and then, dazzled by sleepiness, she stood, she wavered, she fell! Susan flew to her, and spoke all soft, entreating, loving words; but her white lids covered up the blue violets of eyes, and there was no murmur came out of the pale lips. The warm tears that rained down did not awaken her; she lay stiff, and weary with her short life, on Susan's knee. Susan went sick with terror. She carried her upstairs, and laid her tenderly in bed; she dressed herself most hastily, with her trembling fingers. Her father was asleep on the settle downstairs; and useless, and worse than useless, if awake. But Susan flew out of the door, and down the quiet resounding street, towards the nearest doctor's house. Quickly she went, but as quickly a shadow followed, as if impelled by some sudden terror. Susan rang wildly at the nightbell – the shadow crouched near. The doctor looked out from an upstairs window.

"A little child has fallen downstairs, at No. 9 Crown Street, and is very ill – dying, I'm afraid. Please, for God's sake, sir, come directly. No. 9 Crown Street."

"I'll be there directly," said he, and shut the window.

"For that God you have just spoken about – for His sake – tell me, are you Susan Palmer? Is it my child that lies a-dying?" said the shadow, springing forwards, and clutching poor Susan's arm.

"It is a little child of two years old. I do not know whose it is; I love it as my own. Come with me, whoever you are; come with me."

The two sped along the silent streets – as silent as the night were they. They entered the house; Susan snatched up the light, and carried it upstairs. The other followed.

She stood with wild, glaring eyes by the bedside, never looking at Susan, but hungrily gazing at the little, white, still child. She stooped down, and put her hand tight on her own heart, as if to still its beating, and bent her ear to the pale lips. Whatever the result was, she did not speak; but threw off the bedclothes wherewith Susan had tenderly covered up the little creature, and felt its left side.

Then she threw up her arms, with a cry of wild despair.

"She is dead! she is dead!"

She looked so fierce, so mad, so haggard, that, for an instant, Susan was terrified; the next, the holy God had put courage into her heart, and her pure arms were round that guilty, wretched creature, and her tears were falling fast and warm upon her breast. But she was thrown off with violence.

"You killed her – you slighted her – you let her fall down those stairs! you killed her!"

Susan cleared off the thick mist before her, and, gazing at the mother with her clear, sweet angel eyes, said, mournfully –

"I would have laid down my own life for her."

"Oh, the murder is on my soul!" exclaimed the wild, bereaved mother, with the fierce impetuosity of one who has none to love her, and to be beloved, regard to whom might teach self-restraint.

"Hush!" said Susan, her finger on her lips. "Here is the doctor. God may suffer her to live."

The poor mother turned sharp round. The doctor mounted the stair. Ah! that mother was right; the little child was really dead and gone.

And when he confirmed her judgment, the mother fell down in a fit. Susan, with her deep grief, had to forget herself, and forget her darling (her charge for years), and question the doctor what she must do with the poor wretch, who lay on the floor in such extreme of misery.

"She is the mother!" said she.

"Why did she not take better care of the child?" asked he, almost angrily.

But Susan only said, "The little child slept with me; and it was I that left her."

"I will go back and made up a composing draught; and while I am away you must get her to bed."

Susan took out some of her own clothes, and softly undressed the stiff, powerless form. There was no other bed in the house but the one in which her father slept. So she tenderly lifted the body of her darling; and was going to take it downstairs, but the mother opened her eyes, and seeing what she was about, she said —

"I am not worthy to touch her, I am so wicked. I have spoken to you as I never should have spoken; but I think you are very good. May I have my own child to lie in my arms for a little while?"

Her voice was so strange a contrast to what it had been before she had gone into the fit, that Susan hardly recognized it; it was now so unspeakably soft, so irresistibly pleading; the features too had lost their fierce expression, and were almost as placid as death. Susan could not speak, but she carried the little child, and laid it in its mother's arms; then, as she looked at them, something overpowered her, and she knelt down, crying aloud —

"Oh my God, my God, have mercy on her, and forgive and comfort her."

But the mother kept smiling, and stroking the little face, murmuring soft, tender words, as if it were alive. She was going mad, Susan thought; but she prayed on, and on, and ever still she prayed with streaming eyes.

The doctor came with the draught. The mother took it, with docile unconsciousness of its nature as medicine. The doctor sat by her; and soon she fell asleep. Then he rose softly, and, beckoning Susan to the door, he spoke to her there.

"You must take the corpse out of her arms. She will not awake. That draught will make her sleep for many hours. I will call before noon again. It is now daylight. Good-bye."

Susan shut him out; and then, gently extricating the dead child from its mother's arms, she could not resist making her own quiet moan over her darling. She tried to learn off its little placid face, dumb and pale before her.

"Not all the scalding tears of care
Shall wash away that vision fair
Not all the thousand thoughts that rise,
Not all the sights that dim her eyes,
    Shall e'er usurp the place
    Of that little angel-face."

And then she remembered what remained to be done. She saw that all was right in the house; her father was still dead asleep on the settle, in spite of all the noise of the night. She went out through the quiet streets, deserted still, although it was broad daylight, and to where the Leighs lived. Mrs. Leigh, who kept her country hours, was opening her window-shutters. Susan took her by the arm, and, without speaking, went into the house-place. There she knelt down before the astonished Mrs. Leigh, and cried as she had never done before; but the miserable night had overpowered her, and she who had gone through so much calmly, now that the pressure seemed removed, could not find the power to speak.

"My poor dear! What has made thy heart so sore as to come and cry a-this-ons? Speak and tell me. Nay, cry on, poor wench, if thou canst not speak yet. It will ease the heart, and then thou canst tell me."

"Nanny is dead!" said Susan. "I left her to go to father, and she fell downstairs, and never breathed again. Oh, that's my sorrow! But I've more to tell. Her mother is come – is in our house! Come and see if it's your Lizzie."

Mrs. Leigh could not speak, but, trembling, put on her things, and went with Susan in dizzy haste back to Crown Street.

Chapter IV

As they entered the house in Crown Street, they perceived that the door would not open freely on its hinges, and Susan instinctively looked behind to see the cause of the obstruction. She immediately recognized the appearance of a little parcel, wrapped in a scrap of newspaper, and evidently containing money. She stopped and picked it up. "Look!" said she sorrowfully, "the mother was bringing this for her child last night."

But Mrs. Leigh did not answer. So near to the ascertaining if it were her lost child or no, she could not be arrested, but pressed onwards with trembling steps, and a beating, fluttering heart. She entered the bedroom, dark and still. She took no heed of the little corpse over which Susan paused, but she went straight to the bed, and withdrawing the curtain, saw Lizzie; but not the former Lizzie, bright, gay, buoyant, and undimmed. This Lizzie was old before her time; her beauty was gone; deep lines of care, and, alas! of want (or thus the mother imagined) were printed on the cheek, so round, and fair, and smooth, when last she gladdened her mother's eyes. Even in her sleep she bore the look of woe and despair which was the prevalent expression of her face by day; even in her sleep she had forgotten how to smile. But all these marks of the sin and sorrow she had passed through only made her mother love her the more. She stood looking at her with greedy eyes, which seemed as though no gazing could satisfy their longing; and at last she stooped down and kissed the pale, worn hand that lay outside the bedclothes. No touch disturbed the sleeper; the mother need not have laid the hand so gently down upon the counterpane. There was no sign of life, save only now and then a deep sob-like sigh. Mrs. Leigh sat down beside the bed, and still holding back the curtain, looked on and on, as if she could never be satisfied.

Susan would fain have stayed by her darling one; but she had many calls upon her time and thoughts, and her will had now, as ever, to be given up to that of others. All seemed to devolve the burden of their cares on her. Her father, ill-humoured from his last night's intemperance, did not scruple to reproach her with being the cause of little Nanny's death; and when, after bearing his upbraiding meekly for some time, she could no longer restrain herself, but began to cry, he wounded her even more by his injudicious attempts at comfort; for he said it was as well the child was dead; it was none of theirs, and why should they be troubled with it? Susan wrung her hands at this, and came and stood before her father, and implored him to forbear. Then she had to take all requisite steps for the coroner's inquest; she had to arrange for the dismissal of her school; she had to summon a little neighbour, and send his willing feet on a message to William Leigh, who, she felt, ought to be informed of his mother's whereabouts, and of the whole state of affairs. She asked her messenger to tell him to come and speak to her; that his mother was at her house. She was thankful that her father sauntered out to have a gossip at the nearest coachstand, and to relate as many of the night's adventures as he knew; for as yet he was in ignorance of the watcher and the watched, who silently passed away the hours upstairs.

At dinner-time Will came. He looked red, glad, impatient, excited. Susan stood calm and white before him, her soft, loving eyes gazing straight into his.

"Will," said she, in a low, quiet voice, "your sister is upstairs."

"My sister!" said he, as if affrighted at the idea, and losing his glad look in one of gloom. Susan saw it, and her heart sank a little, but she went on as calm to all appearance as ever.

"She was little Nanny's mother, as perhaps you know. Poor little Nanny was killed last night by a fall downstairs." All the calmness was gone; all the suppressed feeling was displayed in spite of every effort. She sat down, and hid her face from him, and cried bitterly. He forgot everything but the wish, the longing to comfort her. He put his arm round her waist, and bent over her. But all he could say, was, "Oh, Susan, how can I comfort you? Don't take on so – pray don't!" He never changed the words, but the tone varied every time he spoke. At last she seemed to regain her power over herself; and she wiped her eyes, and once more looked upon him with her own quiet, earnest, unfearing gaze.

"Your sister was near the house. She came in on hearing my words to the doctor. She is asleep now, and your mother is watching her. I wanted to tell you all myself. Would you like to see your mother?"

"No!" said he. "I would rather see none but thee. Mother told me thou knew'st all." His eyes were downcast in their shame.

But the holy and pure did not lower or veil her eyes. She said, "Yes, I know all – all but her sufferings.

Think what they must have been!"

He made answer, low and stern, "She deserved them all; every jot."

"In the eye of God, perhaps she does. He is the Judge; we are not."

"Oh!" she said, with a sudden burst, "Will Leigh! I have thought so well of you; don't go and make me think you cruel and hard. Goodness is not goodness unless there is mercy and tenderness with it. There is your mother, who has been nearly heart-broken, now full of rejoicing over her child. Think of your mother."

"I do think of her," said he. "I remember the promise I gave her last night. Thou shouldst give me time. I would do right in time. I never think it o'er in quiet. But I will do what is right and fitting, never fear. Thou hast spoken out very plain to me, and misdoubted me, Susan; I love thee so, that thy words cut me. If I did hang back a bit from making sudden promises, it was because not even for love of thee, would I say what I was not feeling; and at first I could not feel all at once as thou wouldst have me. But I'm not cruel and hard; for if I had been, I should na' have grieved as I have done."

He made as if he were going away; and indeed he did feel he would rather think it over in quiet. But Susan, grieved at her incautious words, which had all the appearance of harshness, went a step or two nearer – paused – and then, all over blushes, said in a low, soft whisper —

"Oh, Will! I beg your pardon. I am very sorry. Won't you forgive me?"

She who had always drawn back, and been so reserved, said this in the very softest manner; with eyes now uplifted beseechingly, now dropped to the ground. Her sweet confusion told more than words could do; and Will turned back, all joyous in his certainty of being beloved, and took her in his arms, and kissed her.

"My own Susan!" he said.

Meanwhile the mother watched her child in the room above.

It was late in the afternoon before she awoke, for the sleeping draught had been very powerful. The instant she awoke, her eyes were fixed on her mother's face with a gaze as unflinching as if she were fascinated. Mrs. Leigh did not turn away, nor move; for it seemed as if motion would unlock the stony command over herself which, while so perfectly still, she was enabled to preserve. But by-and-by Lizzie cried out, in a piercing voice of agony —

"Mother, don't look at me; I have been so wicked!" and instantly she hid her face, and grovelled among the bedclothes, and lay like one dead, so motionless was she.

Mrs. Leigh knelt down by the bed, and spoke in the most soothing tones.

"Lizzie, dear, don't speak so. I'm thy mother, darling; don't be afeard of me. I never left off loving thee, Lizzie. I was always a-thinking of thee. Thy father forgave thee afore he died." (There was a little start here, but no sound was heard.) "Lizzie, lass, I'll do ought for thee; I'll live for thee; only don't be afeard of me. Whate'er thou art or hast been, we'll ne'er speak on't. We'll leave th'oud times behind us, and go back to the Upclose Farm. I but left it to find thee, my lass; and God has led me to thee. Blessed be His name. And God is good, too, Lizzie. Thou hast not forgot thy Bible, I'll be bound, for thou wert always a scholar. I'm no reader, but I learnt off them texts to comfort me a bit, and I've said them many a time a day to myself. Lizzie, lass, don't hide thy head so; it's thy mother as is speaking to thee. Thy little child clung to me only yesterday; and if it's gone to be an angel, it will speak to God for thee. Nay, don't sob a-that-'as; thou shalt have it again in heaven; I know thou'lt strive to get there, for thy little Nanny's sake – and listen! I'll tell thee God's promises to them that are penitent – only doan't be afeard."

Mrs. Leigh folded her hands, and strove to speak very clearly, while she repeated every tender and merciful text she could remember. She could tell from the breathing that her daughter was listening; but she was so dizzy and sick herself when she had ended, that she could not go on speaking. It was all she could do to keep from crying aloud.

At last she heard her daughter's voice.

"Where have they taken her to?" she asked quietly.

"She is downstairs. So quiet, and peaceful, and happy she looks."

"Could she speak! Oh, if God – if I might but have heard her little voice! Mother, I used to dream of it. May I see her once again? Oh, mother, if I strive very hard and God is very merciful, and I go to heaven, I shall not know her – I shall not know my own again; she will shun me as a stranger, and cling to Susan Palmer and to you. Oh, woe! Oh, woe!" She shook with exceeding sorrow.

In her earnestness of speech she had uncovered her face, and tried to read Mrs. Leigh's thoughts through her looks. And when she saw those aged eyes brimming full of tears, and marked the quivering lips, she threw her arms round the faithful mother's neck, and wept there as she had done in many a childish sorrow, but with a deeper, a more wretched grief.

Her mother hushed her on her breast; and lulled her as if she was a baby; and she grew still and quiet.

They sat thus for a long, long time. At last, Susan Palmer came up with some tea and bread and butter for Mrs. Leigh. She watched the mother feed her sick, unwilling child, with every fond inducement to eat which she could devise; they neither of them took notice of Susan's presence. That night they lay in each other's arms; but Susan slept on the ground beside them.

They took the little corpse (the little unconscious sacrifice, whose early calling home had reclaimed her poor wandering mother) to the hills, which in her lifetime she had never seen. They dared not lay her by the stern grandfather in Milne Row churchyard, but they bore her to a lone moorland graveyard, where, long ago, the Quakers used to bury their dead. They laid her there on the sunny slope, where the earliest spring flowers blow.

Will and Susan live at the Upclose Farm. Mrs. Leigh and Lizzie dwell in a cottage so secluded that, until you drop into the very hollow where it is placed, you do not see it. Tom is a schoolmaster in Rochdale, and he and Will help to support their mother. I only know that, if the cottage be hidden in a green hollow of the hills, every

sound of sorrow in the whole upland is heard there –
every call of suffering or of sickness for help is listened
to by a sad, gentle-looking woman, who rarely smiles (and
when she does her smile is more sad than other people's
tears), but who comes out of her seclusion whenever there
is a shadow in any household. Many hearts bless Lizzie
Leigh, but she – she prays always and ever for forgiveness
– such forgiveness as may enable her to see her child once
more. Mrs. Leigh is quiet and happy. Lizzie is, to her eyes,
something precious – as the lost piece of silver – found
once more. Susan is the bright one who brings sunshine
to all. Children grow around her and call her blessed.
One is called Nanny; her Lizzie often takes to the sunny
graveyard in the uplands, and while the little creature
gathers the daisies, and makes chains, Lizzie sits by a little
grave and weeps bitterly.

Notes

1   "He for God only, she for God in him:/ His fair large front
    and eye sublime declared / Absolute rule." John Milton (1608-
    1674), *Paradise Lost* (1667) 4.297.
2   Luke 15:11-32.
3   Troubled.
4   Bantering.
5   Cattle shed.
6   The Pharisees were a Jewish sect active around the time of
    Christ and distinguished by their strict observance of the law.
    The term became generally applied to any self-righteous, intol-
    erant person or hypocrite.
7   Handsome.
8   Proud.
9   Harass or worry.
10 Abused.

11 Mary Magdalen is often associated with the unnamed penitent woman whose sins Christ pardoned when she anointed his feet and wiped them with her hair. Luke 7:37-48. A Magdalen has therefore become a generic term for a repentant prostitute.

12 The parable of the Prodigal son: "For this son of mine was dead and has come back to life; he was lost and is found." Luke 15:24.

Source: *Lizzie Leigh and Other Tales*. London: Chapman Hall, 1855.

Elizabeth Gaskell (1810-1865)

The Old Nurse's Story

YOU KNOW, MY DEARS, THAT YOUR MOTHER WAS AN ORPHAN, and an only child; and I dare say you have heard that your grandfather was a clergyman up in Westmoreland, where I come from. I was just a girl in the village school, when, one day, your grandmother came in to ask the mistress if there was any scholar there who would do for a nursemaid; and mighty proud I was, I can tell ye, when the mistress called me up, and spoke to my being a good girl at my needle, and a steady, honest girl, and one whose parents were very respectable, though they might be poor. I thought I should like nothing better than to serve the pretty young lady, who was blushing as deep as I was, as she spoke of the coming baby, and what I should have to do with it. However, I see you don't care so much for this part of my story, as for what you think is to come, so I'll tell you at once. I was engaged and settled at the parsonage before Miss Rosamond (that was the baby, who is now your mother) was born. To be sure, I had little enough to do with her when she came, for she was never out of her mother's arms, and slept by her all night long; and proud enough was I sometimes when missis trusted her to me. There never was such a baby before or since, though you've all of you been fine enough in your turns; but for sweet, winning ways, you've none of you come up to your mother. She took after her mother, who was a real lady born; a Miss Furnivall, a grand-daughter of Lord Furnivall's, in Northumberland. I believe she had neither brother nor sister, and had been brought up in my lord's family till she had married your grandfather, who was just a curate, son to a shopkeeper in Carlisle – but a clever, fine gentleman as ever was – and one who was a right-down hard worker in his parish, which was very wide, and scattered all abroad over the Westmoreland Fells. When your mother, little Miss Rosamond, was about four or five years old, both her parents died in a fortnight – one after the other. Ah! that was a sad time. My pretty young mistress and me was looking for another baby, when my master came home from one of his long rides, wet and tired, and took the fever he died of; and then she never held up her head again, but just lived to see her dead baby, and have it laid on her breast, before she sighed away her life. My mistress had asked me, on her death-bed, never to leave Miss Rosamond; but if she never had spoken a word, I would have gone with the little child to the end of the world.

The next thing, and before we had well stilled our sobs, the executors and guardians came to settle the affairs. They were my poor young mistress's own cousin, Lord Furnivall, and Mr. Esthwaite, my master's brother, a shopkeeper in Manchester; not so well-to-do then as he was afterwards, and with a large family rising about him. Well! I don't know if it were their settling, or because of a letter my mistress wrote on her death-bed to her cousin, my lord; but somehow it was settled that Miss Rosamond and me were to go to Furnivall Manor House, in Northumberland; and my lord spoke as if it had been her mother's wish that she should live with his family, and as if he had no objections, for that one or two more or less could make no difference in so grand a household. So, though that was not the way in which I should have wished the coming of my bright and pretty pet to have been looked at – who was like a sunbeam in any family, be it never so grand – I was well pleased that all the folks in the Dale should stare and admire, when they heard I was going to be young lady's maid at my Lord Furnivall's at Furnivall Manor.

But I made a mistake in thinking we were to go and live where my lord did. It turned out that the family had left Furnivall Manor House fifty years or more. I could not hear that my poor young mistress had ever been there, though she had been brought up in the family; and I was sorry for that, for I should have liked Miss Rosamond's youth to have passed where her mother's had been.

My lord's gentleman, from whom I asked as many questions as I durst, said that the Manor House was at the foot of the Cumberland Fells, and a very grand place; that an old Miss Furnivall, a great-aunt of my lord's, lived there, with only a few servants; but that it was a very healthy place, and my lord had thought that it would suit Miss Rosamond very well for a few years, and that her being there might perhaps amuse his old aunt.

I was bidden by my lord to have Miss Rosamond's things ready by a certain day. He was a stern, proud man, as they say all the Lords Furnivall were; and he never spoke a word more than was necessary. Folk did say he loved my young mistress; but that, because she knew that his father would object, she would never listen to him, and married Mr. Esthwaite; but I don't know. He never married, at any rate. But he never took much notice of Miss Rosamond; which I thought he might have done if he had cared for her dead mother. He sent his gentleman with us to the Manor House, telling him to join him at Newcastle that same evening; so there was no great length of time for him to make us known to all the strangers before he, too, shook us off; and we were left, two lonely young things (I was not eighteen) in the great old Manor House. It seems like yesterday that we drove there. We had left our own dear parsonage very early, and we had both cried as if our hearts would break, though we were travelling in my lord's carriage, which I thought so much of once. And now it was long past noon on a September day, and we stopped to change horses for the last time at a smoky little town, all full of colliers and miners. Miss Rosamond had fallen asleep, but Mr. Henry told me to waken her, that she might see the park and the Manor House as we drove up. I thought it rather a pity; but I did what he bade me, for fear he should complain of me to my lord. We had left all signs of a town, or even a village, and were then inside the gates of a large, wild park – not like the parks here in the south, but with rocks, and the noise of running water, and gnarled thorn-trees, and old oaks, all white and peeled with age.

The road went up about two miles, and then we saw

a great and stately house, with many trees close around it, so close that in some places their branches dragged against the walls when the wind blew, and some hung broken down; for no one seemed to take much charge of the place; – to lop the wood, or to keep the moss-covered carriage-way in order. Only in front of the house all was clear. The great oval drive was without a weed; and neither tree nor creeper was allowed to grow over the long, many-windowed front; at both sides of which a wing projected, which were each the ends of other side fronts; for the house, although it was so desolate, was even grander than I expected. Behind it rose the Fells, which seemed unenclosed and bare enough; and on the left hand of the house, as you stood facing it, was a little old-fashioned flower-garden, as I found out afterwards. A door opened out upon it from the west front; it had been scooped out of the thick, dark wood for some old Lady Furnivall; but the branches of the great forest-trees had grown and over-shadowed it again, and there were very few flowers that would live up there at that time.

When we drove up to the great front entrance, and went into the hall, I thought we should be lost – it was so large, and vast, and grand. There was a chandelier all of bronze, hung down from the middle of the ceiling; and I had never seen one before, and looked at it all in amaze. Then, at one end of the hall, was a great fireplace, as large as the sides of the houses in my country, with massy andirons and dogs to hold the wood; and by it were heavy, old-fashioned sofas. At the opposite end of the hall, to the left as you went in – on the western side – was an organ built into the wall, and so large that it filled up the best part of that end. Beyond it, on the same side, was a door; and opposite, on each side of the fireplace, were also doors leading to the east front; but those I never went through as long as I stayed in the house, so I can't tell you what lay beyond.

The afternoon was closing in, and the hall, which had no fire lighted in it, looked dark and gloomy; but we did not stay there a moment. The old servant, who had opened the door for us, bowed to Mr. Henry, and took us in through the door at the further side of the great organ, and led us through several smaller halls and passages into the west drawing-room, where he said that Miss Furnivall was sitting. Poor little Miss Rosamond held very tight to me, as if she were scared and lost in that great place; and as for myself, I was not much better. The west drawing-room was very cheerful-looking, with a warm fire in it, and plenty of good, comfortable furniture about. Miss Furnivall was an old lady not far from eighty, I should think, but I do not know. She was thin and tall, and had a face as full of fine wrinkles as if they had been drawn all over it with a needle's point. Her eyes were very watchful, to make up, I suppose, for her being so deaf as to be obliged to use a trumpet.[1] Sitting with her, working at the same great piece of tapestry, was Mrs. Stark, her maid and companion, and almost as old as she was. She had lived with Miss Furnivall ever since they both were young, and now she seemed more like a friend than a servant; she looked so cold, and grey, and stony, as if she had never loved or cared for any one; and I don't suppose she did care for any one, except her mistress; and, owing to the great deafness of the latter, Mrs. Stark treated her very much as if she were a child. Mr. Henry gave some message from my lord, and then he bowed good-bye to us all – taking no notice of my sweet little Miss Rosamond's outstretched hand – and left us standing there, being looked at by the two old ladies through their spectacles.

I was right glad when they rung for the old footman who had shown us in at first, and told him to take us to our rooms. So we went out of that great drawing-room, and into another sitting-room, and out of that, and then up a great flight of stairs, and along a broad gallery – which was something like a library, having books all down one side, and windows and writing-tables all down the other – till we came to our rooms, which I was not sorry to hear were just above the kitchens; for I began to think I should be lost in that wilderness of a house. There was an old nursery, that had been used for all the little lords and ladies long ago, with a pleasant fire burning in the grate, and the kettle boiling on the hob, and tea-things spread out on the table; and out of that room was the night-nursery, with a little crib for Miss Rosamond close to my bed. And old James called up Dorothy, his wife, to bid us welcome; and both he and she were so hospitable and kind, that by-and-by Miss Rosamond and me felt quite at home; and by the time tea was over, she was sitting on Dorothy's knee, and chattering away as fast as her little tongue could go. I soon found out that Dorothy was from Westmoreland, and that bound her and me together, as it were; and I would never wish to meet with kinder people than were old James and his wife. James had lived pretty nearly all his life in my lord's family, and thought there was no one so grand as they. He even looked down a little on his wife; because, till he had married her, she had never lived in any but a farmer's household. But he was very fond of her, as well he might be. They had one servant under them, to do all the rough work. Agnes they called her; and she and me, and James and Dorothy, with Miss Furnivall and Mrs. Stark, made up the family; always remembering my sweet little Miss Rosamond! I used to wonder what they had done before she came, they thought so much of her now. Kitchen and drawing-room, it was all the same. The hard, sad Miss Furnivall, and the cold Mrs. Stark, looked pleased when she came fluttering in like a bird, playing and pranking hither and thither, with a continual murmur, and pretty prattle of gladness. I am sure, they were sorry many a time when she flitted away into the kitchen, though they were too proud to ask her to stay with them, and were a little surprised at her taste; though to be sure, as Mrs. Stark said, it was not to be wondered at, remembering what stock her father had come of. The great, old rambling house was a famous place for little Miss Rosamond. She made expeditions all over it, with me at her heels; all, except the east wing, which was never opened, and whither we never thought of going. But in the western and northern part was many a pleasant room; full of things that were curiosities to us, though they might not have been to people who had seen more. The windows were darkened by the sweeping boughs of the trees, and the ivy which had overgrown them; but, in the green gloom, we could manage to see old china jars and carved ivory boxes, and great heavy books, and, above all, the old pictures!

Once, I remember, my darling would have Dorothy go with us to tell who they all were; for they were all portraits of some of my lord's family, though Dorothy could not tell us the names of every one. We had gone through most of the rooms, when we came to the old state drawing-room over the hall, and there was a picture of Miss Furnivall; or, as she was called in those days, Miss Grace, for she was the younger sister. Such a beauty she must have been! but with such a set, proud look, and such scorn looking out of her handsome eyes, with her eyebrows just a little raised, as if she wondered how any one could have the impertinence to look at her, and her lip curled at us, as we stood there gazing. She had a dress on, the like of which I had never seen before, but it was all the fashion when she was young: a hat of some soft white stuff like beaver, pulled a little over her brows, and a beautiful plume of feathers sweeping round it on one side; and her gown of blue satin was open in front to a quilted white stomacher.

"Well, to be sure!" said I, when I had gazed my fill. "Flesh is grass, they do say; but who would have thought that Miss Furnivall had been such an out-and-out beauty, to see her now?"

"Yes," said Dorothy. "Folks change sadly. But if what my master's father used to say was true, Miss Furnivall, the elder sister, was handsomer than Miss Grace. Her picture is here somewhere; but, if I show it you, you must never let on, even to James, that you have seen it. Can the little lady hold her tongue, think you?" asked she.

I was not so sure, for she was such a little sweet, bold, open-spoken child, so I set her to hide herself; and then I helped Dorothy to turn a great picture, that leaned with its face towards the wall, and was not hung up as the others were. To be sure, it beat Miss Grace for beauty; and, I think, for scornful pride, too, though in that matter it might be hard to choose. I could have looked at it an hour, but Dorothy seemed half frightened at having shown it to me, and hurried it back again, and bade me run and find Miss Rosamond, for that there were some ugly places about the house, where she should like ill for the child to go. I was a brave, high-spirited girl, and thought little of what the old woman said, for I liked hide-and-seek as well as any child in the parish; so off I ran to find my little one.

As winter drew on, and the days grew shorter, I was sometimes almost certain that I heard a noise as if some one was playing on the great organ in the hall. I did not hear it every evening; but, certainly, I did very often, usually when I was sitting with Miss Rosamond, after I had put her to bed, and keeping quite still and silent in the bedroom. Then I used to hear it booming and swelling away in the distance. The first night, when I went down to my supper, I asked Dorothy who had been playing music, and James said very shortly that I was a gowk[2] to take the wind soughing[3] among the trees for music; but I saw Dorothy look at him very fearfully, and Bessy, the kitchen-maid, said something beneath her breath, and went quite white. I saw they did not like my question, so I held my peace till I was with Dorothy alone, when I knew I could get a good deal out of her. So, the next day, I watched my time, and I coaxed and asked her who it was that played the organ; for I knew that it was the organ and not the wind well enough, for all I had kept silence before James. But Dorothy had had her lesson, I'll warrant, and never a word could I get from her. So then I tried Bessy, though I had always held my head rather above her, as I was evened to James and Dorothy, and she was little better than their servant. So she said I must never, never tell; and if ever I told, I was never to say *she* had told me; but it was a very strange noise, and she had heard it many a time, but most of all on winter nights, and before storms; and folks did say it was the old lord playing on the great organ in the hall, just as he used to do when he was alive; but who the old lord was, or why he played on stormy winter evenings in particular, she either could not or would not tell me. Well! I told you I had a brave heart;

and I thought it was rather pleasant to have that grand music rolling about the house, let who would be the player; for now it rose above the great gusts of wind, and wailed and triumphed just like a living creature, and then it fell to a softness most complete, only it was always music, and tunes, so it was nonsense to call it the wind. I thought at first, that it might be Miss Furnivall who played, unknown to Bessy; but one day, when I was in the hall by myself, I opened the organ and peeped all about it and around it, as I had done to the organ in Crosthwaite Church once before, and I saw that it was all broken and destroyed inside, though it looked so brave and fine; and then, though it was noon-day, my flesh began to creep a little, and I shut it up, and run away pretty quickly to my own bright nursery; and I did not like hearing the music for some time after that, any more than James and Dorothy did. All this time Miss Rosamond was making herself more and more beloved. The old ladies liked her to dine with them at their early dinner. James stood beside Miss Furnivall's chair, and I behind Miss Rosamond's all in state; and, after dinner, she would play about in a corner of the great drawing-room as still as any mouse, while Miss Furnivall slept, and I had my dinner in the kitchen. But she was glad enough to come to me in the nursery afterwards; for, as she said, Miss Furnivall was so sad, and Mrs. Stark so dull; but she and I were merry enough; and, by-and-by, I got not to care for that weird rolling music, which did no one any harm, if we did not know. where it came from.

That winter was very cold. In the middle of October the frosts began, and lasted many, many weeks. I remember one day, at dinner, Miss Furnivall lifted up her sad, heavy eyes, and said to Mrs. Stark, "I am afraid we shall have a terrible winter," in a strange kind of meaning way. But Mrs. Stark pretended not to hear, and talked very loud of something else. My little lady and I did not care for the frost; not we! As long as it was dry, we climbed up the steep brows behind the house, and went up on the Fells, which were bleak and bare enough, and there we ran races in the fresh, sharp air; and once we came down by a new path, that took us past the two old gnarled holly-trees, which grew about half-way down by the east side of the house. But the days grew shorter and shorter, and the old lord, if it was he, played away, more and more stormily and sadly, on the great organ. One Sunday afternoon – it must have been towards the end of November – I asked Dorothy to take charge of little missy when she came out of the drawing-room, after Miss Furnivall had had her nap; for it was too cold to take her with me to church, and yet I wanted to go. And Dorothy was glad enough to promise, and was so fond of the child, that all seemed well; and Bessy and I set off very briskly, though the sky hung heavy and black over the white earth, as if the night had never fully gone away, and the air, though still, was very biting and keen.

"We shall have a fall of snow," said Bessy to me. And sure enough, even while we were in church, it came down thick, in great large flakes – so thick, it almost darkened the windows. It had stopped snowing before we came out, but it lay soft, thick, and deep beneath our feet, as we tramped home. Before we got to the hall, the moon rose, and I think it was lighter then – what with the moon, and what with the white dazzling snow – than it had been when we went to church, between two and three o'clock. I have not told you that Miss Furnivall and Mrs. Stark never went to church; they used to read the prayers together, in their quiet, gloomy way; they seemed to feel the Sunday very long without their tapestry-work to be busy at. So when I went to Dorothy in the kitchen, to fetch Miss Rosamond and take her upstairs with me, I did not much wonder when the old woman told me that the ladies had kept the child with them, and that she had never come to the kitchen, as I had bidden her, when she was tired of behaving pretty in the drawing-room. So I took off my things and went to find her, and bring her to her supper in the nursery. But when I went into the best drawing-room, there sat the two old ladies, very still and quiet, dropping out a word now and then, but looking as if nothing so bright and merry as Miss Rosamond had ever been near them. Still I thought she might be hiding from me; it was one of her pretty ways, – and that she had persuaded them to look as if they knew nothing about her; so I went softly peeping under this sofa, and behind that chair, making believe I was sadly frightened at not finding her.

"What's the matter, Hester?" said Mrs. Stark sharply. I don't know if Miss Furnivall had seen me, for, as I told you, she was very deaf, and she sat quite still, idly staring into the fire, with her hopeless face. "I'm only looking for my little Rosy Posy," replied I, still thinking that the child was there, and near me, though I could not see her.

"Miss Rosamond is not here," said Mrs. Stark. "She went away, more than an hour ago, to find Dorothy." And she, too, turned and went on looking into the fire.

My heart sank at this, and I began to wish I had never left my darling. I went back to Dorothy and told her. James was gone out for the day, but she, and me, and Bessy, took lights, and went up into the nursery first; and then we roamed over the great, large house, calling and entreating Miss Rosamond to come out of her hiding-place, and not to frighten us to death in that way. But there was no answer; no sound.

"Oh!" said I, at last, "can she have got into the east wing and hidden there?"

But Dorothy said it was not possible, for that she herself had never been in there; that the doors were always locked, and my lord's steward had the keys, she believed; at any rate, neither she nor James had ever seen them; so I said I would go back, and see if, after all, she was not hidden in the drawing-room, unknown to the old ladies; and if I found her there, I said, I would whip her well for the fright she had given me; but I never meant to do it. Well, I went back to the west drawing-room, and I told Mrs. Stark we could not find her anywhere, and asked for leave to look all about the furniture there, for I thought now that she might have fallen asleep in some warm, hidden corner; but no! we looked – Miss Furnivall got up and looked, trembling all over – and she was nowhere there; then we set off again, every one in the house, and looked in all the places we had searched before, but we could not find her. Miss Furnivall shivered and shook so much, that Mrs. Stark took her back into the warm drawing-room; but not before they had made me promise to bring her back to them when she was found. Well-a-day! I began to think she never would be found, when I bethought me to look into the great front court, all covered with snow. I was upstairs when I looked out; but, it was such clear moonlight, I could see, quite plain, two little footprints, which might be traced from the hall-door and round the corner of the east wing. I don't know how I got down, but I tugged open the great stiff hall-door, and, throwing the skirt of my gown over my head for a cloak, I ran out. I turned the east corner, and there a black shadow fell on the snow; but when I came again into the moonlight, there were the little footprints going up – up to the Fells. It was bitter cold; so cold, that the air almost took the skin off my face as I ran; but I ran on, crying to think how my poor little darling must be perished and frightened. I was within sight of the holly-trees, when I saw a shepherd coming down the hill, bearing something in his arms wrapped in his maud. He shouted to me, and asked me if I had lost a bairn; and, when I could not speak for crying, he bore towards me, and I saw my wee bairnie, lying still, and white, and stiff in his arms, as if she had been dead. He told me he had been up the Fells to gather in his sheep, before the deep cold of night came on, and that under the holly-trees (black marks on the hill-side, where no other bush was for miles around) he had found my little lady – my lamb – my queen – my darling – stiff and cold in the terrible sleep which is frost-begotten. Oh! the joy and the tears of having her in my arms once again! for I would not let him carry her; but took her, maud and all, into my own arms, and held her near my own warm neck and heart, and felt the life stealing slowly back again into her little gentle limbs. But she was still insensible when we reached the hall, and I had no breath for speech. We went in by the kitchen-door.

"Bring the warming-pan," said I; and I carried her upstairs, and began undressing her by the nursery fire, which Bessy had kept up. I called my little lammie all the sweet and playful names I could think of, – even while my eyes were blinded by my tears; and at last, oh! at length she opened her large blue eyes. Then I put her into her warm bed, and sent Dorothy down to tell Miss Furnivall that all was well; and I made up my mind to sit by my darling's bedside the live-long night. She fell away into a soft sleep as soon as her pretty head had touched the pillow, and I watched by her till morning light; when she wakened up bright and clear – or so I thought at first – and, my dears, so I think now.

She said, that she had fancied that she should like to go to Dorothy, for that both the old ladies were asleep, and it was very dull in the drawing-room; and that, as she was going through the west lobby, she saw the snow through the high window falling – falling – soft and steady; but she wanted to see it lying pretty and white on the ground; so she made her way into the great hall: and then, going to the window, she saw it bright and soft upon the drive; but while she stood there, she saw a little girl, not so old as she was, "but so pretty," said my darling; "and this little girl beckoned to me to come out; and oh, she was so pretty and so sweet, I could not choose but go." And then this other little girl had taken her by the hand, and side by side the two had gone round the east corner.

"Now you are a naughty little girl, and telling stories," said I. "What would your good mamma, that is in heaven, and never told a story in her life, say to her little Rosamond, if she heard her – and I dare say she does – telling stories!"

"Indeed, Hester," sobbed out my child, "I'm telling you true. Indeed I am!"

"Don't tell me!" said I, very stern. "I tracked you by your foot-marks through the snow; there were only yours to be seen: and if you had had a little girl to go hand-in-hand with you up the hill, don't you think the footprints would have gone along with yours?"

"I can't help it, dear, dear Hester," said she, crying, "if they did not; I never looked at her feet, but she held my hand fast and tight in her little one, and it was very,

very cold. She took me up the Fell-path, up to the holly-trees; and there I saw a lady weeping and crying; but when she saw me, she hushed her weeping, and smiled very proud and grand, and took me on her knee, and began to lull me to sleep; and that's all, Hester – but that is true; and my dear mamma knows it is," said she, crying. So I thought the child was in a fever, and pretended to believe her, as she went over her story – over and over again, and always the same. At last Dorothy knocked at the door with Miss Rosamond's breakfast; and she told me the old ladies were down in the eating parlour, and that they wanted to speak to me. They had both been into the night-nursery the evening before, but it was after Miss Rosamond was asleep; so they had only looked at her – not asked me any questions.

"I shall catch it," thought I to myself, as I went along the north gallery. "And yet," I thought, taking courage, "it was in their charge that I left her; and it's they that's to blame for letting her steal away unknown and un-watched." So I went in boldly, and told my story. I told it all to Miss Furnivall, shouting it close to her ear; but when I came to the mention of the other little girl out in the snow, coaxing and tempting her out, and wiling her up to the grand and beautiful lady by the holly-tree, she threw her arms up – her old and withered arms – and cried aloud, "Oh! Heaven forgive! Have mercy!"

Mrs. Stark took hold of her; roughly enough, I thought; but she was past Mrs. Stark's management, and spoke to me, in a kind of wild warning and authority.

"Hester! keep her from that child! It will lure her to her death! That evil child! Tell her it is a wicked, naughty child." Then, Mrs. Stark hurried me out of the room; where, indeed, I was glad enough to go; but Miss Furnivall kept shrieking out, "Oh, have mercy! Wilt Thou never for-give! It is many a long year ago" —

I was very uneasy in my mind after that. I durst never leave Miss Rosamond, night or day, for fear lest she might slip off again, after some fancy or other; and all the more, because I thought I could make out that Miss Furnivall was crazy, from their odd ways about her; and I was afraid lest something of the same kind (which might be in the family, you know) hung over my darling. And the great frost never ceased all this time; and, whenever it was a more stormy night than usual, between the gusts, and through the wind, we heard the old lord playing on the great organ. But, old lord, or not, wherever Miss Rosamond went, there I followed; for my love for her, pretty, helpless orphan, was stronger than my fear for the grand and terrible sound. Besides, it rested with me to keep her cheerful and merry, as beseemed her age. So we played together, and wandered together, here and there, and everywhere; for I never dared to lose sight of her again in that large and rambling house. And so it happened, that one afternoon, not long before Christmas-day, we were playing together on the billiard-table in the great hall (not that we knew the right way of playing, but she liked to roll the smooth ivory balls with her pretty hands, and I liked to do whatever she did); and, by-and-by, without our noticing it, it grew dusk indoors, though it was still light in the open air, and I was thinking of taking her back into the nursery, when, all of a sudden, she cried out —

"Look, Hester! look! there is my poor little girl out in the snow!"

I turned towards the long narrow windows, and there, sure enough, I saw a little girl, less than my Miss Rosamond – dressed all unfit to be out-of-doors such a bitter night – crying, and beating against the window-panes, as if she wanted to be let in. She seemed to sob and wail, till Miss Rosamond could bear it no longer, and was flying to the door to open it, when, all of a sudden, and close upon us, the great organ pealed out so loud and thundering, it fairly made me tremble; and all the more, when I remembered me that, even in the stillness of that dead-cold weather, I had heard no sound of little battering hands upon the window-glass, although the phantom child had seemed to put forth all its force; and, although I had seen it wail and cry, no faintest touch of sound had fallen upon my ears. Whether I remembered all this at the very moment, I do not know; the great organ sound had so stunned me into terror; but this I know, I caught up Miss Rosamond before she got the hall-door opened, and clutched her, and carried her away, kicking and screaming, into the large, bright kitchen, where Dorothy and Agnes were busy with their mince-pies.

"What is the matter with my sweet one?" cried Dorothy, as I bore in Miss Rosamond, who was sobbing as if her heart would break.

"She won't let me open the door for my little girl to come in; and she'll die if she is out on the Fells all night. Cruel, naughty Hester," she said, slapping me; but she might have struck harder, for I had seen a look of ghastly terror on Dorothy's face, which made my very blood run cold.

"Shut the back-kitchen door fast, and bolt it well," said she to Agnes. She said no more; she gave me raisins and almonds to quiet Miss Rosamond; but she sobbed about the little girl in the snow, and would not touch any of the good things. I was thankful when she cried herself to sleep in bed. Then I stole down to the kitchen, and told Dorothy I had made up my mind. I would carry my darling back to my father's house in Applethwaite; where, if we lived humbly, we lived at peace. I said I had been frightened enough with the old lord's organ-playing; but now that I had seen for myself this little moaning child, all decked out as no child in the neighbourhood could be, beating and battering to get in, yet always without any sound or noise – with the dark wound on its right shoulder; and that Miss Rosamond had known it again for the phantom that had nearly lured her to death (which Dorothy knew was true); I would stand it no longer.

I saw Dorothy change colour once or twice. When I had done, she told me she did not think I could take Miss Rosamond with me, for that she was my lord's ward, and I had no right over her; and she asked me would I leave the child that I was so fond of just for sights and sounds that could do me no harm; and that they had all had to get used to in their turns? I was all in a hot, trembling passion; and I said it was very well for her to talk, that knew what these sights and noises betokened, and that had, perhaps, had something to do with the spectre child while it was alive. And I taunted her so, that she told me all she knew at last; and then I wished I had never been told, for it only made me more afraid than ever.

She said she had heard the tale from old neighbours that were alive when she was first married; when folks used to come to the hall sometimes, before it had got such a bad name on the country side: it might not be true, or it might, what she had been told.

The old lord was Miss Furnivall's father – Miss Grace, as Dorothy called her, for Miss Maude was the elder, and Miss Furnivall by rights. The old lord was eaten up with pride. Such a proud man was never seen or heard of; and his daughters were like him. No one was good enough to wed them, although they had choice enough; for they were the great beauties of their day, as I had seen by their portraits, where they hung in the state drawing-room. But, as the old saying is, "Pride will have a fall;" and these two haughty beauties fell in love with the same man, and he no better than a foreign musician, whom their father had down from London to play music with him at the Manor House. For, above all things, next to his pride, the old lord loved music. He could play on nearly every instrument that ever was heard of; and it was a strange thing it did not soften him; but he was a fierce, dour old man, and had broken his poor wife's heart with his cruelty, they said. He was mad after music, and would pay any money for it. So he got this foreigner to come; who made such beautiful music, that they said the very birds on the trees stopped their singing to listen. And, by degrees, this foreign gentleman got such a hold over the old lord, that nothing would serve him but that he must come every year; and it was he that had the great organ brought from Holland, and built up in the hall, where it stood now. He taught the old lord to play on it; but many and many a time, when Lord Furnivall was thinking of nothing but his fine organ, and his finer music, the dark foreigner was walking abroad in the woods, with one of the young ladies: now Miss Maude, and then Miss Grace.

Miss Maude won the day and carried off the prize,

such as it was; and he and she were married, all unknown to any one; and, before he made his next yearly visit, she had been confined of a little girl at a farm-house on the Moors, while her father and Miss Grace thought she was away at Doncaster Races. But though she was a wife and a mother, she was not a bit softened, but as haughty and as passionate as ever; and perhaps more so, for she was jealous of Miss Grace, to whom her foreign husband paid a great deal of court – by way of blinding her – as he told his wife. But Miss Grace triumphed over Miss Maude, and Miss Maude grew fiercer and fiercer, both with her husband and with her sister; and the former – who could easily shake off what was disagreeable, and hide himself in foreign countries – went away a month before his usual time that summer, and half-threatened that he would never come back again. Meanwhile, the little girl was left at the farm-house, and her mother used to have her horse saddled and gallop wildly over the hills to see her once every week, at the very least; for where she loved she loved, and where she hated she hated. And the old lord went on playing – playing on his organ; and the servants thought the sweet music he made had soothed down his awful temper, of which (Dorothy said) some terrible tales could be told. He grew infirm too, and had to walk with a crutch; and his son – that was the present Lord Furnivall's father – was with the army in America, and the other son at sea; so Miss Maude had it pretty much her own way, and she and Miss Grace grew colder and bitterer to each other every day; till at last they hardly spoke to each other, except when the old lord was by. The foreign musician came again the next summer, but it was for the last time; for they led him such a life with their jealousy and their passions, that he grew weary, and went away, and never was heard of again. And Miss Maude, who had always meant to have her marriage acknowledged when her father should be dead, was left now a deserted wife, whom nobody knew to have been married, with a child that she dared not own, although she loved it to distraction; living with a father whom she feared, and a sister whom she hated. When the next summer passed over, and the dark foreigner never came, both Miss Maude and Miss Grace grew gloomy and sad; they had a haggard look about them, though they looked handsome as ever. But, by-and-by, Miss Maude brightened; for her father grew more and more infirm, and more than ever carried away by his music; and she and Miss Grace lived almost entirely apart, having separate rooms, the one on the west side, Miss Maude on the east – those very rooms which were now shut up. So she thought she might have her little girl with her, and no one need ever know except those who dared not speak about it, and were bound to believe that it was, as she said, a cottager's child she had taken a fancy to. All this, Dorothy said, was pretty well known; but what came afterwards no one knew, except Miss Grace and Mrs. Stark, who was even then her maid, and much more of a friend to her than ever her sister had been. But the servants supposed, from words that were dropped, that Miss Maude had triumphed over Miss Grace, and told her that all the time the dark foreigner had been mocking her with pretended love – he was her own husband. The colour left Miss Grace's cheek and lips that very day for ever, and she was heard to say many a time that sooner or later she would have her revenge; and Mrs. Stark was for ever spying about the east rooms.

One fearful night, just after the New Year had come in, when the snow was lying thick and deep; and the flakes were still falling – fast enough to blind any one who might be out and abroad – there was a great and violent noise heard, and the old lord's voice above all, cursing and swearing awfully, and the cries of a little child, and the proud defiance of a fierce woman, and the sound of a blow, and a dead stillness, and moans and wailings, dying away on the hill-side! Then the old lord summoned all his servants, and told them, with terrible oaths, and words more terrible, that his daughter had disgraced herself, and that he had turned her out of doors – her, and her child – and that if ever they gave her help, or food, or shelter, he prayed that they might never enter heaven. And, all the while, Miss Grace stood by him, white and still as any stone; and, when he had ended, she heaved a great sigh, as much as to say her work was done, and her end was accomplished. But the old lord never touched his organ again, and died within the year; and no wonder! for, on the morrow of that wild and fearful night, the shepherds, coming down the Fell side, found Miss Maude sitting, all crazy and smiling, under the holly-trees, nursing a dead child, with a terrible mark on its right shoulder. "But that was not what killed it," said Dorothy: "it was the frost and the cold. Every wild creature was in its hole, and every beast in its fold, while the child and its mother were turned out to wander on the Fells! And now you know all! and I wonder if you are less frightened now?"

I was more frightened than ever; but I said I was not. I wished Miss Rosamond and myself well out of that dreadful house for ever; but I would not leave her, and I dared not take her away. But oh, how I watched her, and guarded her! We bolted the doors, and shut the window-shutters fast, an hour or more before dark, rather than leave them open five minutes too late. But my little lady still heard the weird child crying and mourning; and not all we could do or say could keep her from wanting to go to her, and let her in from the cruel wind and snow. All this time I kept away from Miss Furnivall and Mrs. Stark, as much as ever I could; for I feared them – I knew no good could be about them, with their grey, hard faces, and their dreamy eyes, looking back into the ghastly years that were gone. But, even in my fear, I had a kind of pity for Miss Furnivall, at least. Those gone down to the pit can hardly have a more hopeless look than that which was ever on her face. At last I even got so sorry for her – who never said a word but what was quite forced from her – that I prayed for her; and I taught Miss Rosamond to pray for one who had done a deadly sin; but often, when she came to those words, she would listen, and start up from her knees, and say, "I hear my little girl plaining and crying, very sad, – oh, let her in, or she will die!"

One night – just after New Year's Day had come at last, and the long winter had taken a turn, as I hoped – I heard the west drawing-room bell ring three times, which was the signal for me. I would not leave Miss Rosamond alone, for all she was asleep – for the old lord had been playing wilder than ever – and I feared lest my darling should waken to hear the spectre child; see her I knew she could not. I had fastened the windows too well for that. So I took her out of her bed, and wrapped her up in such outer clothes as were most handy, and carried her down to the drawing-room, where the old ladies sat at their tapestry-work as usual. They looked up when I came in, and Mrs. Stark asked, quite astounded, "Why did I bring Miss Rosamond there, out of her warm bed?" I had begun to whisper, "Because I was afraid of her being tempted out while I was away, by the wild child in the snow," when she stopped me short (with a glance at Miss Furnivall), and said Miss Furnivall wanted me to undo some work she had done wrong, and which neither of them could see to unpick. So I laid my pretty dear on the sofa, and sat down on a stool by them, and hardened my heart against them, as I heard the wind rising and howling.

Miss Rosamond slept on sound, for all the wind blew so; and Miss Furnivall said never a word, nor looked round when the gusts shook the windows. All at once she started up to her full height, and put up one hand, as if to bid us listen.

"I hear voices!" said she. "I hear terrible screams – I hear my father's voice!"

Just at that moment my darling wakened with a sudden start: "My little girl is crying, oh, how she is crying!" and she tried to get up and go to her, but she got her feet entangled in the blanket, and I caught her up; for my flesh had begun to creep at these noises, which they heard while we could catch no sound. In a minute or two the noises came, and gathered fast, and filled our ears; we, too, heard voices and screams, and no longer heard the winter's wind that raged abroad. Mrs. Stark looked at me, and I at her, but we dared not speak. Suddenly Miss Furnivall went towards the door, out into the ante-room, through the west lobby, and opened the door into the great hall. Mrs. Stark followed, and I durst not be left, though my heart almost stopped beating for fear. I wrapped my darling tight in my arms, and went out with them. In the hall the screams were louder than ever; they seemed to come from the east wing – nearer and nearer – close on the other side of the locked-up doors – close behind them. Then I noticed that the great bronze chandelier seemed all alight, though the hall was dim, and that a fire was blazing in the vast hearth-place, though it gave no heat; and I shuddered up with terror, and folded my darling closer to me. But as I did so the east door shook, and she, suddenly struggling to get free from me, cried "Hester, I must go! My little girl is there! I hear her; she is coming! Hester, I must go!"

I held her tight with all my strength; with a set will, I held her. If I had died, my hands would have grasped her still, I was so resolved in my mind. Miss Furnivall stood listening, and paid no regard to my darling, who had got down to the ground, and whom I, upon my knees now, was holding with both my arms clasped round her neck; she still striving and crying to get free.

All at once, the east door gave way with a thundering crash, as if torn open in a violent passion, and there came into that broad and mysterious light, the figure of a tall old man, with grey hair and gleaming eyes. He drove before him, with many a relentless gesture of abhorrence, a stern and beautiful woman, with a little child clinging to her dress.

"O Hester! Hester!" cried Miss Rosamond; "it's the lady! the lady below the holly-trees; and my little girl is with her. Hester! Hester! let me go to her; they are drawing me to them. I feel them – I feel them. I must go!"

Again she was almost convulsed by her efforts to get away; but I held her tighter and tighter, till I feared I should do her a hurt; but rather that than let her go towards those terrible phantoms. They passed along towards the great hall-door, where the winds howled and ravened for their prey; but before they reached that, the lady turned; and I could see that she defied the old man with a fierce and proud defiance; but then she quailed – and then she threw up her arms wildly and piteously to save her child – her little child – from a blow from his uplifted crutch.

And Miss Rosamond was torn as by a power stronger than mine, and writhed in my arms, and sobbed (for by this time the poor darling was growing faint).

"They want me to go with them to the Fells – they are drawing me to them. Oh, my little girl! I would come, but cruel, wicked Hester holds me very tight." But when she saw the uplifted crutch, she swooned away, and I thanked God for it. Just at this moment – when the tall old man, his hair streaming as in the blast of a furnace, was going to strike the little shrinking child – Miss Furnivall, the old woman by my side, cried out, "O father! father! spare the little innocent child!" But just then I saw – we all saw – another phantom shape itself, and grow clear out of the blue and misty light that filled the hall; we had not seen her till now, for it was another lady who stood by the old man, with a look of relentless hate and triumphant scorn. That figure was very beautiful to look upon, with a soft, white hat drawn down over the proud brows, and a red and curling lip. It was dressed in an open robe of blue satin. I had seen that figure before. It was the likeness of Miss Furnivall in her youth; and the terrible phantoms moved on, regardless of old Miss Furnivall's wild entreaty, – and the uplifted crutch fell on the right shoulder of the little child, and the younger sister looked on, stony, and deadly serene. But at that moment, the dim lights, and the fire that gave no heat, went out of themselves, and Miss Furnivall lay at our feet stricken down by the palsy – death-stricken.

Yes! she was carried to her bed that night never to rise again. She lay with her face to the wall, muttering low, but muttering always: "Alas! alas! what is done in youth can never be undone in age! What is done in youth can never be undone in age!"

Notes

1   Early form of hearing aid.
2   A fool.
3   Sighing.
Source: *Lizzie Leigh and Other Tales*, London: Chapman Hall, 1855.

Biographical Note

Born in Chelsea in 1810, Gaskell was sent to live with her aunt in Knutsford when her mother died a year later. She was educated at home until the age of twelve, and then sent to boarding-school at Barford. She returned to London in 1828 and lived with her father and his new wife until his death in 1829. After a few more years in Knutsford, she married a Unitarian minister, William Gaskell, in 1832. They lived in Manchester, and Gaskell spent the next fifteen years helping her husband with his humanitarian work and looking after her growing family. She began writing tales for *Howitt's Journal* during the 1840s, but it was only after the death of her nine-month-old son from scarlet fever in 1845 that she began to focus her energies on writing. *Mary Barton*, a social-problem novel detailing the grim living conditions of Manchester factory workers, was published anonymously in 1848 to critical and popular acclaim. Dickens began to press her for contributions to his new journal, *Household Words*, during the next year, and "Lizzie Leigh" appeared in the first issue in 1850. But it was *Cranford*, first serialized in *Household Words* and then published in book form in 1853, that firmly established Gaskell's reputation, and, until recently, it was as the author of these stories based on her childhood memories of Knutsford that she was best known. While *Cranford* was being serialized in *Household Words*, Dickens asked Gaskell to write a ghost story for the first special Christmas issue of 1852; the result was "The Old Nurse's Story," one of the most powerful ghost stories of

Nurse's Story," one of the most powerful ghost stories of the century. With the publication of *Ruth* in 1853 Gaskell shocked and offended a number of her readers because of her support and sympathy for the fallen woman and her exposure of the hypocrisy in a society which condemned the victims while tolerating the seducers. Another social problem novel, *North and South*, followed in response to Dickens's request for a full-length novel for *Household Words*. One of Gaskell's friends, Charlotte Brontë, died in 1855, and Brontë's father and husband both asked her to write the offical biography; Gaskell spent the next two years on this *Life* (1857), and it is still considered one of the finest of Victorian biographies. Unfortunately, the initially positive response to the work was soon replaced by protests and threatened law-suits from some of the people mentioned; the second edition was withdrawn and revised. In 1858 the novella *My Lady Ludlow* appeared, followed by *Lois the Witch*, an account of the Salem witch trials, in 1861, and *Sylvia's Lovers* in 1863. *Cousin Phyllis*, an examination of a young girl's sexual awakening, was published by George Smith in the *Cornhill* and ran from November 1863 until February 1864; and Gaskell's last novel, *Wives and Daughters: An Every-Day Story*, also ran in the *Cornhill* from August 1864 to January 1866. While this work was left unfinished, Gaskell had provided Smith with a full synopsis, and so the novel as it stands is virtually complete. Although Gaskell purchased a house in the country to which she hoped to retire eventually with her husband, her health was poor and, on a visit to her new house in November 1865, she suddenly collapsed and died. Gaskell produced many collections of short stories during her literary career, including *Round the Sofa and Other Tales* (1859), *Right at Last, and Other Tales* (1860), *Lois the Witch and Other Tales* (1861), and *The Grey Woman and Other Tales* (1865). As the two stories reprinted here confirm, Gaskell was the pre-eminent short story writer of the early Victorian age.

Selected Modern Reprints:

Cousin Phyllis and Other Tales. Ed. Angus Easson. Oxford:
    Oxford UP, 1981.
Elizabeth Gaskell: Four Short Stories. Intro. Anna Walters. Lon-
    don: Pandora, 1983.
Elizabeth Gaskell: A Portrait in Letters. Ed. J.A.V. Chapple.
    Manchester: Manchester UP, 1980.
Mrs. Gaskell's Tales of Mystery and Horror. Ed. Michael Ashley.
    London: Gollancz, 1978.
My Lady Ludlow and Other Stories. Ed. Edgar Wright. Oxford:
    Oxford UP, 1989.

Selected Secondary Sources:

Easson, Angus, ed. *Elizabeth Gaskell: The Critical Heritage*.
    London: Routledge, 1991.
Gerin, Winifred. *Elizabeth Gaskell: A Biography*. Oxford: Ox-
    ford UP, 1980.
Lansbury, Coral. *Elizabeth Gaskell*. Boston: Twayne, 1984.
—. *Elizabeth Gaskell: The Novel of Social Crisis*. London: Paul
    Elek, 1975.
Stoneman, Patsy. *Elizabeth Gaskell*. Bloomington: Indiana
    UP, 1987.
Thompson, Joanne. "Faith of Our Mothers: Elizabeth
    Gaskell's 'Lizzie Leigh.'" *Victorian Newsletter* 78 (1990):
    22-26.

310   CHARLOTTE PERKINS GILMAN (1860-1935)

Charlotte Perkins Gilman (1860-1935)

The Yellow Wallpaper

IT IS VERY SELDOM THAT MERE ORDINARY PEOPLE LIKE JOHN and myself secure ancestral halls for the summer.

A colonial mansion, a hereditary estate, I would say a haunted house, and reach the height of romantic felicity – but that would be asking too much of fate!

Still I will proudly declare that there is something queer about it.

Else, why should it be let so cheaply? And why have stood so long untenanted?

John laughs at me, of course, but one expects that in marriage.

John is practical in the extreme. He has no patience with faith, an intense horror of superstition, and he scoffs openly at any talk of things not to be felt and seen and put down in figures.

John is a physician, and *perhaps* – (I would not say it to a living soul, of course, but this is dead paper and a great relief to my mind –) *perhaps* that is one reason I do not get well faster.

You see he does not believe I am sick!

And what can one do?

If a physician of high standing, and one's own husband, assures friends and relatives that there is really nothing the matter with one but temporary nervous depression – a slight hysterical tendency – what is one to do?

My brother is also a physician, and also of high standing, and he says the same thing.

So I take phosphates or phosphites – whichever it is, and tonics, and journeys, and air, and exercise, and am absolutely forbidden to "work" until I am well again.

Personally, I disagree with their ideas.

Personally, I believe that congenial work, with excitement and change, would do me good.

But what is one to do?

I did write for a while in spite of them; but it *does* exhaust me a good deal – having to be so sly about it, or else meet with heavy opposition.

I sometimes fancy that in my condition if I had less opposition and more society and stimulus – but John says the worst thing I can do is to think about my condition, and I confess it always makes me feel bad.

So I will let it alone and talk about the house.

The most beautiful place! It is quite alone, standing well back from the road, quite three miles from the village. It makes me think of English places that you read about, for there are hedges and walls and gates that lock, and lots of separate little houses for the gardeners and people.

There is a *delicious* garden! I never saw such a garden – large and shady, full of box-bordered paths, and lined with long grape-covered arbors with seats under them.

There were greenhouses, too, but they are all broken now.

There was some legal trouble, I believe, something about the heirs and co-heirs; anyhow, the place has been empty for years.

That spoils my ghostliness, I am afraid, but I don't care – there is something strange about the house – I can feel it.

I even said so to John one moonlight evening, but he said what I felt was a *draught*, and shut the window.

I get unreasonably angry with John sometimes. I'm sure I never used to be so sensitive. I think it is due to this nervous condition.

But John says if I feel so, I shall neglect proper self-control; so I take pains to control myself – before him, at least, and that makes me very tired.

I don't like our room a bit. I wanted one downstairs that opened on the piazza and had roses all over the window, and such pretty old-fashioned chintz hangings! but John would not hear of it.

He said there was only one window and not room for two beds, and no near room for him if he took another.

He is very careful and loving, and hardly lets me stir without special direction.

I have a schedule prescription for each hour in the day; he takes all care from me, and so I feel basely ungrateful not to value it more.

He said we came here solely on my account, that I was to have perfect rest and all the air I could get. "Your exercise depends on your strength, my dear," said he, "and your food somewhat on your appetite; but air you can absorb all the time." So we took the nursery at the top of the house.

It is a big, airy room, the whole floor nearly, with windows that look all ways, and air and sunshine galore. It was nursery first and then playroom and gymnasium, I should judge; for the windows are barred for little children, and there are rings and things in the walls.

The paint and paper look as if a boys' school had used it. It is stripped off – the paper – in great patches all around the head of my bed, about as far as I can reach, and in a great place on the other side of the room low down. I never saw a worse paper in my life.

One of those sprawling flamboyant patterns committing every artistic sin.

It is dull enough to confuse the eye in following, pronounced enough to constantly irritate and provoke study, and when you follow the lame uncertain curves for a little distance they suddenly commit suicide – plunge off at outrageous angles, destroy themselves in unheard of contradictions.

The color is repellent, almost revolting; a smouldering unclean yellow, strangely faded by the slow-turning sunlight.

It is a dull yet lurid orange in some places, a sickly sulphur tint in others.

No wonder the children hated it! I should hate it myself if I had to live in this room long.

There comes John, and I must put this away, – he hates to have me write a word.

*   *   *   *   *

We have been here two weeks, and I haven't felt like writing before, since that first day.

I am sitting by the window now, up in this atrocious nursery, and there is nothing to hinder my writing as much as I please, save lack of strength.

John is away all day, and even some nights when his cases are serious.

I am glad my case is not serious!

But these nervous troubles are dreadfully depressing.

John does not know how much I really suffer. He knows there is no *reason* to suffer, and that satisfies him.

Of course it is only nervousness. It does weigh on me so not to do my duty in any way!

I meant to be such a help to John, such a real rest and comfort, and here I am a comparative burden already!

Nobody would believe what an effort it is to do what little I am able, – to dress and entertain, and order things.

It is fortunate that Mary is so good with the baby. Such a dear baby!

And yet I *cannot* be with him, it makes me so nervous.

I suppose John never was nervous in his life. He laughs at me so about this wall-paper!

At first he meant to repaper the room, but afterwards he said that I was letting it get the better of me, and that nothing was worse for a nervous patient than to give way to such fancies.

He said that after the wall-paper was changed it would be the heavy bedstead, and then the barred windows, and then that gate at the head of the stairs, and so on.

"You know the place is doing you good," he said, "and really, dear, I don't care to renovate the house for just three months' rental."

"Then do let us go downstairs," I said, "there are such pretty rooms there."

Then he took me in his arms and called me a blessed little goose, and said he would go down cellar, if I wished, and have it whitewashed into the bargain.

But he is right enough about the beds and windows and things.

It is an airy and comfortable room as any one need wish, and, of course, I would not be so silly as to make him uncomfortable just for a whim.

I'm really getting quite fond of the big room, all but that horrid paper.

Out of one window I can see the garden, those mysterious deep-shaded arbors, the riotous old-fashioned flowers, and bushes and gnarly trees.

Out of another I get a lovely view of the bay and a little private wharf belonging to the estate. There is a beautiful shaded lane that runs down there from the house. I always fancy I see people walking in these numerous paths and arbors, but John has cautioned me not to give way to fancy in the least. He says that with my imaginative power and habit of story-making, a nervous weakness like mine is sure to lead to all manner of excited fancies, and that I ought to use my will and good sense to check the tendency. So I try.

I think sometimes that if I were only well enough to write a little it would relieve the press of ideas and rest me.

But I find I get pretty tired when I try.

It is so discouraging not to have any advice and companionship about my work. When I get really well, John says we will ask Cousin Henry and Julia down for a long visit; but he says he would as soon put fireworks in my pillow-case as to let me have those stimulating people about now.

I wish I could get well faster.

But I must not think about that. This paper looks to me as if it *knew* what a vicious influence it had!

There is a recurrent spot where the pattern lolls like a broken neck and two bulbous eyes stare at you upside down.

I get positively angry with the impertinence of it and the everlastingness. Up and down and sideways they crawl, and those absurd, unblinking eyes are everywhere. There is one place where two breadths didn't match, and the eyes go all up and down the line, one a little higher than the other.

I never saw so much expression in an inanimate thing before, and we all know how much expression they have! I used to lie awake as a child and get more entertainment and terror out of blank walls and plain furniture than most children could find in a toy-store.

I remember what a kindly wink the knobs of our big, old bureau used to have, and there was one chair that always seemed like a strong friend.

I used to feel that if any of the other things looked too fierce I could always hop into that chair and be safe.

The furniture in this room is no worse than inharmonious, however, for we had to bring it all from downstairs. I suppose when this was used as a playroom they had to take the nursery things out, and no wonder! I never saw such ravages as the children have made here.

The wall-paper, as I said before, is torn off in spots, and it sticketh closer than a brother – they must have had perseverance as well as hatred.

Then the floor is scratched and gouged and splintered, the plaster itself is dug out here and there, and this great heavy bed which is all we found in the room, looks as if it had been through the wars.

"But I don't mind it a bit – only the paper."

There comes John's sister. Such a dear girl as she is, and so careful of me! I must not let her find me writing.

She is a perfect and enthusiastic housekeeper, and hopes for no better profession. I verily believe she thinks it is the writing which made me sick!

But I can write when she is out, and see her a long way off from these windows.

There is one that commands the road, a lovely shaded winding road, and one that just looks off over the country. A lovely country, too, full of great elms and velvet meadows.

This wallpaper has a kind of sub-pattern in a different shade, a particularly irritating one, for you can only see it in certain lights, and not clearly then.

But in the places where it isn't faded and where the sun is just so – I can see a strange, provoking, formless sort of figure, that seems to skulk about behind that silly and conspicuous front design.

There's sister on the stairs!

*   *   *   *   *

Well, the Fourth of July is over! The people are all gone and I am tired out. John thought it might do me good to see a little company, so we just had mother and Nellie and the children down for a week.

Of course I didn't do a thing. Jennie sees to everything now.

But it tired me all the same.

John says if I don't pick up faster he shall send me to Weir Mitchell[1] in the fall.

But I don't want to go there at all. I had a friend who was in his hands once, and she says he is just like John and my brother, only more so!

Besides, it is such an undertaking to go so far.

I don't feel as if it was worth while to turn my hand over for anything, and I'm getting dreadfully fretful and querulous.

I cry at nothing, and cry most of the time.

Of course I don't when John is here, or anybody else, but when I am alone.

And I am alone a good deal just now. John is kept in town very often by serious cases, and Jennie is good and lets me alone when I want her to.

So I walk a little in the garden or down that lovely lane, sit on the porch under the roses, and lie down up here a good deal.

I'm getting really fond of the room in spite of the wallpaper. Perhaps *because* of the wallpaper.

It dwells in my mind so!

I lie here on this great immovable bed – it is nailed down, I believe – and follow that pattern about by the hour. It is as good as gymnastics, I assure you. I start, we'll say, at the bottom, down in the corner over there where it has not been touched, and I determine for the thousandth time that I *will* follow that pointless pattern to some sort of a conclusion.

I know a little of the principle of design, and I know this thing was not arranged on any laws of radiation, or alternation, or repetition, or symmetry, or anything else that I ever heard of.

It is repeated, of course, by the breadths, but not otherwise.

Looked at in one way each breadth stands alone, the bloated curves and flourishes – a kind of "debased Romanesque" with *delirium tremens* – go waddling up and down in isolated columns of fatuity.

But, on the other hand, they connect diagonally, and the sprawling outlines run off in great slanting waves of optic horror, like a lot of wallowing sea-weeds in full chase.

The whole thing goes horizontally, too, at least it seems so, and I exhaust myself in trying to distinguish the order of its going in that direction.

They have used a horizontal breadth for a frieze, and that adds wonderfully to the confusion.

There is one end of the room where it is almost intact, and there, when the crosslights fade and the low sun shines directly upon it, I can almost fancy radiation after all, – the interminable grotesque seem to form around a common centre and rush off in headlong plunges of equal distraction.

It makes me tired to follow it. I will take a nap I guess.

*   *   *   *   *

I don't know why I should write this.

I don't want to.

I don't feel able.

And I know John would think it absurd. But I *must* say what I feel and think in some way – it is such a relief!

But the effort is getting to be greater than the relief.

Half the time now I am awfully lazy, and lie down ever so much.

John says I mustn't lose my strength, and has me take

cod liver oil and lots of tonics and things, to say nothing of ale and wine and rare meat. Dear John! He loves me very dearly, and hates to have me sick. I tried to have a real earnest reasonable talk with him the other day, and tell him how I wish he would let me go and make a visit to Cousin Henry and Julia.

But he said I wasn't able to go, nor able to stand it after I got there; and I did not make out a very good case for myself, for I was crying before I had finished.

It is getting to be a great effort for me to think straight. Just this nervous weakness I suppose.

And dear John gathered me up in his arms, and just carried me upstairs and laid me on the bed, and sat by me and read to me till it tired my head.

He said I was his darling and his comfort and all he had, and that I must take care of myself for his sake, and keep well.

He says no one but myself can help me out of it, that I must use my will and self-control and not let any silly fancies run away with me.

There's one comfort, the baby is well and happy, and does not have to occupy this nursery with the horrid wall-paper.

If we had not used it, that blessed child would have! What a fortunate escape! Why, I wouldn't have a child of mine, an impressionable little thing, live in such a room for worlds.

I never thought of it before, but it is lucky that John kept me here after all, I can stand it so much easier than a baby, you see.

Of course I never mention it to them any more – I am too wise, – but I keep watch of it all the same.

There are things in that paper that nobody knows but me, or ever will.

Behind that outside pattern the dim shapes get clearer every day.

It is always the same shape, only very numerous.

And it is like a woman stooping down and creeping about behind that pattern. I don't like it a bit. I wonder – I begin to think – I wish John would take me away from here!

*　*　*　*　*

It is so hard to talk with John about my case, because he is so wise, and because he loves me so.

But I tried it last night.

It was moonlight. The moon shines in all around just as the sun does.

I hate to see it sometimes, it creeps so slowly, and always comes in by one window or another.

John was asleep and I hated to waken him, so I kept still and watched the moonlight on that undulating wallpaper till I felt creepy.

The faint figure behind seemed to shake the pattern, just as if she wanted to get out.

I got up softly and went to feel and see if the paper *did* move, and when I came back John was awake.

"What is it, little girl?" he said. "Don't go walking about like that – you'll get cold."

I thought it was a good time to talk, so I told him that I really was not gaining here, and that I wished he would take me away.

"Why, darling!" said he, "our lease will be up in three weeks, and I can't see how to leave before.

"The repairs are not done at home, and I cannot possibly leave town just now. Of course if you were in any danger, I could and would, but you really are better, dear, whether you can see it or not. I am a doctor, dear, and I know. You are gaining flesh and color, your appetite is better, I feel really much easier about you."

"I don't weigh a bit more," said I, "nor as much; and my appetite may be better in the evening when you are here, but it is worse in the morning when you are away!"

"Bless her little heart!" said he with a big hug, "she shall be as sick as she pleases! But now let's improve the shining hours by going to sleep, and talk about it in the morning!"

"And you won't go away?" I asked gloomily.

"Why, how can I, dear? It is only three weeks more

and then we will take a nice little trip of a few days while Jennie is getting the house ready. Really dear you are better!"

"Better in body perhaps —" I began, and stopped short, for he sat up straight and looked at me with such a stern, reproachful look that I could not say another word.

"My darling," said he, "I beg of you, for my sake and for our child's sake, as well as for your own, that you will never for one instant let that idea enter your mind! There is nothing so dangerous, so fascinating, to a temperament like yours. It is a false and foolish fancy. Can you not trust me as a physician when I tell you so?"

So of course I said no more on that score, and we went to sleep before long. He thought I was asleep first, but I wasn't, and lay there for hours trying to decide whether that front pattern and the back pattern really did move together or separately.

*   *   *   *   *

On a pattern like this, by daylight, there is a lack of sequence, a defiance of law, that is a constant irritant to a normal mind.

The color is hideous enough, and unreliable enough, and infuriating enough, but the pattern is torturing.

You think you have mastered it, but just as you get well underway in following, it turns a back-somersault and there you are. It slaps you in the face, knocks you down, and tramples upon you. It is like a bad dream.

The outside pattern is a florid arabesque, reminding one of a fungus. If you can imagine a toadstool in joints, an interminable string of toadstools, budding and sprouting in endless convolutions – why, that is something like it.

That is, sometimes!

There is one marked peculiarity about this paper, a thing nobody seems to notice but myself, and that is that it changes as the light changes.

When the sun shoots in through the east window – I

always watch for that first long, straight ray – it changes so quickly that I never can quite believe it.

That is why I watch it always.

By moonlight – the moon shines in all night when there is a moon – I wouldn't know it was the same paper.

At night in any kind of light, in twilight, candlelight, lamplight, and worst of all by moonlight, it becomes bars! The outside pattern I mean, and the woman behind it is as plain as can be.

I didn't realize for a long time what the thing was that showed behind, that dim sub-pattern, but now I am quite sure it is a woman.

By daylight she is subdued, quiet. I fancy it is the pattern that keeps her so still. It is so puzzling. It keeps me quiet by the hour.

I lie down ever so much now. John says it is good for me, and to sleep all I can.

Indeed he started the habit by making me lie down for an hour after each meal.

It is a very bad habit I am convinced, for you see I don't sleep.

And that cultivates deceit, for I don't tell them I'm awake – O no!

The fact is I am getting a little afraid of John.

He seems very queer sometimes, and even Jennie has an inexplicable look.

It strikes me occasionally, just as a scientific hypothesis, – that perhaps it is the paper!

I have watched John when he did not know I was looking, and come into the room suddenly on the most innocent excuses, and I've caught him several times *looking at the paper!* And Jennie too. I caught Jennie with her hand on it once.

She didn't know I was in the room, and when I asked her in a quiet, a very quiet voice, with the most restrained manner possible, what she was doing with the paper – she turned around as if she had been caught stealing, and looked quite angry – asked me why I should frighten her so!

Then she said that the paper stained everything it

touched, that she had found yellow smooches on all my clothes and John's, and she wished we would be more careful!

Did not that sound innocent? But I know she was studying that pattern, and I am determined that nobody shall find it out but myself!

*   *   *   *   *

Life is very much more exciting now than it used to be. You see I have something more to expect, to look forward to, to watch. I really do eat better, and am more quiet than I was.

John is so pleased to see me improve! He laughed a little the other day, and said I seemed to be flourishing in spite of my wall-paper.

I turned it off with a laugh. I had no intention of telling him it was *because* of the wall-paper – he would make fun of me. He might even want to take me away.

I don't want to leave now until I have found it out. There is a week more, and I think that will be enough.

*   *   *   *   *

I'm feeling ever so much better! I don't sleep much at night, for it is so interesting to watch developments; but I sleep a good deal in the daytime.

In the daytime it is tiresome and perplexing.

There are always new shoots on the fungus, and new shades of yellow all over it. I cannot keep count of them, though I have tried conscientiously.

It is the strangest yellow, that wallpaper! It makes me think of all the yellow things I ever saw – not beautiful ones like buttercups, but old foul, bad yellow things.

But there is something else about that paper – the smell! I noticed it the moment we came into the room, but with so much air and sun it was not bad. Now we have had a week of fog and rain, and whether the windows are open or not, the smell is here.

It creeps all over the house.

I find it hovering in the dining-room, skulking in the parlor, hiding in the hall, lying in wait for me on the stairs.

It gets into my hair.

Even when I go to ride, if I turn my head suddenly and surprise it – there is that smell!

Such a peculiar odor, too! I have spent hours in trying to analyze it, to find what it smelled like.

It is not bad – at first, and very gentle, but quite the subtlest, most enduring odor I ever met.

In this damp weather it is awful, I wake up in the night and find it hanging over me.

It used to disturb me at first. I thought seriously of burning the house – to reach the smell.

But now I am used to it. The only thing I can think of that it is like is the *color* of the paper! A yellow smell.

There is a very funny mark on this wall, low down, near the mopboard. A streak that runs round the room. It goes behind every piece of furniture, except the bed, a long, straight, even *smooch*, as if it had been rubbed over and over.

I wonder how it was done and who did it, and what they did it for. Round and round and round – round and round and round – it makes me dizzy!

*   *   *   *   *

I really have discovered something at last.

Through watching so much at night, when it changes so, I have finally found out.

The front pattern *does* move – and no wonder! The woman behind shakes it!

Sometimes I think there are a great many women behind, and sometimes only one, and she crawls around fast, and her crawling shakes it all over.

Then in the very bright spots she keeps still, and in the very shady spots she just takes hold of the bars and shakes them hard.

And she is all the time trying to climb through. But nobody could climb through that pattern – it strangles so;

I think that is why it has so many heads.

They get through, and then the pattern strangles them off and turns them upside down, and makes their eyes white!

If those heads were covered or taken off it would not be half so bad.

*   *   *   *   *

I think that woman gets out in the daytime!

And I'll tell you why – privately – I've seen her!

I can see her out of every one of my windows!

It is the same woman, I know, for she is always creeping, and most women do not creep by daylight.

I see her in that long shaded lane, creeping up and down. I see her in those dark grape arbors, creeping all around the garden.

I see her on that long road under the trees, creeping along, and when a carriage comes she hides under the blackberry vines.

I don't blame her a bit. It must be very humiliating to be caught creeping by daylight!

I always lock the door when I creep by daylight. I can't do it at night, for I know John would suspect something at once.

And John is so queer now, that I don't want to irritate him. I wish he would take another room! Besides, I don't want anybody to get that woman out at night but myself.

I often wonder if I could see her out of all the windows at once.

But, turn as fast as I can, I can only see out of one at one time.

And though I always see her, she *may* be able to creep faster than I can turn!

I have watched her sometimes away off in the open country, creeping as fast as a cloud shadow in a high wind.

*   *   *   *   *

If only that top pattern could be gotten off from the

under one! I mean to try it, little by little.

I have found out another funny thing, but I shan't tell it this time! It does not do to trust people too much.

There are only two more days to get this paper off, and I believe John is beginning to notice. I don't like the look in his eyes.

And I heard him ask Jennie a lot of professional questions about me. She had a very good report to give.

She said I slept a good deal in the daytime.

John knows I don't sleep very well at night, for all I'm so quiet!

He asked me all sorts of questions, too, and pretended to be very loving and kind.

As if I couldn't see through him!

Still, I don't wonder he acts so, sleeping under this paper for three months.

It only interests me, but I feel sure John and Jennie are secretly affected by it.

*   *   *   *   *

Hurrah! This is the last day, but it is enough. John to stay in town over night, and won't be out until this evening.

Jennie wanted to sleep with me – the sly thing! but I told her I should undoubtedly rest better for a night all alone.

That was clever, for really I wasn't alone a bit! As soon as it was moonlight and that poor thing began to crawl and shake the pattern, I got up and ran to help her.

I pulled and she shook, I shook and she pulled, and before morning we had peeled off yards of that paper.

A strip about as high as my head and half around the room.

And then when the sun came and that awful pattern began to laugh at me, I declared I would finish it to-day!

We go away tomorrow, and they are moving all my furniture down again to leave things as they were before.

Jennie looked at the wall in amazement, but I told her merrily that I did it out of pure spite at the vicious thing.

She laughed and said she wouldn't mind doing it herself, but I must not get tired.

How she betrayed herself that time!

But I am here, and no person touches this paper but me – not *alive*!

She tried to get me out of the room – it was too patent! But I said it was so quiet and empty and clean now that I believed I would lie down again and sleep all I could; and not to wake me even for dinner – I would call when I woke.

So now she is gone, and the servants are gone, and the things are gone, and there is nothing left but that great bedstead nailed down, with the canvas mattress we found on it.

We shall sleep downstairs to-night, and take the boat home to-morrow.

I quite enjoy the room, now it is bare again.

How those children did tear about here!

This bedstead is fairly gnawed!

But I must get to work.

I have locked the door and thrown the key down into the front path.

I don't want to go out, and I don't want to have anybody come in, till John comes.

I want to astonish him.

I've got a rope up here that even Jennie did not find. If that woman does get out, and tries to get away, I can tie her!

But I forgot I could not reach far without anything to stand on!

This bed will *not* move!

I tried to lift and push it until I was lame, and then I got so angry I bit off a little piece at one corner – but it hurt my teeth.

Then I peeled off all the paper I could reach standing on the floor. It sticks horribly and the pattern just enjoys it! All those strangled heads and bulbous eyes and waddling fungus growths just shriek with derision!

I am getting angry enough to do something desperate. To jump out of the window would be admirable exercise, but the bars are too strong even to try.

Besides I wouldn't do it. Of course not. I know well enough that a step like that is improper and might be misconstrued.

I don't like to *look* out of the windows even – there are so many of those creeping women, and they creep so fast.

I wonder if they all come out of that wall-paper as I did?

But I am securely fastened now by my well-hidden rope – you don't get *me* out in the road there!

I suppose I shall have to get back behind the pattern when it comes night, and that is hard!

It is so pleasant to be out in this great room and creep around as I please!

I don't want to go outside. I won't, even if Jennie asks me to.

For outside you have to creep on the ground, and everything is green instead of yellow.

But here I can creep smoothly on the floor, and my shoulder just fits in that long smooch around the wall, so I cannot lose my way.

Why there's John at the door!

It is no use, young man, you can't open it!

How he does call and pound!

Now he's crying for an axe.

It would be a shame to break down that beautiful door!

"John dear!" said I in the gentlest voice, "the key is down by the front steps, under a plantain leaf!"

That silenced him for a few moments.

Then he said – very quietly indeed, "Open the door, my darling!"

"I can't," said I, "The key is down by the front door under a plantain leaf!"

And then I said it again, several times, very gently and slowly, and said it so often that he had to go and see, and he got it of course, and came in. He stopped short by the door.

"What is the matter?" he cried. "For God's sake, what

are you doing!"

I kept on creeping just the same, but I looked at him over my shoulder.

"I've got out at last," said I, "in spite of you and Jane? And I've pulled off most of the paper, so you can't put me back!"

Now why should that man have fainted? But he did, and right across my path by the wall, so that I had to creep over him every time!

Note

1   Silas Weir Mitchell (1829-1914). American physician and specialist in nerve disorders who popularized the "rest cure."

Source: *New England Magazine* 1892.

Biographical Note

Charlotte Perkins Gilman was born in Hartford, Connecticut on 3 July, 1860, and educated primarily at home apart from a brief period at the Rhode Island School of Design. While still in her teens, she began to support herself as artist and governess, and by the age of twenty-one, was writing poems dealing with the limitations imposed upon women in late nineteenth-century New England. At twenty-four she married Charles Stetson, also an artist, and a year later she gave birth to a daughter, Katharine. Gilman experienced severe depression afterwards, and for a time she suffered through the rest cure prescribed for "inappropriately" ambitious women by the famous specialist, S. Weir Mitchell. Mitchell, arguing that woman's health depended on the passivity of the womb being echoed in the woman's life, suggested a complete end to all reading and writing, and advised Gilman to adopt a totally domestic life and to enjoy the constant companionship of her daughter. In her attempts to follow these instructions, Gilman grew steadily worse. She finally broke away and left for California in 1885. Her symptoms finally began to disappear, and in 1888 she moved with her daughter to Pasadena, divorced her husband, and began to support herself by giving public lectures.

"The Yellow Wallpaper" (1892), which draws upon and fictionalizes these experiences, is Gilman's masterpiece and one of the most frequently reprinted short stories by a woman. During the nineties, Gilman began to establish a reputation for herself as a writer, first with a series of satiric poems in the *Nationalist*, and then, in 1893, with a collection of short poems entitled *In This Our World* which reflect her social views with particular reference to women. In 1895 she left California for Chicago; her former husband had married her best friend, Grace Channing, the previous year, and Gilman had sent Katherine to live with them. Over the next three years, she devoted herself completely to her work; she spent much time on the road, lecturing, attending many feminist meetings, and continuing to write. *Women and Economics*, an argument in support of women's rights, appeared in 1898 and made a significant contribution to the women's movement of the time. In 1900 Gilman married her cousin George Houghton Gilman, a lawyer from New York. In 1909 she began to edit her own periodical, the *Forerunner*, for which she wrote poetry, fiction, and articles on women's social and economic issues. Her novels, including *What Diantha Did* (1910), *The Crux* (1911), and the feminist utopian fiction of *Herland* (1915), which celebrates a vigorous female community that exists peacefully and happily without men, were also first published in the *Forerunner* as was *The Man-Made World*, in which Gilman further outlined her views upon the differences between peace-loving, communal women and aggressive, competitive men. After her husband's unexpected death in 1934, Gilman, suffering from cancer, lived near her daughter in Pasadena for a short time and then committed suicide with chloroform. Her autobiography, *The Living of Charlotte Perkins Gilman* (1935), was published soon after.

Selected Modern Reprints:

The Charlotte Perkins Gilman Reader. Ed. and Intro. Ann J. Lane. New York: Pantheon, 1980.
Herland. Intro. Anne J. Lane. New York: Pantheon, 1979.
The Yellow Wallpaper and Other Writings. New York: Bantam, 1989.

Selected Secondary Sources:

Haney-Peritz, Janice. "Monumental Feminism and Literature's Ancestral House: Another Look at 'The Yellow Wallpaper.'" *Women's Studies: An Interdisciplinary Journal* 12.2 (1986): 113-28.

Lane, Ann J. *To Herland and Beyond: The Life and Work of Charlotte Perkins Gilman.* New York: Pantheon, 1990.

Meyering, Sheryl L., ed. *Charlotte Perkins Gilman: The Woman and Her Work.* Rochester, NY: U of Rochester P, 1988.

Scharnhorst, Gary. *Charlotte Perkins Gilman.* Boston: Twayne, 1984.

Schumaker, Conrad. "Realism, Reform, and the Audience: Charlotte Perkins Gilman's Unreadable Wallpaper." *Arizona Quarterly* 47.1 (1991): 81-93.

Treichler, Paula A. "Escaping the Sentence: Diagnosis and Discourse in 'The Yellow Wallpaper.'" *Tulsa Studies in Women's Literature* 3.1-2 (1984): 61-77.

SARAH ORNE JEWETT (1849-1909)

Sarah Orne Jewett (1849-1909)

A White Heron

I

THE WOODS WERE ALREADY FILLED WITH SHADOWS ONE JUNE
evening, just before eight o'clock, though a bright sunset
still glimmered faintly among the trunks of the trees. A little
girl was driving home her cow, a plodding, dilatory, provoking creature in her behavior, but a valued companion for all
that. They were going away from whatever light there was,
and striking deep into the woods, but their feet were familiar with the path, and it was no matter whether their eyes
could see it or not.

There was hardly a night the summer through when
the old cow could be found waiting at the pasture bars;
on the contrary, it was her greatest pleasure to hide herself away among the huckleberry bushes, and though she
wore a loud bell she had made the discovery that if one
stood perfectly still it would not ring. So Sylvia had to
hunt for her until she found her, and call Co'! Co'! with
never an answering Moo, until her childish patience was
quite spent. If the creature had not given good milk and
plenty of it, the case would have seemed very different to
her owners. Besides, Sylvia had all the time there was,
and very little use to make of it. Sometimes in pleasant
weather it was a consolation to look upon the cow's pranks
as an intelligent attempt to play hide and seek, and as the
child had no playmates she lent herself to this amusement
with a good deal of zest. Though this chase had been so
long that the wary animal herself had given an unusual
signal of her whereabouts, Sylvia had only laughed when
she came upon Mistress Moolly at the swampside, and

urged her affectionately homeward with a twig of birch leaves. The old cow was not inclined to wander farther, she even turned in the right direction for once as they left the pasture, and stepped along the road at a good pace. She was quite ready to be milked now, and seldom stopped to browse. Sylvia wondered what her grandmother would say because they were so late. It was a great while since she had left home at half-past five o'clock, but everybody knew the difficulty of making this errand a short one. Mrs. Tilley had chased the horned torment too many summer evenings herself to blame any one else for lingering, and was only thankful as she waited that she had Sylvia nowadays, to give such valuable assistance. The good woman suspected that Sylvia loitered occasionally on her own account; there never was such a child for straying about out-of-doors since the world was made! Everybody said that it was a good change for a little maid who had tried to grow for eight years in a crowded manufacturing town, but, as for Sylvia herself, it seemed as if she never had been alive at all before she came to live at the farm. She thought often with wistful compassion of a wretched geranium that belonged to a town neighbor.

"'Afraid of folks,'" old Mrs. Tilley said to herself, with a smile, after she had made the unlikely choice of Sylvia from her daughter's houseful of children, and was returning to the farm. "'Afraid of folks,' they said! I guess she won't be troubled no great with 'em up to the old place!" When they reached the door of the lonely house and stopped to unlock it, and the cat came to purr loudly, and rub against them, a deserted pussy, indeed, but fat with young robins, Sylvia whispered that this was a beautiful place to live in, and she never should wish to go home.

The companions followed the shady wood-road, the cow taking slow steps and the child very fast ones. The cow stopped long at the brook to drink, as if the pasture were not half a swamp, and Sylvia stood still and waited, letting her bare feet cool themselves in the shoal water, while the great twilight moths struck softly against her. She waded on through the brook as the cow moved away, and listened to the thrushes with a heart that beat fast with pleasure. There was a stirring in the great boughs overhead. They were full of little birds and beasts that seemed to be wide awake, and going about their world, or else saying good-night to each other in sleeping twitters. Sylvia herself felt sleepy as she walked along. However, it was not much farther to the house, and the air was soft and sweet. She was not often in the woods so late as this, and it made her feel as if she were a part of the gray shadows and the moving leaves. She was just thinking how long it seemed since she first came to the farm a year ago, and wondering if everything went on in the noisy town just the same as when she was there; the thought of the great red-faced boy who used to chase and frighten her made her hurry along the path to escape from the shadow of the trees.

Suddenly this little woods-girl is horror-stricken to hear a clear whistle not very far away. Not a bird's whistle, which would have a sort of friendliness, but a boy's whistle, determined, and somewhat aggressive. Sylvia left the cow to whatever sad fate might await her, and stepped discreetly aside into the brushes, but she was just too late. The enemy had discovered her, and called out in a very cheerful and persuasive tone, "Halloa, little girl, how far is it to the road?" and trembling Sylvia answered almost inaudibly, "A good ways."

She did not dare to look boldly at the tall young man, who carried a gun over his shoulder, but she came out of her bush and again followed the cow, while he walked alongside.

"I have been hunting for some birds," the stranger said kindly, "and I have lost my way, and need a friend very much. Don't be afraid," he added gallantly. "Speak up and tell me what your name is, and whether you think I can spend the night at your house, and go out gunning early in the morning."

Sylvia was more alarmed than before. Would not her grandmother consider her much to blame? But who could have foreseen such an accident as this? It did not seem to be her fault, and she hung her head as if the stem of it were broken, but managed to answer "Sylvy," with much effort when her companion again asked her name.

Mrs. Tilley was standing in the doorway when the trio came into view. The cow gave a loud moo by way of explanation.

"Yes, you'd better speak up for yourself, you old trial! Where'd she tucked herself away this time, Sylvy?" But Sylvia kept an awed silence; she knew by instinct that her grandmother did not comprehend the gravity of the situation. She must be mistaking the stranger for one of the farmer-lads of the region.

The young man stood his gun beside the door, and dropped a lumpy game-bag beside it; then he bade Mrs. Tilley good-evening, and repeated his wayfarer's story, and asked if he could have a night's lodging.

"Put me anywhere you like," he said. "I must be off early in the morning, before day; but I am very hungry, indeed. You can give me some milk at any rate, that's plain."

"Dear sakes, yes," responded the hostess, whose long slumbering hospitality seemed to be easily awakened. "You might fare better if you went out to the main road a mile or so, but you're welcome to what we've got. I'll milk right off, and you make yourself at home. You can sleep on husks or feathers," she proffered graciously. "I raised them all myself. There's good pasturing for geese just below here towards the ma'sh. Now step round and set a plate for the gentleman, Sylvy!" And Sylvia promptly stepped. She was glad to have something to do, and she was hungry herself.

It was a surprise to find so clean and comfortable a dwelling in this New England wilderness. The young man had known the horrors of its most primitive housekeeping, and the dreary squalor of that level of society which does not rebel at the companionship of hens. This was the best thrift of an old-fashioned farmstead, though on such a small scale that it seemed like a hermitage. He listened eagerly to the old woman's quaint talk, he watched Sylvia's pale face and shining gray eyes with ever growing enthusiasm, and insisted that this was the best supper he had eaten for a month, and afterward the new-made friends sat down in the door-way together while the moon came up.

Soon it would be berry-time, and Sylvia was a great help at picking. The cow was a good milker, though a plaguy thing to keep track of, the hostess gossiped frankly, adding presently that she had buried four children, so Sylvia's mother, and a son (who might be dead) in California were all the children she had left. "Dan, my boy, was a great hand to go gunning," she explained sadly. "I never wanted for pa'tridges or gray squer'ls while he was at home. He's been a great wanderer, I expect, and he's no hand to write letters. There, I don't blame him, I'd ha' seen the world myself if it had been so I could."

"Sylvy takes after him," the grandmother continued affectionately, after a minute's pause. "There ain't a foot o' ground she don't know her way over, and the wild creatures counts her one o' themselves. Squer'ls she'll tame to come an' feed right out o' her hands, and all sorts o' birds. Last winter she got the jay-birds to bangeing here, and I believe she'd 'a'scanted herself of her own meals to have plenty to throw out amongst'em, if I hadn't kep' watch. Anything but crows, I tell her, I'm willin' to help support – though Dan he had a tamed one o' them that did seem to have reason same as folks. It was round here a good spell after he went away. Dan an' his father they didn't hitch, – but he never held up his head ag'in after Dan had dared him an' gone off."

The guest did not notice this hint of family sorrows in his eager interest in something else.

"So Sylvy knows all about birds, does she?" he exclaimed, as he looked round at the little girl who sat, very demure but increasingly sleepy, in the moonlight. "I am making a collection of birds myself. I have been at it ever since I was a boy." (Mrs. Tilley smiled.) "There are two or three very rare ones I have been hunting for these five years. I mean to get them on my own ground if they can be found."

"Do you cage 'em up?" asked Mrs. Tilley doubtfully, in response to this enthusiastic announcement.

"Oh no, they're stuffed and preserved, dozens and

dozens of them," said the ornithologist, "and I have shot or snared every one myself. I caught a glimpse of a white heron a few miles from here on Saturday, and I have followed it in this direction. They have never been found in this district at all. The little white heron, it is," and he turned again to look at Sylvia with the hope of discovering that the rare bird was one of her acquaintances.

But Sylvia was watching a hop-toad in the narrow footpath.

"You would know the heron if you saw it," the stranger continued eagerly. "A queer tall white bird with soft feathers and long thin legs. And it would have a nest perhaps in the top of a high tree, made of sticks, something like a hawk's nest."

Sylvia's heart gave a wild beat; she knew that strange white bird, and had once stolen softly near where it stood in some bright green swamp grass, away over at the other side of the woods. There was an open place where the sunshine always seemed strangely yellow and hot, where tall, nodding rushes grew, and her grandmother had warned her that she might sink in the soft black mud underneath and never be heard of more. Not far beyond were the salt marshes just this side the sea itself, which Sylvia wondered and dreamed much about, but never had seen, whose great voice could sometimes be heard above the noise of the woods on stormy nights.

"I can't think of anything I should like so much as to find that heron's nest," the handsome stranger was saying. "I would give ten dollars to anybody who could show it to me," he added desperately, "and I mean to spend my whole vacation hunting for it if need be. Perhaps it was only migrating, or had been chased out of its own region by some bird of prey."

Mrs. Tilley gave amazed attention to all this, but Sylvia still watched the toad, not divining, as she might have done at some calmer time, that the creature wished to get to its hole under the door-step, and was much hindered by the unusual spectators at that hour of the evening. No amount of thought, that night, could decide how many wished-for treasures the ten dollars, so lightly spoken of, would buy.

The next day the young sportsman hovered about the woods, and Sylvia kept him company, having lost her first fear of the friendly lad, who proved to be most kind and sympathetic. He told her many things about the birds and what they knew and where they lived and what they did with themselves. And he gave her a jack-knife, which she thought as great a treasure as if she were a desert-islander. All day long he did not once make her troubled or afraid except when he brought down some unsuspecting singing creature from its bough. Sylvia would have liked him vastly better without his gun; she could not understand why he killed the very birds he seemed to like so much. But as the day waned, Sylvia still watched the young man with loving admiration. She had never seen anybody so charming and delightful; the woman's heart, asleep in the child, was vaguely thrilled by a dream of love. Some premonition of that great power stirred and swayed these young creatures who traversed the solemn woodlands with soft-footed silent care. They stopped to listen to a bird's song; they pressed forward again eagerly, parting the branches – speaking to each other rarely and in whispers; the young man going first and Sylvia following, fascinated, a few steps behind, with her gray eyes dark with excitement.

She grieved because the longed-for white heron was elusive, but she did not lead the guest, she only followed, and there was no such thing as speaking first. The sound of her own unquestioned voice would have terrified her – it was hard enough to answer yes or no when there was need of that. At last evening began to fall, and they drove the cow home together, and Sylvia smiled with pleasure when they came to the place where she heard the whistle and was afraid only the night before.

II

Half a mile from home, at the farther edge of the woods, where the land was highest, a great pine-tree stood, the last of its generation. Whether it was left for a boundary mark, or for what reason, no one could say; the wood-choppers who had felled its mates were dead and gone long ago, and a whole forest of sturdy trees, pines and oaks and maples, had grown again. But the stately head of this old pine towered above them all and made a landmark for sea and shore miles and miles away. Sylvia knew it well. She had always believed that whoever climbed to the top of it could see the ocean; and the little girl had often laid her hand on the great rough trunk and looked up wistfully at those dark boughs that the wind always stirred, no matter how hot and still the air might be below. Now she thought of the tree with a new excitement, for why, if one climbed it at break of day could not one see all the world, and easily discover from whence the white heron flew, and mark the place, and find the hidden nest?

What a spirit of adventure, what wild ambition! What fancied triumph and delight and glory for the later morning when she could make known the secret! It was almost too real and too great for the childish heart to bear.

All night the door of the little house stood open and the whippoorwills came and sang on the very step. The young sportsman and his old hostess were sound asleep, but Sylvia's great design kept her broad awake and watching. She forgot to think of sleep. The short summer night seemed as long as the winter darkness, and at last when the whippoorwills ceased, and she was afraid the morning would after all come too soon, she stole out of the house and followed the pasture path through the woods, hastening toward the open ground beyond, listening with a sense of comfort and companionship to the drowsy twitter of a half-awakened bird, whose perch she had jarred in passing. Alas, if the great wave of human interest which flooded for the first time this dull little life should sweep away the satisfactions of an existence heart to heart with nature and the dumb life of the forest!

There was the huge tree asleep yet in the paling moonlight and small and silly Sylvia began with utmost bravery to mount to the top of it, with tingling, eager blood coursing the channels of her whole frame, with her bare feet and fingers, that pinched and held like bird's claws to the monstrous ladder reaching up, up, almost to the sky itself. First she must mount the white oak tree that grew alongside, where she was almost lost among the dark branches and the green leaves heavy and wet with dew; a bird fluttered off its nest, and a red squirrel ran to and fro and scolded pettishly at the harmless housebreaker. Sylvia felt her way easily. She had often climbed there, and knew that higher still one of the oak's upper branches chafed against the pine trunk, just where its lower boughs were set close together. There, when she made the dangerous pass from one tree to the other, the great enterprise would really begin.

She crept out along the swaying oak limb at last, and took the daring step across into the old pine-tree. The way was harder than she thought; she must reach far and hold fast, the sharp dry twigs caught and held her and scratched her like angry talons, the pitch made her thin little fingers clumsy and stiff as she went round and round the tree's great stem, higher and higher upward. The sparrows and robins in the woods below were beginning to wake and twitter to the dawn, yet it seemed much lighter there aloft in the pine-tree, and the child knew she must hurry if her project were to be of any use.

The tree seemed to lengthen itself out as she went up, and to reach farther and farther upward. It was like a great main-mast to the voyaging earth; it must truly have been amazed that morning through all its ponderous frame as it felt this determined spark of human spirit wending its way from higher branch to branch. Who knows how steadily the least twigs held themselves to advantage this light, weak creature on her way! The old pine must have loved his new dependent. More than all the hawks, and bats, and moths, and even the sweet voiced thrushes, was the brave, beating heart of the solitary gray-eyed child. And the tree stood still and frowned away the winds that June morning while the dawn grew bright in the east.

Sylvia's face was like a pale star, if one had seen it from the ground, when the last thorny bough was past, and she stood trembling and tired but wholly triumphant, high in the tree-top. Yes, there was the sea with the dawning sun making a golden dazzle over it, and toward that glorious east flew two hawks with slow-moving pinions. How low they looked in the air from that height when one had only seen them before far up, and dark against the blue sky. Their gray feathers were as soft as moths; they seemed only a little way from the tree, and Sylvia felt as if she too could go flying away among the clouds. Westward, the woodlands and farms reached miles and miles into the distance; here and there were church steeples, and white villages, truly it was a vast and awesome world!

The birds sang louder and louder. At last the sun came up bewilderingly bright. Sylvia could see the white sails of ships out at sea, and the clouds that were purple and rose-colored and yellow at first began to fade away. Where was the white heron's nest in the sea of green branches, and was this wonderful sight and pageant of the world the only reward for having climbed to such a giddy height? Now look down again, Sylvia, where the green marsh is set among the shining birches and dark hemlocks; there where you saw the white heron once you will see him again; look, look! a white spot of him like a single floating feather comes up from the dead hemlock and grows larger, and rises, and comes close at last, and goes by the landmark pine with steady sweep of wing and outstretched slender neck and crested head. And wait! wait! do not move a foot or a finger, little girl, do not send an arrow of light and consciousness from your two eager eyes, for the heron has perched on a pine bough not far beyond yours, and cries back to his mate on the nest and plumes his feathers for the new day!

The child gives a long sigh a minute later when a company of shouting cat-birds comes also to the tree, and vexed by their fluttering and lawlessness the solemn heron goes away. She knows his secret now, the wild, light, slender bird that floats and wavers, and goes back like an arrow presently to his home in the green world beneath. Then Sylvia, well satisfied, makes her perilous way down again, not daring to look far below the branch she stands on, ready to cry sometimes because her fingers ache and her lamed feet slip. Wondering over and over again what the stranger would say to her, and what he would think when she told him how to find his way straight to the heron's nest.

"Sylvy, Sylvy!" called the busy old grandmother again and again, but nobody answered, and the small husk bed was empty and Sylvia had disappeared.

The guest waked from a dream, and remembering his day's pleasure hurried to dress himself that might it sooner begin. He was sure from the way the shy little girl looked once or twice yesterday that she had at least seen the white heron, and now she must really be made to tell. Here she comes now, paler than ever, and her worn old frock is torn and tattered, and smeared with pine pitch. The grandmother and the sportsman stand in the door together and question her, and the splendid moment has come to speak of the dead hemlock-tree by the green marsh.

But Sylvia does not speak after all, though the old grandmother fretfully rebukes her, and the young man's kind, appealing eyes are looking straight in her own. He can make them rich with money; he has promised it, and they are poor now. He is so well worth making happy, and he waits to hear the story she can tell.

No, she must keep silence! What is it that suddenly forbids her and makes her dumb? Has she been nine years growing and now, when the great world for the first time puts out a hand to her, must she thrust it aside for a bird's sake? The murmur of the pine's green branches is in her ears, she remembers how the white heron came flying through the golden air and how they watched the sea and the morning together, and Sylvia cannot speak; she cannot tell the heron's secret and give its life away.

Dear loyalty, that suffered a sharp pang as the guest went away disappointed later in the day, that could have served and followed him and loved him as a dog loves! Many a night Sylvia heard the echo of his whistle haunting the pasture path as she came home with the loitering cow.

She forgot even her sorrow at the sharp report of his gun and the sight of thrushes and sparrows dropping silent to the ground, their songs hushed and their pretty feathers stained and wet with blood. Were the birds better friends than their hunter might have been, – who can tell? Whatever treasures were lost to her, woodlands and summertime, remember! Bring your gifts and graces and tell your secrets to this lonely country child!

Source: *A White Heron and Other Stories*. Boston: Houghton, Mifflin, 1886.

Biographical Note

Jewett, one of the finest regionalist writers in America, was born in South Berwick, Maine, in 1849, the daughter of Theodore Jewett, an affluent country doctor, and the former Caroline Perry, a distant descendent of Anne Bradstreet. She was educated partly at girls' schools, but primarily by her father, and she spent much time as a child accompanying him on his rounds and becoming familiar with the countryside that was to be the focus of her works. By 1867 Jewett was submitting stories to magazines under a variety of pseudonyms; her first published story, "Jenny Garrow's Lovers," appeared in the *Flag of Our Union* in January of 1868. *Deephaven*, her first extended work, began to be serialized in the *Atlantic Monthly* in September, 1873, and after producing some fiction for children she returned to stories and sketches for adults with *Old Friends* in 1879. In 1881 Jewett's next collection, *Country By-Ways*, appeared, dedicated to her father who had died three years earlier. Around this time Jewett began her friendship with Annie Fields, wife of the publisher James T. Fields; after Fields's death in 1881 the two women formed a "Boston marriage" which lasted throughout Jewett's lifetime. The two friends made a number of trips to Europe over the next few years where they visited such literary celebrities as Tennyson, Anne Ritchie, and Christina Rossetti. Their circle of acquaintances at home expanded to include close friendships with many women artists and writers of the day.

A *Country Doctor* was published in 1884, a work which is now receiving renewed attention by feminist critics for its concern with a woman's conflict between love and career, and *A Marsh Island* in 1885. *A White Heron and Other Stories* followed in 1886 and *A Native of Winby and Other Tales* in 1893. Jewett continued to be as prolific throughout the 1890s while managing to travel extensively with Annie Fields; they made two trips to Europe and one to Chicago, took a vacation in Florida, and went on a cruise in the Caribbean. In 1896 Jewett published her masterpiece, *The Country of the Pointed Firs*, described by Willa Cather as one of the three works certain to endure in American literature. Jewett's strength lies primarily in the regionalist sketch; her skills are best revealed in her style and characterization rather than her plots, and her characters are frequently elderly and female. "A White Heron," which has received much recent critical attention and is considered by most her best short story, is generally seen as either an initiation story in which the heroine refuses to be initiated, or as a distinctively female form of *Bildungsroman*. The conflict between the urban and rural values found here is one of Jewett's central themes. There is a 1977 film version of the story shot by Jane Morrison around Jewett's home town of South Berwick. On her fifty-third birthday Jewett was thrown from a carriage and received serious injuries to her head and spine from which she never fully recovered; she suffered a stroke in March of 1909 and died three months later of a cerebral hemorrhage.

Selected Modern Reprints:

The Best Short Stories of Sarah Orne Jewett. 2 vols. Intro. Willa Cather. Boston: Houghton Mifflin, 1925.
The Country of the Pointed Firs and Other Stories. Ed. Mary Ellen Chase, with an introduction by Marjorie Pryse. New York: Norton, 1982.
Deephaven and Other Stories. Ed. Richard Cary. New Haven:

College and University P, 1966.

The Queen's Twin and Other Stories. 1899. New York: Garrett P, 1969.

The Uncollected Short Stories of Sarah Orne Jewett. Ed. Richard Cary. Waterville: Colby College P, 1971.

Selected Secondary Sources:

Ammons, Elizabeth. "The Shape of Violence in Jewett's 'A White Heron.'" *Colby Library Quarterly* 22 (1986): 6-16.

Cary, Richard, ed. *Appreciation of Sarah Orne Jewett: Twenty-Nine Interpretive Essays.* Waterville, ME: Colby College P, 1973.

Donovan, Josephine. *Sarah Orne Jewett.* New York: Ungar, 1980.

Nagel, Gwen L., ed. *Critical Essays on Sarah Orne Jewett.* Boston: G.K. Hall, 1984.

Nagel, Gwen L. and James Nagel, comps. *Sarah Orne Jewett: A Reference Guide.* Boston: G.K. Hall, 1978.

Sherman, Sarah Way. *Sarah Orne Jewett, an American Persephone.* Hanover: UP of New England, 1989.

Smith, Gale L. "The Language of Transcendence in Sarah Ornen Jewett's 'A White Heron.'" *Colby Library Quarterly* 19.1 (1983): 37-44.

348   VERNON LEE (1856-1935)

Vernon Lee (Violet Paget) (1856-1935)

Dionea

From the letters of Doctor Alessandro De Rosis to the Lady Evelyn Savelli, Princess of Sabina.

Montemirto Ligure, *June* 29, 1873.

I TAKE IMMEDIATE ADVANTAGE OF THE GENEROUS OFFER OF your Excellency (allow an old Republican who has held you on his knees to address you by that title sometimes, 'tis so appropriate) to help our poor people. I never expected to come a-begging so soon. For the olive crop has been unusually plenteous. We semi-Genoese don't pick the olives unripe, like our Tuscan neighbours, but let them grow big and black, when the young fellows go into the trees with long reeds and shake them down on the grass for the women to collect – a pretty sight which your Excellency must see some day: the grey trees with the brown, barefoot lads craning, balanced in the branches, and the turquoise sea as background just beneath ... That sea of ours – it is all along of it that I wish to ask for money. Looking up from my desk, I see the sea through the window, deep below and beyond the olive woods, bluish-green in the sunshine and veined with violet under the cloud-bars, like one of your Ravenna mosaics spread out as pavement for the world: a wicked sea, wicked in its loveliness, wickeder than your grey northern ones, and from which must have arisen in times gone by (when Phœnicians or Greeks built the temples at Lerici and Porto Venere) a baleful goddess of beauty, a Venus Verticordia[1], but in the bad sense of the word, overwhelming men's lives in sudden darkness like that squall of last week.

To come to the point. I want you, dear Lady Evelyn, to promise me some money, a great deal of money, as much as would buy you a little mannish cloth frock – for the complete bringing-up, until years of discretion, of a young stranger whom the sea has laid upon our shore. Our people, kind as they are, are very poor, and overburdened with children; besides, they have got a certain repugnance for this poor little waif, cast up by that dreadful storm, and who is doubtless a heathen, for she had no little crosses or scapulars on, like proper Christian children. So, being unable to get any of our women to adopt the child, and having an old bachelor's terror of my housekeeper, I have bethought me of certain nuns, holy women, who teach little girls to say their prayers and make lace close by here; and of your dear Excellency to pay for the whole business.

Poor little brown mite! She was picked up after the storm (such a set-out of ship-models and votive candles as that storm must have brought the Madonna at Porto Venere!) on a strip of sand between the rocks of our castle: the thing was really miraculous, for this coast is like a shark's jaw, and the bits of sand are tiny and far between. She was lashed to a plank, swaddled up close in outlandish garments; and when they brought her to me they thought she must certainly be dead: a little girl of four or five, decidedly pretty, and as brown as a berry, who, when she came to, shook her head to show she understood no kind of Italian, and jabbered some half-intelligible Eastern jabber, a few Greek words embedded in I know not what; the Superior of the College de Propagandà Fidé[2] would be puzzled to know. The child appears to be the only survivor from a ship which must have gone down in the great squall, and whose timbers have been strewing the bay for some days past; no one at Spezia or in any of our ports knows anything about her, but she was seen, apparently making for Porto Venere, by some of our sardine-fishers: a big, lumbering craft, with eyes painted on each side of the prow, which, as you know, is a peculiarity of Greek boats. She was sighted for the last time off the island of Palmaria, entering, with all sails spread, right into the thick of the storm-darkness. No bodies, strangely enough, have been washed ashore.

July 10.

I have received the money, dear Donna Evelina. There was tremendous excitement down at San Massimo when the carrier came in with a registered letter, and I was sent for, in presence of all the village authorities, to sign my name on the postal register.

The child has already been settled some days with the nuns; such dear little nuns (nuns always go straight to the heart of an old priest-hater and conspirator against the Pope, you know), dressed in brown robes and close, white caps, with an immense round straw-hat flapping behind their heads like a nimbus: they are called Sisters of the Stigmata, and have a convent and school at San Massimo, a little way inland, with an untidy garden full of lavender and cherry-trees. Your *protégée* has already half set the convent, the village, the Episcopal See[3], the Order of St. Francis, by the ears. First, because nobody could make out whether or not she had been christened. The question was a grave one, for it appears (as your uncle-in-law, the Cardinal, will tell you) that it is almost equally undesirable to be christened twice over as not to be christened at all. The first danger was finally decided upon as the less terrible; but the child, they say, had evidently been baptized before, and knew that the operation ought not to be repeated, for she kicked and plunged and yelled like twenty little devils, and positively would not let the holy water touch her. The Mother Superior, who always took for granted that the baptism had taken place before, says that the child was quite right, and that Heaven was trying to prevent a sacrilege; but the priest and the barber's wife, who had to hold her, think the occurrence fearful, and suspect the little girl of being a Protestant. Then the question of the name. Pinned to her clothes – striped Eastern things, and that kind of crinkled silk stuff they weave in Crete and Cyprus – was a piece of parchment, a scapular we thought at first, but which was found to contain only the name Διονεα – Dionea, as they pronounce it here. The question was, Could such a name be fitly borne by a young lady at the Convent of the Stigmata? Half the population here have names as unchristian quite – Norma, Odoacer, Archimedes – my housemaid is called Themis – but Dionea seemed to scandalise every one, perhaps because these good folk had a mysterious instinct that the name is derived from Dione[4], one of the loves of Father Zeus, and mother of no less a lady than the goddess Venus. The child was very near being called Maria, although there are already twenty-three other Marias, Mariettas, Mariuccias, and so forth at the convent. But the sister-bookkeeper, who apparently detests monotony, bethought her to look out Dionea first in the Calendar[5], which proved useless; and then in a big vellum-bound book, printed at Venice in 1625, called "Flos Sanctorum, or Lives of the Saints, by Father Ribadeneira, S.J., with the addition of such Saints as have no assigned place in the Almanack, other- wise called the Movable or Extravagant Saints." The zeal of Sister Anna Maddalena has been rewarded, for there, among the Extravagant Saints, sure enough, with a border of palm-branches and hour-glasses, stands the name of Saint Dionea, Virgin and Martyr, a lady of Antioch, put to death by the Emperor Decius.[6] I know your Excellency's taste for historical information, so I forward this item. But I fear, dear Lady Evelyn, I fear that the heavenly patroness of your little sea-waif was a much more extravagant saint than that.

December 21, 1879.

Many thanks, dear Donna Evelina, for the money for Dionea's schooling. Indeed, it was not wanted yet: the ac- complishments of young ladies are taught at a very moder- ate rate at Montemirto: and as to clothes, which you men- tion, a pair of wooden clogs, with pretty red tips, costs sixty- five centimes, and ought to last three years, if the owner is careful to carry them on her head in a neat parcel when out walking, and to put them on again only on entering the vil- lage. The Mother Superior is greatly overcome by your Ex- cellency's munificence towards the convent, and much per- turbed at being unable to send you a specimen of your *protégée*'s skill, exemplified in an embroidered pocket-handkerchief or a pair of mittens; but the fact is that poor Dionea *has* no skill. "We will pray to the Madonna and St. Francis to make her more worthy," remarked the Superior. Perhaps, however, your Excellency, who is, I fear but a Pagan woman (for all the Savelli Popes and St. Andrew Savelli's miracles)[7], and insufficiently appreciative of embroidered pocket-handkerchiefs, will be quite as satisfied to hear that Dionea, instead of skill, has got the prettiest face of any little girl in Montemirto. She is tall, for her age (she is eleven) quite wonderfully well proportioned and extremely strong: of all the convent-full, she is the only one for whom I have never been called in. The features are very regular, the hair black, and despite all the good Sisters' efforts to keep it smooth like a Chinaman's, beautifully curly. I am glad she should be pretty, for she will more easily find a husband; and also because it seems fitting that your *protégée* should be beautiful. Unfortunately her character is not so satisfactory: she hates learning, sewing, washing up the dishes, all equally. I am sorry to say she shows no natural piety. Her companions detest her, and the nuns, although they admit that she is not exactly naughty, seem to feel her as a dreadful thorn in the flesh. She spends hours and hours on the terrace overlooking the sea (her great desire, she confided to me, is to get to the sea – to get *back to the sea*, as she expressed it), and lying in the garden, under the big myrtle-bushes, and, in spring and summer, under the rose-hedge. The nuns say that the rose-hedge and that myrtle-bush are growing a great deal too big, one would think from Dionea's lying under them; the fact, I suppose, has drawn attention to them. "That child makes all the useless weeds grow," remarked Sister Reparata. Another of Dionea's amusements is playing with pigeons. The number of pigeons she collects about her is quite amazing; you would never have thought that San Massimo or the neighbouring hills contained as many. They flutter down like snowflakes, and strut and swell themselves out, and furl and unfurl their tails, and peck with little sharp movements of their silly, sensual heads and a little throb and gurgle in their throats, while Dionea lies stretched out full length in the sun, putting out her lips, which they come to kiss, and uttering strange, cooing sounds; or hopping about, flapping her arms slowly like wings, and raising her little head with much the same odd gesture as they; – 'tis a lovely sight, a thing fit for one of your painters, Burne Jones or Tadema[8], with the myrtle-bushes all round, the bright, white-washed convent walls behind, the white marble chapel steps (all steps are marble in this Carrara country), and the enamel blue sea through the ilex-branches beyond. But the good Sisters abominate these pigeons, who, it appears, are messy little creatures, and they complain that, were it not that the Reverend Director likes a pigeon in his pot on a holiday, they could not stand the bother of perpetually sweeping the chapel steps and the kitchen threshold of all those dirty birds....

August 6, 1882.

Do not tempt me, dearest Excellency, with your invitations to Rome. I should not be happy there, and do but little honour to your friendship. My many years of exile, of wanderings in northern countries, have made me a little bit into a northern man: I cannot quite get on with my own fellow-countrymen, except with the good peasants and fishermen all around. Besides – forgive the vanity of an old man, who has learned to make triple acrostic sonnets to cheat the days and months at Theresienstadt and Spielberg – I have suffered too much for Italy to endure patiently the sight of little parliamentary cabals and municipal wranglings, although they also are necessary in this day as conspiracies and battles were in mine. I am not fit for your roomful of ministers and learned men and pretty women: the former would think me an ignoramus, and the latter – what would afflict me much more – a pedant.... Rather, if your Excellency really wants to show yourself and your children to your father's old *protégé* of Mazzinian times, find a few days to come here next spring. You shall have some very bare rooms with brick floors and white curtains opening out on my terrace; and a dinner of all manner of fish and milk (the white garlic flowers shall be mown away from under the olives lest my cow should eat it) and eggs cooked in herbs plucked in the hedges. Your boys can go and see the big ironclads[9] at Spezia; and you shall come with me up our lanes fringed with delicate ferns and overhung by big olives, and into the fields where the cherry-trees shed their blossoms on to the budding vines, the fig-trees stretching out their little green gloves, where the goats nibble perched on their hind legs, and the cows low in the huts of reeds; and there rise from the ravines, with the gurgle of the brooks, from the cliffs with the boom of the surf, the voices of unseen boys and girls, singing about love and flowers and death, just as in the days of Theocritus, whom your learned Excellency does well to read. Has your Excellency ever read Longus, a Greek pastoral novelist? He is a trifle free, a trifle nude for us readers of Zola; but the old French of Amyot[10] has a wonderful charm, and he gives one an idea, as no one else does, how folk lived in such valleys, by such sea-boards, as these in the days when daisy-chains and garlands of roses were still hung on the olive-trees for the nymphs of the grove; when across the bay, at the end of the narrow neck of blue sea, there clung to the marble rocks not a church of Saint Lawrence, with the sculptured martyr on his gridiron, but the temple of Venus, protecting her harbour.... Yes, dear Lady Evelyn, you have guessed aright. Your old friend has returned to his sins, and is scribbling once more. But no longer at verses or political pamphlets. I am enthralled by a tragic history, the history of the fall of the Pagan Gods.... Have you ever read of their wanderings and disguises, in my friend Heine's little book?[11]

And if you come to Montemirto, you shall see also your *protégée*, of whom you ask for news. It has just missed being disastrous. Poor Dionea! I fear that early voyage tied to the spar did no good to her wits, poor little waif! There has been a fearful row; and it has required all my influence, and all the awfulness of your Excellency's name, and the Papacy, and the Holy Roman Empire, to prevent her expulsion by the Sisters of the Stigmata. It appears that this mad creature very nearly committed a sacrilege: she was discovered handling in a suspicious manner the Madonna's gala frock and her best veil of *pizzo di Cantù*[12], a gift of the late Marchioness Violante Vigalena of Fornovo.

One of the orphans, Zaira Barsanti, whom they call the Rossaccia, even pretends to have surprised Dionea as she was about to adorn her wicked little person with these sacred garments; and, on another occasion, when Dionea had been sent to pass some oil and sawdust over the chapel floor (it was the eve of Easter of the Roses), to have discovered her seated on the edge of the altar, in the very place of the Most Holy Sacrament. I was sent for in hot haste, and had to assist at an ecclesiastical council in the convent parlour, where Dionea appeared, rather out of place, an amazing little beauty, dark, lithe, with an odd, ferocious gleam in her eyes, and a still odder smile, tortuous, serpentine, like that of Leonardo da Vinci's[13] women, among the plaster images of St. Francis, and the glazed and framed samplers before the little statue of the Virgin, which wears in summer a kind of mosquito-curtain to guard it from the flies, who, as you know, are creatures of Satan.

Speaking of Satan, does your Excellency know that on the inside of our little convent door, just above the little perforated plate of metal (like the rose of a watering-pot) through which the Sister-portress peeps and talks, is pasted a printed form, an arrangement of holy names and texts in triangles, and the stigmatised hands of St. Francis, and a variety of other devices, for the purpose, as is explained in a special notice, of baffling the Evil One, and preventing his entrance into that building? Had you seen Dionea, and the stolid, contemptuous way in which she took, without attempting to refute, the various shocking allegations against her, your Excellency would have reflected, as I did, that the door in question must have been accidentally absent from the premises, perhaps at the joiner's for repair, the day that your *protégée* first penetrated into the convent. The ecclesiastical tribunal, consisting of the Mother Superior, three Sisters, the Capuchin Director, and your humble servant (who vainly attempted to be Devil's advocate), sentenced Dionea, among other things, to make the sign of the cross twenty-six times on the bare floor with her tongue. Poor little child! One might almost expect that, as happened when Dame Venus scratched her hand on the thorn-bush, red roses should sprout up between the fissures of the dirty old bricks.

October 14, 1883.

You ask whether, now that the Sisters let Dionea go and do half a day's service now and then in the village, and that Dionea is a grown-up creature, she does not set the place by the ears with her beauty. The people here are quite aware of its existence. She is already dubbed *La bella Dionea*; but that does not bring her any nearer getting a husband, although your Excellency's generous offer of a wedding-portion is well known throughout the district of San Massimo and Montemirto. None of our boys, peasants or fishermen, seem to hang on her steps; and if they turn round to stare and whisper as she goes by straight and dainty in her wooden clogs, with the pitcher of water or the basket of linen on her beautiful crisp dark head, it is, I remark, with an expression rather of fear than of love. The women, on their side, make horns with their fingers as she passes, and as they sit by her side in the convent chapel; but that seems natural. My housekeeper tells me that down in the village she is regarded as possessing the evil eye and bringing love misery. "You mean," I said, "that a glance from her is too much for our lads' peace of mind." Veneranda shook her head, and explained, with the deference and contempt with which she always mentions any of her countryfolk's superstitions to me, that the matter is different: it's not with her they are in love (they would be afraid of her eye), but wherever she goes the young people must needs fall in love with each other, and usually where it is far from desirable. "You know Sora Luisa, the blacksmith's widow? Well, Dionea did a *half-service* for her last month, to prepare for the wedding of Luisa's daughter. Well, now, the girl must say, forsooth! that she won't have Pieriho of Lerici any longer, but will have that ragamuffin Wooden Pipe from Solaro, or go into a convent. And the girl changed her mind the very day that Dionea had come into the house. Then there is the wife of Pippo, the coffee-house keeper; they say she is carrying on with one of the coastguards, and Dionea helped her do her washing six weeks ago. The son of Sor Temistocle has just cut off a finger to avoid the conscription, because he is mad about his cousin and afraid of being taken for a soldier; and it is a fact that some of the shirts which were made for him at the Stigmata had been sewn by Dionea;" ... and thus a perfect string of love misfortunes, enough to make a little "Decameron,"[14] I assure you, and all laid to Dionea's account. Certain it is that the people of San Massimo are terribly afraid of Dionea....

July 17, 1884.

Dionea's strange influence seems to be extending in a terrible way. I am almost beginning to think that our folk are correct in their fear of the young witch. I used to think, as physician to a convent, that nothing was more erroneous than all the romancings of Diderot and Schubert[15] (your Excellency sang me his "Young Nun" once: do you recollect, just before your marriage?), and that no more humdrum creature existed than one of our little nuns, with their pink baby faces under their tight white caps. It appeared the romancing was more correct than the prose. Unknown things have sprung up in these good Sisters' hearts, as unknown flowers have sprung up among the myrtle-bushes and the rose-hedge which Dionea lies under. Did I ever mention to you a certain little Sister Giuliana, who professed only two years ago? – a funny rose and white little creature presiding over the infirmary, as prosaic a little saint as ever kissed a crucifix or scoured a saucepan. Well, Sister Giuliana has disappeared, and the same day has disappeared also a sailor-boy from the port.

August 20, 1884.

The case of Sister Giuliana seems to have been but the beginning of an extraordinary love epidemic at the Convent of the Stigmata: the elder schoolgirls have to be kept under lock and key lest they should talk over the wall in the moonlight, or steal out to the little hunchback who writes love-letters at a penny a-piece, beautiful flourishes and all, under the portico by the Fish-market. I wonder does that wicked little Dionea, whom no one pays court to, smile (her lips like a Cupid's bow or a tiny snake's curves) as she calls the pigeons down around her, or lies fondling the cats under the myrtle-bush, when she sees the pupils going about with swollen, red eyes; the poor little nuns taking fresh penances on the cold chapel flags; and hears the long-drawn guttural vowels, *amore* and *morte* and *mio bene*[16], which rise up of an evening, with the boom of the surf and the scent of the lemon-flowers, as the young men wander up and down, arm-in-arm, twanging their guitars along the moonlit lanes under the olives?

October 20, 1885.

A terrible, terrible thing has happened! I write to your Excellency with hands all a-tremble; and yet I *must* write, I must speak, or else I shall cry out. Did I ever mention to you Father Domenico of Casoria, the confessor of our Convent of the Stigmata? A young man, tall, emaciated with fasts and vigils, but handsome like the monk playing the virginal in Giorgione's "Concert,"[17] and under his brown serge still the most stalwart fellow of the country all round? One has heard of men struggling with the tempter. Well, well, Father Domenico had struggled as hard as any of the Anchorites recorded by St. Jerome,[18] and he had conquered. I never knew anything comparable to the angelic serenity of gentleness of this victorious soul. I don't like monks, but I loved Father Domenico. I might have been his father, easily, yet I always felt a certain shyness and awe of him; and yet men have accounted me a clean-lived man in my generation; but I felt, whenever I approached him, a poor worldly creature, debased by the knowledge of so many mean and ugly things. Of late Father Domenico had seemed to me less calm than usual: his eyes had grown strangely bright, and red spots had formed on his salient cheekbones. One day last week, taking his hand, I felt his pulse flutter, and all his strength as it were, liquefy under my touch. "You are ill," I said. "You have fever, Father Domenico. You have been overdoing yourself – some new privation, some new penance. Take care and do not tempt Heaven; remember the flesh is weak." Father Domenico withdrew his hand quickly. "Do not say that," he cried; "the flesh is strong!" and turned away his face. His eyes were glistening and he shook all over. "Some quinine," I ordered. But I felt it was no case for quinine. Prayers might be more useful, and could I have given them he should not have wanted. Last night I was suddenly sent for to Father Domenico's monastery above Montemirto: they told me he was ill. I ran up through the dim twilight of moonbeams and olives with a sinking heart. Something told me my monk was dead. He was lying in a little low whitewashed room; they had carried him there from his own cell in hopes he might still be alive. The windows were wide open; they framed some olive-branches, glistening in the moonlight, and far below, a strip of moonlit sea. When I told them that he was really dead, they brought some tapers and lit them at his head and feet, and placed a crucifix between his hands. "The Lord has been pleased to call our poor brother to Him," said the Superior. "A case of apoplexy, my dear Doctor – a case of apoplexy. You will make out the certificate for the authorities." I made out the certificate. It was weak of me. But, after all, why make a scandal? He certainly had no wish to injure the poor monks.

Next day I found the little nuns all in tears. They were gathering flowers to send as a last gift to their confessor. In the convent garden I found Dionea, standing by the side of a big basket of roses, one of the white pigeons perched on her shoulder.

"So," she said, "he has killed himself with charcoal, poor Padre Domenico!"

Something in her tone, her eyes, shocked me.

"God has called to Himself one of His most faithful servants," I said gravely.

Standing opposite this girl, magnificent, radiant in her beauty, before the rose-hedge, with the white pigeons furling and unfurling, strutting and pecking all round, I seemed to see suddenly the whitewashed room of last night, the big crucifix, that poor thin face under the yellow waxlight. I felt glad for Father Domenico; his battle was over.

"Take this to Father Domenico from me," said Dionea, breaking off a twig of myrtle starred over with white blossom; and raising her head with that smile like the twist of a young snake, she sang out in a high guttural voice a strange chaunt, consisting of the word *Amor – amor – amor*. I took the branch of myrtle and threw it in her face.

January 3, 1886.

It will be difficult to find a place for Dionea, and in this neighbourhood well-nigh impossible. The people associate her somehow with the death of Father Domenico, which has confirmed her reputation of having the evil eye. She left the convent (being now seventeen) some two months back, and is at present gaining her bread working with the masons at our notary's new house at Lerici: the work is hard, but our women often do it, and it is magnificent to see Dionea, in her short white skirt and tight white bodice, mixing the smoking lime with her beautiful strong arms; or, an empty sack drawn over her head and shoulders, walking majestically up the cliff, up the scaffoldings with her load of bricks.... I am, however, very anxious to get Dionea out of the neighbourhood, because I cannot help dreading the annoyances to which her reputation for the evil eye exposes her, and even some explosion of rage if ever she should lose the indifferent contempt with which she treats them. I hear that one of the rich men of our part of the world, who owns a whole flank of marble mountain, is looking out for a maid for his daughter, who is about to be married; kind people and patriarchal in their riches, the old man still sitting down to table with all his servants; and his nephew, who is going to be his son-in-law, a splendid young fellow, who has worked like Jacob, in the quarry and at the saw-mill, for love of his pretty cousin. That whole house is so good, simple, and peaceful, that I hope it may tame down even Dionea. If I do not succeed in getting Dionea this place (and all your Excellency's illustriousness and all my poor eloquence will be needed to counteract the sinister reports attaching to our poor little waif), it will be best to accept your suggestion of taking the girl into your household at Rome, since you are curious to see what you call our baleful beauty. I am amused, and a little indignant at what you say about your footmen being handsome: Don Juan himself, my dear Lady Evelyn, would be cowed by Dionea....

May 29, 1886.

Here is Dionea back upon our hands once more! but I cannot send her to your Excellency. Is it from living among these peasants and fishing-folk, or is it because, as people pretend, a sceptic is always superstitious? I could not muster courage to send you Dionea, although your boys are still in sailor-clothes and your uncle, the Cardinal, is eighty-four; and as to the Prince, why, he bears the most potent amulet against Dionea's terrible powers in your own dear capricious person. Seriously, there is something eerie in this coincidence. Poor Dionea! I feel sorry for her, exposed to the passion of a once patriarchally respectable old man. I feel even more abashed at the incredible audacity, I should almost say sacrilegeous madness, of the vile old creature. But still the coincidence is strange and uncomfortable. Last week the lightning struck a huge olive in the orchard of Sor Agostino's house above Sarzana. Under the olive was Sor Agostino himself, who was killed on the spot; and opposite, not twenty paces off, drawing water from the well, unhurt and calm, was Dionea. It was the end of a sultry afternoon: I was on a terrace in one of those villages of ours, jammed, like some hardy bush, in the gash of a hill-side. I saw the storm rush down the valley, a sudden blackness, and then, like a curse, a flash, a tremendous crash, re-echoed by a dozen hills. "I told him," Dionea said very quietly, when she came to stay with me the next day (for Sor Agostino's family would not have her for another half-minute), "that if he did not leave me alone Heaven would send him an accident."

July 15, 1886.

My book? Oh, dear Donna Evelina, do not make me blush by talking of my book! Do not make an old man, respectable, a Government functionary (communal physician of the district of San Massimo and Montemirto Ligure), confess that he is but a lazy unprofitable dreamer, collecting materials as a child picks hips out of a hedge, only to throw them away, liking them merely for the little occupation of scratching his hands and standing on tiptoe, for their pretty redness.... You remember what Balzac says about projecting any piece of work? – *"C'est fumer des cigarettes enchantées."*....[19] Well, well! The data obtainable about the ancient gods in their days of adversity are few and far between: a quotation here and there from the Fathers; two or three legends; Venus reappearing; the persecutions of Apollo in Styria; Prosperina going, in Chaucer, to reign over the fairies; a few obscure religious persecutions in the Middle Ages on the score of Paganism; some strange rites practised till lately in the depths of a Breton forest near Lannion.... As to Tannhäuser, he was a real knight, and a sorry one, and a real Minnesinger not of the best. Your Excellency will find some of his poems in Von der Hagen's four immense volumes, but I recommend you to take your notions of Ritter Tannhäuser's poetry rather from Wagner.[20] Certain it is that the Pagan divinities lasted much longer than we suspect, sometimes in their own nakedness, sometimes in the stolen garb of the Madonna or the saints. Who knows whether they do not exist to this day? And, indeed, is it possible they should not? For the awfulness of the deep woods, with their filtered green light, the creak of the swaying, solitary reeds, exists, and is Pan[21]; and the blue, starry May night exists, the sough of the waves, the warm wind carrying the sweetness of the lemon-blossoms, the bitterness of the myrtle on our rocks, the distant chaunt of the boys cleaning out their nets, of the girls sickling the grass under the olives, *Amor – amor – amor*, and all this is the great goddess Venus. And opposite to me, as I write, between the branches of the ilexes, across the blue sea, streaked like a Ravenna mosaic with purple and green, shimmer the white houses and walls, the steeple and towers, an enchanted Fata Morgana[22] city, of dim Porto Venere;... and I mumble to myself the verse of Catullus, but addressing a greater and more terrible goddess than he did: –

"Procul a mea sit furor omnis, Hera, domo; alios; age incitatos, alios age rabidos."[23]

March 25, 1887.

Yes; I will do everything in my power for your friends. Are you well-bred folk as well bred as we, Republican *bourgeois*, with the coarse hands (though you once told me mine were psychic hands when the mania of palmistry had not yet been succeeded by that of the Reconciliation between Church and State), I wonder, that you should apologise, you whose father fed me and housed me and clothed me in my exile, for giving me the horrid trouble of hunting for lodgings? It is like you, dear Donna Evelina, to have sent me photographs of my future friend Waldemar's statue.... I have no love for modern sculpture, for all the hours I have spent in Gibson's and Dupré's studio:[24] 'tis a dead art we should do better to bury. But your Waldemar has something of the old spirit: he seems to feel the divineness of the mere body, the spirituality of a limpid stream of mere physical life. But why among these statues only men and boys, athletes and fauns? Why only the bust of that thin, delicate-lipped little Madonna wife of his? Why no wide-shouldered Amazon or broad-flanked Aphrodite?

April 10, 1887.

You ask me how poor Dionea is getting on. Not as your Excellency and I ought to have expected when we placed her with the good Sisters of the Stigmata: although I wager that, fantastic and capricious as you are, you would be better pleased (hiding it carefully from that grave side of you which bestows devout little books and carbolic acid upon the indigent) that your *protégée* should be a witch than a serving-maid, a maker of philters rather than a knitter of stockings and sewer of shirts.

A maker of philters. Roughly speaking, that is Dionea's profession. She lives upon the money which I dole out to her (with many useless objurgations) on behalf of your Excellency; and her ostensible employment is mending nets, collecting olives, carrying bricks, and other miscellaneous jobs; but her real status is that of village sorceress. You think our peasants are sceptical? Perhaps they do not believe in thought-reading, mesmerism, and ghosts, like you, dear Lady Evelyn. But they believe very firmly in the evil eye, in magic and in love-potions. Every one has his little story of this or that which happened to his brother or cousin or neighbour. My stable-boy and male factotum's brother-in-law, living some years ago in Corsica, was seized with a longing for a dance with his beloved at one of those balls which our peasants give in the winter, when the snow makes leisure in the mountains. A wizard anointed him for money, and straightway he turned into a black cat, and in three bounds was over the seas, at the door of his uncle's cottage, and among the dancers. He caught his beloved by the skirt to draw her attention; but she replied with a kick which sent him squealing back to Corsica. When he returned in summer he refused to marry the lady, and carried his left arm in a sling. "You broke it when I came to the Veglia!" he said, and all seemed explained. Another lad, returning from working in the vineyards near Marseilles, was walking up to his native village, high in our hills, one moonlight night. He heard sounds of fiddle and fife from a roadside barn, and saw yellow light from its chinks; and then entering, he found many women dancing, old and young, and among them his affianced. He tried to snatch her round the waist for a waltz (they play *Mme. Angot* at our rustic balls), but the girl was unclutchable, and whispered, "Go; for these are witches, who will kill thee; and I am a witch also. Alas! I shall go to hell when I die."

I could tell your Excellency dozens of such stories. But love-philters are among the commonest things to sell and buy. Do you remember the sad little story of Cervantes' Licentiate[25], who, instead of a love-potion, drank a philter which made him think he was made of glass, fit emblem of a poor mad poet?... It is love-philters that Dionea prepares. No; do not misunderstand; they do not give love of her, still less her love. Your seller of love-charms is as cold as ice, as pure as snow. The priest has crusaded against her, and stones have flown at her as she went by from dissatisfied lovers; and the very children, paddling in the sea and making mud-pies in the sand, have put out forefinger and little finger and screamed, "Witch, witch! ugly witch!" as she passed with basket or brick load; but Dionea has only smiled, that snake-like, amused smile, but more ominous than of yore. The other day I determined to seek her and argue with her on the subject of her evil trade. Dionea has a certain regard for me; not, I fancy, a result of gratitude, but rather the recognition of a certain admiration and awe which she inspires in your Excellency's foolish old servant. She has taken up her abode in a deserted hut, built of dried reeds and thatch, such as they keep cows in, among the olives on the cliffs. She was not there, but about the hut pecked some white pigeons, and from it, startling me foolishly with its unexpected sound, came the eerie bleat of her pet goat.... Among the olives it was twilight already, with streakings of faded rose in the sky, and faded rose, like long trails of petals, on the distant sea. I clambered down among the myrtle-bushes and came to a little semicircle of yellow sand, between two high and jagged rocks, the place where the sea had deposited Dionea after the wreck. She was seated there on the sand, her bare foot dabbling in the waves; she had twisted a wreath of myrtle and wild roses on her black, crisp hair. Near her was one of our prettiest girls, the Lena of Sor Tullio the blacksmith, with ashy, terrified face under her flowered kerchief. I determined to speak to the child, but without startling her now, for she is a nervous, hysteric little thing. So I sat on the rocks, screened by the myrtle-bushes, waiting till the girl had gone. Dionea, seated listless on the sands, leaned over the sea and took some of its water in the hollow of her hand. "Here," she said to the Lena of Sor Tullio, "fill your bottle with this and give it to drink to Tommasino the Rosebud." Then she set to singing: —

"Love is salt, like the sea-water – I drink and I die of thirst.... Water! water! Yet the more I drink, the more I burn. Love! thou art bitter as the seaweed."

April 20, 1887.

Your friends are settled here, dear Lady Evelyn. The house is built in what was once a Genoese fort, growing like a grey spiked aloes out of the marble rocks of our bay; rock and wall (the walls existed long before Genoa was ever heard of) grown almost into a homogeneous mass, delicate grey, stained with black and yellow lichen, and dotted here and there with myrtle-shoots and crimson snapdragon. In what was once the highest enclosure of the fort, where your friend Gertrude watches the maids hanging out the fine white sheets and pillow-cases to dry (a bit of the North, of Hermann and Dorothea[26] transferred to the South), a great twisted fig-tree juts out like an eccentric gargoyle over the sea, and drops its ripe fruit into the deep blue pools. There is but scant furniture in the house, but a great oleander overhangs it, presently to burst into pink splendour; and on all the window-sills, even that of the kitchen (such a background of shining brass saucepans Waldemar's wife has made of it!) are pipkins and tubs full of trailing carnations, and tufts of sweet basil and thyme and mignonette. She pleases me most, your Gertrude, although you foretold I should prefer the husband; with her thin white face, a Memling Madonna[27] finished by some Tuscan sculptor, and her long, delicate white hands ever busy, like those of a mediaeval lady, with some delicate piece of work; and the strange blue, more limpid than the sky and deeper than the sea, of her rarely lifted glance.

It is in her company that I like Waldemar best; I prefer to the genius that infinitely tender and respectful, I would not say *lover* – yet I have no other word – of his pale wife. He seems to me, when with her, like some fierce, generous, wild thing from the woods, like the lion of Una[28], tame and submissive to this saint.... This tenderness is really beautiful on the part of that big lion Waldemar, with his odd eyes, as of some wild animal – odd, and, your Excellency remarks, not without a gleam of latent ferocity. I think that hereby hangs the explanation of his never doing any but male figures: the female figure, he says (and your Excellency must hold him responsible, not me, for such profanity), is almost inevitably inferior in strength and beauty; woman is not form, but expression, and therefore suits painting, not sculpture. The point of a woman is not her body, but (and here his eyes rested very tenderly on his wife) her soul. "Still," I answered, "the ancients, who understood such matters, did manufacture some tolerable female statues: the Fates of the Parthenon, the Phidian Pallas, the Venus of Milo."...

"Ah! yes," exclaimed Waldemar, smiling, with that savage gleam of his eyes; "but those are not women, and the people who made them have left as the tales of Endymion, Adonis, Anchises: a goddess might sit for them."...[29]

May 5, 1887.

Has it ever struck your Excellency in one of your La Rochefoucauld[30] fits (in Lent say, after too many balls) that not merely maternal but conjugal unselfishness may be a very selfish thing? There! you toss your little head at my words; yet I wager I have heard you say that *other* women may think it right to humour their husbands, but as to you, the Prince must learn a wife's duty is as much to chasten her husband's whims as to satisfy them. I really do feel indignant that such a snow-white saint should wish another woman to part with all instincts of modesty merely because that other woman would be a good model for her husband; really it is intolerable. "Leave the girl alone," Waldemar said, laughing. "What do I want with the unaesthetic sex, as Schopenhauer calls it?"[31] But Gertrude has set her heart on his doing a female figure; it seems that folk have twitted him with never having produced one. She has long been on the look-out for a model for him. It is odd to see this pale, demure diaphanous creature, not the more earthly for approaching motherhood, scanning the girls of our village with the eyes of a slave-dealer.

"If you insist on speaking to Dionea," I said, "I shall insist on speaking to her at the same time, to urge her to refuse your proposal." But Waldemar's pale wife was indifferent to all my speeches about modesty being a poor girl's only dowry. "She will do for a Venus," she merely answered.

We went up to the cliffs together, after some sharp words, Waldemar's wife hanging on my arm as we slowly clambered up the stony path among the olives. We found Dionea at the door of her hut, making faggots of myrtle-branches. She listened sullenly to Gertrude's offer and explanations; indifferently to my admonitions not to accept. The thought of stripping for the view of a man, which would send a shudder through our most brazen village girls, seemed not to startle her, immaculate and savage as she is accounted. She did not answer, but sat under the olives, looking vaguely across the sea. At that moment, Waldemar came up to us; he had followed with the intention of putting an end to these wranglings.

"Gertrude," he said, "do leave her alone. I have found a model – a fisher-boy, whom I much prefer to any woman."

Dionea raised her head with that serpentine smile. "I will come," she said.

Waldemar stood silent; his eyes were fixed on her, where she stood under the olives, her white shift loose about her splendid throat, her shining feet bare in the grass. Vaguely, as if not knowing what he said, he asked her name. She answered that her name was Dionea; for the rest, she was an Innocentina, that is to say, a foundling; then she began to sing: –
"Flower of the myrtle!
My father is the starry sky;
The mother that made me is the sea."

June 22, 1887.

I confess that I was an old fool to have grudged Waldemar his model. As I watch him gradually building up his statue, watch the goddess gradually emerging from the clay heap, I ask myself – and the case might trouble a more subtle moralist than me – whether a village girl, an obscure, useless life within the bounds of what we choose to call right and wrong, can be weighed against the possession by mankind of a great work of art, a Venus immortally beautiful? Still,

I am glad that the two alternatives need not be weighed against each other. Nothing can equal the kindness of Gertrude, now that Dionea has consented to sit to her husband; the girl is ostensibly merely a servant like any other; and, lest any report of her real functions should get abroad and discredit her at San Massimo or Montemirto, she is to be taken to Rome, where no one will be the wiser, and where, by the way, your Excellency will have an opportunity of comparing Waldemar's goddess of love with our little orphan of the Convent of the Stigmata. What reassures me still more is the curious attitude of Waldemar towards the girl. I could never have believed that an artist could regard a woman so utterly as a mere inanimate thing, a form to copy, like a tree or flower. Truly he carries out his theory that sculpture knows only the body, and the body scarcely considered as human. The way in which he speaks to Dionea after hours of the most rapt contemplation of her is almost brutal in its coldness. And yet to hear him exclaim, "How beautiful she is! Good God, how beautiful!" No love of mere woman was ever so violent as this love of woman's mere shape.

June 27, 1887.

You asked me once, dearest Excellency, whether there survived among our people (you had evidently added a volume on folk-lore to that heap of half-cut, dog's-eared books that litter about among the Chineseries and mediaeval brocades of your rooms) any trace of Pagan myths. I explained to you then that all our fairy mythology, classic gods, and demons and heroes, teemed with fairies, ogres, and princes. Last night I had a curious proof of this. Going to see the Waldemar, I found Dionea seated under the oleander at the top of the old Genoese fort, telling stories to the two little blonde children who were making the falling pink blossoms into necklaces at her feet; the pigeons, Dionea's white pigeons, which never leave her, strutting and pecking among the basil pots, and the white gulls flying round the rocks overhead. This is what I heard.... "And the three fairies said to the youngest son of the King, to the one who had been brought up as a shepherd, 'Take this apple, and give it to her among us who is most beautiful.' And the first fairy said, 'If thou give it to me thou shalt be Emperor of Rome, and have purple clothes, and have a gold crown and gold armour, and horses and courtiers;' and the second said, 'If thou give it to me thou shalt be Pope, and wear a mitre, and have the keys of heaven and hell;' and the third fairy said, 'Give the apple to me, for I will give thee the most beautiful lady to wife.' And the youngest son of the King sat in the green meadow and thought about it a little, and then said, 'What use is there in being Emperor or Pope? Give me the beautiful lady to wife, since I am young myself.' And he gave the apple to the third of the three fairies.".…[32]

Dionea droned out the story in her half-Genoese dialect, her eyes looking far away across the blue sea, dotted with sails like white sea-gulls, that strange serpentine smile on her lips.

"Who told thee that fable?" I asked.

She took a handful of oleander-blossoms from the ground, and throwing them into the air, answered listlessly, as she watched the little shower of rosy petals descend on her black hair and pale breast —

"Who knows?"

July 6, 1887.

How strange is the power of art! Has Waldemar's statue shown me the real Dionea, or has Dionea really grown more strangely beautiful than before? Your Excellency will laugh; but when I meet her I cast down my eyes after the first glimpse of her loveliness; not with the shyness of a ridiculous old pursuer of the Eternal Feminine, but with a sort of religious awe – the feeling with which, as a child kneeling by my mother's side, I looked down on the church flags when the Mass bell told the elevation of the Host.… Do you remember the story of Zeuxis and the ladies of Crotona, five of the fairest not being too much for his Juno?[33] Do you remember – you, who have read everything – all the bosh of our writers about the Ideal in Art? Why, here is a girl who disproves all this nonsense in a minute; she is far, far more beautiful than Waldemar's statue of her. He said so angrily, only yesterday, when his wife took me into his studio (he has made a studio of the long-desecrated chapel of the old Genoese fort, itself, they say, occupying the site of the temple of Venus).

As he spoke that odd spark of ferocity dilated in his eyes, and seizing the largest of his modelling tools, he obliterated at one swoop the whole exquisite face. Poor Gertrude turned ashy white, and a convulsion passed over her face....

July 15.

I wish I could make Gertrude understand, and yet I could never, never bring myself to say a word. As a matter of fact, what is there to be said? Surely she knows best that her husband will never love any woman but herself. Yet ill, nervous as she is, I quite understand that she must loathe this unceasing talk of Dionea, of the superiority of the model over the statue. Cursed statue! I wish it were finished, or else that it had never been begun.

July 20.

This morning Waldemar came to me. He seemed strangely agitated: I guessed he had something to tell me, and yet I could never ask. Was it cowardice on my part? He sat in my shuttered room, the sunshine making pools on the red bricks and tremulous stars on the ceiling, talking of many things at random, and mechanically turning over the manuscript, the heap of notes of my poor, never-finished book on the Exiled Gods. Then he rose, and walking nervously round my study, talking disconnectedly about his work, his eye suddenly fell upon a little altar, one of my few antiquities, a little block of marble with a carved garland and rams' heads, and a half-effaced inscription dedicating it to Venus, the mother of Love.

"It was found," I explained, "in the ruins of the temple, somewhere on the site of your studio: so, at least, the man said from whom I bought it."

Waldemar looked at it long. "So," he said, "this little

cavity was to burn the incense in; or rather, I suppose, since it has two little gutters running into it, for collecting the blood of the victim? Well, well! they were wiser in that day, to wring the neck of a pigeon or burn a pinch of incense than to eat their own hearts out, as we do, all along of Dame Venus;" and he laughed, and left me with that odd ferocious lighting-up of his face. Presently, there came a knock at my door. It was Waldemar. "Doctor," he said very quietly, "will you do me a favour? Lend me your little Venus altar – only for a few days, only till the day after to-morrow. I want to copy the design of it for the pedestal of my statue: it is appropriate." I sent the altar to him: the lad who carried it told me that Waldemar had set it up in the studio, and calling for a flask of wine, poured out two glasses. One he had given to my messenger for his pains; of the other he had drunk a mouthful, and thrown the rest over the altar, saying some unknown words. "It must be some German habit," said my servant. What odd fancies this man has!

July 25.

You ask me, dearest Excellency, to send you some sheets of my book: you want to know what I have discovered. Alas! dear Donna Evelina, I have discovered, I fear, that there is nothing to discover; that Apollo was never in Styria; that Chaucer, when he called the Queen of the Fairies Prosperine, meant nothing more than an eighteenth century poet when he called Dolly or Betty Cynthia or Amaryllis; that the lady who damned poor Tannhäuser was not Venus, but a mere little Suabian mountain sprite; in fact, that poetry is only the invention of poets, and that that rogue, Heinrich Heine, is entirely responsible for the existence of *Dieux en Exil*.... My poor manuscript can only tell you what St. Augustine, Tertullian, and sundry morose old Bishops thought about the loves of Father Zeus and the miracles of the Lady Isis, none of which is much worth your attention[34].... Reality, my dear Lady Evelyn, is always prosaic: at least when investigated into by bald old gentlemen like me.

And yet, it does not look so. The world, at times,

seems to be playing at being poetic, mysterious, full of wonder and romance. I am writing, as usual, by my window, the moonlight brighter in its whiteness than my mean little yellow-shining lamp. From the mysterious greyness, the olive groves and lanes beneath my terrace, rises a confused quaver of frogs, and buzz and whirr of insects: something, in sound, like the vague trails of countless stars, the galaxies on galaxies blurred into mere blue shimmer by the moon, which rides slowly across the highest heaven. The olive twigs glisten in the rays: the flowers of the pomegranate and oleander are only veiled as with bluish mist in their scarlet and rose. In the sea is another sea, of molten, rippled silver, or a magic causeway leading to the shining vague offing, the luminous pale sky-line, where the islands of Palmaria and Tino float like unsubstantial, shadowy dolphins. The roofs of Montemirto glimmer among the black, pointing cypresses: farther below, at the end of that half-moon of land, is San Massimo: the Genoese fort inhabited by our friends is profiled black against the sky. All is dark: our fisher-folk go to bed early; Gertrude and the little ones are asleep: they at least are, for I can imagine Gertrude lying awake, the moonbeams of her thin Madonna face, smiling as she thinks of the little ones around her, of the other tiny thing that will soon lie on her breast.... There is a light in the old desecrated chapel, the thing that was once the temple of Venus, they say, and is now Waldemar's workshop, its broken roof mended with reeds and thatch. Waldemar has stolen in, no doubt to see his statue again. But he will return, more peaceful for the peacefulness of the night, to his sleeping wife and children. God bless and watch over them! Good-night, dearest Excellency.

July 26.

I have your Excellency's telegram in answer to mine. Many thanks for sending the Prince. I await his coming with feverish longing; it is still something to look forward to. All does not seem over. And yet what can he do?

The children are safe: we fetched them out of their

bed and brought them up here. They are still a little shaken by the fire, the bustle, and by finding themselves in a strange house; also, they want to know where their mother is; but they have found a tame cat, and I hear them chirping on the stairs.

It was only the roof of the studio, the reeds and thatch, that burned, and a few old pieces of timber. Waldemar must have set fire to it with great care; he had brought armfuls of faggots of dry myrtle and heather from the bakehouse close by, and thrown into the blaze quantities of pine-cones, and of some resin, I know not what, that smelt like incense. When we made our way, early this morning, through the smouldering studio, we were stifled with a hot church-like perfume: my brain swam, and suddenly I remembered going into Saint Peter's on Easter Day as a child.

It happened last night, while I was trying to write to you. Gertrude had gone to bed, leaving her husband in the studio. About eleven the maids heard him come out and call Dionea to get up and come and sit to him. He had had this craze once before, of seeing her and his statue by an artificial light: you remember he had theories about the way in which the ancients lit up the statues in their temples. Gertrude, the servants say, was overheard creeping downstairs a little later.

Do you see it? I have seen nothing else these hours, which have seemed weeks and months. He had placed Dionea on the big marble block behind the altar, a great curtain of dull red brocade – you know that Venetian brocade with the gold pomegranate pattern – behind her, like a Madonna of Van Eyck's.[35] He showed her to me once before like this, the whiteness of her neck and breast, the whiteness of the drapery round her flanks, toned to the colour of old marble by the light of the resin burning in pans all round.... Before Dionea was the altar – the altar of Venus which he had borrowed from me. He must have collected all the roses about it, and thrown the incense upon the embers when Gertrude suddenly entered. And then, and then....

We found her lying across the altar, her pale hair

among the ashes of the incense, her blood – she had but little to give, poor white ghost! – trickling among the carved garlands and rams' heads, blackening the heaped-up roses. The body of Waldemar was found at the foot of the castle cliff. Had he hoped, by setting the place on fire, to bury himself among its ruins, or had he not rather wished to complete in this way the sacrifice, to make the whole temple an immense votive pyre? It looked like one, as we hurried down the hills to San Massimo: the whole hillside, dry grass, myrtle, and heather, all burning, the pale short flames waving against the blue moonlit sky, and the old fortress outlined black against the blaze.

August 30.

Of Dionea I can tell you nothing certain. We speak of her as little as we can. Some say they have seen her, on stormy nights, wandering among the cliffs: but a sailor-boy assures me, by all the holy things, that the day after the burning of the Castle Chapel – we never call it anything else – he met at dawn, off the island of Palmaria, beyond the strait of Porto Venere, a Greek boat, with eyes painted on the prow, going full sail to sea, the men singing as she went. And against the mast, a robe of purple and gold about her, and a myrtle-wreath on her head, leaned Dionea, singing words in an unknown tongue, the white pigeons circling around her.

Notes

1. Verticordia is one of the names given to Venus because she was invoked to "turn the hearts" of women to virtue and chastity.
2. College of the Propagation of the Faith.
3. The see is the town or place where the bishop's cathedral is located and from which he takes his title.

4. According to Homer, Dione is the daughter of Oceanus and Tethys and the mother of Aphrodite by Zeus. According to Hesiod, Aphrodite sprang from the foam of the sea that gathered about the severed parts of the god Uranus when he was castrated by his son Cronus; Hesiod also links Aphrodite with Cyprus. Venus, originally an obscure Italian goddess, soon became identified by the Romans with Aphrodite and acquired her mythology. The myrtle is her tree, the dove her bird.

5. The calendar of the saints.

6. Gaius Messius Quintus Decius, Emperor from 249-251 AD, and notorious persecutor of Christians.

7. The Savellis were one of the oldest and most important families in Rome from the late twelfth century until 1712.

8. Sir Edward Coley Burne Jones (1833-1898), English painter, illustrator and designer; his style is self-consciously aesthetic and dreamlike, but at the same time reflects a classical influence. Sir Laurence Alma-Tadema (1836-1912), Dutch born painter who lived in England; his paintings, usually of beautiful women, are often sentimental or titillating.

9. Warships.

10. Theocritus (c.308-c.240 BC), Hellenistic Greek poet, the originator of pastoral poetry. Nothing is known about Longus except that he wrote *Daphnis and Chloe* (mid-third century AD), a pastoral romance. Émile Zola (1840-1902), leading figure in the French school of naturalistic fiction. Jacques Amyot (1513-1593), translated Plutarch's *Lives* into French.

11. Heinrich Heine (1797-1856). *The Gods in Exile* depicts the return of the pagan gods as emigrants forced to take up trades in a bourgeois world.

12. Lace from Cantú.

13. Leonardo da Vinci (1452-1519), Florentine artist best known for the enigmatic *Mona Lisa* and the mural painting of *The Last Supper*.

14. *The Decameron* is a collection of tales by Giovanni Boccaccio (1313-1375).

15. Denis Diderot (1713-1784), French philosopher and man of letters; Franz Schubert (1797-1828), French composer highly regarded for his songs.

16. Love, death, and my good.

17. Giorgione Da Castelfranco (1476/8-1510), highly influential Venetian painter. "The Concert Champêtre" is still disputed between Giorgione and Titian.

18. St. Jerome (c.347-419/20), scholar and ascetic; he lived for several years as a hermit or anchorite in the Syrian desert.

19. Honoré de Balzac (1799-1850), French novelist, author of the ninety one works that constitute the *Comédie Humaine*. "It's like smoking enchanted cigarettes."

20. Pluto and Proserpine have a connubial dispute in January's garden in Chaucer's "The Merchant's Tale." Tannhäuser was a German Minnesinger or lyric poet of the thirteenth century, and the subject of the legend about the knight who spends seven years with Venus in the Venusberg. His story was made into an opera by Richard Wagner that was first performed in 1845.

21. In Greek mythology, Pan, half-man, half-goat, is the god of pastures, forests, flocks, and herds. Plutarch relates the story of how, at the time of the crucifixion, passengers in a ship sailing along the coast of Greece heard a great voice cry "the Great God Pan is dead"; the responses of the pagan oracles were said to then cease for ever.

22. A fata morgana is an illusion or mirage.

23. Gaius Valerius Catullus (c.84-c.54 BC), Roman poet. Poem 63. The line that he is misquoting actually addresses "Era," or "mistress," not Hera: "Let your maddening anger, mistress, / alight far away; / agitate others; / drive others mad" (Translation: Bob Solomon).

24. John Gibson (1790-1866), English Neoclassical sculptor who became notorious with his *Tinted Venus*. Jules Dupré (1811-1889), French landscape painter of the Barbizon school.

25. Miguel de Cervantes Saavedra (1547-1616). Spanish novelist best known for *Don Quixote*.

26. *Hermann und Dorothea* (1797), a poem by Goethe founded on the expulsion of the Protestants by the Archbishop of Salzburg in 1732.

27. Hans Memling (c.1430/40-1494). German born Netherlandish painter; in many of his paintings he has a diptych with the Madonna and child on one side and the donor on the other.

28. Character in Spenser's *Faerie Queene* who typifies singleness of the true religion and is protected by a lion.

29. In classical mythology, Endymion is a shepherd loved by the moon goddess Selene; Adonis is the beloved of Aphrodite and is killed by a wild boar; Anchises, King of Dardanus and Aphrodite are the parents of Aeneas. All three are mortal.

30. La Rochefoucauld (1630-1680). French courtier, soldier and moralist, author of *Maximes*, a series of brief reflections best summarized by the epigraph to the collection, "Our virtues are mostly vices in disguise."

31. Arthur Schopenhauer (1788-1860). German philosopher; his many writings include the bitter essay "On Women."

32. This is a revised version of the story of the Judgement of Paris. Eris (Discord) throws down a golden apple inscribed "for the most beautiful"; Hera, Athena, and Aphrodite all claim it and apply to Paris to settle the dispute. Aphrodite offers him the most beautiful woman in the world, he gives her the apple, and, with her help, carries off Helen and initiates the Trojan war.

33. Zeuxis, Greek painter, Pliny dates him 397 BC. Lee is perhaps confused here. His "Helen of Troy" is an ideal picture compiled from the five most beautiful women he could find.

34. St. Augustine (354-430), Bishop of Hippo in North Africa and author of the *Confessions*. Tertullian (fl 200), North African Christian writer and apologist. Isis is an Egyptian goddess representing the female productive force of nature; Herodotus later identified her with the Greek Demeter.

35. Jan van Eyck (died 1441). Renowned Netherlandish painter, best known for the massive altarpiece at Ghent.

Source: *Hauntings: Fantastic Stories*. London: Heinemann, 1890.

Biographical Note

Vernon Lee, born Violet Paget in a chateau outside of Boulogne, was the daughter of Matilda Adams and her second husband, Henry Ferguson Paget. Mrs. Paget directed most of her affection to her son from her first marriage, the poet Eugene Lee-Hamilton, but resolved that her daughter would become a writer and provided her with an impressive education. Lee's childhood was spent travelling around Europe, where she soon developed a passionate interest in art. At twenty-four, she published *Studies of the Eighteenth Century in Italy* (1880), which was well-received by the critics, and she soon became a minor literary celebrity. In 1881 she visited London for the first time and stayed with the poet and novelist Mary Robinson; here she met many of the leading artists and authors of the day, including Walter Pater, whose work she greatly admired. While Lee's own philosophy of art was linked to that of Pater's and she believed art's primary function to be the creation of pleasure, she was not a pure aesthete. Her first novel, *Miss Brown* (1884), was a satire on aestheticism and dedicated to Henry James; it was not a success, and Lee unfortunately made enemies of such influential figures as Wilde, Rossetti, and Morris. Soon after, she began to focus her attention on the short story and the essay; with the story of "Lady Tal," she made another mistake by basing the central figure of Marion, an American psychological novelist who becomes the victim of his own artistic detachment, on Henry James; James was not pleased.

Lee's most important relationship was with Kit Anstruther-Thomson; they lived together in Florence for many years, and collaborated on several works dealing with aesthetic issues. The most significant of these is *Beauty and Ugliness: and Other Studies in Psychological Aesthetics* (1912), in which Lee develops her aesthetics of "empathy," a term she is generally credited with introducing. The art critic Bernard Berenson unfairly accused the two women of plagiarism; the charge resulted in a lengthy and unpleasant feud. At the outbreak of World War One, Lee adopted a strong pacifist stance and alienated even more of her friends; in 1920, she brought out a war trilogy entitled *Satan the Waster* which was strongly condemned for many years until the changing political climate allowed the work to be seen as a powerful anti-war satire. Lee also produced three historical novels—*Ottile* (1883), *Penelope Brandling* (1903), and *Louis Norbert* (1914)—and a play, *Ariadne in Mantua* (1899). She is best known, however, for her critical essays and her fantasies and ghost stories. Her essays on fiction, collected in *The Handling of Words* (1923), are considered some of the first examples of close literary analysis. Such collections as *Vanitas* (1892) and *Pope Jacynth, and Other Fantastic Tales* (1904) prove her to be one of the most innovative short story writers of the age.

The story reprinted here is one of four published in the impressive collection entitled *Hauntings* (1890). In "Amor Dure," a Polish scholar working in the archives of a small Italian town becomes obsessed by an evil dead woman, Medea da Carpi. In "Oke of Okehurst," better known to avid readers of ghost stories by its subtitle, "The Phantom Lover," the sinister past again impinges on the present when a woman becomes possessed by the spirit of a murderous ancestor. In "A Wicked Voice," set in a corrupt and decadent Venice, a young composer is haunted by the voice of a singer who had used his talents to seduce and destroy. And in "Dionea," a young girl, perhaps the incarnation of a pagan goddess, awakens violent passions in the Christian inhabitants of a small island community.

Selected Modern Reprints:

Hauntings: Fantastic Stories. 1890. New York: Books for Libraries P, 1971.

Pope Jacynth and More Supernatural Tales: Excursions into Fantasy. 1904. London: Peter Owen, 1956.

The Snake Lady and Other Stories. Ed. Horace Gregory. New York: Grove, 1954.

A Vernon Lee Anthology. Selections from the Earlier Works Made by Irene Cooper Willis. 1929. Folcroft, PA: Folcroft Library Editions, 1977.

Selected Secondary Sources:

Colby, Vineta. "The Puritan Aesthete: Vernon Lee." *The Singular Anomaly: Women Novelists of the Nineteenth Century.* New York: New York UP, 1970. 235-304.

Gunn, Peter. *Vernon Lee. Violet Paget, 1856-1935*. London: Oxford UP, 1964.

Mannocchi, Phyllis F. "'Vernon Lee': A Reintroduction and Primary Bibliography." *English Literature in Transition.* 26.4 (1983): 268-312.

—. "Vernon Lee and Kit Anstruther-Thomson: A Study of Love and Collaboration between Romantic Friends." *Women's Studies: An Interdisciplinary Journal* 12.2 (1986): 129-48.

Markgraf, Carl. "'Vernon Lee': A Commentary and Annotated Bibliography of Writings About Her." *English Literature in Transition* 26.4 (1983): 268-312.

384   L.M. MONTGOMERY (1874-1942)

L.M. Montgomery (1874-1942)

The Red Room

YOU WOULD HAVE ME TELL YOU THE STORY, GRANDCHILD? 'tis a sad one and best forgotten — few remember it now. There are always sad and dark stories in old families such as ours.

Yet I have promised and must keep my word. So sit down here at my feet and rest your bright head on my lap, that I may not see in your young eyes the shadows my story will bring across their bonny blue. I was a mere child when it all happened, yet I remember it but too well, and I can recall how pleased I was when my father's stepmother, Mrs. Montressor — she not liking to be called grandmother, seeing she was but turned of fifty and a handsome woman still — wrote to my mother that she must send little Beatrice up to Montressor Place for the Christmas holidays. So I went joyfully, though my mother grieved to part with me; she had little to love save me, my father, Conrad Montressor, having been lost at sea when but three months wed.

My aunts were wont to tell me how much I resembled him, being, so they said, a Montressor to the backbone; and this I took to mean commendation, for the Montressors were a well-descended and well-thought-of family, and the women were noted for their beauty. This I could well believe, since of all my aunts there was not one but was counted a pretty woman. Therefore I took heart of grace when I thought of my dark face and spindling shape, hoping that when I should be grown up I might be counted not unworthy of my race.

The Place was an old-fashioned, mysterious house, such as I delighted in, and Mrs. Montressor was ever kind to me, albeit a little stern, for she was a proud woman and cared but little for children, having none of her own.

But there were books there to pore over without let or hindrance — for nobody questioned of my whereabouts if I but kept out of the way — and strange, dim family portraits on the walls to gaze upon, until I knew each proud old face well, and had visioned a history for it in my own mind — for I was given to dreaming and was older and wiser than my years, having no childish companions to keep me still a child.

There were always some of my aunts at the Place to kiss and make much of me for my father's sake — for he had been their favourite brother. My aunts — there were eight of them — had all married well, so said people who knew, and lived not far away, coming home often to take tea with Mrs. Montressor, who had always gotten on well with her stepdaughters, or to help prepare for some festivity or other — for they were notable housekeepers, every one.

They were all at Montressor Place for Christmas, and I got more petting than I deserved, albeit they looked after me somewhat more strictly than did Mrs. Montressor, and saw to it that I did not read too many fairy tales or sit up later at nights than became my years.

But it was not for fairy tales and sugarplums nor yet for petting that I rejoiced to be at the Place at that time. Though I spoke not of it to anyone, I had a great longing to see my Uncle Hugh's wife, concerning whom I had heard much, both good and bad.

My Uncle Hugh, albeit the oldest of the family, had never married until now, and all the countryside rang with talk of his young wife. I did not hear as much as I wished, for the gossips took heed to my presence when I drew anear and turned to other matters. Yet, being somewhat keener of comprehension than they knew, I heard and understood not a little of their talk.

And so I came to know that neither proud Mrs. Montressor nor my good aunts, nor even my gentle mother, looked with overmuch favour on what my Uncle Hugh had done. And I did hear that Mrs. Montressor had chosen a wife for her stepson, of good family and some beauty, but that my Uncle Hugh would none of her — a thing Mrs. Montressor found hard to pardon, yet might so have done had not my uncle, on his last voyage to the Indies — for he went often in his own vessels — married and brought home a foreign bride, of whom no one knew aught save that her beauty was a thing to dazzle the day and that she was of some strange alien blood such as ran not in the blue veins of the Montressors.

Some had much to say of her pride and insolence, and wondered if Mrs. Montressor would tamely yield her mistress-ship to the stranger. But others, who were taken with her loveliness and grace, said that the tales told were born of envy and malice, and that Alicia Montressor was well worthy of her name and station.

So I halted between two opinions and thought to judge for myself, but when I went to the Place my Uncle Hugh and his bride were gone for a time, and I had even to swallow my disappointment and bide their return with all my small patience.

But my aunts and their stepmother talked much of Alicia, and they spoke slightingly of her, saying that she was but a light woman and that no good would come of my Uncle Hugh's having wed her, with other things of a like nature. Also they spoke of the company she gathered around her, thinking her to have strange and unbecoming companions for a Montressor. All this I heard and pondered much over, although my good aunts supposed that such a chit as I would take no heed to their whisperings.

When I was not with them, helping to whip eggs and stone raisins, and being watched to see that I ate not more than one out of five, I was surely to be found in the wing hall, poring over my book and grieving that I was no more allowed to go into the Red Room.

The wing hall was a narrow one and dim, connecting the main rooms of the Place with an older wing, built in a curious way. The hall was lighted by small, square-paned windows, and at its end a little flight of steps led up to the Red Room.

Whenever I had been at the Place before — and this was often — I had passed much of my time in this same

Red Room. It was Mrs. Montressor's sitting-room then, where she wrote her letters and examined household accounts, and sometimes had an old gossip in to tea. The room was low ceilinged and dim, hung with red damask, and with odd, square windows high up under the eaves and a dark wainscoting all around it. And there I loved to sit quietly on the red sofa and read my fairy tales, or talk dreamily to the swallows fluttering crazily against the tiny panes.

When I had gone this Christmas to the Place I soon bethought myself of the Red Room — for I had a great love for it. But I had got no further than the steps when Mrs. Montressor came sweeping down the hall in haste and, catching me by the arm, pulled me back as roughly as if it had been Bluebeard's chamber itself into which I was venturing.

Then, seeing my face, which I doubt not was startled enough, she seemed to repent of her haste and patted me gently on the head.

"There, there, little Beatrice! Did I frighten you, child? Forgive an old woman's thoughtlessness. But be not too ready to go where you are not bidden, and never venture foot in the Red Room now, for it belongs to your Uncle Hugh's wife, and let me tell you she is not over fond of intruders."

I felt sorry overmuch to hear this, nor could I see why my new aunt should care if I went in once in a while, as had been my habit, to talk to the swallows and misplace nothing. But Mrs. Montressor saw to it that I obeyed her, and I went no more to the Red Room, but busied myself with other matters.

For there were great doings at the Place and much coming and going. My aunts were never idle; there was to be much festivity Christmas week and a ball on Christmas Eve. And my aunts had promised me — though not till I had wearied them of my coaxing — that I should stay up that night and see as much of the gaiety as was good for me. So I did their errands and went early to bed every night without complaint — though I did this the more readily for that, when they thought me safely asleep, they would come in and talk around my bedroom fire, saying that of Alicia which I should not have heard.

At last came the day when my Uncle Hugh and his wife were expected home — though not until my scanty patience was well nigh wearied out — and we were all assembled to meet them in the great hall, where a ruddy firelight was gleaming.

My Aunt Frances had dressed me in my best white frock and my crimson sash, with much lamenting over my skinny neck and arms, and bade me behave prettily, as became my bringing up. So I slipped in a corner, my hands and feet cold with excitement, for I think every drop of blood in my body had gone to my head, and my heart beat so hardly that it even pained me.

Then the door opened and Alicia — for so I was used to hearing her called, nor did I ever think of her as my aunt in my own mind — came in, and a little in the rear my tall, dark uncle.

She came proudly forward to the fire and stood there superbly while she loosened her cloak, nor did she see me at all at first, but nodded, a little disdainfully, it seemed, to Mrs. Montressor and my aunts, who were grouped about the drawing-room door, very ladylike and quiet.

But I neither saw nor heard aught at the time save her only, for her beauty, when she came forth from her crimson cloak and hood, was something so wonderful that I forgot my manners and stared at her as one fascinated — as indeed I was, for never had I seen such loveliness and hardly dreamed it.

Pretty women I had seen in plenty, for my aunts and my mother were counted fair, but my uncle's wife was as little like to them as a sunset glow to pale moonshine or a crimson rose to white day-lilies. Nor can I paint her to you in words as I saw her then, with the long tongues of firelight licking her white neck and wavering over the rich masses of her red-gold hair.

She was tall — so tall that my aunts looked but insignificant beside her, and they were of no mean height, as became their race; yet no queen could have carried herself more royally, and all the passion and fire of her foreign nature burned in her splendid eyes, that might have been dark or light for aught that I could ever tell, but which seemed always like pools of warm flame, now tender, now fierce.

Her skin was like a delicate white rose leaf, and when she spoke I told my foolish self that never had I heard music before; nor do I ever again think to hear a voice so sweet, so liquid, as that which rippled over her ripe lips.

I had often in my own mind pictured this, my first meeting with Alicia, now in one way, now in another, but never had I dreamed of her speaking to me at all, so that it came to me as a great surprise when she turned and, holding out her lovely hands, said very graciously:

"And is this the little Beatrice? I have heard much of you — come, kiss me, child."

And I went, despite my Aunt Elizabeth's black frown, for the glamour of her loveliness was upon me, and I no longer wondered that my Uncle Hugh should have loved her.

Very proud of her was he too; yet I felt, rather than saw for I was sensitive and quick of perception, as old-young children ever are — that there was something other than pride and love in his face when he looked on her, and more in his manner than the fond lover — as it were, a sort of lurking mistrust.

Nor could I think, though to me the thought seemed as treason, that she loved her husband overmuch, for she seemed half condescending and half disdainful to him; yet one thought not of this in her presence, but only remembered it when she had gone.

When she went out it seemed to me that nothing was left, so I crept lonesomely away to the wing hall and sat down by a window to dream of her; and she filled my thoughts so fully that it was no surprise when I raised my eyes and saw her coming down the hall alone, her bright head shining against the dark old walls.

When she paused by me and asked me lightly of what I was dreaming, since I had such a sober face, I answered her truly that it was of her — whereat she laughed, as one not ill pleased, and said half mockingly:

"Waste not your thoughts so, little Beatrice. But come with me, child, if you will, for I have taken a strange fancy to your solemn eyes. Perchance the warmth of your young life may thaw out the ice that has frozen around my heart ever since I came among these cold Montressors."

And, though I understood not her meaning, I went, glad to see the Red Room once more. So she made me sit down and talk to her, which I did, for shyness was no failing of mine; and she asked me many questions, and some that I thought she should not have asked, but I could not answer them, so 'twere little harm.

After that I spent a part of every day with her in the Red Room. And my Uncle Hugh was there often, and he would kiss her and praise her loveliness, not heeding my presence — for I was but a child.

Yet it ever seemed to me that she endured rather than welcomed his caresses, and at times the ever-burning flame in her eyes glowed so luridly that a chill dread would creep over me, and I would remember what my Aunt Elizabeth had said, she being a bitter-tongued woman, though kind at heart — that this strange creature would bring on us all some evil fortune yet.

Then would I strive to banish such thoughts and chide myself for doubting one so kind to me.

When Christmas Eve drew nigh my silly head was full of the ball day and night. But a grievous disappointment befell me, for I awakened that day very ill with a most severe cold; and though I bore me bravely, my aunts discovered it soon, when, despite my piteous pleadings, I was put to bed, where I cried bitterly and would not be comforted. For I thought I should not see the fine folk and, more than all, Alicia.

But that disappointment, at least, was spared me, for at night she came into my room, knowing of my longing — she was ever indulgent to my little wishes. And when I saw her I forgot my aching limbs and burning brow, and even the ball I was not to see, for never was mortal creature so lovely as she, standing there by my bed.

Her gown was of white, and there was nothing I could liken the stuff to save moonshine falling athwart a frosted pane, and out from it swelled her gleaming breast and arms, so bare that it seemed to me a shame to look upon them. Yet it could not be denied they were of wondrous beauty, white as polished marble.

And all about her snowy throat and rounded arms, and in the masses of her splendid hair, were sparkling, gleaming stones, with hearts of pure light, which I know now to have been diamonds, but knew not then, for never had I seen aught of their like.

And I gazed at her, drinking in her beauty until my soul was filled, as she stood like some goddess before her worshipper. I think she read my thought in my face and liked it — for she was a vain woman, and to such even the admiration of a child is sweet.

Then she leaned down to me until her splendid eyes looked straight into my dazzled ones.

"Tell me, little Beatrice — for they say the word of a child is to be believed — tell me, do you think me beautiful?"

I found my voice and told her truly that I thought her beautiful beyond my dreams of angels — as indeed she was. Whereat she smiled as one well pleased.

Then my Uncle Hugh came in, and though I thought that his face darkened as he looked on the naked splendour of her breast and arms, as if he liked not that the eyes of other men should gloat on it, yet he kissed her with all a lover's fond pride, while she looked at him half mockingly.

Then said he, "Sweet, will you grant me a favour?"

And she answered, "It may be that I will."

And he said, "Do not dance with that man tonight, Alicia. I mistrust him much."

His voice had more of a husband's command than a lover's entreaty. She looked at him with some scorn, but when she saw his face grow black — for the Montressors brooked scant disregard of their authority, as I had good reason to know — she seemed to change, and a smile came to her lips, though her eyes glowed balefully.

Then she laid her arms about his neck and — though it seemed to me that she had as soon strangled as embraced him — her voice was wondrous sweet and caressing as she murmured in his ear.

He laughed and his brow cleared, though he said still sternly, "Do not try me too far, Alicia."

Then they went out, she a little in advance and very stately.

After that my aunts also came in, very beautifully and modestly dressed, but they seemed to me as nothing after Alicia. For I was caught in the snare of her beauty, and the longing to see her again so grew upon me that after a time I did an undutiful and disobedient thing.

I had been straitly charged to stay in bed, which I did not, but got up and put on a gown. For it was in my mind to go quietly down, if by chance I might again see Alicia, myself unseen.

But when I reached the great hall I heard steps approaching and, having a guilty conscience, I slipped aside into the blue parlour and hid me behind the curtains lest my aunts should see me.

Then Alicia came in, and with her a man whom I had never before seen. Yet I instantly bethought myself of a lean black snake, with a glittering and evil eye, which I had seen in Mrs. Montressor's garden two summers agone, and which was like to have bitten me. John, the gardener, had killed it, and I verily thought that if it had a soul, it must have gotten into this man.

Alicia sat down and he beside her, and when he had put his arms about her, he kissed her face and lips. Nor did she shrink from his embrace, but even smiled and leaned nearer to him with a little smooth motion, as they talked to each other in some strange, foreign tongue.

I was but a child and innocent, nor knew I aught of honour and dishonour. Yet it seemed to me that no man should kiss her save only my Uncle Hugh, and from that hour I mistrusted Alicia, though I understood not then what I afterwards did.

And as I watched them — not thinking of playing the spy — I saw her face grow suddenly cold, and she straightened herself up and pushed away her lover's arms.

Then I followed her guilty eyes to the door, where stood my Uncle Hugh, and all the pride and passion of the Montressors sat on his lowering brow. Yet he came forward quietly as Alicia and the snake drew apart and stood up.

At first he looked not at his guilty wife but at her lover, and smote him heavily in the face. Whereat he, being a coward at heart, as are all villains, turned white and slunk from the room with a muttered oath, nor was he stayed.

My uncle turned to Alicia, and very calmly and terribly he said, "From this hour you are no longer wife of mine!"

And there was that in his tone which told that his forgiveness and love should be hers nevermore.

Then he motioned her out and she went, like a proud queen, with her glorious head erect and no shame on her brow.

As for me, when they were gone I crept away, dazed and bewildered enough, and went back to my bed, having seen and heard more than I had a mind for, as disobedient people and eavesdroppers ever do.

But my Uncle Hugh kept his word, and Alicia was no more wife to him, save only in name. Yet of gossip or scandal there was none, for the pride of his race kept secret his dishonour, nor did he ever seem other than a courteous and respectful husband.

Nor did Mrs. Montressor and my aunts, though they wondered much among themselves, learn aught, for they dared question neither their brother nor Alicia, who carried herself as loftily as ever, and seemed to pine for neither lover nor husband. As for me, no one dreamed I knew aught of it, and I kept my own counsel as to what I had seen in the blue parlour on the night of the Christmas ball.

After the New Year I went home, but ere long Mrs. Montressor sent for me again, saying that the house was lonely without little Beatrice. So I went again and found all unchanged, though the Place was very quiet, and Alicia went out but little from the Red Room.

Of my Uncle Hugh I saw little, save when he went and came on the business of his estate, somewhat more gravely and silently than of yore, or brought to me books and sweetmeats from town.

But every day I was with Alicia in the Red Room, where she would talk to me, oftentimes wildly and strangely, but always kindly. And though I think Mrs. Montressor liked our intimacy none too well, she said no word, and I came and went as I listed with Alicia, though never quite liking her strange ways and the restless fire in her eyes.

Nor would I ever kiss her, after I had seen her lips pressed by the snake's, though she sometimes coaxed me, and grew pettish and vexed when I would not; but she guessed not my reason.

March came in that year like a lion, exceedingly hungry and fierce, and my Uncle Hugh had ridden away through the storm nor thought to be back for some days.

In the afternoon I was sitting in the wing hall, dreaming wondrous day-dreams, when Alicia called me to the Red Room. And as I went, I marvelled anew at her loveliness, for the blood was leaping in her face and her jewels were dim before the lustre of her eyes. Her hand, when she took mine, was burning hot, and her voice had a strange ring.

"Come, little Beatrice," she said, "come talk to me, for I know not what to do with my lone self today. Time hangs heavily in this gloomy house. I do verily think this Red Room has an evil influence over me. See if your childish prattle can drive away the ghosts that riot in these dark old corners — ghosts of a ruined and shamed life! Nay, shrink not — do I talk wildly? I mean not all I say — my brain seems on fire, little Beatrice. Come; it may be you know some grim old legend of this room — it must surely have one. Never was place fitter for a dark deed! Tush! never be so frightened, child — forget my vagaries. Tell me now and I will listen."

Whereat she cast herself lithely on the satin couch and turned her lovely face on me. So I gathered up my small wits and told her what I was not supposed to know — how that, generations agone, a Montressor had disgraced himself and his name, and that, when he came home to his mother, she had met him in that same Red Room and flung at him taunts and reproaches, forgetting whose breast had nourished him; and that he, frantic with shame and despair, turned his sword against his own heart and so died. But his mother went mad with her remorse, and was kept a prisoner in the Red Room until her death.

So lamely told I the tale, as I had heard my Aunt Elizabeth tell it, when she knew not I listened or understood. Alicia heard me through and said nothing, save that it was a tale worthy of the Montressors. Whereat I bridled, for I too was a Montressor, and proud of it.

But she took my hand soothingly in hers and said, "Little Beatrice, if tomorrow or the next day they should tell you, those cold, proud women, that Alicia was unworthy of your love, tell me, would you believe them?"

And I, remembering what I had seen in the blue parlour, was silent — for I could not lie. So she flung my hand away with a bitter laugh, and picked lightly from the table anear a small dagger with a jewelled handle.

It seemed to me a cruel-looking toy and I said so whereat she smiled and drew her white fingers down the thin, shining blade in a fashion that made me cold

"Such a little blow with this," she said, "such a little blow — and the heart beats no longer, the weary brain rests, the lips and eyes smile never again! T'were a short path out of all difficulties, my Beatrice."

And I, understanding her not, yet shivering begged her to cast it aside, which she did carelessly and, putting a hand under my chin, she turned up my face to hers.

"Little, grave-eyed Beatrice, tell me truly, would it grieve you much if you were never again to sit here with Alicia in this same Red Room?"

And I made answer earnestly that it would, glad that I could say so much truly. Then her face grew tender and she sighed deeply.

Presently she opened a quaint, inlaid box and took from it a shining gold chain of rare workmanship and exquisite design, and this she hung around my neck, nor would suffer me to thank her but laid her hand gently on my lips.

"Now go," she said. "But ere you leave me, little Beatrice, grant me but the one favour — it may be that I shall never ask another of you. Your people, I know — those cold Montressors — care little for me, but with all my faults, I have ever been kind to you. So, when the morrow's come, and they tell you that Alicia is as one worse than dead, think not of me with scorn only but grant me a little pity for I was not always what I am now, and might never have become so had a little child like you been always anear me, to keep me pure and innocent. And I would have you but the once lay your arms about my neck and kiss me."

And I did so, wondering much at her manner — for it had in it a strange tenderness and some sort of hopeless longing. Then she gently put me from the room, and I sat musing by the hall window until night fell darkly — and a fearsome night it was, of storm and blackness. And I thought how well it was that my Uncle Hugh had not to return in such a tempest. Yet, ere the thought had grown cold, the door opened and he strode down the hall his cloak drenched and wind-twisted, in one hand a whip, as though he had but then sprung from his horse, in the other what seemed like a crumpled letter.

Nor was the night blacker than his face, and he took no heed of me as I ran after him, thinking selfishly of the sweetmeats he had promised to bring me — but I thought no more of them when I got to the door of the Red Room.

Alicia stood by the table, hooded and cloaked as for a journey, but her hood had slipped back, and her face rose from it marble-white, save where her wrathful eyes burned out, with dread and guilt and hatred in their depths, while she had one arm raised as if to thrust him back.

As for my uncle, he stood before her and I saw not his face, but his voice was low and terrible, speaking words I understood not then, though long afterwards I came to know their meaning.

And he cast foul scorn at her that she should have thought to fly with her lover, and swore that naught should again thwart his vengeance, with other threats, wild and dreadful enough.

Yet she said no word until he had done, and then she spoke, but what she said I know not, save that it was full of hatred and defiance and wild accusation, such as a mad woman might have uttered.

And she defied him even then to stop her flight, though he told her to cross that threshold would mean her death; for he was a wronged and desperate man and thought of nothing save his own dishonour. Then she made as if to pass him, but he caught her by her white wrist; she turned on him with fury, and I saw her right hand reach stealthily out over the table behind her, where lay the dagger.

"Let me go!" she hissed.

And he said, "I will not."

Then she turned herself about and struck at him with the dagger — and never saw I such a face as was hers at the moment.

He fell heavily, yet held her even in death, so that she had to wrench herself free, with a shriek that rings yet in my ears on a night when the wind wails over the rainy moors. She rushed past me unheeding, and fled down the hall like a hunted creature, and I heard the heavy door clang hollowly behind her.

As for me, I stood there looking at the dead man, for I could neither move nor speak and was like to have died of horror. And presently I knew nothing, nor did I come to my recollection for many a day, when I lay abed, sick of a fever and more like to die than live.

So that when at last I came out from the shadow of death, my Uncle Hugh had been long cold in his grave, and the hue and cry for his guilty wife was well nigh over, since naught had been seen or heard of her since she fled the country with her foreign lover.

When I came rightly to my remembrance, they questioned me as to what I had seen and heard in the Red

Room. And I told them as best I could, though much aggrieved that to my questions they would answer nothing save to bid me to stay still and think not of the matter.

Then my mother, sorely vexed over my adventures which in truth were but sorry ones for a child — took me home. Nor would she let me keep Alicia's chain, but made away with it, how I knew not and little cared, for the sight of it was loathsome to me.

It was many years ere I went again to Montressor Place, and I never saw the Red Room more, for Mrs. Montressor had the old wing torn down, deeming its sorrowful memories dark heritage enough for the next Montressor.

So, Grandchild, the sad tale is ended, and you will not see the Red Room when you go next month to Montressor Place. The swallows still build under the eaves, though — I know not if you will understand their speech as I did.

Source: *Waverly Magazine*, July 1898.

Biographical Note

Best known as the author of the children's classic *Anne of Green Gables*, Lucy Maud Montgomery was born in Clifton, Prince Edward Island, on November 30, 1874. After her mother died two years later, she went to live with her maternal grandparents in Cavendish. Her first poem appeared in the Charlottetown *Patriot* when she was fifteen, and her first story, "The Wreck of the Marco Polo," in the Montreal *Witness* two years later. From that point on, Montgomery's short fiction was published widely in both American and Canadian magazines and newspapers. In 1893, she attended the Prince of Wales College in Charlottetown and studied for a teaching licence. She then taught school at Bideford for a year before attending Dalhousie University in Halifax, where she studied English Language and Literature. After teaching for another two years, Montgomery returned to live with her grandmother in Cavendish after her grandfather died. She assisted at the Post Office, ran the household, and continued to write. In 1901 she spent several months in Halifax working for the *Daily Echo*: she edited the page of "Society Letters" and, under the pseudonym "Cynthia," produced a column called "Around the Tea-Table." She returned to her grandmother's home in Cavendish a year later. Montgomery's first novel, *Anne of Green Gables*, was rejected by several publishers and left in a cupboard for three years before finally being published by L.C. Page of Boston in 1908. Within six months the book went through six editions. Her red-haired heroine seized the imagination of both children and adults, and brought Montgomery instant success and international acclaim. Anne's popularity has endured, and the novel has been made into a musical (annually staged in Charlottetown), a film, and a television miniseries. Seven sequels followed which chronicled the development of this imaginative adolescent and her search for love and self-knowledge.

In 1911 Montgomery married the Reverend Ewan Macdonald and they moved to Ontario where she continued to write. At a reception of the Canadian Women's Press Club in Toronto that year she also met the novelist Marian Keith (Mrs. Donald McGregor), and the two remained lifelong friends. In 1920 L.C. Page published, without her permission, the *Further Chronicles of Avonlea*, a collection of Montgomery's stories previously published in magazines; the legal battle that ensued lasted for nine years. During the 1920s she also began a new, and a more autobiographical, series of books with a writer-heroine called Emily, and in 1934 she published *Courageous Women* with Marian Keith and Mabel Burns McKinley. In 1935 she was awarded the OBE. She died on April 24, 1942, and was buried in a grave overlooking the house known as "Green Gables."

Montgomery was a prolific writer: she produced 22 books of fiction, a book of poetry, and approximately 450 other poems and 500 short stories; she also kept a journal, and, at her death, left behind over 5000 pages which provide a fascinating record of her life. A melodramatic thriller which shows a less famililar side of the popular author, "The Red Room" is particularly interesting for Montgomery's questioning of the responses to beauty and her use of the innocent child narrator to depict the lurid scenes of adultery and murder.

Selected Modern Reprints:

The Doctor's Sweetheart and Other Stories. L.M. Montgomery. Selected and with an introduction by Catherine McLay. Toronto: McGraw-Hill Ryerson, 1979.

L.M. Montgomery. Akin to Anne: Tales of Other Orphans. Ed. Rea Wilmshurst. Toronto: McClelland and Stewart, 1988.

L.M. Montgomery. Along the Shore: Tales by the Sea. Ed. Rea Wilmshurst. Toronto: McClelland and Stewart, 1989.

L.M. Montgomery. Among the Shadows: Tales from the Darker Side. Ed. Rea Wilmshurst. Toronto: McClelland and Stewart, 1990.

The Selected Journals of L.M. Montgomery, 1889-1910. Ed. Mary Rubio and Elizabeth Waterston. Toronto: Oxford UP, 1985.

Selected Secondary Sources:

Ahmansson, Gabriella. *A Life and Its Mirrors: A Feminist Reading of L.M. Montgomery's Fiction.* Uppsala: Uppsala U, 1991.

Gillen, Mollie. *The Wheel of Things: A Biography of L.M. Montgomery.* Toronto: Fitzhenry and Whiteside, 1975.

Russell, Ruth Webber, D.W. Russell, and Rea Wilmhurst. *Lucy Maud Montgomery, a Preliminary Bibliography.* Waterloo, ON: U of Waterloo Library, 1986.

Sorfleet, John Robert, ed. *L.M. Montgomery: An Assessment.* Guelph, ON: Canadian Children's P, 1976.

402   MARGARET OLIPHANT (1828-1897)

Margaret Oliphant (1828-1897)

A Story of a
Wedding Tour

Chapter I

THEY HAD BEEN MARRIED EXACTLY A WEEK WHEN THIS incident occurred.

It was not a love marriage. The man, indeed, had been universally described as being "very much in love," but the girl was not by any one supposed to be in that desirable condition. She was a very lonely little girl, without parents, almost without relations. Her guardian was a man who had been engaged in business relations with her father, and who had accepted the charge of the little orphan as his duty. But neither he nor his wife had any love to expend on her, and they did not feel that such visionary sentiments came within the line of duty. He was a very honourable man, and took charge of her small – very small – property with unimpeachable care.

If anything, he wronged himself rather than Janey, charging her nothing for the transfers which he made of her farthing's worth of stock from time to time, to get a scarcely appreciable rise of interest and income for her. The whole thing was scarcely appreciable, and to a large-handed man like Mr Midhurst, dealing with hundreds of thousands, it was almost ridiculous to give a moment's attention to what a few hundreds might produce. But he did so; and if there is any angel who has to do with trade affairs, I hope it was carefully put to his account to balance some of the occasions on which he was not perhaps so particular. Nor did Mrs Midhurst shrink from her duty in all substantial and real good offices to the girl. She, who spent hundreds at the dressmaker's every year on account of her many daughters, did not disdain to get Janey's serge frocks at a cheaper shop, and to have them made by an inexpensive workwoman, so that the girl should have the very utmost she could get for her poor little money.

Was not this real goodness, real honesty, and devotion to their duty? But to love a little thing like that with no real claim upon them, and nothing that could be called specially attractive about her, who could be expected to do it? They had plenty – almost more than enough – of children of their own. These children were big boys and girls, gradually growing, in relays, into manhood and womanhood, when this child came upon their hands. There was no room for her in the full and noisy house. When she was grown up most of the Midhurst children were married, but there was one son at home, who, in the well-known contradictiousness of young people – it being a very wrong and, indeed, impossible thing – was quite capable of falling in love with Janey – and one daughter, with whom it was also possible that Janey might come into competition.

The young Midhursts were nice-looking young people enough; but Janey was very pretty. If Providence did but fully consider all the circumstances, it cannot but be felt that Providence would not carry out, as often is done, such ridiculous arrangements. Janey was very pretty. Could anything more inconvenient, more inappropriate, be conceived?

The poor little girl had, accordingly, spent most of her life at school, where she had, let it not be doubted, made many friendships and little loves; but these were broken up by holidays, by the returning home of the other pupils, while she stayed for ever at school: and not at one school, but several – for in his extreme conscientiousness her guardian desired to do her "every justice," as he said, and prepare her fully for the life – probably that of a governess – which lay before her. Therefore, when she had become proficient in one part of her education she was carried on to another, with the highest devotion to her commercial value no doubt, but a sublime indifference to her little feelings. Thus, she had been in France for two years, and in Germany for two years, so as to be able to state that French and German acquired in these countries were among the list of her accomplishments. English, of course, was the foundation of all; and Janey had spent some time at a famous academy of music, – her guardian adding something out of his own pocket to her scanty means, that she might be fully equipped for her profession. And then she was brought, I will not say home: Janey fondly said home, but she knew very well it did not mean home. And it was while Mrs Midhurst was actually writing out the advertisement for 'The Times,' and the 'Morning Post,' and 'The Guardian,' which was to announce to all the world that a young lady desired an engagement as governess, that her husband burst in with the extraordinary news that Mr Rosendale, who had chanced to travel with Janey from Flushing, on her return, and who afterwards, by a still greater chance, met her when asked to lunch at the Midhursts', and stared very much at her, as they all remarked – had fallen in love with, and wanted to marry, this humble little girl.

"Fallen in love with Janey!" Mrs Midhurst cried. "Fallen in love with you, Janey!" said Agnes Midhurst, with a little emphasis on the pronoun. He was not, indeed, quite good enough to have permitted himself the luxury of falling in love with Mr Midhurst's daughter, but he was an astonishing match for Janey. He was a man who was very well off: he could afford himself such a caprice as that. He was not handsome. There was a strain of Jewish blood in him. He was a thick-set little man, and did not dress or talk in perfect taste; but – in love! These two words had made all the difference. Nobody had ever loved her, much less been "in love" with her. Janey consented willingly enough for the magic of these two words. She felt that she was going to be like the best of women at last – to have some one who loved her, some one who was in love with her. He might not be "joli, joli,"[1] as they say in France. She might not feel any very strong impulse on her own part towards him; but if he were in love with her – in love! Romeo was no more than that with Juliet. The thought went to Janey's head. She married him quite willingly for the sake of this.

I am afraid that Janey, being young, and shy, and strange, was a good deal frightened, horrified, and even revolted, by her first discoveries of what it meant to be in love. She had made tremendous discoveries in the course of a week. She had found out that Mr Rosendale, her husband, was in love with her beauty, but as indifferent to herself as any of the persons she had quitted to give herself to him. He did not care at all what she thought, how she felt, what she liked or disliked. He did not care even for her comfort, or that she should be pleased and happy, which, in the first moment even of such a union, and out of pure self-regard to make a woman more agreeable to himself, a man – even the most brutal – generally regards more or less. He was, perhaps, not aware that he did not regard it. He took it for granted that, being his wife, she would naturally be pleased with what pleased him, and his mind went no further than this.

Therefore, as far as Janey liked the things he liked, all went well enough. She had these, but no other. Her wishes were not consulted further, nor did he know that he failed in any way towards her. He had little to say to her, except expressions of admiration. When he was not telling her that she was a little beauty, or admiring her pretty hair, her pretty eyes, the softness of her skin, and the smallness of her waist, he had nothing to say. He read his paper, disappearing behind it in the morning; he went to sleep after his midday meal (for the weather was warm;) he played billiards in the evening in the hotels to which he took her on their wedding journey; or he overwhelmed her with caresses from which she shrank in disgust, almost in terror. That was all that being in love meant, she found; and to say that she was disappointed cruelly was to express in the very mildest way the dreadful downfall of all her expectations and hopes which happened to Janey before she had been seven days a wife. It is not disagreeable to be told that you are a little beauty, prettier than any one else. Janey would have been very well pleased to put up with that; but to be petted like a little lapdog and then left as a lapdog is – to be quiet and not to trouble in the intervals of petting – was to the poor little girl, unaccustomed to love and athirst for it, who had hoped to be loved, and to find a companion to whom she would be truly dear, a disenchantment and disappointment which was almost more than flesh and blood could bear.

She was in the full bitterness of these discoveries when the strange incident occurred which was of so much importance in her life. They were travelling through France in one of those long night journeys to which we are all accustomed nowadays; and Janey, pale and tired, had been contemplating for some time the figure of her husband thrown back in the corner opposite, snoring complacently with his mouth open, and looking the worst that a middle-aged man can look in the utter abandonment of self-indulgence and rude comfort, when the train began to slacken its speed, and to prepare to enter one of those large stations which look so ghastly in the desertion of the night.

Rosendale jumped up instinctively, only half awake, as the train stopped. The other people in the carriage were leaving it, having attained the end of their journey, but he pushed through them and their baggage to get out, with the impatience which some men show at any pause of the kind, and determination to stretch their legs, or get something to drink, which mark the breaks in their journey. He did not even say anything to Janey as he forced his way out, but she was so familiar with his ways by this time that she took no notice. She did take notice, however, when, her fellow-passengers and their packages having all been cleared away, she suddenly became sensible that the train was getting slowly into motion again without any sign of her husband.

She thought she caught a glimpse of him strolling about on the opposite platform before she was quite sure of what was happening. And then there was a scurry of hurrying feet, a slamming of doors, and as she rose and ran to the window bewildered, she saw him, along with some other men, running at full speed, but quite hopelessly, to catch the train. The last she saw was his face, fully revealed by the light of the lamp, convulsed with rage and astonishment, evidently with a yell of denunciation on the lips. Janey trembled at the sight. There was that in him, too, though as yet in her submissiveness she had never called it forth, a temper as unrestrained as his love-making, and as little touched by any thought save that of his own gratification. Her first sensation was fright, a terror that she was in fault and was about to be crushed to pieces in his rage: and then Janey sank back in her corner, and a flood of feeling of quite another kind took possession of her breast.

Was it possible that she was alone? Was it possible that for the first time since that terrible moment of her marriage she was more safely by herself than any locked door or even watchful guardian could keep her, quite unapproachable in the isolation of the train? Alone!

"Safe!" Janey ventured to say to herself, clasping her hands together with a mingled sensation of excitement and terror and tremulous delight which words could not tell.

She did not know what to think at first. The sound of the train plunging along through the darkness, through the unknown country, filled her mind as if some one was talking to her. And she was fluttered by the strangeness of the incident and disturbed by alarms. There was a fearful joy in thus being alone, in having a few hours, perhaps a whole long tranquil night, to herself: whatever came of it, that was always so much gained. But then she seemed to see him in the morning coming in upon her heated and angry. She had always felt that the moment would come when he would be angry, and more terrible to confront than any governess, or even principal of a ladies' college. He would come in furious, accusing her of being the cause of the accident, or doing something to set the train in motion; or else he would come in fatigued and dusty, claiming her services as if she were his valet – a thing which had, more or less, happened already, and against which Janey's pride and her sense of what was fit had risen in arms. She thought of this for a little time with trouble, and of the difficulties she would have in arriving, and where she would go to, and what she would say. It was an absurd story to tell, not to his advantage, "I lost my husband at Montbard." How could she say it? The hotel people would think she was a deceiver. Perhaps they would not take her in. And how would he know where to find her when he arrived? He would feel that he had lost her, as much as she had lost him.

Just as this idea rose in her mind, like a new thing full of strange suggestions, the train began to shorten speed again, and presently stopped once more. She felt it to do so with a pang of horror. No doubt he had climbed up somewhere, at the end or upon the engine, and was now to be restored to his legitimate place, to fall upon her either in fondness or in rage, delighted to get back to her, or angry with her for leaving him behind: she did not know which would be the worst. Her heart began to beat with fright and anticipation. But to her great relief it was only the guard who came to the door. He wanted to know if madame was the lady whose husband had been left behind; and to offer a hundred apologies and explanations. One of those fools at Montbard had proclaimed twenty minutes' pause when there were but five. If he had but heard he would have put it right, but he was at the other end of the train. But madame must not be too much distressed; a few hours would put it all right.

"Then there is another train?" said Janey, her poor little head buzzing between excitement and relief.

"Not for some hours," said the guard. "Madame will understand that there is not more than one *rapide*[2] in the middle of the night; but in the morning quite early there is the train omnibus. Oh, very early, at five o'clock. Before madame is ready for her dinner monsieur will be at her side."

"Not till evening, then?" said Janey, with again a sudden acceleration of the movement of her heart.

The guard was desolated. "Not before evening. But if madame will remain quietly in the carriage when the train arrives at the station, I will find the omnibus of the hotel for her – I will see to everything! Madame, no doubt, knows which hotel to go to?"

Janey, as a matter of fact, did not know. Her husband had told her none of the details of the journey; but she said with a quick breath of excitement –

"I will go to the one that is nearest, the one at the Gare.³ There will be no need for any omnibus."

"And the baggage? Madame has her ticket?"

"I have nothing," cried Janey, "except my travelling-bag. You must explain that for me. But otherwise – otherwise, I think I can manage."

"Madame speaks French so well," the man said, with admiration. It was, indeed, a piece of good fortune that she had been made to acquire the language in the country: that she was not frightened to find herself in a foreign place, and surrounded by people speaking a strange tongue, as many a young English bride would have been. There was a moment of tremendous excitement and noise at the station while all was explained to a serious *chef de Gare*,⁴ and a gesticulating band of porters and attendants, whose loud voices, as they all spoke together, would have frightened an ordinary English girl out of her wits. But Janey, in the strange excitement which had taken possession of her, and in her fortunate acquaintance with the language, stood still as a little rock amid all the confusion. "I will wait at the hotel till my husband comes," she said, taking out the travelling-bag and her wraps, and maintaining a composure worthy of all admiration. Not a tear, not an outcry. How astonishing are these English, cried the little crowd, with that swift classification which the Frenchman loves.

Janey walked into the hotel with her little belongings, not knowing whether she was indeed walking upon her feet or floating upon wings. She was quite composed. But if any one could only have seen the commotion within that youthful bosom! She locked the door of the little delightful solitary room in which she was placed. It was not delightful at all. But to Janey it was a haven of peace, as sweet, as secluded from everything alarming and terrible, as any bower. Not till evening could he by any possibility arrive – the man who had caused such a revolution in her life. She had some ten hours of divine quiet before her, of blessed solitude, of thought. She did not refuse to take the little meal that was brought to her, the breakfast of which she stood in need; and she was glad to be able to bathe her face, to take off her dusty dress, and put on the soft and fresh one, which, happily, had folded into very small space, and therefore could be put into her bag. Her head still buzzed with the strangeness of the position, yet began to settle a little. When she had made all these little arrangements she sat down to consider. Perhaps you will think there was very little to consider, nothing but how to wait till the next train brought him, which, after all, was not a very great thing to do. Appalling, perhaps, to a little inexperienced bride; but not to Janey, who had travelled alone so often, and knew the language, and all that.

But whoever had been able to look into Janey's mind would have seen that something more was there, – a very, very different thing from the question of how best to await his coming back. Oh, if he had loved her, Janey would have put up with many things! She would have schooled herself out of all her private repugnances; she would have been so grateful to him, so touched by the affection which nobody had ever bestowed upon her before! But he did not love her. He cared nothing about herself, Janey; did not even know her, or want to know her, or take into consideration her ways or her wishes. He was in love with her pretty face, her fresh little beauty, her power of pleasing him. If ever that power ceased, which it was sure to do, sooner or later, she would be to him less than nothing, the dreary little wife whom everybody has seen attached to a careless man: Janey felt that this was what was in store for her. She felt the horror of him, and his kind of loving, which had been such a miserable revelation to her. She felt the relief, the happiness, ah, the bliss, of having lost him for a moment, of being alone.

She took out her purse from her pocket, which was full of the change she had got in Paris of one of the ten-pound notes which her guardian had given her when she left his house on her wedding morning. She took out the clumsy pocket-book, an old one, in which there were still nine ten-pound notes. It was all her fortune, except a very, very small investment which brought her in some seven pounds a year. This was the remainder of another small investment which had been withdrawn in order to provide her with her simple trousseau, leaving this sum of a hundred pounds which her guardian had given her, advising her to place it at once for security in her husband's hands. Janey had not done this, she scarcely could tell why. She spread them on the table – the nine notes, the twelve napoleons of shining French money. A hundred pounds; she had still the twelve francs which made up the sum. She had spent nothing. There were even the few coppers over for the *agio*.[5] She spread them all out, and counted them from right to left, and again from left to right. Nine ten-pound notes, twelve and a-half French napoleons – or louis, as people call them nowadays – making a hundred pounds. A hundred pounds is a big sum in the eyes of a girl. It may not be much to you and me, who know that it means only ten times ten pounds, and that ten pounds goes like the wind as soon as you begin to spend it. But to Janey! Why, she could live upon a hundred pounds for – certainly for two years; for two long delightful years, with nobody to trouble her, nobody to scold, nobody to interfere. Something mounted to her head like the fumes of wine. Everything began to buzz again, to turn round, to sweep her away as on a rapidly mounting current. She put back all the money in the pocket-book – her fortune, the great sum that made her independent; and she put back her things into the bag. A sudden energy of resolution seized her. She put on her hat again, and as she looked at herself in the glass encountered the vision of a little face which was new to her. It was not that of Janey, the little governess-pupil; it was not young Mrs. Rosendale. It was full of life, and meaning, and energy, and strength. Who was it? Janey? Janey herself, the real woman, whom nobody had ever seen before.

Chapter II

It is astonishing how many things can be done in sudden excitement and passion which could not be possible under any other circumstances. Janey was by nature a shy girl and easily frightened, accustomed indeed to do many things for herself, and to move quietly without attracting observation through the midst of a crowd; but she had never taken any initiative, and since her marriage had been reduced to such a state of complete dependence on her husband's wishes and plans that she had not attempted the smallest step on her own impulse.

Now, however, she moved about with a quiet assurance and decision which astonished herself. She carried her few possessions back again to the railway station, leaving the small gold piece of ten francs to pay, and much overpay, her hour's shelter and entertainment at the hotel.

Nobody noticed her as she went through the bustle of the place and back to the crowded station, where a little leisurely local train was about starting – a slow train occupied by peasants and country folk, and which stopped at every station along the line. English people abound in that place at all hours, except at this particular moment, when the *rapide* going towards Italy had but newly left and the little country train was preparing in peace. Nobody seemed to notice Janey as she moved about with her bag on her arm. She took her ticket in her irreproachable French "acquired in the country," which attracted no attention. She got into a second-class carriage in which there were already various country people, and especially a young mother with a baby, and its nurse in a white round cap with long streaming ribbons. Janey's heart went out to these people. She wondered if the young woman was happy, if her husband loved her, if it was not very sweet to have a child – a child must love you; it would not mind whether your cheeks were rosy or pale, whether you were pretty or not, whether you had accomplishments or languages acquired in the country.

Looking at this baby, Janey almost forgot that she was

going out upon the world alone, and did not know where. It is a tremendous thing to do this, to separate from all the world you are acquainted with, to plunge into the unknown. Men do it often enough, though seldom without some clue, some link of connection with the past and way of return. Janey was about to cut herself off as by the Fury's shears[6] from everything. She would never join her husband again. She would never fear her guardian again. She must drop out of sight like a stone into the sea. There was no longing love to search for her, no pardon to be offered, no one who would be heart-struck at the thought of the little girl lost and unhappy. Only anger would be excited by her running away, and a desire to punish, to shake her little fragile person to pieces, to make her suffer. She knew that if she did it at all, it must be final. But this did not overwhelm her. What troubled Janey a great deal more than the act of severance which she was about to accomplish, was the inevitable fib or fibs she must tell in order to account for her appearance in the unknown. She did not like to tell a fib, even a justifiable one. It was against all her traditions, against her nature. She felt that she could never do it anything but badly, never without exciting suspicions; and she must needs have some story, some way of accounting for herself.

This occupied her mind while the slow train crawled from station to station. It was the most friendly, idle, gossiping little train. It seemed to stop at the merest signal-box to have a talk, to drink as it were a social glass administered through that black hose, with a friend; it stopped wherever there were a few houses, it carried little parcels, it took up a leisurely passenger going next door, and the little electric bell went on tingling, and the guard cried "En voiture!"[7] and the little bugle sounded. Janey was amused by all these little sounds and sights, and the country all flooded with sunshine, and the flowers everywhere, though it was only March, and dark black weather when she had left home.

Left home! and she had no home now, anywhere, no place to take refuge in, nobody to write to, to appeal to, to tell if she was happy or unhappy. But Janey did not care! She felt a strange elation of ease and relief. All alone, but everybody smiling upon her, the young mother opposite beginning to chatter, the baby to crow to her, the nurse to smile and approve of the *bonne petite*[8] dame who took so much notice of the child. Her head was swimming, but with pleasure, and the blessed sensation of freedom – pleasure tinctured with the exhilaration of escape, and the thrill of fright which added to the excitement. Yet at that moment she was certainly in no danger. He was toiling along no doubt, fuming and perhaps swearing, on another slow train on the other side of Marseilles. Janey laughed to herself a little guiltily at the thought.

And she had escaped! It was not her doing primarily. She might have gone on all her life till she had died, but for that accident which was none of her doing. It was destiny that had done it, fate. The cage door had been opened and the bird had flown away. And how nice it would be to settle down, with this little mother, just about her own age, for a neighbour, and to help to bring the baby up! The kind, sweet faces they all had, mother and baby and *bonne*[9] all smiling upon her! When Janey looked out on the other side she saw the sea flashing in the sunshine, the red porphyry rocks reflecting themselves in the brilliant blue, and village after village perched upon a promontory or in the hollow of a bay. She had never in all her life before felt that sensation of blessedness, of being able to do what she liked, of having no one to call to her account. She did not know where she was going, but that was part of the pleasure. She did not want to know where she was going.

Then suddenly this sentiment changed, and she saw in a moment a place that smiled at her like the smiling of the mother and baby. It was one of those villages in a bay: a range of blue mountains threw forth a protecting arm into the sea to shield it: the roofs were red, the houses were white, they were all blazing in the sun. Soft olives and palms fringed the deep green of the pines that rolled back in waves of verdure over the country behind, and strayed down in groups and scattered files to the shore below. Oh, what a cheerful, delightsome place! and this was where the little group with the baby were preparing to get out. "I will go too," said Janey to herself; and her heart gave a little bound of pleasure. She was delighted to reach the place where she was going to stay – just as she had been delighted to go on in the little pottering train, not knowing where she was going; and not wishing to know.

This was how Janey settled herself on the day of her flight from the world. She scarcely knew what story it was she told to the young woman whose face had so charmed her, and whom she asked whether she would be likely to find lodgings anywhere, lodgings that would not be too expensive.

"My husband is – at sea," Janey heard herself saying. She could scarcely tell what it was that put those words into her head.

"Oh, but yes," the other young woman cried with rapture. Nothing was more easy to get than a lodging in St Honorat, which was beginning to try to be a winter resort, and was eager to attract strangers. Janey had dreamed of a cottage and a garden, but she was not dissatisfied when she found herself in a sunbright room on the second floor of a tall white house facing the sea. It had a little balcony all to itself. The water rippled on the shore just over the road, the curve of the blue mountains was before her eyes.

I do not say that when she had settled down, when the thrill of movement was no longer in her brain, Janey was not without a shiver at the thought of what she had done. When the sun set, and that little chill which comes into the air of the south at the moment of its setting breathed a momentary cold about her, and when the woman of the house carefully closed the shutters and shut out the shining of the bay, and she was left alone with her candle, something sank in Janey's heart – something of the unreasonable elation, the fantastic happiness, of the day. She thought of "Mr. Rosendale" (she had never got so near her husband as to call him by any other name) arriving, of the fuss there would be about her and the inquiries.

Was it rash to have come to a place so near as this –

within an hour or two of where he was? Was there a danger that some one might have seen her? that it might be found out that she had taken her ticket? But then she had taken her ticket for a place much farther along the coast. She thought she could see him arrive all flaming with anger and eagerness, and the group that would gather round him, and how he would be betrayed by his bad French, and the rage he would get into! Again she laughed guiltily; but then got very grave again trying to count up all the chances – how some porter might have noticed and might betray her, how he might yet come down upon her furiously, to wreak upon her all the fury of his discomfiture. Janey knew by instinct that though it was in no way her fault, her husband would wreak his vengeance upon her even for being left behind by the train. She became desperate as she sat and thought it all over. It would be better for her to leap from the window, to throw herself into the sea, than to fall into his hands. There would be no forgiveness for her if he once laid hands upon her. Now that she had taken this desperate step, she must stand by it to the death.

Chapter III

Ten years had passed away since the time of that wedding tour.

Ten years! It is a very long time in a life. It makes a young man middle-aged, and a middle-aged man old. It takes away the bloom of youth, and the ignorance of the most inexperienced; and yet what a little while it is! – no more than a day when you look back upon it. The train from Marseilles to Nice, which is called the *rapide*, goes every day, and most people one time or another have travelled by it.

One day last winter one of the passengers in this train, established very comfortably in the best corner of a sleeping carriage in which he had passed the night luxuriously, and from which he was now looking out upon the shining sea, the red rocks, the many bays and headlands of the coast, suddenly received such a shock and sensation as seldom occurs to any one. He was a man of middle-age and not of engaging aspect. His face was red, and his eyes were dull yet fiery. He had the air of a man who had indulged himself much and all his inclinations, had loved good living and all the joys of the flesh, had denied himself nothing – and was now paying the penalties. Such men, to tell the truth, are not at all unusual apparitions on that beautiful coast or in the train *rapide*. No doubt appearances are deceitful, and it is not always a bad man who bears that aspect or who pays those penalties: but in this case few people would have doubted.

His eyes were bloodshot, he had a scowl upon his brow, his foot was supported upon a cushion. He had a servant with him to whom he rarely spoke but with an insult. Not an agreeable man – and the life he was now leading, whatever it had been, was not an agreeable life. He was staring out at the window upon the curves of the coast, sometimes putting up the collar of his fur coat over his ears, though it was a warm morning, and the sun had all the force of April. What he was thinking of it would be difficult to divine – perhaps of the good dinner that awaited him at Monte Carlo when he got there, perhaps of his good luck in being out of England when the east winds began to blow, perhaps of something quite different – some recollection of his past. The *rapide* does not stop at St Honorat, which indeed had not succeeded in making itself a winter resort. It was still a very small place. There were a few people on the platform when the train rushed through. It seemed to pass like a whirlwind, yet notwithstanding, in that moment two things happened. The gentleman in the corner of the carriage started in his seat, and flung himself half out of the window, with a sudden roar which lost itself in the tunnel into which the train plunged. There was an awful minute in that tunnel: for the servant thought his master had taken a fit, and there was no light to see what convulsions he might have fallen into, while at the same time he fought furiously against the man's efforts to loose his wrappings and place him in a recumbent position, exclaiming furiously all the time. He had not taken a fit, but when the train emerged into the light he was as near to it as possible – purple-red in his face, and shouting with rage and pain.

"Stop the train! stop the train!" he shouted. "Do you hear, you fool? stop the train! Ring the bell or whatever it is! break the — thing! Stop the train!"

"Sir, sir! if you will only be quiet, I will get your medicine in a moment!"

"Medicine, indeed!" cried the master, indignantly, and every furious name that he could think of mounted to his lips – fool, idiot, ass, swine – there was no end to his epithets. "I tell you I saw her, I saw her!" he shouted. "Stop the train! Stop the train!"

On the other hand, among the few insignificant persons, peasants and others, who had been standing on the platform at St Honorat when the *rapide* dashed past, there had been a woman and a child. The woman was not a peasant: she was very simply dressed in black, with one of the small bonnets which were a few years ago so distinctively English, and with an air which corresponded to that simple coiffure. She was young, and yet had the air of responsibility and motherhood which marks a woman who is no longer in the first chapter of life. The child, a boy of nine or ten, standing close by her side, had seized her hand just as the train appeared impatiently to call her attention to something else; but, by some strange spell of attraction or coincidence, her eyes fixed upon that window out of which the gouty traveller was looking. She saw him as he saw her, and fell back dragging the boy with her as if she would have sunk into the ground. It was only a moment and the *rapide* was gone, screaming and roaring into the tunnel, making too much noise with the rush and sweep of its going to permit the shout of the passenger to be heard.

Ten years, ten long years, during which life had undergone so many changes! They all seemed to fly away in a moment, and the girl who had arrived at the little station of St Honorat alone, a fugitive, elated and intoxicated with her freedom, suddenly felt herself again the little Janey who had emancipated herself so strangely, – though she had for a long time been frightened by every train that passed and every stranger who came near.

In the course of these long years all this had changed. Her baby had been born, her forlorn state had called forth great pity, great remark and criticism, in the village where she had found refuge, – great censure also, for the fact of her marriage was not believed by everybody. But she was so lonely, so modest, and so friendly, that the poor little English stranger was soon forgiven. Perhaps her simple neighbours were glad to find that a prim English-woman, supposed to stand so fierce on her virtue, was in reality so fallible – or perhaps pity put all other sentiments out of court. She told her real story to the priest when the boy was baptised, and though he tried to persuade her to return to her husband, he only half believed in that husband, since the story was not told under any seal of confession. Janey never became absolutely one of his flock. She was a prim little Protestant in her heart, standing strong against the saints, but devoutly attending church, believing with simple religiousness that to go to church was better than not to go to church, whatever the rites might be, and reading her little English service steadily through all the prayers of the Mass, which she never learned to follow. But her boy was like the other children of St Honorat, and learned his catechism and said his lessons with the rest.

There were various things which she did to get a living, and got it very innocently and sufficiently, though in the humblest way. She taught English to the children of some of the richer people in the village: she taught them music. She had so much credit in this latter branch, that she often held the organ in church on a holiday and pleased everybody. Then she worked very well with her needle, and would help on an emergency at first for pure kindness, and then, as her faculties and her powers of service became known, for pay, with diligence and readiness. She found a niche in the little place which she filled perfectly, though only accident seemed to have made it for her. She had fifty pounds of her little fortune laid by for the boy. She had a share of a cottage in a garden – not an English cottage indeed, but the upper floor of a two-storeyed French house; and she and her boy did much in the garden, cultivating prettinesses which do not commend themselves much to the villagers of St Honorat. Whether she ever regretted the step she had taken nobody ever knew. She might have been a lady with a larger house than any in St Honorat, and servants at her call. Perhaps she sometimes thought of that; perhaps she felt herself happier as she was; sometimes, I think, she felt that if she had known the boy was coming she might have possessed her soul in patience, and borne even with Mr Rosendale. But then at the time the decisive step was taken she did not know.

She hurried home in a great fright, not knowing what to do; then calmed herself with the thought that even if he had recognised her, there were many chances against his following her, or at least finding her, with no clue, and after so many years. And then a dreadful panic seized her at the thought that he might take her boy from her. He had known nothing about the boy: but if he discovered that fact it would make a great difference. He could not compel Janey to return to him, but he could take the boy. When this occurred to her she started up again, having just sat down, and put on her bonnet and called the child.

"Are you going out again, mother?" he cried.

"Yes, directly, directly: come, John, come, come!" she said, putting his cap upon his head and seizing him by the hand. She led him straight to the presbytery, and asked for the *curé*,[10] and went in to the good priest in great agitation, leaving the boy with his housekeeper.

"M. l'Abbé," she said, with what the village called her English directness, "I have just seen my husband go past in the train!"

"Not possible!" said M. l'Abbé, who only half believed there was a husband at all.

"And he saw me. He will come back, and I am afraid he will find me. I want you to do something for me."

"With pleasure," said the priest; "I will come and meet Monsieur your husband, and I will explain —"

"That is not what I want you to do. I want you to let John stay with you, to keep him here till – till — He will want to take him away from me!" she cried.

"He will want to take you both away, *chère petite dame.*[11] He has a right to do so."

"No, no! but I do not ask you what is his right. I ask you to keep John safe; to keep him here – till the danger has passed away!"

The priest tried to reason, to entreat, to persuade her that a father, not to say a husband, had his rights. But Janey would hear no reason: had she heard reason either from herself or another, she would not have been at St Honorat now. And he gave at last a reluctant consent. There was perhaps no harm in it after all. If a man came to claim his rights, he would not certainly go away again without some appeal to the authorities – which was a thing it must come to sooner or later, – if there was indeed a husband at all, and the story was true.

Janey then went back to her home. She thought she could await him there and defy him. "I will not go with you," she would say. "I may be your wife, but I am not your slave. You have left me alone for ten years. I will not go with you now!" She repeated this to herself many times, but it did not subdue the commotion in her being. She went out again when it became too much for her, locking her door with a strange sense that she might never come back again. She walked along the sea shore, repeating these words to herself, and then she walked up and down the streets, and went into the church and made the round of it, passing all the altars and wondering if the saints did pay attention to the poor women who were there, as always, telling St. Joseph or the Blessed Mary all about it. She sunk down in a dark corner, and said —

"Oh, my God! oh, my God!"

She could not tell Him about it in her agitation, with her heart beating so, but only call His attention, as the woman in the Bible touched the Redeemer's robe.[12] And then she went out and walked up and down again. I cannot tell what drew her back to the station – what fascination, what dreadful spell. Before she knew what she was doing she found herself there, walking up and down, up and down.

As if she were waiting for some one! "You have come to meet a friend?" some one said to her, with an air of suspicion. And she first nodded and then shook her head; but still continued in spite of herself to walk up and down. Then she said to herself that it was best so – that to get it over would be a great thing, now John was out of the way; he would be sure to find her sooner or later – far better to get it over! When the train came in, the slow local train, coming in from the side of Italy, she drew herself back a little to watch. There was a great commotion when it drew up at the platform. A man got out and called all the loungers about to help to lift out a gentleman who was ill, – who had had a bad attack in the train.

"Is there anywhere here we can take him to? Is there any decent hotel? Is there a room fit to put my master in?" he cried.

He was English with not much French at his command, and in great distress. Janey, forgetting herself and her terrors, and strong in the relief of the moment that he whom she feared had not come, went up to offer her help. She answered the man's questions; she called the right people to help him; she summoned the *chef de Gare* to make some provision for carrying the stricken man to the hotel.

"I will go with you," she said to the servant, who felt as if an angel speaking English had suddenly come to his help. She stood by full of pity, as they lifted that great inert mass out of the carriage. Then she gave a great cry and fell back against the wall.

It was a dreadful sight the men said afterwards, enough to overcome the tender heart of any lady, especially of one so kind as Madame Jeanne. A huge man, helpless, unconscious, with a purple countenance, staring eyes, breathing so that you could hear him a mile off. No wonder that she covered her eyes with her hands not to see him: but finally she hurried away to the hotel to prepare for him, and to call the doctor, that no time should be lost. Janey felt as if she was restored for the moment to life when there was something she could do. The questions were all postponed. She did not think of flight or concealment, or even of John at the presbytery. "He is my husband," she said, with awe in her heart.

This was how the train brought back to Janey the man whom the train had separated from her ten years before. The whole tragedy was one of the railway, the noisy carriages, the snorting locomotives. He was taken to the hotel, but he never came to himself again, and died there the next day, without being able to say what his object was, or why he had got out of the *rapide*, though unable to walk, and insisted on returning to St Honorat. It cost him his life; but then his life was not worth a day's purchase, all the doctors said, in the condition in which he was.

Friends had to be summoned, and men of business, and it was impossible but that Janey's secret should be made known. When she found herself and her son recognised, and that there could be no doubt that the boy was his father's heir, she was struck with a great horror which she never quite got over all her life. She had not blamed herself before; but now seemed to herself no less than the murderer of her husband: and could not forgive herself, nor get out of her eyes the face she had seen, nor out of her ears the dreadful sound of that labouring breath.

Notes

1   Pretty.
2   Express train.
3   Station.
4   Stationmaster.
5   Exchange.
6   In classical mythology, the Furies were the goddesses of vengeance. Oliphant seems to be confusing them with the Fates, one of whom – Atropos – severs the thread of life.
7   Travelling!
8   Pretty little lady.

9   Nursemaid.

10 Priest.

11 Dear little lady.

12 A sick woman touched the robe of Christ believing that she would then be healed. Christ turned around saying "Who touched me? Somebody hath touched me: for I perceive that the virtue is gone out of me." When he saw the woman he comforted her and told her that her faith had made her whole again. Matthew 9:20-22; Mark 5:25-34; Luke 8:43-48.

Source: *A Widow's Tale and Other Stories.* Intro. J.M. Barrie. Edinburgh: Blackwood, 1898.

Biographical Note

Oliphant, one of the most prolific women writers of the nineteenth century and Queen Victoria's favorite novelist, was born in Wallyford, Scotland, on April 4, 1828. She spent most of her early years in Lasswade, near Edinburgh, and then in Glasgow, before moving first to Liverpool, then Birkenhead, where her father worked in custom and excise. Oliphant's first published work, a Scottish regionalist novel entitled *Passages in the Life of Mrs. Margaret Maitland,* appeared in 1849, the first of the nearly 100 books that were to follow. In the early 1850s she came to London, and on May 4, 1852 married her cousin, Francis William Oliphant, an artist specializing in stained glass. He was a talented man, but not much of a provider, and Oliphant soon found herself forced to support both him and her alcoholic brother William. She began writing for *Blackwood's Magazine* in 1853 and went on to publish the many highly successful novels that turned her into a minor literary celebrity in London. In 1859, her husband's declining health necessitated the family's move to Italy; he died soon after, and Oliphant was left heavily in debt and, for the third time, pregnant. Her ten-year-old daughter Maggie died in Rome five years later; Oliphant continued to support her brother, and, finally, after returning to England, she also undertook the support of her widowed brother Frank, a failed businessman with four children. Oliphant's best-known works, the tales of English provincial life entitled "Chronicles of Carlingford," began to appear in *Blackwood's* during this difficult decade. They included *The Rector and the Doctor's Family* (1863) and the highly melodramatic *Salem Chapel* (1863). In addition to writing novels, Oliphant tried her hand at biography, produced an excellent history of Blackwood's publishing house, and was a prolific reviewer and essayist, producing over 200 articles for such magazines as *Blackwood's* and the *Cornhill*. She began a successful series of travel books during the 1870s and produced some of the century's best supernatural stories which dealt with the attempts at reunion between the dead and the living under the general title of *Tales of the Seen and the Unseen*; "The Open Door" in particular is considered a masterpiece. A number of previously unpublished stories were collected after her death in 1897 by J. M. Barrie in *A Widow's Tale* (1898). "A Story of a Wedding Tour," probably written sometime during the 1870s, is representative of most of the stories in this collection in its bleak presentation of a woman's encounter with male sexuality. While Oliphant was never a supporter of women's suffrage, her female characters are, like Janey and Oliphant herself, women of great resilience, women who manage their lives without the support, financial or otherwise, of men, and women who, by struggling against the limitations imposed upon them by society, finally attain some small measure of independence.

Selected Modern Reprints:

The Autobiography of Margaret Oliphant: The Complete Text. Ed. Elizabeth Jay. Oxford: Oxford UP, 1990.

The Beleaguered City and Other Stories. Ed. Merryn Williams. Oxford: Oxford UP, 1988.

The Doctor's Family and Other Stories. Ed. Merryn Williams. Oxford: Oxford UP, 1986.

Margaret Oliphant: Selected Stories of the Supernatural. Ed. Margaret K. Gray. Scottish Academic P, 1985.

Selected Secondary Sources:

Clarke, John Stock. *Margaret Oliphant: A Bibliography*. U of Queensland, 1986.

Colby, Vineta and Robert A. *The Equivocal Virtue: Mrs. Oliphant and the Victorian Literary Market Place*. New York: Archon, 1966.

Harris, Janice. "Not Suffering and Not Still: Women Writers at the Cornhill Magazine, 1860-1900." *Modern Language Quarterly* 47.4 (1988): 382-92.

Williams, Merryn. *Margaret Oliphant: A Critical Biography*. New York: St. Martin's P, 1986.

428   MARY SHELLEY (1797-1851)

Mary Shelley (1797-1851)

The Parvenue

WHY DO I WRITE MY MELANCHOLY STORY? IS IT AS A LESSON, to prevent any other from wishing to rise to rank superior to that in which they are born? No, miserable as I am, others might have been happy, I doubt not, in my position: the chalice has been poisoned for me alone! Am I evil-minded – am I wicked? What have been my errors, that I am now an outcast and wretched? I will tell my story – let others judge me; my mind is bewildered, I cannot judge myself.

My father was land steward to a wealthy nobleman. He married young, and had several children. He then lost his wife, and remained fifteen years a widower, when he married again a young girl, the daughter of a clergyman, who died, leaving a numerous offspring in extreme poverty. My maternal grandfather had been a man of sensibility and genius; my mother inherited many of his endowments. She was an angel on earth; all her works were charity, all her thoughts were love.

Within a year after her marriage, she gave birth to twins – I and my sister; soon after she fell into ill-health, and from that time was always weakly. She could endure no fatigue, and seldom moved from her chair. I see her now; – her white, delicate hands employed in needlework, her soft, love-lighted eyes fixed on me. I was still a child when my father fell into trouble, and we removed from the part of the country where we had hitherto lived, and went to a distant village, where we rented a cottage, with a little land adjoining. We were poor, and all the family assisted each other. My elder half-sisters were strong, industrious, rustic young women, and submitted to a life of labour with great cheerfulness. My father held the plough, my half-brothers worked in the barns; all was toil, yet all seemed enjoyment.

How happy my childhood was! Hand in hand with my dear twin-sister, I plucked the spring flowers in the hedges, turned the hay in the summer meadows, shook the apples from the trees in the autumn, and at all seasons, gambolled in delicious liberty beneath the free air of heaven; or at my mother's feet, caressed by her, I was taught the sweetest lessons of charity and love. My elder sisters were kind; we were all linked by strong affection. The delicate, fragile existence of my mother gave an interest to our monotony, while her virtues and her refinement threw a grace over our homely household.

I and my sister did not seem twins, we were so unlike. She was robust, chubby, full of life and spirits; I, tall, slim, fair, and even pale. I loved to play with her, but soon grew tired, and then I crept to my mother's side, and she sang me to sleep, and nursed me in her bosom, and looked on me with her own angelic smile. She took pains to instruct me, not in accomplishments, but in all real knowledge. She unfolded to me the wonders of the visible creation, and to each tale of bird and beast, of fiery mountain or vast river, was appended some moral, derived from her warm heart and ardent imagination. Above all, she impressed upon me the precepts of the gospel, charity to every fellow-creature, the brotherhood of mankind, the rights that every sentient creature possesses to our service. I was her almoner; for, poor as she was, she was the benefactress of those who were poorer. Being delicate, I helped her in her task of needlework, while my sister aided the rest in their household or rustic labours.

When I was seventeen, a miserable accident happened. A hayrick caught fire; it communicated to our outhouses, and at last to the cottage. We were roused from our beds at midnight, and escaped barely with our lives. My father bore out my mother in his arms, and then tried to save a portion of his property. The roof of the cottage fell in on him. He was dug out after an hour, scorched, maimed, crippled for life.

We were all saved, but by a miracle only was I preserved. I and my sister were awoke by cries of fire. The cottage was already enveloped in flames. Susan, with her accustomed intrepidity, rushed through the flames, and escaped; I thought only of my mother, and hurried to her room. The fire raged around me; it encircled – hemmed me in. I believed that I must die, when suddenly I felt myself seized upon and borne away. I looked on my pre-server – it was Lord Reginald Desborough.

For many Sundays past, when at church, I knew that Lord Reginald's eyes were fixed on me. He had met me and Susan in our walks; he had called at our cottage. There was fascination in his eye, in his soft voice and earnest gaze, and my heart throbbed with gladness, as I thought that he surely loved me. To have been saved by him was to make the boon of life doubly precious.

There is to me much obscurity in this part of my story. Lord Reginald loved me, it is true; why he loved me, so far as to forget pride of rank and ambition for my sake, he who afterwards showed no tendency to disregard the prejudices and habits of rank and wealth, I cannot tell; it seems strange. He had loved me before, but from the hour that he saved my life, love grew into an overpowering pas-sion. He offered us a lodge on his estate to take refuge in; and while there, he sent us presents of game, and still more kindly, fruits and flowers to my mother, and came himself, especially when all were out except my mother and myself, and sat by us and conversed. Soon I learnt to expect the soft asking look of his eyes, and almost dared answer it. My mother once perceived these glances, and took an opportunity to appeal to Lord Reginald's good feelings, not to make me miserable for life, by implanting an attachment that could only be productive of unhappi-ness. His answer was to ask me in marriage.

I need not say that my mother gratefully consented; that my father, confined to his bed since the fire, thanked God with rapture; that my sisters were transported by de-light: I was the least surprised then, though the most happy. Now, I wonder much, what could he see in me? So many girls of rank and fortune were prettier. I was an untaught, low-born, portionless girl. It was very strange.

Then I only thought of the happiness of marrying

him, of being loved, of passing my life with him. My wedding day was fixed. Lord Reginald had neither father nor mother to interfere with his arrangements. He told no relation; he became one of our family during the interval. He saw no deficiencies in our mode of life – in my dress; he was satisfied with all; he was tender, assiduous, and kind, even to my elder sisters; he seemed to adore my mother, and became a brother to my sister Susan. She was in love, and asked him to intercede to gain her parents' consent for her choice. He did so; and though before, Lawrence Cooper, the carpenter of the place, had been disdained, supported by him, he was accepted. Lawrence Cooper was young, well-looking, well disposed, and fondly attached to Susan.

My wedding day came. My mother kissed me fondly, my father blessed me with pride and joy, my sisters stood round, radiant with delight. There was but one drawback to the universal happiness – that immediately on my marriage I was to go abroad.

From the church door I stepped into the carriage. Having once and again been folded in my dear mother's embrace, the wheels were in motion, and we were away. I looked out from the window; there was the dear group: my old father, white-headed and aged, in his large chair; my mother, smiling through her tears, with folded hands and upraised looks of gratitude, anticipating long years of happiness for her child; Susan and Lawrence standing side by side, unenvious of my greatness, happy in themselves; my sisters conning over with pride and joy the presents made to them, and the prosperity that flowed in from my husband's generosity. All looked happy, and it seemed as if I were the cause of all this happiness. We had been indeed saved from dreadful evils; ruin had ensued from the fire, and we had been sunk in adversity through that very event from which our good fortune took its rise. I felt proud and glad. I loved them all. I thought, I make them happy – they are prosperous through me! And my heart warmed with gratitude towards my husband at the idea.

We spent two years abroad. It was rather lonely for

me, who had always been surrounded, as it were, by a populous world of my own, to find myself cast upon foreigners and strangers; the habits of the different sexes in the higher ranks so separate them from each other, that, after a few months, I spent much of my time in solitude. I did not repine; I had been brought up to look upon the hard visage of life, if not unflinchingly, at least with resignation. I did not expect perfect happiness. Marriages in humble life are attended with so much care. I had none of this; my husband loved me; and though I often longed to see the dear familiar faces that thronged my childhood's home, and, above all, pined for my mother's caresses and her wise maternal lessons, yet for a time I was content to think of them, and hope for a reunion.

Still many things pained me. I had, poor myself, been brought up among the poor, and nothing, since I can remember forming an idea, so much astonished and jarred with my feelings as the thought of how the rich could spend so much on themselves, while any of their fellow-creatures were in destitution. I had none of the patrician charity (though such is praiseworthy), which consists in distributing thin soup and coarse flannel petticoats – a sort of instinct or sentiment of justice, the offspring of my lowly paternal hearth, and my mother's enlightened piety, was deeply implanted in my mind, that all had as good a right to the comforts of life as myself, or even as my husband. My charities, they were called – they seemed to me the payment of my debts to my fellow-creatures – were abundant. Lord Reginald peremptorily checked them; but as I had a large allowance for my own expenses, I denied myself a thousand luxuries, for the sake of feeding the hungry. Nor was it only that charity impelled me, but that I could not acquire a taste for spending money on myself – I disliked the apparatus of wealth. My husband called my ideas sordid, and reproved me severely, when, instead of outshining all competitors at a fête, I appeared dowdily dressed, and declared warmly that I could not, I would not, spend twenty guineas for a gown, while I could dress many sad faces in smiles, and bring much joy to many drooping hearts, by the same sum.

Was I right? I firmly believe that there is not one among the rich who will not affirm that I did wrong; that to please my husband, and do honour to his rank, was my first duty. Yet, shall I confess it? even now, rendered miserable by this fault – I cannot give it that name – I can call it a misfortune – I have wasted at the slow fire of knowing that I lost my husband's affections because I performed what I believed to be a duty.

But I am not come to that yet. It was not till my return to England that the full disaster crushed me. We had often been applied to for money by my family, and Lord Reginald had acceded to nearly all their requests. When we reached London, after two years' absence, my first wish was to see my dear mother. She was at Margate for her health. It was agreed that I should go there alone, and pay a short visit. Before I went, Lord Reginald told me what I did not know before, that my family had often made exorbitant demands on him, with which he was resolved not to comply. He told me that he had no wish to raise my relatives from their station in society; and that, indeed, there were only two among them whom he conceived had any claims upon me – my mother and my twin-sister: that the former was incapable of any improper request, and the latter, by marrying Cooper, had fixed her own position, and could in no way be raised from the rank of her chosen husband. I agreed to much that he said. I replied that he well knew that my own taste led me to consider mediocrity the best and happiest situation; that I had no wish, and would never consent, to supply any extravagant demands on the part of persons, however dear to me, whose circumstances he had rendered easy.

Satisfied with my reply, we parted most affectionately, and I went on my way to Margate with a light and glad heart; and the cordial reception I received from my whole family collected together to receive me, was calculated to add to my satisfaction. The only drawback to my content was my mother's state; she was wasted to a shadow. They all talked and laughed around her, but it was evident to me that she had not long to live.

There was no room for me in the small furnished

house in which they were all crowded, so I remained at the hotel. Early in the morning, before I was up, my father visited me. He begged me to intercede with my husband; that on the strength of his support he had embarked in a speculation which required a large capital; that many families would be ruined, and himself dishonoured, if a few hundreds were not advanced. I promised to do what I could, resolving to ask my mother's advice, and make her my guide. My father kissed me with an effusion of gratitude, and left me.

I cannot enter into the whole of these sad details; all my half brothers and sisters had married, and trusted to their success in life to Lord Reginald's assistance. Each evidently thought that they asked little in not demanding an equal share of my luxuries and fortune; but they were all in difficulty – all needed large assistance – all depended on me.

Lastly, my own sister Susan appealed to me – but hers was the most moderate request of all – she only wished for twenty pounds. I gave it her at once from my own purse.

As soon as I saw my mother I explained to her my difficulties. She told me that she expected this, and that it broke her heart: I must summon courage and resist these demands. That my father's imprudence had ruined him, and that he must encounter the evil he had brought on himself; that my numerous relatives were absolutely mad with the notion of what I ought to do for them. I listened with grief – I saw the torments in store for me – I felt my own weakness, and knew that I could not meet the rapacity of those about me with any courage or firmness. That same night my mother fell into convulsions; her life was saved with difficulty. From Susan I learned the cause of her attack. She had had a violent altercation with my father: she insisted that I should not be appealed to; while he reproached her for rendering me undutiful, and bringing ruin and disgrace on his grey hairs. When I saw my pale mother trembling, fainting, dying – when I was again and again assured that she must be my father's victim unless I yielded, what wonder that, in the agony of my distress, I wrote to my husband to implore his assistance.

Oh, what thick clouds now obscured my destiny! how do I remember, with a sort of thrilling horror, the boundless sea, white cliffs, and wide sands of Margate! The summer day that had welcomed my arrival changed to bleak wintry weather during this interval – while I waited with anguish for my husband's answer. Well do I remember the evening on which it came: the waves of the sea showed their white crests, no vessel ventured to meet the gale with any canvas except a topsail, the sky was bared clear by the wind, the sun was going down fiery red. I looked upon the troubled waters – I longed to be borne away upon them, away from care and misery. At this moment a servant followed me to the sands with my husband's answer – it contained a refusal. I dared not communicate it. The menaces of bankruptcy; the knowledge that he had instilled false hopes into so many; the fears of disgrace, rendered my father, always rough, absolutely ferocious. Life flickered in my dear mother's frame, it seemed on the point of expiring when she heard my father's step; if he came in with a smooth brow, her pale lips wreathed into her own sweet smile, and a delicate pink tinged her fallen cheeks; if he scowled, and his voice was high, every limb shivered, she turned her face to her pillow, while convulsive tears shook her frame, and threatened instant dissolution. My father sought me alone one day, as I was walking in melancholy guise upon the sands; he swore that he would not survive his disgrace. "And do you think, Fanny," he added, "that your mother will survive the knowledge of my miserable end?" I saw the resolution of despair in his face as he spoke. – I asked the sum needed, the time when it must be given. – A thousand pounds in two days was all that was asked. I set off to London to implore my husband to give this sum.

No! no! I cannot step by step record my wretchedness – the money was given – I extorted it from Lord Reginald, though I saw his heart closed on me as he wrote the cheque. Worse had happened since I had left him. Susan had used the twenty pounds I gave her to reach town, to throw herself at my husband's feet, and implore his compassion. Rendered absolutely insane by the idea of having a lord for a brother-in-law, Cooper had launched into a system of extravagance, incredible as it was wicked. He was many thousands of pounds in debt, and when at last Lord Reginald wrote to refuse all further supply, the miserable man committed forgery. Two hundred pounds prevented exposure, and preserved him from an ignominious end. Five hundred more were advanced to send him and his wife to America, to settle there, out of the way of temptation. I parted from my dear sister – I loved her fondly; she had no part in her husband's guilt, yet she was still attached to him, and her child bound them together; they went into solitary, miserable exile. "Ah! had we remained in virtuous poverty," cried my broken-hearted sister, "I had not been forced to leave my dying mother."

The thousand pounds given to my father was but a drop of water in the ocean. Again I was appealed to; again I felt the slender thread of my mother's life depended on my getting a supply. Again, trembling and miserable, I implored the charity of my husband.

"I am content," he said, "to do what you ask, to do more than you ask; but remember the price you pay – either give up your parents and your family, whose rapacity and crimes deserve no mercy, or we part for ever. You shall have a proper allowance; you can maintain all your family on it if you please; but their names must never be mentioned to me again. Choose between us – you never see them more, or we part for ever."

Did I do right – I cannot tell – misery is the result – misery frightful, endless, unredeemed. My mother was dearer to me than all the world. I did not reply – I rushed to my room, and that night, in a delirium of grief and horror, I set out for Margate – such was my reply to my husband.

Three years have passed since then; and during all this time I was grateful to Heaven for being permitted to do my duty by my mother; and though I wept over the alienation of my husband, I did not repent. But she, my angelic support, is no more. My father survived my mother but two months; remorse for all he had done, and made me suffer, cut short his life. His family by his first wife are gathered round me; they importune, they rob, they destroy me. Last week I wrote to Lord Reginald. I communicated the death of my parents; I represented that my position was altered; and that if he still cared for his unhappy wife all might be well. Yesterday his answer came. – It was too late, he said; – I had myself torn asunder the ties that united us – they never could be knit together again.

By the same post came a letter from Susan. She is happy. Cooper, awakened to a manly sense of the duties of life, is thoroughly reformed. He is industrious and prosperous. Susan asks me to join her. I am resolved to go. Oh! my home, and recollections of my youth, where are ye now? envenomed by serpents' stings, I long to close my eyes on every scene I have ever viewed. Let me seek a strange land, a land where a grave will soon be opened for me. I desire to die. I am told that Lord Reginald loves another, a high-born girl; that he openly curses our union as the obstacle to his happiness. The memory of this will poison the oblivion I go to seek. He will soon be free. Soon will the hand he once so fondly took in his and made his own, which, now flung away, trembles with misery as it traces these lines, moulder in its last decay.

Source: *Keepsake* (1837).

Biographical Note

Shelley, best known as the author of *Frankenstein*, was the daughter of Mary Wollstonecraft, pioneer feminist and author of *A Vindication of the Rights of Woman* (1792), and William Godwin, philosopher and novelist. Wollstonecraft died of puerperal poisoning ten days after the birth of her daughter, and four years later Godwin married the widowed Mrs. Mary Jane Clairmont. In 1814, Mary began a relationship with Percy Bysshe Shelley who was, along with his wife Harriet, a frequent visitor to the Godwin's home, and in the summer of 1814 Mary and Shelley eloped, accompanied by Mary's stepsister, Jane (later "Claire") Clairmont. They spent some time in Europe and returned to London in the autumn. In May of 1816 Claire, Mary, and Shelley spent the summer at Lake Geneva in the company of Byron and his friend and personal physician, John Polidori. It was during this time, in response to a ghost story competition devised by Byron, that Mary conceived the idea for *Frankenstein*. In December of the same year, Harriet Shelley was found drowned in the Serpentine, and Mary and Shelley were immediately married. They left for Italy in 1818, shortly after the anonymous publication of *Frankenstein; or, The Modern Prometheus*. Before Mary Shelley was twenty-two she had given birth to, and lost, three children. After Shelley's death by drowning in August of 1822, she returned to England. She published five other novels, including *Valperga: or, The Life and Adventures of Castruccio, Prince of Lucca* (1823), a romance set in fourteenth-century Italy, and *The Last Man* (1826), a story set in the twenty-first century, about the gradual destruction of the human race through a plague. Her novella *Mathilda*, the account of a father's incestuous desire for his daughter, was completed in 1819, but not published in her lifetime. Shelley was also a frequent contributor of such short stories as "The Parvenue" to the Annuals, wrote a number of essays and reviews, travel books, mythological dramas, and five volumes of the lives of various European writers in Lardner's *Cabinet Cyclopedia*. She also edited her husband's *Poetical Works* (1839) and his *Essays, Letters from*

Abroad, Translations and Fragments (1839), both marred by distortions and suppressions which resulted in the over-idealized portrait of the poet and his work that has only recently come to be questioned. Shelley's last work was a travelogue, *Rambles in Germany and Italy* (1844), which related her continental travels with her son, Percy Florence, in the early 1840s. She died in London at the age of fifty-three.

Selected Modern Reprints:

The Journals of Mary Shelley. 1814-1844. 2 vols. Ed. Paula R. Feldman and Diana Scott-Kilvert. Oxford: Clarendon P, 1987.

The Letters of Mary Wollstonecraft Shelley. 3 vols. Ed. Betty T. Bennett. Baltimore: Johns Hopkins UP, 1980.

Mary Shelley: Collected Tales and Stories. Ed. Charles E. Robinson. Baltimore: Johns Hopkins UP, 1976.

The Mary Shelley Reader. Ed. Betty T. Bennett and Charles E. Robinson. New York: Oxford UP, 1991.

Tales and Stories by Mary Wollstonecraft Shelley. Intro. Richard Garnett. London: Paterson, 1891. Rpt. with intro by Joanna Russ. Boston: Hall, 1975.

Selected Secondary Sources:

Mellor, Anne K. *Mary Shelley: Her Life, Her Fiction, Her Monsters.* New York: Methuen, 1988.

Pollin, Burton R. "Mary Shelley as the Parvenue." *A Review of English Literature* 8.3 (July 1967): 9-21.

Spark, Muriel. *Child of Light: A Reassessment of Mary Shelley.* 1951. New York: E.P. Dutton, 1987.

Sunstein, Emily W. *Mary Shelley: Romance and Reality.* Toronto: Little, Brown, 1989.

Walling, William A. *Mary Shelley.* New York: Twayne, 1972.

442   HARRIET PRESCOTT SPOFFORD (1835-1921)

Harriet Prescott Spofford (1835-1921)

Circumstance

SHE HAD REMAINED, DURING ALL THAT DAY, WITH A SICK NEIGH-
bor, – those eastern wilds of Maine in that epoch frequently
making neighbors and miles synonymous, – and so busy had
she been with care and sympathy that she did not at first ob-
serve the approaching night. But finally the level rays, red-
dening the snow, threw their gleam upon the wall, and, hastily donning cloak and hood, she bade her friends farewell
and sallied forth on her return. Home lay some three miles
distant, across a copse, a meadow, and a piece of woods, –
the woods being a fringe on the skirts of the great forests
that stretch far away into the North. That home was one of
a dozen log-houses lying a few furlongs apart from each
other, with their half-cleared demesnes[1] separating them at
the rear from a wilderness untrodden save by stealthy native
or deadly panther tribes.

She was in a nowise exalted frame of spirit, – on the
contrary, rather depressed by the pain she had witnessed
and the fatigue she had endured; but in certain tempera-
ments such a condition throws open the mental pores, so
to speak, and renders one receptive of every influence.
Through the little copse she walked slowly, with her cloak
folded about her, lingering to imbibe the sense of shelter,
the sunset filtered in purple through the mist of woven
spray and twig, the companionship of growth not sufficiently dense to band against her, the sweet home-feeling
of a young and tender wintry wood. It was therefore just
on the edge of the evening that she emerged from the
place and began to cross the meadowland. At one hand
lay the forest to which her path wound; at the other the
evening star hung over a tide of falling orange that slowly
slipped down the earth's broad side to sadden other hemi-

spheres with sweet regret. Walking rapidly now, and with her eyes wide-open, she distinctly saw in the air before her what was not there a moment ago, a winding-sheet, – cold, white, and ghastly, waved by the likeness of four wan hands, – that rose with a long inflation, and fell in rigid folds, while a voice, shaping itself from the hollowness above, spectral and melancholy, sighed, – "The Lord have mercy on the people! The Lord have mercy on the people!" Three times the sheet with its corpse-covering outline waved beneath the pale hands, and the voice, awful in its solemn and mysterious depth, sighed, "The Lord have mercy on the people!" Then all was gone, the place was clear again, the gray sky was obstructed by no deathly blot; she looked about her, shook her shoulders decidedly, and, pulling on her hood, went forward once more.

She might have been a little frightened by such an apparition, if she had led a life of less reality than frontier settlers are apt to lead; but dealing with hard fact does not engender a flimsy habit of mind, and this woman was too sincere and earnest in her character, and too happy in her situation, to be thrown by antagonism, merely, upon superstitious fancies and chimeras of the second-sight. She did not even believe herself subject to an hallucination, but smiled simply, a little vexed that her thought could have framed such a glamour from the day's occurrences, and not sorry to lift the bough of the warder of the woods and enter and disappear in their sombre path. If she had been imaginative, she would have hesitated at her first step into a region whose dangers were not visionary; but I suppose that the thought of a little child at home would conquer that propensity in the most habituated. So, biting a bit of spicy birch, she went along. Now and then she came to a gap where the trees had been partially felled, and here she found that the lingering twilight was explained by that peculiar and perhaps electric film which sometimes sheathes the sky in diffused light for many hours before a brilliant aurora. Suddenly, a swift shadow, like the fabulous flying-dragon, writhed through the air before her, and she felt herself instantly seized and borne aloft. It was that wild beast – the most savage and serpentine and subtle and fearless of our latitudes – known by hunters as the Indian Devil,[2] and he held her in his clutches on the broad floor of a swinging fir-bough. His long sharp claws were caught in her clothing, he worried them sagaciously a little, then, finding that ineffectual to free them, he commenced licking her bare arm with his rasping tongue and pouring over her the wide streams of his hot, foetid breath. So quick had this flashing action been that the woman had had no time for alarm; moreover, she was not of the screaming kind: but now, as she felt him endeavoring to disentangle his claws, and the horrid sense of her fate smote her, and she saw instinctively the fierce plunge of those weapons, the long strips of living flesh torn from her bones, the agony, the quivering disgust, itself a worse agony, – while by her side, and holding her in his great lithe embrace, the monster crouched, his white tusks whetting and gnashing, his eyes glaring through all the darkness like balls of red fire, – a shriek, that rang in every forest hollow, that startled every winter-housed thing, that stirred and woke the least needle of the tasselled pines, tore through her lips. A moment afterward, the beast left the arm, once white, now crimson, and looked up alertly.

She did not think at this instant to call upon God. She called upon her husband. It seemed to her that she had but one friend in the world; that was he; and again the cry, loud, clear, prolonged, echoed through the woods. It was not the shriek that disturbed the creature at his relish; he was not born in the woods to be scared of an owl, you know; what then? It must have been the echo, most musical, most resonant, repeated and yet repeated, dying with long sighs of sweet sound, vibrated from rock to river and back again from depth to depth of cave and cliff. Her thought flew after it; she knew, that, even if her husband heard it, he yet could not reach her in time; she saw that while the beast listened he would not gnaw, – and this she *felt* directly, when the rough, sharp, and multiplied stings of his tongue retouched her arm. Again her lips opened by instinct, but the sound that issued thence came by reason. She had heard that music charmed wild beasts, – just this point between life and death intensified every faculty, – and when she opened her lips the third time, it was not for shrieking, but for singing.

A little thread of melody stole out, a rill of tremulous motion; it was the cradle-song with which she rocked her baby; – how could she sing that? And then she remembered the baby sleeping rosily on the long settee before the fire. – the father cleaning his gun, with one foot on the green wooden rundle, – the merry light from the chimney dancing out and through the room, on the rafters of the ceiling with their tassels of onions and herbs, on the log walls painted with lichens and festooned with apples, on the king's-arm slung across the shelf with the old pirate's-cutlass, on the snow-pile of the bed, and on the great brass clock, – dancing, too, and lingering on the baby, with his fringed-gentian eyes, his chubby fists clenched on the pillow, and his fine breezy hair fanning with the notion of his father's foot. All this struck her in one, and made a sob of her breath, and she ceased.

Immediately the long red tongue thrust forth again. Before it touched, a song sprang to her lips, a wild sea-song, such as some sailor might be singing far out on trackless blue water that night, the shrouds whistling with frost and the sheets glued in ice, – a song with the wind in its burden and the spray in its chorus. The monster raised his head and flared the fiery eyeballs upon her, then fretted the imprisoned claws a moment and was quiet; only the breath like the vapor from some hell-pit still swathed her. Her voice, at first faint and fearful, gradually lost its quaver, grew under her control and subject to her modulation; it rose on long swells, it fell in subtile cadences, now and then its tones pealed out like bells from distant belfries on fresh sonorous mornings. She sung the song through, and, wondering lest his name of Indian Devil were not his true name, and if he would not detect her, she repeated it. Once or twice now, indeed, the beast stirred uneasily, turned, and made the bough sway at his movement. As she ended, he snapped his jaws together, and tore away the fettered member, curling it under him with a snarl, – when she burst into the gayest reel that ever answered a fiddle-bow. How many a time she had heard her husband play it on the homely fiddle made by himself from birch and cherry-wood! how many a time she had seen it danced on the floor of their one room, to the patter of wooden clogs and the rustle of homespun petticoat! how many a time she had danced it herself! – and did she not remember once, as they joined clasps for eight-hands-round, how it had lent its gay, bright measure to her life? And here she was singing it alone, in the forest, at midnight, to a wild beast! As she sent her voice trilling up and down its quick oscillations between joy and pain, the creature who grasped her uncurled his paw and scratched the bark from the bough; she must vary the spell; and her voice spun leaping along the projecting points of tune of a hornpipe. Still singing, she felt herself twisted about with a low growl and a lifting of the red lip from the glittering teeth; she broke the hornpipe's thread, and commenced unravelling a lighter, livelier thing, an Irish jig. Up and down and round about her voice flew, the beast threw back his head so that the diabolical face fronted hers, and the torrent of his breath prepared her for his feast as the anaconda slimes his prey. Frantically she darted from tune to tune; his restless movements followed her. She tired herself with dancing and vivid national airs, growing feverish and singing spasmodically as she felt her horrid tomb yawning wider. Touching in this manner all the slogan and keen clan cries, the beast moved again, but only to lay the disengaged paw across her with heavy satisfaction. She did not dare to pause; through the clear cold air, the frosty starlight, she sang. If there were yet any tremor in the tone, it was not fear, – she had learned the secret of sound at last; nor could it be chill, – far too high a fever throbbed her pulses; it was nothing but the thought of the log-house and of what might be passing within it. She fancied the baby stirring in his sleep and moving his pretty lips, – her husband rising and opening the door, looking out after her, and wondering at her absence. She fancied the light pouring through the chink and then shut in again with all the safety and comfort and joy, her husband taking down the fiddle and playing lightly with his head inclined, playing while she sang, while she sang for her life to an Indian Devil. Then she knew he was fumbling for and finding some shining fragment and scoring it down the yellowing hair, and unconsciously her voice forsook the wild war-tunes and drifted into the half-gay, half-melancholy Rosin the Bow.

Suddenly she woke pierced with a pang, and the daggered tooth penetrating her flesh; – dreaming of safety, she had ceased singing and lost it. The beast had regained the use of all his limbs, and now, standing and raising his back, bristling and foaming, with sounds that would have been hisses but for their deep and fearful sonority, he withdrew step by step toward the trunk of the tree, still with his flaming balls upon her. She was all at once free, on one end of the bough, twenty feet from the ground. She did not measure the distance, but rose to drop herself down, careless of any death, so that it were not this. Instantly, as if he scanned her thoughts, the creature bounded forward with a yell and caught her again in his dreadful hold. It might be that he was not greatly famished; for, as she suddenly flung up her voice again, he settled himself composedly on the bough, still clasping her with invincible pressure to his rough, ravenous breast, and listening in a fascination to the sad, strange U-la-lu that now moaned forth in loud, hollow tones above him. He half closed his eyes, and sleepily reopened and shut them again.

What rending pains were close at hand! Death! and what a death! worse than any other that is to be named! Water, be it cold or warm, that which buoys up blue icefields, or which bathes tropical coasts with currents of balmy bliss, is yet a gentle conqueror, kisses as it kills, and draws you down gently through darkening fathoms to its heart. Death at the sword is the festival of trumpet and bugle and banner, with glory ringing out around you and distant hearts thrilling through yours. No gnawing disease can bring such hideous end as this; for that is a fiend bred of your own flesh, and this – is it a fiend, this living lump of appetites? What dread comes with the thought of perishing in flames! but fire, let it leap and hiss never so hotly, is something too remote, too alien, to inspire us with such loathly horror as a wild beast; if it have a life, that life is too utterly beyond our comprehension. Fire is not half ourselves; as it devours, arouses neither hatred nor disgust; is not to be known by the strength of our lower natures let loose; does not drip our blood into our faces from foaming chaps, nor mouth nor slaver above us with vitality. Let us be ended by fire, and we are ashes, for the winds to bear, the leaves to cover; let us be ended by wild beasts, and the base, cursed thing howls with us forever through the forest. All this she felt as she charmed him, and what force it lent to her song God knows. If her voice should fail! If the damp and cold should give her any fatal hoarseness! If all the silent powers of the forest did not conspire to help her! The dark, hollow night rose indifferently over her; the wide, cold air breathed rudely past her, lifted her wet hair and blew it down again; the great boughs swung with a ponderous strength, now and then clashed their iron lengths together and shook off a sparkle of icy spears or some long-lain weight of snow from their heavy shadows. The green depths were utterly cold and silent and stern. These beautiful haunts that all the summer were hers and rejoiced to share with her their bounty, these heavens that had yielded their largess, these stems that had thrust their blossoms into her hands, all these friends of three moons ago forgot her now and knew her no longer.

Feeling her desolation, wild, melancholy, forsaken songs rose thereon from that frightful aerie, – weeping, wailing tunes, that sob among the people from age to age, and overflow with otherwise unexpressed sadness, – all rude, mournful ballads, – old tearful strains, that Shakespeare heard the vagrants sing, and that rise and fall like the wind and tide, – sailor-songs, to be heard only in lone mid-watches beneath the moon and stars, – ghastly rhyming romances, such as that famous one of the Lady Margaret, when

"She slipped on her gown of green

A piece below the knee, —
And 'twas all a long cold winter's night
A dead corse followed she."[3]

Still the beast lay with closed eyes, yet never relaxing his
grasp. Once a half-whine of enjoyment escaped him, – he
fawned his fearful head upon her; once he scored her cheek
with his tongue: savage caresses that hurt like wounds. How
weary she was! and yet how terribly awake! How fuller and
fuller of dismay grew the knowledge that she was only prolonging her anguish and playing with death! How appalling
the thought that with her voice ceased her existence! Yet
she could not sing forever; her throat was dry and hard; her
very breath was a pain; her mouth was hotter than any de-
sert-worn pilgrim's; – if she could but drop upon her burning tongue one atom of the ice that glittered about her! –
but both of her arms were pinioned in the giant's vice. She
remembered the winding-sheet, and for the first time in her
life shivered with spiritual fear. Was it hers? She asked herself, as she sang, what sins she had committed, what life she
had led, to find her punishment so soon and in these pangs,
– and then she sought eagerly for some reason why her husband was not up and abroad to find her. He failed her, –
her one sole hope in life; and without being aware of it, her
voice forsook the songs of suffering and sorrow for old
Covenanting hymns,[4] – hymns with which her mother had
lulled her, which the class-leader pitched in the chimney-cor-
ners, – grand and sweet Methodist hymns, brimming with
melody and all fantastic involutions of tune to suit that ec-
static worship, – hymns full of the beauty of holiness, stead-
fast, relying, sanctified by the salvation they had lent to
those in worse extremity than hers, – for they had found
themselves in the grasp of hell, while she was but in the jaws
of death. Out of this strange music, peculiar to one character of faith, and than which there is none more beautiful in
its degree nor owning a more potent sway of sound, her
voice soared into the glorified chants of churches. What to
her was death by cold or famine or wild beasts? "Though He
slay me, yet will I trust in him,"[5] she sang. High and clear
through the frore[6] fair night, the level moonbeams splinter-

ing in the wood, the scarce glints of stars in the shadowy roof of branches, these sacred anthems rose, – rose as a hope from despair, as some snowy spray of flower-bells from blackest mould. Was she not in God's hands? Did not the world swing at his will? If this were in his great plan of providence, was it not best, and should she not accept it?

"He is the Lord our God; his judgments are in all the earth."[7]

Oh, sublime faith of our fathers, where utter self-sacrifice alone was true love, the fragrance of whose unrequired subjection was pleasanter than that of golden censers swung in purple-vapored chancels!

Never ceasing in the rhythm of her thoughts, articulated in music as they thronged, the memory of her first communion flashed over her. Again she was in that distant place on that sweet spring morning. Again the congregation rustled out, and the few remained, and she trembled to find herself among them. How well she remembered the devout, quiet faces, too accustomed to the sacred feast to glow with their inner joy! how well the snowy linen at the altar, the silver vessels slowly and silently shifting! and as the cup approached and passed, how the sense of delicious perfume stole in and heightened the transport of her prayer, and she had seemed, looking up through the windows where the sky soared blue in constant freshness, to feel all heaven's balms dripping from the portals, and to scent the lilies of eternal peace! Perhaps another would not have felt so much ecstasy as satisfaction on that occasion; but it is a true, if a later disciple, who has said, "The Lord bestoweth his blessings there, where he findeth the vessels empty."

"And does it need the walls of a church to renew my communion?" she asked. "Does not every moment stand a temple four-square to God? And in that morning, with its buoyant sunlight, was I any dearer to the Heart of the World than now? – 'My beloved is mine, and I am his,"[8] she sang over and over again, with all varied inflection and profuse tune. How gently all the winter-wrapt things bent toward her then! into what relation to her had they grown! how this common dependence was the spell of their intimacy! how at one with Nature had she become! how all the night and the silence and the forest seemed to hold its breath, and to send its soul up to God in her singing! It was no longer despondency, that singing. She had left imploring, "How long wilt thou forget me, O Lord? Lighten mine eyes, lest I sleep the sleep of death! For in death there is no remembrance of thee,"[9] – with countless other such fragments of supplication. She cried rather, "Yea, though I walk through the valley of the shadow of death, I will fear no evil: for thou art with me; thy rod and thy staff, they comfort me,"[10] – and lingered, and repeated, and sang again, "I shall be satisfied, when I awake, with thy likeness."[11]

Then she thought of the Great Deliverance, when he drew her up out of many waters, and the flashing old psalm pealed forth triumphantly: —

"The Lord descended from above,
and bow'd the heavens hie:
And underneath his feet he cast
the darknesse of the skie.
On cherubs and on cherubins
full royally he road:
And on the wings of all the winds
came flying all abroad."[12]

She forgot how recently, and with what a strange pity for her own shapeless form that was to be, she had quaintly sung, —

"O lovely appearance of death!
What sight upon earth is so fair?
Not all the gay pageants that breathe
Can with a dead body compare!"

She remembered instead, – "In thy presence is fulness of joy; at thy right hand there are pleasures forevermore. God will redeem my soul from the power of the grave: for he shall receive me. He will swallow up death in victory."[13] Not once now did she say, "Lord, how long wilt thou look on;

rescue my soul from their destructions, my darling from the lions,"[14] – for she knew that the young lions roar after their prey and seek their meat from God.[15] "O Lord, thou preservest man and beast!"[16] she said.

She had no comfort or consolation in this season, such as sustained the Christian martyrs in the amphitheatre. She was not dying for her faith; there were no palms in heaven for her to wave; but how many a time had she declared, – "I had rather be a doorkeeper in the house of my God, than to dwell in the tents of wickedness!"[17] And as the broad rays here and there broke through the dense covert of shade and lay in rivers of lustre on crystal sheathing and frozen fretting of trunk and limb and on the great spaces of refraction, they builded up visibly that house, the shining city on the hill, and singing, "Beautiful for situation, the joy of the whole earth, is Mount Zion, on the sides of the North, the city of the Great King,"[18] her vision climbed to that higher picture where the angel shows the dazzling thing, the holy Jerusalem descending out of heaven from God, with its splendid battlements and gates of pearls, and its foundations, the eleventh a jacinth, the twelfth an amethyst, – with its great white throne, and the rainbow round about it, in sight like unto an emerald: "And there shall be no night there, – for the Lord God giveth them light,"[19] she sang.

What whisper of dawn now rustled through the wilderness? How the night was passing! And still the beast crouched upon the bough, changing only the posture of his head, that again he might command her with those charmed eyes; – half their fire was gone; she could almost have released herself from his custody; yet, had she stirred, no one knows what malevolent instinct might have dominated anew. But of that she did not dream; long ago stripped of any expectation, she was experiencing in her divine rapture how mystically true it is that "he that dwelleth in the secret place of the Most High shall abide under the shadow of the Almighty."[20]

Slow clarion cries now wound from the distance as the cocks caught the intelligence of day and re-echoed it faintly from farm to farm, – sleepy sentinels of night, sounding the foe's invasion, and translating that dim intuition to ringing notes of warning. Still she chanted on. A remote crash of brushwood told of some other beast on his depredations, or some night-belated traveller groping his way through the narrow path. Still she chanted on. The far, faint echoes of the chanticleers died into distance, the crashing of the branches grew nearer. No wild beast that, but a man's step, – a man's form in the moonlight, stalwart and strong, – on one arm slept a little child, in the other hand he held his gun. Still she chanted on.

Perhaps, when her husband last looked forth, he was half ashamed to find what a fear he felt for her. He knew she would never leave the child so long but for some direst need, – and yet he may have laughed at himself, as he lifted and wrapped it with awkward care, and, loading his gun and strapping on his horn, opened the door again and closed it behind him, going out and plunging into the darkness and dangers of the forest. He was more singularly alarmed than he would have been willing to acknowledge; as he had sat with his bow hovering over the strings, he had half believed to hear her voice mingling gayly with the instrument, till he paused and listened if she were not about to lift the latch and enter. As he drew nearer the heart of the forest, that intimation of melody seemed to grow more actual, to take body and breath, to come and go on long swells and ebbs of the night-breeze, to increase with tune and words, till a strange shrill singing grew ever clearer, and, as he stepped into an open space of moonbeams, far up in the branches, rocked by the wind, and singing, "How beautiful upon the mountains are the feet of him that bringeth good tidings, that publisheth peace,"[21] he saw his wife, – his wife, – but, great God in heaven! how? Some mad exclamation escaped him, but without diverting her. The child knew the singing voice, though never heard before in that unearthly key, and turned toward it through the veiling dreams. With a celerity almost instantaneous, it lay, in the twinkling of an eye, on the ground at the father's feet, while his gun was raised to his shoulder and levelled at the monster covering his wife with shaggy form and flaming gaze, – his wife so ghastly white, so rigid, so stained with blood, her eyes so fixedly bent above, and her lips, that had indurated into the chiselled pallor of marble, parted only with that flood of solemn song.

I do not know if it were the mother-instinct that for a moment lowered her eyes, – those eyes, so lately riveted on heaven, now suddenly seeing all life-long bliss possible. A thrill of joy pierced and shivered through her like a weapon, her voice trembled in its course, her glance lost its steady strength, fever-flushes chased each other over her face, yet she never once ceased chanting. She was quite aware, that, if her husband shot now, the ball must pierce her body before reaching any vital part of the beast, – and yet better that death, by his hand, than the other. But this her husband also knew, and he remained motionless, just covering the creature with the sight. He dared not fire, lest some wound not mortal should break the spell exercised by her voice, and the beast, enraged with pain, should rend her in atoms; moreover, the light was too uncertain for his aim. So he waited. Now and then he examined his gun to see if the damp were injuring its charge, now and then he wiped the great drops from his forehead. Again the cocks crowed with the passing hour, – the last time they were heard on that night. Cheerful home sound then, how full of safety and all comfort and rest it seemed! what sweet morning incidents of sparkling fire and sunshine, of gay household bustle, shining dresser, and cooing baby, of steaming cattle in the yard, and brimming milk-pails at the door! what pleasant voices! what laughter! what security! and here —

Now, as she sang on in the slow, endless, infinite moments, the fervent vision of God's peace was gone. Just as the grave had lost its sting, she was snatched back again into the arms of earthly hope. In vain she tried to sing, "There remaineth a rest for the people of God,"[22] – her eyes trembled on her husband's, and she could only think of him, and of the child, and of happiness that yet might be, but with what a dreadful gulf of doubt between! She shuddered now in the suspense; all calm forsook her; she was tortured with dissolving heats or frozen with icy blasts; her face contracted, growing small and pinched; her voice was hoarse and sharp, – every tone cut like a knife, – the notes became heavy to lift, – withheld by some hostile pressure, impossible. One gasp, a convulsive effort, and then there was silence, – she had lost her voice.

The beast made a sluggish movement, – stretched and fawned like one awaking, – then, as if he would have yet more of the enchantment, stirred her slightly with his muzzle. As he did so, a sidelong hint of the man standing below with the raised gun smote him; he sprung round furiously, and, seizing his prey, was about to leap into some unknown airy den of the topmost branches now waving to the slow dawn. The late moon had rounded through the sky so that her gleam at last fell full upon the bough with fairy frosting; the wintry morning light did not yet penetrate the gloom. The woman, suspended in mid-air an instant, cast only one agonized glance beneath, – but across and through it, ere the lids could fall, shot a withering sheet of flame, – a rifle-crack, half-heard, was lost in the terrible yell of desperation that bounded after it and filled her ears with savage echoes, and in the wide arc of some eternal descent she was falling; – but the beast fell under her.

I think that the moment following must have been too sacred for us, and perhaps the three have no special interest again till they issue from the shadows of the wilderness upon the white hills that skirt their home. The father carries the child hushed again into slumber, the mother follows with no such feeble step as might be anticipated. It is not time for reaction, – the tension not yet relaxed, the nerves still vibrant, she seems to herself like some one newly made; the night was a dream; the present stamped upon her in deep satisfaction, neither weighed nor compared with the past; if she has the careful tricks of former habit, it is as an automaton; and as they slowly climb the steep under the clear gray vault and the paling morning star, and as she stops to gather a spray of the red-rose berries or a feathery tuft of dead grasses for the chimney-piece of the log-house, or a handful of brown cones for the child's play, – of these quiet, happy folk you would scarcely dream how lately they had stolen from under the banner and encampment of the great King Death. The husband proceeds a step or two in advance; the wife lingers over a singular foot-print in the snow, stoops and examines it, then looks up with a hurried word. Her husband stands alone on the hill, his arms folded across the babe, his gun fallen, – stands defined as a silhouette against the pallid sky. What is there in their home, lying below and yellowing in the light, to fix him with such a stare? She springs to his side. There is no home there. The log-house, the barns, the neighboring farms, the fences, are all blotted out and mingled in one smoking ruin. Desolation and death were indeed there, and beneficence and life in the forest. Tomahawk and scalping-knife, descending during that night, had left behind them only this work of their accomplished hatred and one subtle foot-print in the snow.

For the rest, – the world was all before them, where to choose.[23]

Notes

1   Grounds belonging to an estate.
2   Panther.
3   Sir Walter Scott (1771-1832). "Lay of the Last Minstrel" (1805).
4   Presbyterian hymns associated with the National Covenant of 1638. When Charles I attempted to introduce a liturgy on the English model into Scotland, the Covenanters swore to uphold their own forms of worship.
5   Job 13:15.
6   Frosty.
7   Psalms 105:7.
8   Song of Solomon 2:16.
9   Psalms 13:1-6.
10 Psalms 23:4.
11 Psalms 17:15.
12 Psalms 18:9-10.

13 Isaiah 25:6-8.
14 Psalms 35:17.
15 Psalms 104:21.
16 Psalms 36:6.
17 Psalms 84:10.
18 Psalms 48:2.
19 The description of the new Jerusalem comes from Revelation, particularly 20, 21, and 22:5.
20 Psalms 91:1.
21 Isaiah 52:7.
22 Hebrews 4:9.
23 John Milton (1608-1674), *Paradise Lost* (1667). The lines refer to the departure of Adam and Eve from Eden, 12:646.

Source: *The Amber Gods and Other Stories*. Boston: Ticknor Fields, 1863.

Biographical Note

Born in Calais, Maine, on April 3, 1835, Harriet Prescott Spofford was the oldest of the seven children of Joseph Newmarch Prescott, a merchant and politician, and Sarah Bridges. Spofford sporadically attended a private school, where her literary talents soon became evident, but the family's financial problems eventually led her father to seek his fortune in Oregon, while her mother moved in with a married sister in Newburyport, Massachusetts. Spofford attended the famous Putnam Free School and, later, in Derry, New Hampshire, the Pinkerton Academy. In 1856, her father returned, plagued by ill-health; her mother soon also became an invalid, and Spofford became a hack writer for various Boston papers in an attempt to support her family. At the same time, she was beginning to write more serious fiction, and when "In A Cellar," a detective story, was published in the *Atlantic Monthly* in 1859, she was immediately acclaimed as a author of considerable talent. Her first novel, a Gothic romance called *Sir Rohan's Ghost*, appeared in 1860, and her first and best known collection of short stories, *The Amber Gods and Other Stories*, in 1863. The title story of this collection, with its unsympathetic and completely self-absorbed, sensuous female narrator, Yone, is a striking portrait in egoism, and focuses on two of Spofford's recurrent concerns: the position of women in society, and the nature of the artistic imagination. In 1864 she published a second novel, *Azarian*. The strong vein of the romanticism she always found so congenial resulted in a severe review from Henry James, in a document that is often considered one of the first expressions of the American realist movement. She was not converted by the criticism, but she was influenced, and, as demonstrated in such works as *A Scarlet Poppy and Other Stories* (1894), eventually became proficient in the realistic sketch produced by many later nineteenth-century American women writers.

She married Richard Spofford, a successful lawyer and politician, in 1865; their only child was born in January of 1867 and died later that same year. They spent the early years of their married life alternately in Washington, D.C., and Newburyport; in 1874 they bought Deer Island in the Merrimack River where Spofford became renowed as a literary hostess. After her husband died in 1888, she spent much of her time in Boston, where she became part of the Boston circle of writers that included Sarah Orne Jewett and Rose Terry Cooke. By the end of the century, she was one of the most popular American women writers. *Old Madame and Other Tragedies* (1900) contains "Her Story," originally published in *Lippincott's* (1872), and an early forerunner of Charlotte Perkins Gilman's "The Yellow Wallpaper"; this, along with the title story, are two of her best works. Spofford also produced some of the best supernatural tales of the time, including "The Godmothers" (*The Cosmopolitan* [1896]), and "The Mad Lady" (*Scribner's* [1916]). Her last collection, *The Elder's People* was published in 1920; one year later she died on Deer Island. "Circumstance," first published in Atlantic Monthly (1860), has variously been read as an expression of the problems faced by the woman artist, an account of a religious experience, and an exploration of a woman's encounter with sexuality, with the animal in human nature.

Selected Modern Reprints:

The Amber Gods and Other Stories. Ed. and Intro. Alfred
Bendixen. New Brunswick: Rutgers UP, 1989.
The Scarlet Poppy and Other Stories. New York: Irvington,
1972.

Selected Secondary Sources:

Dalke, Anne. "'Circumstance' and the Creative Woman:
Harriet Prescott Spofford." *Arizona Quarterly* 41.1
(1985): 71-85.
Garbowsky, Maryanne M. "A Maternal Muse for Emily Dick-
inson." *Dickinson Studies* 41 (1981): 12-17.
Halbeisen, Elizabeth K. *Harriet Prescott Spofford: A Romantic
Survival.* Philadelphia: U of Pennsylvania P, 1935.
James, Henry. Rev. of *Azarian. North American Review* (Jan
1865): 268-77.
Shinn, Thelma J. "Harriet Prescott Spofford: A Reconsid-
eration." *Turn of the Century Women* 1.1 (1984): 36-45.

462   FLORA ANNIE STEEL (1847-1929)

Flora Annie Steel (1847-1929)

Mussumât Kirpo's Doll

THEY HAD GATHERED ALL THE SCHOOLS INTO THE MISSION house compound, and set them out in companies on the bare ground like seedlings in a bed, – a perfect garden of girls, from five to fifteen, arrayed in rainbow hues; some of them in their wedding dresses of scarlet, most of them bedecked with the family jewelry, and even the shabbiest boasting a row or two of tinsel on bodice or veil.

And down the walks, drawn with mathematical accuracy between these hotbeds of learning, a few English ladies with eager, kindly faces, trotting up and down, conferring excitedly with portly native Christian Bible-women, and pausing occasionally to encourage some young offshoot of the Tree of Knowledge – uncertain either of its own roots or of the soil it grew in – by directing its attention to the tables set out with toys which stood under a group of date-palms and oranges. Behind these tables sat in a semicircle more of those eager, kindly foreign faces, not confined here to one sex, but in fair proportion male and female; yet, bearded like the pard[1] or feminine to a fault, all with the same expression, the same universal kindly benevolence towards the horticultural exhibition spread out before their eyes.

At the table, pale or flushed with sheer good feeling, two or three of the chief Mission ladies, and between them, with a mundane, married look about her, contrasting strongly with her surroundings, the Commissioner's wife, about to give away the prizes. A kindly face also, despite its half-bewildered look, as one after another of the seedlings comes up to receive the reward of merit. One after another solemnly, for dotted here and there behind the screen of walls and bushes squats many a critical mother, determined that her particular plant shall receive its fair share of watering, or cease to be part of the harvest necessary for a good report. The Commissioner's wife has half-a-dozen children of her own, and prides herself on understanding them; but these bairns are a race apart. She neither comprehends them, nor the fluent, scholastic Hindustani with which her flushed, excited countrywomen introduce each claimant to her notice. Still she smiles, and says, '*Bohut uchcha*' (very good), and nods as if she did. In a vague way she is relieved when the books are finished and she begins upon the dolls. There is something familiar and cosmopolitan in the gloating desire of the large dark eyes, and the possessive clutch of the small hands over the treasure.

'Standard I. Mussumât Kirpo,'[2] reads out the secretary, and a tall girl of about fifteen comes forward. A sort of annoyed surprise passes among the ladies in quick whispers. Clearly, a Japanese baby-doll with a large bald head is not the correct thing here; but it is so difficult, so almost impossible with hundreds of girls who attend school so irregularly, and really Julia Smith might have explained! This the lady in question proceeds to do almost tearfully, until she is cut short by superior decision.

'Well, we must give it her now as there isn't anything else for her. So, dear Mrs. Gordon, if you please! Of course, as a rule, we always draw the line about dolls when a girl is married. Sometimes it seems a little hard, for they are so small, you know; still it is best to have a rule; all these tiny trifles help to emphasize our views on the child-marriage question. But if you will be kind enough in this case – just to avoid confusion – we will rectify the mistake to-morrow.'

Mussumât Kirpo took her doll stolidly; – a sickly, stupid-looking girl, limping as she walked dully, stolidly back to her place.

'*Ari!*'[3] giggled the women behind the bushes. 'That's all she is likely to get in that way. Lo! they made a bad bargain in brides in Gungo's house, and no mistake. But 'twas ill luck, not ill management; for they tell me Kirpo was straight and sound when she was betrothed. May the gods keep my daughters-in-law healthy and handsome.'

Then they forgot the joke in tender delight over more suitable gifts to the others; and so the great day passed to its ending.

'I do believe poor Kirpo's getting that doll was the only *contretemps*,'[4] said the superintendent triumphantly, 'and that, dear Julia, you can easily remedy to-morrow, so don't fret about it.'

With this intention Julia Smith went down at the first opportunity to her school in the slums of the city. A general air of slackness pervaded the upstairs room, where only a row of little mites sat whispering to each other, while their mistress, full of yawns and stretchings, talked over the events of yesterday with her monitor. Briefly, if the Miss-*sahib*[5] thought she was going to slave as she had done for the past year for a paltry eight yards of *sussi*-trousering,[6] which would not be enough to cut into the 'fassen'[7] – why, the Miss-*sahib* was mistaken. And then with the well-known footfall on the stairs came smiles and flattery. But Kirpo was not at school. Why should she be, seeing that she was a paper-pupil and the prize-giving was over? If the Miss-*sahib* wanted to see her, she had better go round to Gungo's house in the heart of the Hindu quarter. So Julia Smith set off again to thread her way through the byeways, till she reached the mud steps and closed door which belonged to Kuniya, the head-man of the comb-makers. This ownership had much to do with the English lady's patience in regard to Kirpo who, to tell the truth, had been learning the alphabet for five years. But the girl's father-in-law was a man of influence, and Julia's gentle, proselytising eyes cast glances of longing on every house where she had not as yet found entrance. Hence her reluctance to quarrel definitely with her pupil, or rather her pupil's belongings, since poor Kirpo did not count for much in that bustling Hindu household. But for the fact that she was useful at the trade and as a general drudge, *Mai* Gungo[8] would long ago have found some excuse for sending the girl, who had so woefully disappointed all expectations, back to her people, – those people who had taken the wedding gifts and given a half-crippled, half-silly bride in exchange. Unparalleled effrontery and wickedness, to be avenged on the only head within reach.

'She wants none of your dolls or your books,' shrilled *Mai* Gungo, who was in a bad temper; 'they aren't worth anything, and I expected nothing less than a suit of clothes, or a new veil at least, else would I never have sent her from the comb-making to waste her time. Lo! Miss-*sahib*,' here the voice changed to a whine, 'we are poor folk, and she costs to feed – she who will never do her duty as a wife. Yet must not Kuniya's son remain sonless; thus is there the expense of another wife in the future.'

So the complaints went on, while Kirpo, in full hearing, sat filing away at the combs without a flicker of expression on her face.

But when Julia had settled the business with eight annas from her private pocket, and was once more picking her way through the drain-like alley, she heard limping steps behind her. It was Kirpo and the Japanese doll.

'The Miss-*sahib* has forgotten it,' she said stolidly. Julia Smith stood in the sunlight, utterly unmindful of a turgid stream of concentrated filth which at that moment came sweeping along the gutter. Her gentle, womanly eyes saw something she recognised in the childlike, yet unchildlike face looking into hers.

'Would you like to keep it, dear?' she asked gently. Kirpo nodded her head.

'She needn't know,' she explained. 'I could keep it in the cow-shed, and they will sell the book you left for me. They would sell this too. That is why I brought it back.'

This admixture of cunning rather dashed poor Julia's pity; but in the end Kirpo went back to her work with the Japanese doll carefully concealed in her veil, and for the next year Julia Smith never caught sight of it again. Things went on as if it had not been in that straggling Hindu house, with its big courtyard and dark slips of rooms. Perhaps Kirpo got up at night to play with it; perhaps she never played with it at all, but, having wrapped it in a napkin and buried it away somewhere, was content in its possession like the man with his one talent; for this miserliness belongs, as a rule, to those who have few things, not many. Once or twice, when Julia Smith found the opportunity, she would ask after the doll's welfare. Then Kirpo would nod her head mysteriously; but this was not often, for, by degrees, Julia's visits to the house and Kirpo's to the schools became less frequent. The former, because *Mai* Gungo's claims grew intolerable, and the Mission lady had found firm footing in less rapacious houses. The latter, because to *Mai* Gungo's somewhat grudging relief her daughter-in-law, after nearly four years of married life, seemed disposed to save the family from the expense of another bride by presenting it with a child. Nothing, of course, could alter the fact of the girl's ugliness and stupidity and lameness; still, if she did her duty in this one point *Mai* Gungo could put up with her, especially as she really did very well at the combs. She was not worked quite so hard now, since that might affect the future promise. Perhaps this gave Kirpo more time to play with the Japanese doll, perhaps it did not. Outwardly, at any rate, life went on in the courtyard as though no such thing existed.

'She may die, the crippled ones often do,' said the gossips, scarcely lowering their voices; 'but it will be a great saving, *Mai* Gungo, if the grandson comes without another daughter-in-law; they quarrel so. Besides, it is in God's hands. May He preserve both to you.' *Mai* Gungo echoed the wish, with the reservation that if the whole wish was impossible, the child at least might not suffer. Kirpo herself understood the position perfectly, and felt dimly that if she could do her duty she would be quite content to give up the comb-making once and for all. It was niggly, cramping work to sit with your crippled legs tucked under you, filing away at the hard wood all day long, while mother-in-law bustled about, scolding away in her shrill voice. It had been much greater fun at the school; and as for the prize-giving days! Kirpo had four of those red-letter glimpses of the world to recollect, but she always gave the palm of pleasure to the last, when they had laughed at her and the Japanese doll. Perhaps because she remembered it best; for, as has been said, poor Kirpo's was not a brilliant intellect.

So just about the time when the Mission House was once more buying large consignments of dolls and books, and laying in yards on yards of *sussi*-trousering and Manchester veiling⁹ against another prize-giving, the mistress of the little schoolroom up two pair of stairs said to Julia Smith,

'Kirpo had a son last week. *Mai* Gungo hath given offerings galore.'

'And Kirpo herself?'

'She ails, they say; but that is likely. The hour of danger is over.'

That same afternoon Julia Smith once more picked her way along the gutters to the mud steps and closed door of Kuniya's house. Kirpo was lying alone on a bed in the shadow of a grass thatch.

'And where is the baby?' asked Julia, cheerfully.

'Mother-in-law hath it. 'Tis a son – doubtless the Miss hath heard so.' There was the oddest mixture of pride and regret in the girl's dull face.

'She will let thee have it when thou art stronger,' said her visitor quickly. 'Thou must give me back the dolly, Kirpo, now thou hast a live one of thine own.'

The girl's head shifted uneasily on the hard pillow.

'Ay! and the prize-giving day must be close, I have been thinking. If the Miss-*sahib* will look behind the straw yonder she will find the doll. It is not hurt. And the Miss can give it to some one else. I don't want it any more. She might give it to a little girl this time. She could play with it.'

'*Mai* Gungo!' said Julia severely, as, on her way out, she found the mother-in-law surrounded by her gossips, exhibiting the baby to them with great pride, 'you must look to Kirpo; she thrives not. And give her the baby – she pines after it.'

'The Miss doth not understand,' flounced Gungo. 'What can Kirpo do with a baby? She is a fool; besides, a mother like that hath evil influences till the time of purification hath passed.'

Ten days afterwards the mistress of the school told

Julia that Kirpo had the fever, and they did not think she would recover. It was never safe for such as she to have sons, and nothing else was to be expected.

Perhaps it was not; for Julia found her on the bare ground of the courtyard where she had been set to die. The oil lamps flared smokily at her head and her feet, and *Mai* Gungo, with the fortnight-old baby in her arms, cried '*Rám! Rám!*'[10] lustily. But the girl lingered in life, turning her head restlessly from side to side on Mother Earth's bosom.

'Give her the baby – only for a minute,' pleaded Julia with tears in her eyes. Mai Gungo frowned; but a neighbour broke in hastily —

'Ay, give it to her, gossip, lest in her evil ways she returns for it when she is dead.'

So they laid the baby beside her; but the restless head went on turning restlessly from side to side.

'My doll! my doll! I like my doll best.'

Before they could fetch it from the Mission compound Kirpo was dead.

Notes

1   Panther.
2   [Steel's note]: Title of honour equivalent to our "mistress".
3   Expression of surprise (Hindustani).
4   An inopportune occurrence.
5   The term of address for an unmarried woman; Mem-sahib would refer to a married woman.
6   An East Indian fabric. In the Punjab it is a striped stuff used for women's trousers.
7   Possibly Anglo-Indian for fashion.
8   Mother Ganges. Both men and women can be named after the sacred river Ganges.
9   Manchester was an important manufacturing centre for textiles.
10 Ráma is an incarnation of Vishnu and the hero of the Hindu epic *Ramayana*. He is widely venerated in Northern India.

Biographical Note

The daughter of a Scottish parliamentary agent and an heiress to a Jamaican plantation, Steel was born in Harrow, Middlesex, and spent her adolescence in Scotland; she was primarily educated at home except for six months in a school in Brussels. In 1867 she married Henry William Steel of the Indian Civil Service, and they lived in India from 1868 until 1889. Within a year of the marriage, Steel gave birth to a still-born daughter; another daughter, Mabel, was born two years later. Steel became actively involved in many aspects of Indian life. She founded a school for Indian girls at the station of Kasur in 1884, became medical advisor to the local population, campaigned for improvements in local living conditions, and produced many plays and musical events within the community. She became particularly involved with academic administration in India, fighting for the education of Indian women and eventually becoming inspector of girls' schools and a member of the Provincial Education Board. After returning from India at the age of forty-two, Steel lived first in Scotland and then in Talgarth, in mid-Wales, where she began to devote herself earnestly to writing. She produced twenty novels beginning with *Miss Stuart's Legacy* (1893), the story of an unconventional young woman in love with an Anglo-Indian officer, and including *On the Face of the Waters* (1896), the account of the Indian Mutiny with which she established her reputation. She also produced collections of folk and fairy tales, including *Wide Awake Stories* (1884), later reprinted as *Tales of the Punjab* (1894) with illlustrations by J.L. Kipling (Rudyard Kipling's father). Steel became an active member of the Women Writers Suffrage League, marched in the suffrage demonstration of 1910, and produced a pamphlet called *The Fruit of the Tree* (1920) on the subjection of women. In later life, she became something of an eccentric, claiming that several of her tales had been told to her by a mysterious apparition, Nathaniel James Craddock. After her husband's death in 1923, Steel began to study philosophy, and grew convinced that sexuality was the cause of all human problems; this became the subject of her last novel, *The Curse of Eve*, which also advocates birth control and was published posthumously in 1929, and is also discussed in her unfinished autobiography, *The Garden of Fidelity* (1926). Steel was highly active until the end of her life, and even in her eighties she managed to sail to Jamaica to visit relatives and continued her research by joining her grandson at Oxford in order to read in the Bodleian. She died in Talgarth on April 12, 1929.

Selected Modern Reprints:

Indian Scene: Collected Short Stories of Flora Annie Steel. Intro. Mabel Webster. London: Edward Arnold, 1933.

Selected Secondary Sources:

Hennessey, Rosemary. "The Construction of Woman in Three Popular Texts of Empire: Towards a Critique of Materialist Feminism." *Textual Practice* 3.3 (1989): 323-59.

Paxton, Nancy. "Feminism Under the Raj: Complicity and Resistance in the Writings of Flora Annie Steel and Annie Besant." *Women's Studies International Forum* 13.4 (1990): 333-46.

Powell, Violet. *Flora Annie Steel: Novelist of India.* London: Heinemann, 1981.

Saunders, Rebecca. "Gender, Colonialism, and Exile: Flora Annie Steel and Sara Jeanette Duncan in India." *Women's Writing in Exile.* Ed. Mary Lyne Broe and Angela Ingram. Chapel Hill: U of North Carolina P, 1989. 303-24.

472　CONSTANCE FENIMORE WOOLSON (1840-1894)

Constance Fenimore Woolson
(1840-1894)

Felipa

Glooms of the live-oaks, beautiful-braided and woven,
With intricate shades of the vines that, myriad cloven,
Clamber the forks of the multiform boughs.
                                        ....Green colonnades
Of the dim sweet woods, of the dear dark woods,
Of the heavenly woods and glades,
That run to the radiant marginal sand-beach within
The wide sea-marshes of Glynn.
                                        ....Free
By a world of marsh that borders a world of sea.
Sinuous southward and sinuous northward the shimmering
                                        band
Of the sand-beach fastens the fringe of the marsh to the folds
                                        of the land.

Inward and outward to northward and southward the beach-
                                        lines linger and curl
As a silver-wrought garment that clings to and follows the
                                        firm, sweet limbs of a girl.
A league and a league of marsh-grass, waist-high, broad in
                                        the blade,
Green, and all of a height, and unflecked with a light or a
                                        shade.
                                        SIDNEY LANIER.[1]

CHRISTINE AND I FOUND HER THERE. SHE WAS A SMALL, DARK-skinned, yellow-eyed child, the offspring of the ocean and the heats, tawny, lithe and wild, shy yet fearless – not unlike one of the little brown deer that bounded through the open reaches of the pine-barren behind the house. She did not come to us – we came to her; we loomed into her life like genii from another world, and she was partly afraid and partly proud of us. For were we not her guests? proud thought! and, better still, were we not women? "I have only seen three women in all my life," said Felipa, inspecting us gravely, "and I like women. I am a woman too, although these clothes of the son of Pedro make me appear as a boy; I wear them on account of the boat and the hauling in of the fish. The son of Pedro being dead at a convenient age, and his clothes fitting me, what would you have? It was a chance not to be despised. But when I am grown I shall wear robes long and beautiful like the señora's." The little creature was dressed in a boy's suit of dark-blue linen, much the worse for wear, and torn.

"If you are a girl, why do you not mend your clothes?" I said.

"Do you mend, señora?"

"Certainly: all women sew and mend."

"The other lady?"

Christine laughed as she lay at ease upon the brown carpet of pine-needles, warm and aromatic after the tropic day's sunshine. "The child has divined me already, Catherine," she said.

Christine was a tall, lissome maid, with an unusually long stretch of arm, long sloping shoulders, and a long fair throat; her straight hair fell to her knees when unbound, and its clear flaxen hue had not one shade of gold, as her clear gray eyes had not one shade of blue. Her small, straight, rose-leaf lips parted over small, dazzlingly white teeth, and the outline of her face in profile reminded you of an etching in its distinctiveness, although it was by no means perfect according to the rules of art. Still, what a comfort it was, after the blurred outlines and smudged profiles many of us possess – seen to best advantage, I think, in church on Sundays, crowned with flower-decked bonnets, listening calmly serene to favorite ministers, unconscious of noses! When Christine had finished her laugh – and she never hurried anything – she stretched out her arm carelessly and patted Felipa's curly head. The child caught the descending hand and kissed the long white fingers.

It was a wild place where we were, yet not new or crude – the coast of Florida, that old-new land, with its deserted plantations, its skies of Paradise, and its broad wastes open to the changeless sunshine. The old house stood on the edge of the dry land, where the pine-barren ended and the salt-marsh began; in front curved the tide-water river that seemed ever trying to come up close to the barren and make its acquaintance, but could not quite succeed, since it must always turn and flee at a fixed hour, like Cinderella at the ball, leaving not a silver slipper behind, but purple driftwood and bright sea-weeds, brought in from the Gulf Stream outside. A planked platform ran out into the marsh from the edge of the barren, and at its end the boats were moored; for, although at high tide the river was at our feet, at low tide it was far away out in the green waste somewhere, and if we wanted it we must go and seek it. We did not want it, however; we let it glide up to us twice a day with its fresh salt odors and flotsam of the ocean, and the rest of the time we wandered over the barrens or lay under the trees looking up into the wonderful blue above, listening to the winds as they rushed across from sea to sea. I was an artist, poor and painstaking. Christine was my kind friend. She had brought me South because my cough was troublesome, and here because Edward Bowne recommended the place. He and three fellow sportsmen were down at the Madre Lagoon, farther south; I thought it probable we should see him, without his three fellow sportsmen, before very long.

"Who are the three women you have seen, Felipa?" said Christine.

"The grandmother, an Indian woman of the Seminoles[2] who comes sometimes with baskets, and the wife of Miguel of the island. But they are all old, and their skins are curled: I like better the silver skin of the señora."

Poor little Felipa lived on the edge of the great salt-marsh alone with her grandparents, for her mother was dead. The yellow old couple were slow-witted Minorcans,[3] part pagan, part Catholic, and wholly ignorant; their minds rarely rose above the level of their orange-trees and their fish-nets. Felipa's father was a Spanish sailor, and, as he had died only the year before, the child's Spanish was fairly correct, and we could converse with her readily, although we were slow to comprehend the patois of the old people, which seemed to borrow as much from the Italian tongue and the Greek as from its mother Spanish. "I know a great deal," Felipa remarked confidently, "for my father taught me. He had sailed on the ocean out of sight of land, and he knew many things. These he taught to me. Do the gracious ladies think there is anything else to know?"

One of the gracious ladies thought not, decidedly. In answer to my remonstrance, expressed in English, she said, "Teach a child like that, and you ruin her."

"Ruin her?"

"Ruin her happiness – the same thing."

Felipa had a dog, a second self – a great, gaunt yellow creature of unknown breed, with crooked legs, big feet, and the name Drollo. What Drollo meant, or whether it was an abbreviation, we never knew; but there was a certain satisfaction in it, for the dog was droll: the fact that the Minorcan title, whatever it was, meant nothing of that sort, made it all the better. We never saw Felipa without Drollo. "They look a good deal alike," observed Christine – "the same coloring."

"For shame!" I said.

But it was true. The child's bronzed yellow skin and soft eyes were not unlike the dog's, but her head was crowned with a mass of short black curls, while Drollo had only his two great flapping ears and his low smooth head. Give him an inch or two more of skull, and what a creature a dog would be! For love and faithfulness even now what man can match him? But, although ugly, Felipa was a picturesque little object always, whether attired in boy's clothes or in her own forlorn bodice and skirt. Ol-ive-hued and meager-faced, lithe and thin, she flew over the pine-barrens like a creature of air, laughing to feel her short curls toss and her thin childish arms buoyed up on the breeze as she ran, with Drollo barking behind. For she loved the winds, and always knew when they were coming, whether down from the north, in from the ocean, or across from the Gulf of Mexico: she watched for them, sitting in the doorway, where she could feel their first breath, and she taught us the signs of the clouds. She was a queer little thing: we used to find her sometimes danc-ing alone out on the barren in a circle she had marked out with pine-cones, and once she confided to us that she talked to the trees. "They hear," she said in a whisper; "you should see how knowing they look, and how their leaves listen."

Once we came upon her most secret lair in a dense thicket of thorn-myrtle and wild smilax – a little bower she had made, where was hidden a horrible-looking image formed of the rough pieces of saw-palmetto grubbed up by old Bartolo from his garden. She must have dragged these fragments thither one by one, and with infinite pains bound them together with her rude withes of strong marsh-grass, until at last she had formed a rough trunk with crooked arms and a sort of head, the red hairy sur-face of the palmetto looking not unlike the skin of some beast, and making the creature all the more grotesque. This fetich was kept crowned with flowers, and after this we often saw the child stealing away with Drollo to carry to it portions of her meals or a new-found treasure – a sea-shell, a broken saucer, or a fragment of ribbon. The food always mysteriously disappeared, and my suspicion is that Drollo used to go back secretly in the night and devour it, asking no questions and telling no lies: it fitted in nicely, however, Drollo merely performing the ancient part of the priests of Jupiter, men who have been much admired. "What a little pagan she is!" I said.

"Oh, no, it is only her doll," replied Christine.

I tried several times to paint Felipa during these first weeks, but those eyes of hers always evaded me. They were, as I have said before, yellow – that is, they were brown with yellow lights – and they stared at you with the most inflexible openness. The child had the full-curved, half-open mouth of the tropics, and a low Greek forehead. "Why isn't she pretty?" I said.

"She is hideous," replied Christine; "look at her elbows."

Now Felipa's arms *were* unpleasant: they were brown and lean, scratched and stained, and they terminated in a pair of determined little paws that could hold on like grim Death. I shall never forget coming upon a tableau one day out on the barren – a little Florida cow and Felipa, she holding on by the horns, and the beast with its small fore feet stubbornly set in the sand; girl pulling one way, cow the other; both silent and determined. It was a hard contest, but the girl won.

"And if you pass over her elbows, there are the feet," continued Christine languidly. For she was a sybaritic lover of the fine linens of life, that friend of mine – a pre-Raphaelite[4] lady with clinging draperies and a mediaeval clasp on her belt. Her whole being rebelled against ugliness, and the mere sight of a sharp-nosed, light-eyed woman on a cold day made her uncomfortable.

"Have we not feet too?" I replied sharply.

But I knew what she meant. Bare feet are not pleasant to the eye nowadays, whatever they may have been in the days of the ancient Greeks; and Felipa's little brown insteps were half the time torn or bruised by the thorns of the chaparral. Besides, there was always the disagreeable idea that she might step upon something cold and squirming when she prowled through the thickets knee-deep in the matted grasses. Snakes abounded, although we never saw them; but Felipa went up to their very doors, as it were, and rang the bell defiantly.

One day old Grandfather Bartolo took the child with him down to the coast; she was always wild to go to the beach, where she could gather shells and sea-beans, and chase the little ocean-birds that ran along close to the waves with that swift gliding motion of theirs, and where she could listen to the roar of the breakers. We were several miles up the salt-marsh, and to go down to the ocean was quite a voyage to Felipa. She bade us good-by joyously; then ran back to hug Christine a second time, then to the boat again; then back.

"I thought you wanted to go, child?" I said, a little impatiently; for I was reading aloud, and these small irruptions were disturbing.

"Yes," said Felipa, "I want to go; and still — Perhaps if the gracious señora would kiss me again —"

Christine only patted her cheek and told her to run away: she obeyed, but there was a wistful look in her eyes, and, even after the boat had started, her face, watching us from the stern, haunted me.

"Now that the little monkey has gone, I may be able at last to catch and fix a likeness of her," I said; "in this case a recollection is better than the changing quicksilver reality."

"You take it as a study of ugliness?"

"Do not be hard upon the child, Christine."

"Hard? Why, she adores me," said my friend, going off to her hammock under the tree.

Several days passed, and the boat returned not. I accomplished a fine amount of work, and Christine a fine amount of swinging in the hammock and dreaming. At length one afternoon I gave my final touch, and carried my sketch over to the pre-Raphaelite lady for criticism. "What do you see?" I said.

"I see a wild-looking child with yellow eyes, a mat of curly black hair, a lank little bodice, her two thin brown arms embracing a gaunt old dog with crooked legs, big feet, and turned-in toes."

"Is that all?"

"All."

"You do not see latent beauty, courage, and a possible great gulf of love in that poor wild little face?"

"Nothing of the kind," replied Christine decidedly. "I see an ugly little girl; that is all."

The next day the boat returned, and brought back five persons, the old grandfather, Felipa, Drollo, Miguel of the island, and - Edward Bowne.

"Already?" I said.

"Tired of the Madre, Kitty; thought I would come up here and see you for a while. I knew you must be pining for me."

"Certainly," I replied; "do you not see how I have wasted away?"

He drew my arm through his and raced me down the plank-walk toward the shore, where I arrived laughing and out of breath.

"Where is Christine?" he asked.

I came back into the traces at once. "Over there in the hammock. You wish to go to the house first, I suppose?"

"Of course not."

"But she did not come to meet you, Edward, although she knew you had landed."

"Of course not, also."

"I do not understand you two."

"And of course not, a third time," said Edward, looking down at me with a smile. "What do you peaceful little artists know about war?"

"Is it war?"

"Something very like it, Kitty. What is that you are carrying?"

"Oh! my new sketch. What do you think of it?"

"Good, very good. Some little girl about here, I suppose?"

"Why, it is Felipa!"

"And who is Felipa? Seems to me I have seen that old dog, though."

"Of course you have; he was in the boat with you, and so was Felipa; but she was dressed in boy's clothes, and that gives her a different look."

"Oh! that boy? I remember him. His name is Philip. He is a funny little fellow," said Edward calmly.

"Her name is Felipa, and she is not a boy or a funny little fellow at all," I replied.

"Isn't she? I thought she was both," replied Ned carelessly; and then he went off toward the hammock. I turned away, after noting Christine's cool greeting, and went back to the boat.

Felipa came bounding to meet me. "What is his name?" she demanded.

"Bowne."

"Buon – Buona; I can not say it."

"Bowne, child – Edward Bowne."

"Oh, Eduardo; I know that. Eduardo – Eduardo – a name of honey."

She flew off singing the name, followed by Drollo carrying his mistress's palmetto basket in his big patient mouth; but when I passed the house a few moments afterward she was singing, or rather talking volubly of, another name – "Miguel," and "the wife of Miguel," who were apparently important personages on the canvas of her life. As it happened, I never really saw that wife of Miguel, who seemingly had no name of her own; but I imagined her. She lived on a sand-bar in the ocean not far from the mouth of our salt-marsh; she drove pelicans like ducks with a long switch, and she had a tame eagle; she had an old horse also, who dragged the driftwood across the sand on a sledge, and this old horse seemed like a giant horse always, outlined as he was against the flat bar and the sky. She went out at dawn, and she went out at sunset, but during the middle of the burning day she sat at home and polished sea-beans, for which she obtained untold sums; she was very tall, she was very yellow, and she had but one eye. These items, one by one, had been dropped by Felipa at various times, and it was with curiosity that I gazed upon the original Miguel, the possessor of this remarkable spouse. He was a grave-eyed, yellow man, who said little and thought less, applying *cui bono?*[5] to mental much as the city man applies it to bodily exertion, and therefore achieving, I think, a finer degree of inanition. The tame eagle, the pelicans, were nothing to him; and, when I saw his lethargic, gentle countenance, my own curiosity about them seemed to die away in haze, as though I had breathed an invisible opiate. He came, he went, and that was all; exit Miguel.

Felipa was constantly with us now. She and Drollo followed the three of us wherever we went – followed the two also whenever I staid behind to sketch, as I often staid, for in those days I was trying to catch the secret of the salt-marsh; a hopeless effort – I know it now. "Stay with me, Felipa," I said; for it was natural to suppose that the lovers might like to be alone. (I call them lovers for want of a better name, but they were more like haters; however, in such cases it is nearly the same thing.) And then Christine, hearing this, would immediately call "Felipa!" and the child would dart after them, happy as a bird. She wore her boy's suit now all the time, because the señora had said she "looked well in it." What the señora really said was, that in boy's clothes she looked less like a grasshopper. But this had been translated as above by Edward Bowne when Felipa suddenly descended upon him one day and demanded to be instantly told what the gracious lady was saying about her; for she seemed to know by intuition when we spoke of her, although we talked in English and mentioned no names. When told, her small face beamed, and she kissed Christine's hand joyfully and bounded away. Christine took out her handkerchief and wiped the spot.

"Christine," I said, "do you remember the fate of the proud girl who walked upon bread?"

"You think that I may starve for kisses some time?" said my friend, going on with the wiping.

"Not while I am alive," called out Edward from behind. His style of courtship *was* of the sledge-hammer sort sometimes. But he did not get much for it on that day; only lofty tolerance, which seemed to amuse him greatly.

Edward played with Felipa very much as if she was a rubber toy or a little trapeze performer. He held her out at arm's length in mid-air, he poised her on his shoulder, he tossed her up into the low myrtle-trees, and dangled her by her little belt over the claret-colored pools on the barren; but he could not frighten her; she only laughed and grew wilder and wilder, like a squirrel. "She has muscles and nerves of steel," he said admiringly.

"Do put her down; she is too excitable for such games." I said in French, for Felipa seemed to divine our English now. "See the color she has."

For there was a trail of dark red over the child's thin oval cheeks which made her look unlike herself. As she caught our eyes fixed upon her, she suddenly stopped her climbing and came and sat at Christine's feet. "Some day I shall wear robes like the señora's," she said, passing her hand over the soft fabric; "and I think," she added after some slow consideration, "that my face will be like the señora's too."

Edward burst out laughing. The little creature stopped abruptly and scanned his face.

"Do not tease her," I said.

Quick as a flash she veered around upon me. "He does not tease me," she said angrily in Spanish; "and, besides, what if he does? I like it." She looked at me with gleaming eyes and stamped her foot.

"What a little tempest!" said Christine.

Then Edward, man-like, began to explain. "You could not look much like this lady, Felipa," he said, "because you are so dark, you know."

"Am I dark?"

"Very dark; but many people are dark, of course; and for my part I always like dark eyes," said this mendacious person.

"Do you like my eyes?" asked Felipa anxiously.

"Indeed I do; they are like the eyes of a dear little calf I once owned when I was a boy."

The child was satisfied, and went back to her place beside Christine. "Yes, I shall wear robes like this," she said dreamily, drawing the flowing drapery over her knees clad in the little linen trousers, and scanning the effect; "they would trail behind me – so." Her bare feet peeped out below the hem, and again we all laughed, the little brown toes looked so comical coming out from the silk and the snowy embroideries. She came down to reality again, looked at us, looked at herself, and for the first time seemed to comprehend the difference. Then suddenly she threw herself down on the ground like a little animal, and buried her head in her arms. She would not speak, she would not look up: she only relaxed one arm a little to take in Drollo, and then lay motionless. Drollo looked at us out of one eye solemnly from his uncomfortable position, as much as to say: "No use, leave her to me." So after a while we went away and left them there.

That evening I heard a low knock at my door. "Come in," I said, and Felipa entered. I hardly knew her. She was dressed in a flowery muslin gown which had probably belonged to her mother, and she wore her grandmother's stockings and large baggy slippers; on her mat of curly hair was perched a high-crowned, stiff white cap adorned with a ribbon streamer; and her lank little neck, coming out of the big gown, was decked with a chain of large sea-beans, like exaggerated lockets. She carried a Cuban fan in her hand which was as large as a parasol, and Drollo, walking behind, fairly clanked with the chain of sea-shells which she had wound around him from head to tail. The droll tableau and the supreme pride on Felipa's countenance overcame me, and I laughed aloud. A sudden cloud of rage and disappointment came over the poor child's face: she threw her cap on the floor and stamped on it; she tore off her necklace and writhed herself out of her big flowered gown, and, running to Drollo, nearly strangled him in her fierce efforts to drag off his shell chains. Then, a half-dressed, wild little phantom, she seized me by the skirts and dragged me toward the looking-glass. "You are not pretty either," she cried. "Look at yourself! look at yourself!"

"I did not mean to laugh at you, Felipa," I said gently; "I would not laugh at any one; and it is true I am not pretty, as you say. I can never be pretty, child; but, if you will try to be more gentle, I could teach you how to dress yourself so that no one would laugh at you again. I could make you a little bright-barred skirt and a scarlet bodice: you could help, and that would teach you to sew. But a little girl who wants all this done for her must be quiet and good."

"I am good," said Felipa; "as good as everything."

The tears still stood in her eyes, but her anger was forgotten: she improvised a sort of dance around my room, followed by Drollo dragging his twisted chain, stepping on it with his big feet, and finally winding himself up into a knot around the chair-legs.

"Couldn't we make Drollo something too? dear old Drollo!" said Felipa, going to him and squeezing him in an enthusiastic embrace. I used to wonder how his poor ribs stood it: Felipa used him as a safety-valve for her impetuous feelings.

She kissed me good night, and then asked for "the other lady."

"Go to bed, child," I said; "I will give her your good night."

"But I want to kiss her too," said Felipa.

She lingered at the door and would not let go; she played with the latch, and made me nervous with its clicking; at last I ordered her out. But on opening my door half an hour afterward there she was sitting on the floor outside in the darkness, she and Drollo, patiently waiting. Annoyed, but unable to reprove her, I wrapped the child in my shawl and carried her out into the moonlight, where Christine and Edward were strolling to and fro under the pines. "She will not go to bed, Christine, without kissing you," I explained.

"Funny little monkey!" said my friend, passively allowing the embrace.

"Me too," said Edward, bending down. Then I carried my bundle back satisfied.

The next day Felipa and I in secret began our labors: hers consisted in worrying me out of my life and spoiling material – mine in keeping my temper and trying to sew. The result, however, was satisfactory, never mind how we got there. I led Christine out one afternoon: Edward followed. "Do you like tableaux?" I said. "There is one I have arranged for you."

Felipa sat on the edge of the low, square-curbed Spanish well, and Drollo stood behind her, his great yellow body and solemn head serving as a background. She wore a brown petticoat barred with bright colors, and a little scarlet bodice fitting her slender waist closely; a chemisette of soft cream-color with loose sleeves covered her neck and arms, and set off the dark hues of her cheeks and eyes; and around her curly hair a red scarf was twisted, its fringed edges forming a drapery at the back of her head, which, more than anything else, seemed to bring out the latent character of her face. Brown moccasins, red stockings, and a quantity of bright beads completed her costume.

"By Jove!" cried Edward, "the little thing is almost pretty."

Felipa understood this, and a great light came into her face: forgetting her pose, she bounded forward to Christine's side. "I am pretty, then?" she said with exultation; "I *am* pretty, then, after all? For now you yourself have said it – have said it."

"No, Felipa," I interposed, "the gentleman said it." For the child had a curious habit of confounding the two identities which puzzled me then as now. But this afternoon, this happy afternoon, she was content, for she was allowed to sit at Christine's feet and look up into her fair face unmolested. I was forgotten, as usual.

"It is always so," I said to myself. But cynicism, as Mr. Aldrich[6] says, is a small brass field-piece that eventually bursts and kills the artilleryman. I knew this, having been blown up myself more than once; so I went back to my painting and forgot the world. Our world down there on the edge of the salt-marsh, however, was a small one: when two persons went out of it there was a vacuum.

One morning Felipa came sadly to my side. "They have gone away," she said.

"Yes, child."

"Down to the beach to spend all the day."

"Yes, I know it."

"And without me!"

This was the climax. I looked up. Her eyes were dry, but there was a hollow look of disappointment in her face that made her seem old; it was as though for an instant you caught what her old-woman face would be half a century on.

"Why did they not take me?" she said. "I am pretty now: she herself said it."

"They can not always take you, Felipa," I replied, giving up the point as to who had said it.

"Why not? I am pretty now; she herself said it," persisted the child. "In these clothes, you know: she herself said it. The clothes of the son of Pedro you will never see more: they are burned."

"Burned?"

"Yes, burned," replied Felipa composedly. "I carried them out on the barren and burned them. Drollo singed his paw. They burned quite nicely. But they are gone, and I am pretty now, and yet they did not take me! What shall I do?"

"Take these colors and make me a picture," I suggested. Generally, this was a prized privilege, but to-day it did not attract; she turned away, and a few moments after I saw her going down to the end of the plank-walk, where she stood gazing wistfully toward the ocean. There she staid all day, going into camp with Drollo, and refusing to come to dinner in spite of old Dominga's calls and beckonings. At last the patient old grandmother went down herself to the end of the long walk where they were, with some bread and venison on a plate. Felipa ate but little, but Drollo, after waiting politely until she had finished, devoured everything that was left in his calmly hungry way, and then sat back on his haunches with one paw on the plate, as though for the sake of memory. Drollo's hunger was of the chronic kind; it seemed impossible either to assuage it or to fill him. There was a gaunt leanness about him which I am satisfied no amount of food could ever fatten. I think he knew it too, and that accounted for his resignation. At length, just before sunset, the boat returned, floating up the marsh with the tide, old Bartolo steering and managing the brown sails. Felipa sprang up joyfully; I thought she would spring into the boat in her eagerness. What did she receive for her long vigil? A short word or two; that was all. Christine and Edward had quarreled.

How do lovers quarrel ordinarily? But I should not ask that, for these were no ordinary lovers: they were extraordinary.

"You should not submit to her caprices so readily," I said the next day while strolling on the barren with Edward. (He was not so much cast down, however, as he might have been.)

"I adore the very ground her foot touches, Kitty."

"I know it. But how will it end?"

"I will tell you: some of these days I will win her, and then – she will adore me."

Here Felipa came running after us, and Edward immediately challenged her to a race: a game of romps began. If Christine had been looking from her window she might have thought he was not especially disconsolate over her absence; but she was not looking. She was never looking out of anything or for anybody. She was always serenely content where she was. Edward and Felipa strayed off among the pine-trees, and gradually I lost sight of them. But as I sat sketching an hour afterward Edward came into view, carrying the child in his arms. I hurried to meet them.

"I shall never forgive myself," he said; "the little thing has fallen and injured her foot badly, I fear."

"I do not care at all," said Felipa; "I like to have it hurt. It is *my* foot, isn't it?"

These remarks she threw at me defiantly, as though I had laid claim to the member in question. I could not help laughing.

"The other lady will not laugh," said the child proudly. And in truth Christine, most unexpectedly, took up the *rôle* of nurse. She carried Felipa to her own room – for we each had a little cell opening out of the main apartment – and as white-robed Charity she shone with new radiance. "Shone" is the proper word; for through the open door of the dim cell, with the dark little face of Felipa on her shoulder, her white robe and skin seemed fairly to shine, as white lilies shine on a dark night. The old grandmother left the child in our care and watched our proceedings wistfully, very much as a dog watches the human hands that extract the thorn from the swollen foot of her puppy. She was grateful and asked no questions; in fact, thought was not one of her mental processes. She did not think much; she felt. As for Felipa, the child lived in rapture during those days in spite of her suffering. She scarcely slept at all – she was too happy: I heard her voice rippling on through the night, and Christine's low replies. She adored her beautiful nurse.

The fourth day came: Edward Bowne walked into the cell. "Go out and breathe the fresh air for an hour or two," he said in the tone more of a command than a request.

"The child will never consent," replied Christine sweetly.

"Oh, yes, she will; I will stay with her," said the young man, lifting the feverish little head on his arm and passing his hand softly over the bright eyes.

"Felipa, do you not want me?" said Christine, bending down.

"He stays; it is all the same," murmured the child.

"So it is. – Go, Christine," said Edward with a little smile of triumph.

Without a word Christine left the cell. But she did not go to walk; she came to my room, and, throwing herself on my bed, fell in a moment into a deep sleep, the reaction after her three nights of wakefulness. When she awoke it was long after dark, and I had relieved Edward in his watch.

"You will have to give it up," he said as our lily came forth at last with sleep-flushed cheeks and starry eyes shielded from the light. "The spell is broken; we have all been taking care of Felipa, and she likes one as well as the other."

Which was not true, in my case at least, since Felipa had openly derided my small strength when I lifted her, and beat off the sponge with which I attempted to bathe her hot face, "They" used no sponges, she said, only their nice cool hands; and she wished "they" would come and take care of her again. But Christine had resigned *in toto*.[7] If Felipa did not prefer her to all others, then Felipa should not have her; she was not a common nurse. And indeed she was not. Her fair face, ideal grace, cooing voice, and the strength of her long arms and flexible hands, were like magic to the sick, and – distraction to the well; the well in this case being Edward Bowne looking in at the door.

"You love them very much, do you not, Felipa?" I said one day when the child was sitting up for the first time in a cushioned chair.

"Ah yes; it is so strong when they carry me," she replied. But it was Edward who carried her.

"He is very strong," I said.

"Yes; and their long soft hair, with the smell of roses in it too," said Felipa dreamily. But the hair was Christine's.

"I shall love them for ever and ever, and they will love me for ever," continued the child. "Drollo too." She patted the dog's head as she spoke, and then concluded to kiss him on his little inch of forehead; next she offered him all her medicines and lotions in turn, and he smelled at them grimly. "He likes to know what I am taking," she explained.

I went on: "You love them, Felipa, and they are fond of you. They will always remember you, no doubt."

"Remember!" cried Felipa, starting up from her cushions like a Jack-in-the-box. "They are not going away? Never! never!"

"But of course they must go some time, for —"

But Felipa was gone. Before I could divine her intent she had flung herself out of her chair down on the floor, and was crawling on her hands and knees toward the outer room. I ran after her, but she reached the door before me, and, dragging her bandaged foot behind her, drew herself toward Christine. "You are *not* going away! You are not! you are not!" she sobbed, clinging to her skirts.

Christine was reading tranquilly; Edward stood at the outer door mending his fishing-tackle. The coolness between them remained, unwarmed by so much as a breath. "Run away, child; you disturb me," said Christine, turning over a leaf. She did not even look at the pathetic little bundle at her feet. Pathetic little bundles must be taught some time what ingratitude deserves.

"How can she run, lame as she is?" said Edward from the doorway.

"You are not going away, are you? Tell me you are

not," sobbed Felipa in a passion of tears, beating on the floor with one hand, and with the other clinging to Christine.

"I am not going," said Edward. "Do not sob so, you poor little thing!"

She crawled to him, and he took her up in his arms and soothed her into stillness again; then he carried her out on the barren for a breath of fresh air.

"It is a most extraordinary thing how that child confounds you two," I said. "It is a case of color-blindness, as it were – supposing you two were colors."

"Which we are not," replied Christine carelessly. "Do not stray off into mysticism, Catherine."

"It is not mysticism; it is a study of character –"

"Where there is no character," replied my friend.

I gave it up, but I said to myself: "Fate, in the next world make me one of those long, lithe, light-haired women, will you? I want to see how it feels."

Felipa's foot was well again, and spring had come. Soon we must leave our lodge on the edge of the pine-barren, our outlook over the salt-marsh, with the river sweeping up twice a day, bringing in the briny odors of the ocean; soon we should see no more the eagles far above us or hear the night-cry of the great owls, and we must go without the little fairy flowers of the barren, so small that a hundred of them scarcely made a tangible bouquet, yet what beauty! what sweetness! In my portfolio were sketches and studies of the salt-marsh, and in my heart were hopes. Somebody says somewhere: "Hope is more than a blessing; it is a duty and a virtue." But I fail to appreciate preserved hope – hope put up in cans and served out in seasons of depression. I like it fresh from the tree. And so when I hope it *is* hope, and not that well-dried, monotonous cheerfulness which makes one long to throw the persistent smilers out of the window. Felipa danced no more on the barrens; her illness had toned her down; she seemed content to sit at our feet while we talked, looking up dreamily into our faces, but no longer eagerly endeavoring to comprehend. We were there; that was enough.

"She is growing like a reed," I said; "her illness has left her weak."

"-Minded," suggested Christine.

At this moment Felipa stroked the lady's white hand tenderly and laid her brown cheek against it.

"Do you not feel reproached?" I said.

"Why? Must we give our love to whoever love us? A fine parcel of paupers we should all be, wasting our inheritance in pitiful small change! Shall I give a thousand beggars a half hour's happiness, or shall I make one soul rich his whole life long?"

"The latter," remarked Edward, who had come up unobserved.

They gazed at each other unflinchingly. They had come to open battle during those last days, and I knew that the end was near. Their words had been cold as ice, cutting as steel, and I said to myself, "At any moment." There would be a deadly struggle, and then Christine would yield. Even I comprehended something of what that yielding would be.

"Why do they hate each other so?" Felipa said to me sadly.

"Do they hate each other?"

"Yes, for I feel it here," she answered, touching her breast with a dramatic little gesture.

"Nonsense! Go and play with your doll, child." For I had made her a respectable, orderly doll to take the place of the ungainly fetich out on the barren.

Felipa gave me a look and walked away. A moment afterward she brought the doll out of the house before my very eyes, and, going down to the end of the dock, deliberately threw it into the water; the tide was flowing out, and away went my toy-woman out of sight, out to sea.

"Well!" I said to myself. "What next?"

I had not told Felipa we were going; I thought it best to let it take her by surprise. I had various small articles of finery ready as farewell gifts, which should act as sponges to absorb her tears. But Fate took the whole matter out of my hands. This is how it happened: One evening in the jasmine arbor, in the fragrant darkness of the warm spring night, the end came; Christine was won. She glided in like a wraith, and I, divining at once what had happened, followed her into her little room, where I found her lying on her bed, her hands clasped on her breast, her eyes open and veiled in soft shadows, her white robe drenched with dew. I kissed her fondly – I never could help loving her then or now – and next I went out to find Edward. He had been kind to me all my poor gray life; should I not go to him now? He was still in the arbor, and I sat down by his side quietly; I knew that the words would come in time. They came; what a flood! English was not enough for him. He poured forth his love in the rich-voweled Spanish tongue also; it has sounded doubly sweet to me ever since.

"Have you felt the wool of the beaver?
Or swan's down ever?
Or have smelt the bud o' the brier?
Or the nard in the fire?
Or ha' tasted the bag o' the bee?
Oh so white, oh so soft, oh so sweet is she!"[8]

said the young lover; and I, listening there in the dark fragrant night, with the dew heavy upon me, felt glad that the old simple-hearted love was not entirely gone from our tired metallic world.

It was late when we returned to the house. After reaching my room I found that I had left my cloak in the arbor. It was a strong fabric; the dew could not hurt it, but it could hurt my sketching materials and various trifles in the wide inside pockets – *objets de luxe*[9] to me, souvenirs of happy times, little artistic properties that I hang on the walls of my poor studio when in the city. I went softly out into the darkness again and sought the arbor; groping on the ground I found, not the cloak, but – Felipa! She was crouched under the foliage, face downward; she would not move or answer.

"What is the matter, child?" I said, but she would not speak. I tried to draw her from her lair, but she tangled herself stubbornly still farther among the thorny vines, and I could not move her. I touched her neck; it was cold. Frightened, I ran back to the house for a candle.

"Go away," she said in a low hoarse voice when I flashed the light over her. "I know all, and I am going to die. I have eaten the poison things in your box, and just now a snake came on my neck and I let him. He has bitten me, and I am glad. Go away; I am going to die."

I looked around; there was my color-case rifled and empty, and the other articles were scattered on the ground. "Good Heavens, child!" I cried, "what have you eaten?"

"Enough," replied Felipa gloomily. "I knew they were poisons; you told me so. And I let the snake stay."

By this time the household, aroused by my hurried exit with the candle, came toward the arbor. The moment Edward appeared Felipa rolled herself up like a hedgehog again and refused to speak. But the old grandmother knelt down and drew the little crouching figure into her arms with gentle tenderness, smoothing its hair and murmuring loving words in her soft dialect.

"What is it?" said Edward; but even then his eyes were devouring Christine, who stood in the dark vine-wreathed doorway like a picture in a frame. I explained.

Christine smiled. "Jealousy," she said in a low voice. "I am not surprised."

But at the first sound of her voice Felipa had started up, and, wrenching herself free from old Domingo's arms, threw herself at Christine's feet. "Look at *me* so," she cried – "me too; do not look at him. He has forgotten poor Felipa; he does not love her any more. But *you* do not forget, señora; *you* love me – *you* love me. Say you do, or I shall die!"

We were all shocked by the pallor and the wild, hungry look of her uplifted face. Edward bent down and tried to lift her in his arms; but when she saw him a sudden fierceness came into her eyes; they shot out yellow light and seemed to narrow to a point of flame. Before we knew it she had turned, seized something, and plunged it into his encircling arm. It was my little Venetian dagger.

We sprang forward; our dresses were spotted with the

fast-flowing blood; but Edward did not relax his hold on the writhing, wild little body he held until it lay exhausted in his arms. "I am glad I did it," said the child, looking up into his face with her inflexible eyes. "Put me down – put me down, I say, by the gracious señora, that I may die with the trailing of her white robe over me." And the old grandmother with trembling hands received her and laid her down mutely at Christine's feet.

Ah, well! Felipa did not die. The poisons racked but did not kill her, and the snake must have spared the little thin brown neck so despairingly offered to him. We went away; there was nothing for us to do but to go away as quickly as possible and leave her to her kind. To the silent old grandfather I said: "It will pass; she is but a child."

"She is nearly twelve, señora. Her mother was married at thirteen."

"But she loved them both alike, Bartolo. It is nothing; she does not know."

"You are right, lady; she does not know," replied the old man slowly; "but *I* know. It was two loves, and the stronger thrust the knife."

Notes

1   Sidney Lanier (1842-1881) was a Southern American poet, musician and critic. *The Marshes of Glynn* appeared in 1877.
2   Florida tribe of North American Indians of Muskhogean stock.
3   Minorca is the second largest of the Balearic islands.
4   The Pre-Raphaelite Brotherhood, a group of mid-nineteenth century artists headed by Dante Gabriel Rossetti, William Holman Hunt, and John Everett Millais, favored an unusual type of female beauty exemplified by such models as Elizabeth Siddal and Jane Morris; the previous physical descriptions of Christine link her with this type.
5   Who will be the better for it? (Lat.)

6   Thomas Bailey Aldrich (1836-1907) was an American poet, editor, and short story writer.
7   Altogether.
8   Ben Jonson (1572[3]-1637), *Under-Wood.*
9   Objects of value.

Source: *Rodman the Keeper: Southern Sketches.* Appleton, 1880.

Biographical Note

Constance Fenimore Woolson, the grand-niece of James Fenimore Cooper, was born on March 5, 1840, in Claremont, New Hampshire, the sixth of nine children, three of whom died of scarlet fever soon after her birth. The family moved to Cleveland where Woolson attended the Cleveland Seminary; she graduated from Madame Chagary's school in New York City in 1858. Although she wrote from an early age, it was only after her father's death in 1869 left her and her mother financially insecure that she began to publish. Her first stories, one a sketch of the Zoarites in Ohio, the other a sketch of Mackinac Island, where the family spent summers, appeared within a year of her father's death. Her first book, *The Old Stone House* (1873) was for children. In 1877 she published her first volume of collected fiction, *Castle Nowhere: Lake Country Sketches* (1875), and became a reviewer for the *Atlantic Monthly*. Like many American women writers in the last half of the century, Woolson was at her best with the regional sketch, but since she travelled extensively, first with her mother through the Southern and Eastern States, and later throughout Europe, she never limited herself to a specific region. She had a particular interest in analysing both the effects of dominant upon developing cultures, and the effects of isolation and exile upon women. Woolson herself was increasingly reclusive. During her thirties, she became subject to crippling bouts of depression, something to which she believed women writers were especially susceptible. She never married, but had complex and platonic friendships with many literary men, the most notorious of which was with Henry James. After her mother's death she left for Europe in 1879 with a letter of introduction to James; they met in Florence in 1880. She spent the remaining years of her life abroad.

In 1880 Woolson published *Rodman the Keeper: Southern Sketches*. Three stories in this collection deal particularly effectively with the lonely woman artist who eventually becomes isolated from even her own art: "Miss Elisabetha," "In the Cotton Country," and the story reprinted here, "Felipa," first published in *Lippincott's* in 1876. Catherine, the repressed woman artist in "Felipa," may share the same desires as the Minorcan child, but she has used art to smother her feelings, and art, as Felipa seems to suggest when she eats the "poison things" in the paint box, can destroy when used in the cause of repression. Other later stories which deal with the question of the woman artist include "At the Chateau of Corinne" (1886) and "Miss Grief" (1880). Woolson's best novel, *East Angels* (1886), is a critique of the ideology of self-sacrifice and repression—although the irony is so subtle that it was completely overlooked by James, who praised it for its exaltation of a sense of duty. At the age of fifty-three, Woolson died in Venice after either falling, but more likely jumping, from her balcony. A collection of travel sketches and what are probably her best works, the Italian stories collected in *The Front Yard* (1895) and *Dorothy* (1896), were published posthumously.

Selected Modern Reprints:

Rodman the Keeper: Southern Sketches. 1880. New York: Irvington, 1986.

Women Artists, Women Exiles: "Miss Grief" and Other Stories. Ed. and Intro. Joan Myers Weimer. New Brunswick: Rutgers UP, 1988.

Selected Secondary Sources:

Kern, John D. *Constance Fenimore Woolson: Literary Pioneer*. Philadelphia: U of Pennsylvania P, 1934.

Kitterman, Mary P. Edwards. "Henry James and the Artist-Heroine in the Tales of Constance Fenimore Woolson." *Nineteenth-Century Women Writers of the English-Speaking World*. Ed. Rhoda R. Nathan. Westport, CT: Greenwood, 1986. 45-59.

Moore, Rayburn S. *Constance Fenimore Woolson*. New York: Twayne, 1963.

Torsney, Cheryl B. *Constance Fenimore Woolson: The Grief of Artistry*. U of Georgia P, 1989.

Weimer, Joan Myers. "Women Artists as Exiles in the Fiction of Constance Fenimore Woolson." *Legacy: A Journal of Nineteenth-Century American Women Writers* 3.1 (1986): 3-15.

A Guide to Further Reading

The following list is necessarily selective rather than complete; it is supplemented by the guide to other anthologies which follows. Wherever possible I have referred the reader to modern reprints or collections. The nationality of the author is indicated at the end of each entry—A: American; B: British; C: Canadian.

Austin, Mary. *Stories from the Country of Lost Borders*. Ed. Marjorie Pryse. New Brunswick: Rutgers UP, 1987. (A)

Baldwin, Louisa. *The Shadow on the Blind, and Other Ghost Stories*. London: Dent, 1895. (B)

Barlow, Jane. *A Creel of Irish Stories*. New York: Dodd, Mead, 1899. (B)

Broughton, Rhoda. *Tales for Christmas Eve*. Leipzig: Tauchnitz, 1872. (B)

Cary, Alice. *Clovernook Sketches and Other Stories*. Ed. Judith Fetterley. New Brunswick: Rutgers UP, 1988. (A)

Cooke, Rose Terry. *"How Celia Changed Her Mind" and Selected Stories*. Ed. Elizabeth Ammons. New Brunswick: Rutgers UP, 1986. (A)

Craik, Dinah Mulock. *Nothing New; Tales*. London: Hurst and Blackett, 1857. (B)

Croker, Bitha Mary. *To Let*. London: Chatto, 1893. (B)

Fleming, May Agnes. *Married for Money and Other Stories*. New York: Ogilvie, 1891. (C)

Frere, Mary. *Old Deccan Days*. 1868. London: Murray, 1881. (B)

Gore, Catherine. *Mary Raymond and Other Tales*. 3 vols. Philadelphia: Lea and Blanchard, 1838. (B)

Grand, Sarah. *Our Manifold Nature: Stories from Life*. 1894. New York: Books for Libraries, 1969. (B)

Henniker, Florence. *In Scarlet and Grey: Stories of Soldiers and Others*. London: John Lane, 1896. (B)

Jackson, Helen Hunt. *Sax Holm's Stories*. 1874-78. 2 vols. New York: Irvington, 1988. (A)

King, Grace. *Balcony Stories*. 1893. Ed. Alfred Bendixon. Albany, NY: New Coll UP, 1990. (A)

Linton, Eliza Lynn. *Witch Stories*. 1861. Detroit: Grand River Books, 1971. (B)

Mitford, Mary. *Our Village*. London: Whittaker, Treacher, 1827-1832. (B)

Molesworth, Louisa. *Uncanny Tales*. London: Hutchinson, 1896. (B)

Moodie, Susanna. *Voyages. Short Narratives of Susanna Moodie*. Ed. John Thurston. Ottawa: U of Ottawa P, 1991.

Peattie, Elia Wilkinson. *The Shape of Fear and Other Ghostly Tales*. 1898. Rpt. Freeport, NY: Books for Libraries P, 1969. (A)

Riddell, Charlotte. *The Banshee's Warning and Other Tales*. London: Remington, 1894. (B)

—. *Handsome Phil and Other Stories*. London: White, 1899.

Rossetti, Christina. *Commonplace, and Other Stories*. London, 1870. (B)

Schreiner, Olive. *Dreams*. 1891. Willow Springs, MO: Select Books, 1971.

Sedgewick, Catherine. *Tales and Sketches*. Philadelphia: Carey, Lea, and Blanchard, 1835. (A)

Somerville and Ross [Edith Somerville and Violet Martin] *Some Experiences of an Irish R.M.* 1899. London: Folio, 1984.

Stowe, Harriet Beecher. *Sam Lawson's Oldtown Fireside Stories*. 1868. (A)

Ward, Elizabeth Stuart (Phelps). *Men, Women, and Ghosts*. 1869. New York: Garrett P, 1969. (A)

—. *Sealed Orders*. 1879. New York: Garrett P, 1979.

Wood, Ellen. *Adam Grainger, and Other Stories*. London: Bentley, 1890. (B)

—. *Lady Grace and Other Stories*. London: Bentley, 1892.

Anthologies:

Bendixen, Alfred, ed. *Haunted Women: The Best Supernatural Tales by American Women Writers*. New York: Ungar, 1985.

Cowasjee, Saros, ed. *Women Writers of the Raj*. London: Grafton, 1990.

Cox, Michael, and R.A. Gilbert, intro. *Victorian Ghost Stories: An Oxford Anthology*. Oxford: Oxford UP, 1991.

Dalby, Richard, ed. *The Virago Book of Victorian Ghost Stories*. London: Virago, 1992.

Fetterley, Judith, ed. *Provisions: A Reader from Nineteenth-Century American Women*. Bloomington: Indiana UP, 1985.

Haining, Peter. ed. *The Gentlewomen of Evil: An Anthology of Rare Supernatural Stories from the Pens of Victorian Ladies*. London: Hale, 1967.

Koppelman, Susan, ed. *Old Maids: Short Stories by Nineteenth-Century U.S. Women Writers*. Boston: Pandora P, 1984.

—. *"May Your Days Be Merry and Bright" and Other Christmas Stories by Women*. Detroit: Wayne State UP, 1988.

—. *The Other Woman: Stories of Two Women and A Man*. New York: Feminist P, 1984.

—. *Women's Friendships: A Collection of Stories*. Norman: U of Oklahoma P, 1991.

Madden-Simpson, Janet. *Woman's Part: An Anthology of Short Fiction by and about Irish Women, 1890-1960*. Dublin: Arlen House, 1984.

Parker, Jeri, ed. *Uneasy Survivors: Five Women Writers*. Salt Lake City: Peregrine Smith, 1975.

Salmonson, Jessica Amanda, ed. *What Did Miss Darrington See? An Anthology of Feminist Supernatural Fiction*. Intro. Rosemary Jackson. New York: Feminist P, 1989.

Shockley, Ann Allen, ed. *Afro-American Women Writers 1746-1933: An Anthology and Critical Guide*. Boston: G.K. Hall, 1988.

Sullivan, Rosemary, ed. *Stories By Canadian Women*. Toronto: Oxford UP, 1984.

Westbrook, Arlene G. R. and Perry D. Westbrook, eds. *The Writing Women of New England, 1630-1900: An Anthology*. Metuchen: Scarecrow, 1982.

Selected Secondary Sources:

Ammons, Elizabeth. *Conflicting Stories: American Women Writers at the Turn into the Twentieth Century.* New York: Oxford UP, 1991.

Alston, R.C. *A Checklist of Women Writers, 1801-1900: Fiction, Verse, Drama.* London: British Library, 1990.

Auerbach, Nina. *Communities of Women: An Idea in Fiction.* Cambridge, MA: Harvard UP, 1978.

Boos, Florence, ed. with Lynn Miller. *Bibliography of Women and Literature* 2 vols. New York: Holmes, 1989.

Carpenter, Lynette and Wendy K. Kolmar. *Haunting the House of Fiction: Feminist Perspectives on Ghost Stories by American Women.* Knoxville: U of Tennessee P, 1991.

Cooke, Rose Terry. *Our Famous Women.* Hartford: Worthington, 1884.

Conrad, Susan Phinney. *Perish the Thought: Intellectual Women in Romantic America 1830-1860.* New York: Oxford UP, 1976.

Cunningham, Gail. *The New Woman and the Victorian Novel.* New York: Barnes and Noble, 1978.

Donovan, Josephine. *New England Local Color Literature: A Woman's Tradition.* NY: Ungar, 1983.

Douglas, Ann. "The Literature of Impoverishment: The Women Local Colorists in America 1865-1914." *Women's Studies* 1 (1972): 3-40.

Duke, Maurice, Jackson R. Bryer, and M. Thomas Inge, eds. *American Women: Bibliographical Essays.* Westport: Greenwood P, 1983.

Fleenor, Juliann E. *The Female Gothic.* Montreal: Eden P, 1983.

Gilbert, Sandra, and Susan Gubar. *The Madwoman in the Attic: The Woman Writer and the Nineteenth-Century Literary Imagination.* New Haven: Yale UP, 1979.

Harris, Wendell V. *British Short Fiction in the Nineteenth Century: A Literary and Bibliographic Guide.* Detroit: Wayne State UP, 1979.

Jones, Anne Goodwyn. *Tomorrow is Another Day: The Woman Writer in the South, 1859-1936.* Baton Rouge: Louisiana State UP, 1981.

Kelley, Mary. *Private Woman, Public Stage: Literary Domesticity in Nineteenth-Century America.* New York: Oxford UP, 1984.

Kolodny, Annette. *The Land Before Her: Fantasy and Experience of the American Frontier 1630-1860.* Chapel Hill: U of North Carolina P, 1984.

Lohafer, Susan. *Coming to Terms with the Short Story.* Baton Rouge: Louisiana State UP, 1983.

Maniero, Lina, ed. *American Women Writers: A Critical Reference Guide from Colonial Times to the Present.* 3 vols. New York: Ungar, 1980.

McMullen, Lorraine, ed. and intro. *Re(Dis)covering Our Foremothers: Nineteenth-Century Canadian Women Writers.* Ottawa: U of Ottawa P, 1990.

Moers, Ellen. *Literary Women.* Garden City, NJ: Doubleday, 1976.

Mussell, Kay. *Women's Gothic and Romantic Fiction: A Reference Guide.* Westport, CT: Greenwood, 1981.

Nathan, Rhoda B. *Nineteenth-Century Women Writers of the English-Speaking World.* New York: Greenwood P, 1986.

Pykett, Lyn. *The Improper Feminine: The Women's Sensation Novel and the New Woman Writing.* New York: Routledge, 1992.

Schlueter, Paul, and June Schlueter, eds. *Encyclopedia of British Women Writers.* New York: Garland, 1988.

Shapiro, Ann R. *Unlikely Heroines: Nineteenth-Century American Women Writers and the Woman Question.* New York: Greenwood P, 1987.

Showalter, Elaine. *A Literature of Their Own: British Women Novelists from Brontë to Lessing.* Princeton: Princeton UP, 1977.

Spacks, Patricia Meyer. *The Female Imagination.* New York: Knopf, 1975.

Stubbs, Patricia. *Women and Fiction: Feminism and the Novel, 1880-1920.* Brighton: Harvester P, 1979.

Sundquist, Eric J., ed. *American Realism: New Essays.* Baltimore: Johns Hopkins UP, 1982.

Todd, Janet, ed. *British Women Writers: A Critical Reference Guide.* New York: Continuum, 1989.

Tompkins, Jane. *Sensational Designs: The Cultural Work of*

American Fiction 1790-1860. New York: Oxford UP, 1986.

Toth, Emily, ed. *Regionalism and the Female Imagination*. New York: Human Sciences P, 1985.

Westbrook, Perry. *Acres of Flint: Sarah Orne Jewett and Her Contemporaries*. 1951. Metuchen, NJ: Scarecrow, 1981.

Warren, Joyce. *The American Narcissus: Individualism and Women in Nineteenth-Century American Fiction*. New Brunswick: Rutgers UP, 1984.

Yellin, Jean Fagan, and Cynthia D. Bond, comp. *The Pen is Ours: A Listing of Writings by and about African-American Women before 1910 With Secondary Bibliography to the Present*. New York: Oxford UP, 1991.